James A Robson

THE DAM BUSTERS

THE WAR-TIME LEADERS OF THE "DAM BUSTERS" SQUADRON

Wing Commander Guy Gibson, V.C.,
D.S.O. and Bar, D.F.C. and Bar.

Group Captain Leonard Cheshire,
V.C., D.S.O. and 2 Bars, D.F.C.

Air Chief Marshal the Hon. Sir Ralph Cochrane, G.B.E., K.C.B., A.F.C.

Wing Commander J. B. Tait,
D.S.O. and 3 Bars, D.F.C. and Bar

Air Commodore J. E. Fauquier,
D.S.O. and 2 Bars, D.F.C.

THE
DAM BUSTERS

by

PAUL BRICKHILL

With a Foreword by
Marshal of the Royal Air Force
THE LORD TEDDER, G.C.B.

LONDON
EVANS BROTHERS LIMITED

First Published, 1951
Reprinted (before publication)
Reprinted October, 1951
Reprinted December, 1951
Reprinted January, 1952
Reprinted April, 1952
Reprinted March, 1953
Reprinted July, 1953
Reprinted October, 1953
Reprinted May, 1954

PRINTED IN GREAT BRITAIN BY THE WHITEFRIARS PRESS LTD.
LONDON AND TONBRIDGE
Z. 5028   P.R. 6984

To the men living and dead
who did these things.

CONTENTS

LIST OF ILLUSTRATIONS

FOREWORD

617 SQUADRON, originally formed to carry out one specific operation with a weapon specially designed for that purpose, had, by the end of the war, built up a record of individual and collective courage and skill which is unique. The story which is told in this book cannot but make its readers feel humble in the face of such devotion, such self-sacrifice, and such courage.

Nevertheless this story does more than set out the history of one individual squadron ; it throws a spotlight on many of the factors which lay behind the successful and decisive employment of air power. It shows scientist, commander and operator working together as a close-knit team, each contributing towards the common aim of greater efficiency ; it shows efficiency interpreted in the short term as " accuracy," and in the long term as " maximum effect with minimum effort." There have been those who allege that the air weapon is necessarily indiscriminate and that the aim of air power is destruction for the sake of destruction. This book is the story of a team that gave the lie to that allegation ; a team whose work had a profound influence on the conduct of air operations, a team whose initiative, skill and self sacrifice on the one hand saved many an air crew who would otherwise have been lost on abortive operations, and on the other hand obviated much useless destruction and pointless loss of life in Europe. Here also is a story of inspired leadership under conditions of almost unbelievable strain, leadership at all levels—within the individual crews, leadership by the Squadron Commander and leadership by the Group Commander—leadership which inspired men to face up to, and overcome, " impossibilities." May their example be an inspiration to us, now and in the future.

TEDDER.

BRIEFING

ONCE I asked an Air Marshal what he thought 617 Squadron was worth, and after a while he said, " Well, one can't really say but I suppose they were worth ten other squadrons." He pondered a little longer and added : " No, that isn't quite so either. Ten other squadrons couldn't have done what they did, and then of course you've got to consider that inventor chap and the freak weapons he gave them. I suppose 617 was the most effective unit of its size the British ever had."

This is a story of quality as against quantity, demonstrating that exceptional skills and ingenuity can give one man or one unit the effectiveness of ten. It seems that this is a rather British synthesis of talents, and perhaps this story will reassure those who are dismayed by the fact that the British and their allies are outnumbered in this not too amicable world.

What is probably more important, the talents that made 617 what they were evolved a new form of precision bombing which enabled a specific military target to be hit accurately and destroyed. Already this is pointing a way towards the end of " carpet " bombing of cities, that dreadfully inescapable feature of recent war.

Forgive me for cloaking occasional characters in tactful anonymity. They are still alive. Some details of Wallis's strange bombs must likewise stay veiled till more fraternal days.

There is so much to tell that some of the " 617 " men, like David Wilson, Arthur Kell, Bunny Clayton, Bob Knights and many others cannot be given full credit for their brave competence. Likewise there are too many to name in thanking those who told me about 617. They were too modest to talk about themselves, so I got them to tell me about the others. And *vice versa*.

The famous dams raid was just the start of it all. Guy Gibson wrote some of the wonderful story of this affair towards the end of his excellent " Enemy Coast Ahead."

must draw on this, and I am most grateful
to do so, in addition to my own researches.
also to Air Commodore Pat Huskinson for the
from " Vision Ahead " ; to Air Vice-Marshal
.H. Bilney; John Nerney, Chief of R.A.F. Historical
rds; Tom Cochrane, Deputy Chief Information Officer;
Mr. A. J. Charge, Keeper of Photographs at the Imperial War
Museum; and, by no means least, to Wing Commander
Willie Tait for the inspiration of his fine accounts.

PAUL BRICKHILL.

CHAPTER I

A WEAPON IS CONCEIVED

THE day before the war started Barnes Wallis drove for five hours back to Vickers' works at Weybridge, leaving his wife and family in the quiet Dorset bay where they had pitched tents for a holiday.

He had that morning reluctantly decided that war was not only inevitable but imminent, and he was going to be needed at his drawing-board. No point bringing the family back yet to a house near an aircraft factory till it became clear what influence the Luftwaffe was going to have on one's expectation of life.

Wallis did not look like a man who was going to have much influence on the war; he looked more like a diffident and gentle cleric. At 53 his face was unlined and composed, the skin smooth and pink and the eyes behind the horn-rimmed glasses mild and grey; crisp white hair like a woolly cap enhanced the effect of benevolence. Many people who stood in his way in the next three years were deceived by this, having failed to note the long upper lip which gave stubbornness to the mouth and was the only visible clue to his persistent refusal to be diverted from his purpose. Even his friends did not quite understand this because Wallis, in a vaguely indefinable way, was a little insulated from the rough and tumble of ordinary life by a mind virtually on another plane, immersed in figures and theories. They knew him as a gentle, if rather detached, aircraft designer, and it was not till later that they began to use the word " genius."

He spent the last night of peace alone in his house near Effingham, and in the morning, like most people, listened to the oddly inspiring speech of Chamberlain's. Afterwards he sat in silence and misery, not even swearing because the strongest words in his vocabulary were inadequate.

One thought had been haunting him since the previous morning's decision: what could he, as an aircraft designer and engineer, do to shorten the war ? The thought stayed

with him for a long time and through remarkable events
before it was honourably discharged. None of the strange
ideas that emerged from it came in a flash of inspiration.
There was no one moment in which Barnes Wallis shouted,
" Eureka, I have it ! " Scientific minds seldom work in that
spectacular and convenient fashion. Ideas germinated slowly
in his head, a fertile breeding ground, feeding on study and
thought, amorphous and unrecognisable at first like any
embryo till gradually they took shape and were recognised.

He had been designing for Vickers since before the first
world war. When that started he was designing an early
British airship, but a potentate in the upper strata of government decided that work on it should stop as the war was not
going to last longer than three months ; so Wallis enlisted
in the Artists' Rifles as a private. As the war, after three
months, was disconcertingly remote from ending, the potentate ordered work resumed on the airship, and Wallis was
brought back to his drawing board.

In the twenties he designed the R.100, the most successful
British dirigible. In the thirties he invented the geodetic
form of aircraft construction and, using this, designed the
Wellesley which captured the world's non-stop distance
record, and the Wellington, which was the mainstay of
Bomber Command for the first three years of the war (and in
1951 was still being used for advanced training).

Vickers' works, nestled in the banked perimeter of the old
Brooklands motor-racing track, was turning out Wellingtons
as fast as it could, and Wallis was designing its proposed
successor, the Warwick. At this time he was on the design
of the Warwick's tailplane, which was being troublesome.
Clearly any additional work would have to be done in his own
spare time and there was, also quite clearly, not going to be
much spare time.

Bombers and bombs were the directions in which he was
most qualified to help. Bombs, particularly, seemed a fruitful
field. He knew something about R.A.F. bombs, their size,
shape, weight and so on ; the knowledge had been essential
when he was designing the Wellington, so that it could carry
the required bombs over the required distance. It was not

knowledge which, in Wallis, inspired complacency. The heaviest bomb was only 500 lb., and aiming was so unpredictable that the Air Force was forced to indulge in stick bombing—you dropped them one after another in the pious hope that one would hit the target. One hoped then that it would go off. Too many didn't. Years of placid peace and the diffidence of the Treasury had inhibited development of bombs, a natural consequence of a war to end all wars but regrettable in the face of reality. Lack of development had been assisted by the presence here and there in the Services of a few of those officers who thrive only in peacetime, lacking neither in courage nor devotion to Regulations and afternoon tea but lamentably deficient in the vitality and intellectual resilience that lead to actual work being done.

R.A.F. bombs, too, were old, very old. Nearly all were stocks hoarded from 1919. There had been an attempt in 1921 to design a better bomb, and in 1938 they actually started to produce them, but in 1940 there were still very few of them. Both new bombs and old were filled with a mediocre explosive called amatol (and only 25 per cent. of the weight consisted of explosive). There *was* a far better explosive called RDX, but production of that had been stopped in 1937. (It was not till 1942 that the R.A.F. was able to use RDX-filled bombs.) Meantime Luftwaffe bombs contained a much more powerful explosive than amatol—and half the weight of the German bomb was explosive.

Wallis knew there had been an attempt in 1926 to make 1,000-lb. bombs for the R.A.F. but they never even got to the testing stage. The Treasury was against them ; the Air Staff thought they would never need a bomb larger than 500 lb., and anyway Air Force planes were designed to carry 500-pounders. Thousand-pound bombs would need new and costlier planes for the whole Air Force and the country could not afford it. Not till 1939 did the Air Staff begin to think seriously again of the 1,000-pounder, and six months *after* the war started they placed an order for some.

These shortcomings were not so obvious then, particularly as (as Wallis knew) all air forces favoured small bombs designed to attack surface targets. The blast of bigger bombs was curiously local against buildings, and a lot of little bombs seemed better than an equal weight of larger ones. Even larger bombs needed a direct hit to cause much damage, and there was more chance of a direct hit with a lot of little bombs.

To Wallis's methodically logical mind there was a serious flaw to all this. Factories and transport could be dispersed ; in fact *were* dispersed all over Germany. Bombing (vintage 1939) would not damage enough factories to make much difference.

He started wondering *where* and *how* bombing could hurt Germany most. If one could not hit the dispersed war effort perhaps there were key points. Perhaps the sources of the effort. And here the probing mind was fastening on a new principle.

The sources of Germany's effort, in war or peace, lay in power. Not political power (that was dispersed too, and hidden in deep shelters at the approach of aircraft). Physical power ! Great sources of energy too massive to move or hide—coal mines, oil dumps and wells, and " white coal "— hydro-electric power from dams. Without them there could be no production and no transport. No weapons. No war.

But they were too massive to dent by existing bombs. One might as well kick them with a dancing pump ! The next step—in theory anyway—was easy. Bigger bombs. Much bigger !

But that meant bigger aircraft ; much bigger than existing ones. All right then—bigger aircraft too.

That was the start of it. It sounds simple but it was against the tenets of the experts of every air force in the world.

Wallis started calculating and found the blast of bigger bombs *was* puny against steadfast targets like coal mines, buried oil and dams. Particularly dams, ramparts of ferro-concrete anchored in the earth.

Then perhaps a new *type* of bomb. But there Wallis did not know enough about bombs and the logic stopped short.

The war was a few weeks old when the dogged scientist dived into engineering and scientific libraries and at lunchtimes, when he pushed the problem of the Warwick's tail-plane aside for an hour or so, he sent out for sandwiches, stayed at his desk and started to learn about bombs.

His designing office was evacuated to an old house at Burhill, near Weybridge, which had been built by Wellington, and there he studied the chemistry and behaviour of high explosives, aerodynamic bomb design, the forging, casting and milling, the theories of light and heavy case bombs, the fusing and the aiming. And at night at home he did the same, absorbed and lost to his family for hours. If a bomb had gone off near by he possibly would not have noticed, or if he did his first thought would probably have been to inquire into the chemical nature of its explosive or the type of casing, or the charge/weight ratio. As the hard winter of 1939 arrived he progressed to the study of the sources of power.

Coal mines ! Impossible to collapse the galleries and tunnels hundreds of feet underground. Possible, he decided, that a heavy bomb might collapse the winding shaft so that the lift would not work. No lift. No work. No coal. But that could soon be repaired.

Oil ! Rumanian oil fields were too far for existing bombers, but a possibility for a future bomber. Germany's synthetic refineries were massive and well defended ; perhaps a target for bigger bombs.

Dams ! Three German dams stood out—the Moehne, the Eder and the Sorpe. All in the Ruhr, they accounted for nearly all the water supply to that monstrous arsenal. Wallis knew that the German method needed eight tons of water to produce a ton of steel. The possibilities were intriguing.

The Moehne dammed Moehne Lake where the Heve flowed into the Ruhr River, maintaining the level so that barges with coal and steel and tanks could go to and from the foundries. Moehne Lake held 134 million tons of water. The Eder dammed the Eder River in Eder Lake, 212 million tons of water. It controlled the level of Germany's second most important waterway, the Mittelland Canal. Even Kassel, forty miles away, got its water from the Eder. The Sorpe dammed another tributary of the Ruhr River in Sorpe Lake.

The Moehne was 112 feet thick at the base, 130 feet high and 25 feet thick at the top where a roadway ran; the Eder was even bigger. Wallis acknowledged that they were formidable. A 500-lb. bomb would hardly scratch the concrete. No less formidable the Sorpe, an earth dam, two sloping mounds of earth sealed and buttressed in the centre by a core of concrete.

In an engineering library Wallis unearthed accounts of their construction compiled by the proud engineers who had built them and found it hard to discipline his excitement as he read what the effects of breaching the dams could be.

It would not merely destroy hydro-electric power and deprive foundries of essential water, but affect other war factories which needed water for their processes. Disrupting them might cause a dozen critical bottlenecks in the completion of tanks, locomotives, guns, aircraft—almost anything one cared to name. It would deprive the populace of water too, which was no cause for joy in a gentle soul like Wallis but would at least induce in them a lessening of zest for the war as well as some testy sentiments directed not only at the R.A.F. but at Hitler too. Humanity is not inclined to limit its censure for discomfort to the direct cause only. Indirect sources get their share; another and intriguing way, thought Wallis whimsically, of attacking the enemy at the source of power.

There was still more to it. Breaches in the dams would send enormous floods ripping down the valleys, tearing away roads, bridges and railway lines, smashing factories and houses, so that some factories, rather than be deprived of water, would receive somewhat too much.

All this was fine, Wallis thought . . . logical ideas; but again one big flaw. The dams were so colossal that bombs twenty times bigger than existing ones were not going to hurt them.

His figures showed that when a 1,000-pounder exploded the charge expanded as a gas bubble, but at the end the bubble was only 20 feet across. A lot of damage was done beyond this 10-foot radius, however, by flying fragments, by blast and by the pressure pulse, or " shock wave." Wallis well remembered the pedantic description of shock waves

. . . " there is no motion of the transmitting medium other than the usual oscillation of particles to and fro about their position of rest as the wave passes through them." Thin air gave scope to flying fragments and blast but the shock wave soon dissipated.

It would vibrate a structure, but not enough. To be destructive, shock waves had to travel through a more solid medium than air. And somewhere in Wallis's brain a little cell awoke and stirred restlessly, an old memory, locked up and almost forgotten. He felt there was something he knew about shock waves that he should remember, tried to think what it was—it was a long time ago—but the harder he tried the farther it receded. Memory can be so tantalising. He thought about it for the rest of the day, trying irritatedly to isolate it, but it had gone. Memory is like a woman; it was only when he put it out of his mind that it sneaked insidiously back to him again.

It was something he had read, something about concrete. And then it hit him. Waterloo Bridge! Concrete piles being driven into the bed of the Thames! That was years ago. The piles had kept shattering mysteriously and there had been an investigation. He started searching his book-cases and in a quarter of an hour had found it, an article in a 1935 journal of the Institution of Civil Engineers. The great drop-hammers had been slamming the piles into the river-bed and the tops of the piles had been exploding upwards.

Investigation narrowed the cause to the shock waves. The sudden blows sent shock waves shivering down the piles; at the bottom they met the blunt resistance of the clay and bounced back up the pile at something like 15,000 feet a second, reaching the top just after the hammer had bounced off, so there was nothing to rebound from again and they passed out and away, and in their wake you got a tension after the compression. A sort of crush and then a sharp stretch, almost in the same moment; enough to make a structure split—to shatter it.

Concrete, the article concluded sagely, well resisted compression but poorly withstood tension. Wallis docketed the fact in his mind, thinking of dams.

You needed a solid medium to get destructive shock waves !

Of course, if you could bury a bomb *deep* in . . . But you couldn't slice a big bomb deep into ferro-concrete. No, but you might be able to inject it deep into some less solid medium before it exploded. You'd get the shock waves then. The expanding gas effects would be greater too ; tamped by the encircling solids they would have to burst their way out.

He was aware that bombs and shells often buried themselves 3 or 4 feet in the ground before exploding, but that was so shallow the explosion forced its way easily to the top, causing a small crater, and the shock waves dissipated into the air. It was less effective than a surface explosion because the blast and shock waves went straight up instead of outwards.

But if you could *lock* the explosion underground so it could not break out you would get a sort of seismic disturbance . . . an earthquake ! An earthquake bomb !

The idea shaped in his mind while he was sitting in a deep chair in his home at Effingham, an unspectacular setting for the birth of something so powerful.

But how to sink a bomb deeply into a resisting medium? You could not put one deep into a concrete dam. But a dam is set in water !

Water ! It might not transmit a shock wave as well as earth but it would do so better than air. The tamping effect of water would produce a concentrated explosion and carry the " shock " punch. Wallis was starting to feel he might be getting somewhere.

And how about sinking the bomb in earth? A schoolboy knew the two principles. The heavier the bomb, the more power and speed it developed in falling. Wallis had learned the classic example in school. Drop a mouse down a well and at the bottom it will be able to get up and run. Drop a horse down and the horse will probably burst. Because it was heavier it would hit *harder*. And the *farther* it fell, the *faster* it would fall !

So there it was : a bomb as heavy as possible (and as slim as possible) dropped from as high as possible.

Wallis looked up more books, studied the propagation of waves in soil, the effects of underground explosions at depth, and even found pages on the penetrative powers into soils of shells and light bombs. There was a piece about an enormous land mine exploded under a German-held hill at Messines Ridge in World War I. A colossal charge sent shock waves ripping into the earth, the hill was destroyed and the shock was felt in Kassel—300 miles away.

Wallis pulled out a pad and pencil and worked for a week, covering sheets with calculations, equations, formulæ— accelerations, resistances, kinetic energy, stresses, friction, charge/weight ratios—and came up with a preliminary theoretical answer. A 10-ton bomb, with 7 tons of explosive in an ærodynamically-designed case of special steel, dropped from 40,000 feet, would reach a speed of 1,440 feet per second, or 982 m.p.h.—well over the speed of sound. At that rate it should penetrate an average soil to a depth of 135 feet.

A charge of that size should theoretically " camouflet " (not break the surface) at a depth of 130 feet. What it *would* do is cause a violent earthquake movement on the surface, resulting in a hump forming.

" Such earth movements," said a learned paper, " are capable of doing much damage at great distances."

It looked as though Wallis had found his answer. Or part of it.

CHAPTER II

—AND REJECTED

HE worked out theoretical effects, more pages of figures, and decided there was a chance that a 10-ton bomb exploding deep in water by a dam wall would punch out a hole a hundred feet across.

Supposing the bomb did not go as deeply into the earth as the figures predicted? Wallis worked out the effects of a 10-tonner exploding about 40 feet deep. In theory it would throw out the staggering amount of 12,000 tons of earth, leaving a crater 70 feet deep, with lips 250 feet across. He worked out the circumference of the crater and from that the maximum number of men and machines that could gather round the edges. Working day and night they could not fill it in under fourteen days ! Supposing one such bomb was dropped accurately in a marshalling yard ! Or on a vital railway or canal or road where ground contours prohibited a detour !

Wallis did not get too excited. No bomber in the world would carry a 10-ton bomb. Or for that matter even a 5-ton bomb far enough to get it to a target.

Back to pencil and paper. He knew the limitations of aircraft design in 1940 and in a couple of weeks he knew it was possible to build a 50-ton bomber to carry a 10-ton bomb 4,000 miles at 320 m.p.h. and a height of 45,000 feet. He drew up rough specifications and christened it the " Victory Bomber."

The methodical mind did not overlook anything. At 40,000 feet would constant cloud obscure the targets ? Back to the library. The weather should be clear enough on one day in three. That was reasonable.

Could a bomb-aimer pick up a small target from 40,000 feet ? Wallis came across a scientific report which showed that a test object a few feet wide could be visible from 35,000 feet.

Winds ? Stratospheric winds sometimes reached 200 m.p.h.

He set that against bomb-aiming techniques and decided that, whatever the faults of present bomb-aiming, the winds could be allowed for.

And the aiming of bombs—notoriously hit and miss, mostly miss. Wallis found that increasing height did not greatly increase the problems and estimated that new bomb sights being developed and special training could put the bombs near enough to a target to destroy it.

That was the beauty of this 10-ton bomb. It should not have to be a direct hit ! The earthquake shock would be so great that a near miss should shake a target to destruction. And another thing—a big bomb exploding 130 feet deep would not crater the surface but cause a huge subterranean cavern. Put such a bomb alongside a bridge or viaduct, and if the shock wave did not shake it to pieces the cavern underneath would knock its support away. An opening trapdoor— a hangman's drop ! The bridge would collapse into it.

There was one other possibility in it—perhaps the greatest of all. A few such bombs, accurately aimed, might shatter the roots of a nation's war effort. That could mean the end of the dreadful " Guernica " carpet bombing, which saturated an area with bombs so limited in effect that the area had to be saturated to make their use militarily worth while. Wiping out cities and civilians at the same time !

But it was only a revolutionary and complicated theory. The Army, Navy and Air Force were deluged with revolutionary, complicated and crackpot theories. The next problem—maybe the biggest—was to get them to listen to this one, to believe and accept it.

Wallis spent weeks setting it all out on paper and took it to people he knew in the R.A.F. and the Ministry of Aircraft Production. It was Dunkirk time. A potent new weapon had never been better timed.

Wallis's paper on the " earthquake bomb " roused three main emotions in officials : (1) Lukewarm interest. (2) Incomprehension. (3) Tactful derision.

One man understood and did what he could : Arthur Tedder, a quiet, intensely likeable man smoking a pipe, chained to a desk in Whitehall. But he was only an air vice-marshal then and did not have the influence he acquired later as Eisenhower's deputy in the invasion, and then as Lord Tedder, Marshal of the R.A.F. and Chief of the Air Staff. He brought the bomb and Victory Bomber to the attention of several people in high places but the only result seemed to be a ubiquitous manifestation of courteous but implacable inactivity, often the only defence of hard-working officials plagued by importunate and impractical inventors. Every machine in the country was working overtime on other vital things and the ambitious and excellent four-engined bomber project was just getting under way. It was a fair assumption that it might be disastrous to dislocate that in favour of the Victory Bomber, which would inevitably take much longer to develop. That automatically prejudiced the shock-wave bomb, because there was therefore no aircraft in sight which could drop it from Wallis's prescribed height of 40,000 feet. The new bombers would probably not be able to lift it or, if they could, to carry it far enough to drop it from higher than 20,000 feet, which was not likely to be enough.

And then on July 19, out of the blue, Wallis got an urgent summons to see Lord Beaverbrook, the bright-eyed fire-cracker who was Minister for Aircraft Production. With " The Beaver " interested anything could happen, and probably at speed. He caught the first train to London, cooled his heels a few minutes in an ante-room and then the big door opened and a young man said :

" Lord Beaverbrook will see you now, sir."

Wallis jumped up, cuddling his calculations under his arm, and crossed the threshold, nervous with anticipation; and there was the little man with the wide, mobile mouth, sitting slightly hunched in his chair. It was the speed with which things happened that shook Wallis as much as the things themselves. No gracious, measured preliminaries. He was still in the middle of the floor, walking, when the little man barked :

" Will you go to America for me ? "

For a moment Wallis was rattled. He collected himself.

" I'd rather stay here for you, sir."

" What would you do for me here ? " Crisply and fast, like repartee.

" Build you a ten-ton bomb and a Victory Bomber to carry it, sir." Wallis was standing his ground better than most. The little man looked at him a moment.

" What good would that do ? "

" End the war," Wallis said simply. " An earthquake bomb. I've got it set out here," he touched the papers under his arm.

" All right, never mind that now. Have a look at this," and Beaverbrook tossed over a newspaper clipping. " Look into it and come back and see me to-morrow."

Wallis lost track of the interview after that, probably because there was no more interview. He found himself outside the door ; from start to finish it had lasted a bare forty seconds and as his thoughts re-assembled he felt disappointment like a shock. Beaverbrook had never heard of his ideas ; it was some other wretched thing he had wanted. Automatically he began to walk away and it was not till he got to the front door that he bagan to wonder what the other thing was and remembered the clipping.

It was not in his hand. He searched his pockets. Not there. It was a pretty position ; he did not even know what Beaverbrook wanted and he had to advise him to-morrow about it. He could not go back and ask what the subject was . . . he shuddered slightly at the thought. Agitated, he ploughed through his pockets again and in the last one, a fob, when hope had gone, he felt the cutting, drew it out and read it.

It was a report from America about work on pressurised aircraft cabins for high flight. " The Beaver " evidently wanted him to go across and see how it was done.

Very amusing ! Wallis had already done experimental work on pressurised cabins and knew how it was done. He went back to Weybridge.

Next day he saw Beaverbrook again, armed this time by experience and was not rattled. He told the Minister he had all the information needed on pressurising aircraft cabins and there was no need to go to America.

" All right," said Beaverbrook. " What's this about a ten-ton bomb ? "

Wallis told him as concisely as he could ; difficult for a scientist, who always feels compelled to go into technicalities, but he kept it short and lucid and Beaverbrook was interested.

" You know how short we are of stuff," he said. " This thing's only a theory. We'd have to stop work on other vital things to make it and then it might be a flop."

" It won't be that," Wallis said stubbornly.

" We'd still have to stop work on other things."

" It will be worth it."

" Take too long, wouldn't it ? " said " The Beaver." " A ten-ton bomb and a bomber twice the size of anything else sounds like something in the distant future."

" We can do it in stages, sir," Wallis said. " I've got drawings for two-ton and six-ton bombs on the same principle. My Wellingtons can carry the two-tonner all right. The new four-engined ones can carry the six-tonner. They'll be operating in a year."

" Well, I'll see my experts about it," Beaverbrook said. " If it's going to mean diverting too much effort I don't like your chances."

Wallis came out with a sigh of hope and relief, spent some days simplifying his designs and on August 9 took a train to Sheffield to get the advice of steel experts on manufacture of the tempered casings. They would have to be immensely strong to withstand the shock of hitting at 1,000 m.p.h. without breaking, and as light and roomy as possible so the maximum amount of explosive could be crammed into them. Big bomb design is incredibly complicated, but the blitz had started and it was a good time for discussing big bombs to throw back.

Little seemed to happen for a while but behind the scenes things were removing in a ponderous government way. Little snippets filtered through to Wallis, particularly from that astute ally, Arthur Tedder. Nothing much ; just that So-and-so had consented to look into the idea and that So-

and-so had expressed mild interest. Out of this came one
or two more converts. One was Air Commodore Pat
Huskinson, a grey-haired, burly man who was Director of
Armament Development for the R.A.F., renowned for his
blunt aggression in forcing new weapons through bottlenecks.
But most of Huskinson's time was filled with dozens of other
problems, and then a bomb fell on his flat. Huskinson lived
but was blinded.

Wallis thought the prospects were still favourable. Sir
Charles Craven, managing director of Vickers, was sympa-
thetic and felt confident enough on November 1 to write to
Beaverbrook suggesting he gave permission to go ahead on
both 10-ton bomb and Victory Bomber.

Then Tedder was posted to take over the R.A.F. in the
Middle East and Wallis had lost his keenest supporter in the
sacred and essential precincts of Whitehall. It was soon
after that Craven sent for him.

" I'm afraid I haven't very encouraging news for you,"
Craven said as kindly as he could. " Air Council seem too
wary of big bombs. They still believe stick bombing is
necessary."

" But can't they *see* what a really big bomb would do ? "
Wallis said pleadingly.

" Apparently not. They say that from experience they
would rather drop four 250-pound bombs than a thousand-
pounder. Much less a 22,000-pounder."

" Could they understand my calculations, sir ? "

Craven did not comment on their understanding. He said
diplomatically that he doubted whether the members would
have the *time* to go individually through all the calculations.
Which was probably true. And then gently : " They say
that anyone who thinks of ten-ton bombs is mad."

Wallis went back to Weybridge in anger, but in the morning
the anger had mostly gone and in its place was outraged
stubbornness. He started writing a treatise on his 10-ton
bomb and called it " A note on a method of attacking the
Axis Powers," the kind of obscure title so favoured by
scientists ; the word " note " being particularly misleading,
as such things are often as long as a book.

Wallis's was.   He started by outlining his theory of crip-
pling an enemy by destroying the sources of energy, and went
on to discuss in exhaustive detail the physical qualities of
the targets, shock waves, blast, penetration, bomb design,
aircraft design, charge/weight ratios, aiming problems,
possible effects, repair potentialities, backed up with pages
of graphs and formulæ and equations.   It was a *tour de force*,
explaining step by step so lucidly that a layman could follow
it if he took the mathematics for granted.

The " note " took Wallis several months, and then he had
it roneoed and bound and posted copies to seventy influential
men in science, politics and the services.

Results were not long coming.   A secret service man called
on him with a copy of the " note " under his arm.

" Did you send this to Mr. —— ? " he asked.

" Yes," Wallis said.   " Why ? "

" I'm afraid you shouldn't have done so, Mr. Wallis."

" Why ? "

" It's very secret stuff.   This sort of thing must be handled
very carefully and only reach authorised persons.   Mr. ——
was very surprised when this arrived in the post.   We were
concerned too.   I quite realise you didn't mean to be . . ."

" I sent out seventy of them," Wallis said calmly, and the
Secret Service was appalled.

" Seventy ! " he said.   " *Seventy !*   Who ?   To whom ?
But you shouldn't have.   This is vital and very secret ! "

" Is it ? " said Wallis mildly.   " When I showed it to the
authorised persons they said I was mad.   I'm supposed to
be a crackpot and this is regarded by authorised persons as
fiddle-faddle."

The secret service man said, " Oh ! "   He asked for the
names of the seventy.   Wallis read them out and the secret
service man, who seemed a little uncertain of his ground,
went back to London to investigate further.

He appeared again a couple of days later.

" Well, it's all right," he said, " this time.   We've decided
that as so many were sent out so openly it's actually rather
a good form of security.   No one will dream it's at all so
secret.   But please don't do it again."

Wallis bowed gravely. " I hope it will not be necessary again," he said and the incident was closed.

A few days later there was another result. A copy had reached a Group Captain Winterbotham, who had an office in the City and was used to dealing with unorthodox aspects of the war. He had found it convincing, called on Wallis, and Wallis explained more fully. Winterbotham caught some of his enthusiasm. He knew Sir Henry Tizard, who was scientific adviser to the Ministry of Aircraft Production, and drew his special attention to Wallis's paper.

Tizard read it carefully ; as a scientist he could follow the intricate calculations. He went down to see Wallis at Weybridge and was impressed.

" I'd better form a committee to study this more fully," he said. " It would have to have pretty solid backing from expert opinion. You'll understand, I know. It would divert effort from other important things if we were to go ahead with it and we've got to be reasonably sure it would be worth while."

" Of course," Wallis said. He felt like singing.

Not long after, Wallis met the committee. At the head was Dr. Pye, Director of Scientific Research at the Ministry of Supply, and the others were scientists too. Wallis explained his ideas and described the probable effect on Germany's war industries if the dams were breached. There was only one really worthwhile time of the year to breach them, and that was in May, when the storage lakes were full after the winter thaw and spring rains, and before the sluice gates were opened to water the country and canals for summer. Then you would get the greatest floods, the most serious loss of water and power. Dr. Pye said the committee would be a few days considering.

A week later Wallis faced the committee to hear their findings. His worst fears were soon over ; the report was favourable, but, as they read on, a little disappointingly so. They thought that the dams showed possibilities and the upshot was another committee. This one focused the aim more definitely ; it was to be called " The Air Attack on Dams Committee."

The members were again scientists and engineers and in a

mood to be interested in something new because even German bombs, though they were more efficient than R.A.F. bombs and killed thousands of civilians, had demonstrated the limitations of small bombs. The machine shop in an English factory, for instance, had been hit by seven Nazi 250-lb. bombs and they had damaged only twenty-four out of the 500 machines in the factory. All except two were repairable and the machine shop was running as usual almost immediately. Because aiming was so inaccurate it was obvious that 75 per cent. of such bombs were wasted.

" With this big bomb," Wallis earnestly impressed on them, " you don't have to get a direct hit. I think a ten-ton bomb dropped fifty feet away stands a good chance of knocking a hole in a dam like the Moehne. A near miss like that ought to be simple enough to organise."

One of the members, Dr. Glanville, of the Road Research Laboratories at Harmondsworth, suggested building a model dam and testing the theories with scaled-down charges of explosive. Wallis accepted delightedly.

Over the next few months, whenever he could spare time from his arduous work at Vickers, Wallis helped Glanville design and painstakingly build a model dam one-fiftieth the size of the Moehne with tiny cubes of concrete, scale models of the huge masonry blocks in the real dam. The model was about 30 feet long, 33 inches high and up to 2 feet thick, a low wall arched between earthen banks, secluded from prying outside eyes in a walled garden.

They flooded the ground at one side to simulate the lake, and Wallis exploded a few ounces of gelignite under the surface 4 feet from the model to give the effect of a 10-tonner going off 200 feet away. There was a commotion on the water and a fountain of muddy water gushed up ; on the model a couple of patches of concrete flaked and chipped.

" Not so good there," Wallis said. " Let's try it closer."

He exploded more gelignite 3 feet from the dam, and there was a little more damage. He set off another charge 2 feet away and still found only minor chipping.

At a distance of 12 inches (representing a 10-tonner 50 feet from the dam) the gelignite caused a couple of cracks in the outer structure ; but they were small cracks, not enough to harm the dam significantly. They tried several more charges but the cumulative effect was not encouraging.

Months had passed since the first hopeful meeting of the committee, and Wallis could see that their early co-operation was congealing. Glanville built another model, and Wallis tried bigger charges to see what *would* smash the models at a distance. One day a few extra ounces of gelignite a foot away sent a mushroom of water spraying over the wall round the garden and as the spume cleared they saw the water of the little lake gushing through the burst dam. Slabs of concrete had cracked and spilled out and there was the breach that Wallis had been wanting. He calculated the scaled-up charge which, dropped 50 feet away, would smash such a hole in the Moehne. The answer was something like 30,000 lb. of the new explosive RDX, and the gentle scientist did not need pencil and paper to estimate the significance.

Thirty thousand pounds was nearly 14 tons. That was the explosive alone. Add the weight of the thick case of special steel—another 40,000 odd lb. It meant a bomb weighing 70,000 lb.—over 30 tons, and the Victory Bomber, still only on paper and straining the limits of feasible aircraft construction, would carry only a 10-tonner.

The next meeting of the Air Attack on Dams Committee was in a fortnight and it required little thought to foresee it would be the last meeting.

Wallis would not give up.

Supposing, he thought, a bomb could be exploded *against* the dam wall. The shock wave punch would be much greater. So the explosive needed would be smaller. So would the bomb casing.

But how to get a big bomb in the exact spot—deep enough for the shock punch and pressed against the wall to make the most of it ? Or, if it required more than one bomb, how could you get them all in the exact spot ? A torpedo ? But the dams had heavy torpedo netting in front of them. You could drop a bomb very low to cut down the error, but it would be almost horizontal when it hit the water and would ricochet off ; so that was no good. If you dropped it from high

enough to enter cleanly, the aim would not be good enough.
Wallis probed at the problem for days.

He does not remember exactly when the idea came to him,
born of that last holiday in Dorset before the war started.
The children had played a game that all youngsters play in
water, and out of that memory an idea grew imperceptibly ;
such a weird idea that it took him days to recognise it. People
afterwards thought it was crazy even when Wallis proved it
to them.

Always sensitive to ridicule, Wallis told no one the details,
not even his friend Mutt Summers, chief test pilot for
Vickers and the man who had tested his old warhorse, the
Wellington. Captain Summers was a hefty extrovert and not
the type to take a freak idea seriously. Unable to keep
completely silent, he did say to Summers cagily :

" Mutt, I think I've got an idea about these dams. Something I saw on my last holiday with the youngsters." He was
mysterious about it and would say no more. Summers,
looking at him curiously, noted that he was " quite excited."

Wallis dragged a tub into the garden of his house at
Effingham, filled it with water and, screened from the world
by a fence and hedges, started playing children's games.
Certain officials, had they seen him, would have felt they
were right when they called him mad. He used a rough bit
of apparatus he had carved out of wood and played for hours,
making himself wet but happy because his idea seemed to
work.

The day of the meeting of the Air Attack on Dams Committee he went early to London, buttonholed the chairman,
Dr. Pye, and privately explained his new theory, so earnestly
that Pye did not laugh though he looked a little sideways.

" I'd rather you didn't tell the others yet," Wallis said.
" They might think it a bit far-fetched."

" Yes," said Dr. Pye. " I see that. What do you want
me to do ? "

" Give me time to find out how much RDX will blow a
hole in the Moehne Dam if it's pressed up against the wall."

Pye talked eloquently to the committee without giving
Wallis's secret away. The members were reluctant when

they heard the results of the last model's test and Wallis was like a cat on hot bricks till they consented to one more experiment.

Glanville built him a new model dam, and Wallis started with small charges, sinking them in the water and exploding them when they were lying against the slabs of concrete. The effect was shattering—literally. He smashed wall after wall seeking the smallest charge needed, and soon he knew that in a contact explosion tamped by water a tiny plug of a few ounces of gelignite blasted a satisfying hole through a concrete wall 6 inches thick. From that he calculated he would need only 6,000 lb. of RDX to breach the Moehne Dam. With his new idea he could cut the case weight down to a little over 3,000 lb., making the complete bomb about 9,500 lb. Less than 5 tons. The new four-engined Lancasters would carry that to the Ruhr without trouble.

CHAPTER III

THE GREEN LIGHT

ARMED with sums and theories, Wallis faced the task of convincing officials in their brick and stone lairs along Whitehall and other influential thoroughfares that he could put his bomb in the exact spot, an awkward task because they were all allergic to weird inventions. Literally one in a thousand was any good, and that usually not good enough to justify diverting effort. Most were obviously " crackpot," and Wallis's must have looked like one of those. He called on Professor Patrick Blackett, director of an " operational research " branch, and Blackett, a spare, rather intense man, listened to his ideas, carefully examined the calculations, riffled them back into a neat pile and said quietly :

" We've been looking for this for two years."

Wallis was electrified.

" I'd like you to leave these with me for a while," Blackett said. " There are one or two people I know who would be interested."

Blackett moved fast. As soon as Wallis had left he went to see Sir Henry Tizard and told him what he had heard. Tizard also moved with unorthodox haste, driving down to Weybridge next morning, where Wallis eagerly explained it all again.

" It seems," Tizard said when he had finished, " that the main thing to establish is whether this freak of yours will really work, and if so how we go about putting it into practice."

At Teddington, he said, was a huge ship-testing tank which would be ideal for experiments. He also thought there should be more tests to check how much explosive would theoretically punch a hole in a dam.

" I think I know just the thing," said Wallis, whose " damology " researches had been fanatical. " There's a small disused dam in Radnorshire ; no earthly use any more as a dam and won't ever be. We could try and knock it down."

" Who owns it ? " Tizard asked.

" Birmingham Corporation." Wallis knew all the answers.

" We'll try them," Tizard said, and Birmingham Corporation, with a little prodding, said yes.

It was a nice little dam, about 150 feet long and quite thick, curving gracefully across the mouth of a reach of Rhayader Lake, high in the Welsh hills west of Leominster. The corporation had built a bigger dam across the mouth of the lake to feed a little river that tumbled out of the hills.

Wallis estimated that the old dam should have a fifth of the resistance of the Moehne, an ideal test model. He calculated the smallest charge that should knock it down and set off with a packet of RDX and some explosives engineers. Wrapped against the raw mountain wind, he wasted little time, measured out the charge, tamped it in a sealed casing and lowered it deep into the water against the dam wall. Behind the rocks, his mouth dry with anxiety, he pressed the plunger and the hills echoed with sound. Water spurted a hundred feet high, the lake whipped into fury, and as the water plunged back into the void the concrete crumbled and a hissing flood burst into the main lake. Wallis, pink with glee, saw there was a ragged hole in the dam 15 feet across and about 12 feet deep.

For the next five months he experimented whenever he could in the tank at Teddington, an enormous thing hundreds of feet long, plunging strangely shaped pellets into the dirty green water and watching their antics under the surface. Progress was steady rather than meteoric, but the results confirmed his theory. He carved larger " bombs " and made these, too, perform his trick, and by the middle of 1942 he was satisfied he knew enough to make a 9,000-lb. bomb behave.

Tizard was pleased, but Tizard was an adviser, not all-powerful ; the task was to get executive officials keen. Wallis thought he had proved his point, and as an innocent scientist he can perhaps be excused for optimism. In government there are " proper channels " and few short cuts, and the proper channels were preoccupied with other vital work.

Wallis saw several officials, received tea and courtesy, even compliments, but not enough action to please him. Two high executives in particular who could have started things moving seemed irritatingly cautious. They shall be nameless, because they are good men who worked hard and brilliantly in other directions, and no honest man should be censured for failing to understand Wallis any more than he should be condemned for failing to follow Einstein.

But it was so *maddening!* Wallis knew he had proved his theories and still he was up against a barrier that seemed as solid as a dam wall. He got the ear of a great scientist who had access to Churchill, expounded his ideas and showed his calculations. The scientist was not impressed, and said so. Yet there were other officials, like Dr. Pye, who were encouraging him.

The phone rang one day and a man named Lane, speaking from London, said he wanted to talk to Wallis about " a secret matter." He was, he said, from one of the committees dealing with new and secret weapons. Wallis felt his heart skip.

" What's it about ? " he asked.

" It's to do with aircraft and water," said the man, " but I mustn't say any more over the phone. Can I come and see you ? "

" To-morrow," said Wallis, " as early as you like."

Lane walked into his office in the morning, an alert young man, and Wallis welcomed him warmly. Lane showed his credentials and said :

" Do you remember an idea of yours back in 1941 about putting a smoke screen round a fleet ? "

" Smoke screen ? " Wallis said, not understanding for a moment ; and then he remembered. Many other things besides earthquake bombs had germinated in his fertile mind since 1939, and one of them had been for a radio-controlled pilotless plane which could be catapulted from a cruiser or battleship to lay a smoke screen ; cheaper and faster than laying a screen by destroyers.

" Yes," he said heavily. " I remember."

" We're interested in it now," Lane said. " Have been for some time, but we couldn't do everything at once. Can you tell me a little more about it ? "

Wallis spent the next hour going into detail, and when he had finished and Lane was thanking him and rising to go Wallis said a little wistfully :

" You know, it's very disappointing. I thought you wanted to see me about my pet idea that nobody seems to want."

" Oh ? " said Lane politely, reaching for his hat. " What's that ? "

Wallis started to tell him, and as he described his tests the casual attention on Lane's face changed to a look of startled interest. He sat down again and listened for another hour ; afterwards, when he rose to go again, he said, " I'll tell my chief about this one. I think he might be interested."

Lane's chief rang Wallis next morning and an hour later he was in Wallis's office in the old house at Burhill, listening. Hours later he went back to London as nearly convinced as a man can be by figures.

Things began to happen in a more practical way. Through Lane's chief Wallis got permission to build six half-size prototypes of his new bomb, purely for experiment, and was told he could convert a Wellington to drop them.

In a few weeks the casings were finished. Wallis filled them with a harmless substitute the same weight as RDX, and at 3 p.m. on December 4, 1942, the converted Wellington took off from Weybridge with the first bomb on board and Mutt Summers in the pilot's seat, Wallis crouched in the nose as bomb-aimer, to test-drop off Chesil Beach on the south coast.

They had had to take the bomb-doors off, and the strange shape hanging underneath changed the outline of the plane. Naval gunners at Portland could not make out the strange aircraft, so they rightly gave themselves the benefit of the doubt and opened fire and the gentle scientist was intrigued to see black puffs of flak staining the sky. He thought they were tiny clouds and his scientific mind wondered at the phenomenon until a wing tip flicked up and the Wellington peeled off out of range. Wallis saw Summers muttering explosively, realised what had happened and thought, wryly, the flak was carrying official obstructionism a little too far.

Off Chesil Beach Summers dived over the water, Wallis pressed the button and watched his bomb rattle clear of its stowage. It took so long it seemed like slow-motion, and then it hit and spray hid it. The spray cleared slowly and Wallis saw that the bomb had worked—in a way—but not quite as he had hoped. He had a mixed emotion, neither pleasure nor acute disappointment. Something had gone a little wrong and on the flight back to Weybridge he decided that the case had not been strong enough and had crushed a little under the impact. When they landed he ordered the cases of the remaining bombs strengthened.

On December 12 he and Summers took off with a strengthened bomb, Summers prudently avoiding Portland. Off Chesil Beach, Wallis watched the bomb going down, holding his breath ; again the spout of water as it hit, and as the spray cleared Wallis gave a yell of delight. It worked beautifully. In the next three days he and Summers dropped three more and the bomb worked every time. They took a movie cameraman with them on these flights and got undeniable evidence that it worked.

On the strength of that Winterbotham arranged an interview for Wallis with the Ministry of Supply's scientific tribunal to assess new weapons. The tribunal watched his films and let it be known that the report would be favourable.

With his films Wallis made a new assault on the two cautious officials. They were still non-committal, but it seemed to Wallis a little less inflexibly so. On February 2 he had another interview with the scientist who had influence with Churchill, and the scientist this time did not say a flat no ; neither did he say yes.

Wallis got a call the same day from one of the two cautious ones, giving him permission to go ahead with the preliminary design of a full-sized bomb, and he felt the fierce joy of a front-row forward who has heaved manfully in the scrum and gained an inch. The official tempered his joy by telling him not to expect too much. Further work would depend on whether it would dislocate work on a new bomber. It is perhaps fair to say that the official *had* to be cautious. He could *not* do everything he wanted to.

This was early February, 1943, and the best time to smash the dams was in May, when they were full. To leave it later might annoy the Germans but not seriously incommode them. There was still just time. Wallis worked late over his plans and on the eighth day had them virtually finished when the bombshell dropped. One of the cautious ones phoned, ordering him to stop work on the big bomb. There was to be no further action on it.

Wallis went grimly next day to the big tank at Teddington, sank two glass airtight tanks in the water, put an arc light in one and induced a slight young woman to go into the other with a movie camera. She and the camera could just fit in. He dropped a model bomb into the water and the girl filmed its under-water progress. It was a beautiful film ; clearly it showed the bomb plunging under the surface and crawling into position against the side of the tank.

Next he bailed up Summers and demanded an interview with Air Marshal Sir Arthur Harris, chief of Bomber Command. Summers had known Harris for years, well enough to call him by his first name, which few people dared to do. Harris, it was freely acknowledged, could crush a seaside landlady with a look.

Summers and Wallis drove into the wood outside High Wycombe where Harris had his headquarters, and as Wallis put his foot on the threshold of Harris's office the booming voice hit him like a shock wave :

" What the hell is it you want? I've no time for you damned inventors. My boys' lives are too precious to be wasted by your crazy notions ! "

It was enough to strike fear into the heart of the sturdiest inventor. Wallis almost baulked, then pressed on and there was the bulky figure of Harris, grey eyes staring coldly over the half-moon glasses perched on his nose.

" Well? " Harris was a man of few words and forceful ones.

" I have an idea for destroying German dams," Wallis said. " The effects on Germany would be enormous."

" I've heard about it. It's far-fetched."

Wallis said he'd like to explain it, and Harris gave a grunt which Wallis took for yes and went ahead, trying not to be too involved and yet show how he had proved the theory. At the end the bomber chief had absorbed it all. Not that there was any encouraging reaction. Harris said bluntly :

" If you think you're going to walk in and get a squadron of Lancasters out of me you've made a mistake. You're not ! "

Wallis started to bristle and Summers, who knew Wallis's obstinacy and Harris's explosive temperament, kicked Wallis's shin under the desk. Wallis controlled himself.

" We don't want a squadron," he said, " . . . yet. We'd like a chance to prove it in trials with one Lancaster first."

Harris eyed him stonily. " Maybe," he said. " You *really* think you can knock a dam down with that thing."

" Yes," Wallis said. " Or it may take three or four. We can put them all in the same place."

Summers said peaceably, " We'll prove it'll work, Bert."

" Prove it and I'll arrange a squadron," Harris said, and then with his old fierceness, staring at Wallis, " but I'm tired of half-baked inventors trying to run things."

Summers kicked Wallis once more under the desk and broke the tension by saying, " We've got some films here that show clearly how it works."

" All right. Let's see them." They trooped out to the Command projection room, picking up Harris's chief lieutenant, Air Vice-Marshal Saundby, on the way. Harris curtly told the projectionist to clear out. " If it's as good as you say," he told Wallis, " there's no point letting everyone know. Saundby can run the films through."

Saundby's training had not concentrated much on film projection work and for a while there was a tangle of celluloid, but eventually he sorted it out, clicked the lights off and they watched in silence the antics of the bombs dropped at Chesil Beach and the tricks of the model under the water at Teddington.

When the lights went up Harris had his poker face on. " Very interesting," he grunted. " I'll think it over."

Wallis and Summers went back to Weybridge ; Summers, who was a tough customer, amused by the interview, and

Wallis with mixed feelings. He did not know why Harris
distrusted inventors so much.

[*It had started (so the story says) back about* 1916, *when
Major Arthur Harris led a squadron of fighters in England whose
job it was to down German Zeppelins. An inventor was sent to him
to try out a new idea, to dangle an explosive charge like a football
on a long line under a fighter, which then flew over a Zeppelin so
that the football grenade hit the Zeppelin, to the mortification of
the Germans. Harris, already a firebrand, tried it and found
that the long clothes-line dangling underneath was more of a
menace to the plane.*

"*. . . So why not,*" *he said to the inventor,* "*dispense with
the clothes-line and just drop the grenade.*"

"*Ah, that's a good idea,*" *said the inventor.* "*Let's try
that.*"

"*Just a minute,*" *Harris said.* "*If you're going to drop it
by itself wouldn't it be better to streamline it so it'll fall faster
and more accurately ?*"

"*Yes, yes,*" *the inventor said.* "*Excellent. Let's do that.*"

"*Just a minute,*" *said Harris, and pointed to his plane
standing near by.* "*What the hell d'you think those are under
the wings ?*"

"*Those*" *were little anti-Zeppelin bombs.*]

Not long after, Wallis got a summons to a senior executive
whom he knew quite well and who in the past had encouraged
his bomb work.

"Wallis," he said, "I've been asked by ―――" (one of
the two cautious ones) "to tell you to stop your nonsense
about destroying dams. He tells me you're making a nuisance
of yourself at the Ministry."

For a moment Wallis was stunned, then recovered and
answered quietly, "If you think I'm not acting in the best
interests of the war effort, I think I should offer to resign from
all my work and try something else."

For the first and last time he saw the executive lose his
temper. The man shot to his feet, smashed his fist on the
desk and shouted "Mutiny !" Smashed his fist down again

with another " Mutiny ! " And again with a third explosive " Mutiny ! " He subsided, red and quivering, and Wallis walked out of the room. He had lunch somewhere but does not remember where, and afterwards went and told the whole story to Sir Thomas Merton, one of the Supply Ministry's inventions tribunal. Merton promised support, but Wallis came away still depressed, knowing of nothing more he could do ; it seemed too late now to organise things for the coming May, and after a couple of days he was resigned to it.

That was the day, February 26, he got a summons to the office of one of the cautious ones, and there he also found the senior executive who had shouted " Mutiny ! " Proceedings opened by the cautious one saying, a little stiffly :

" Mr. Wallis, orders have been received that your dams project is to go ahead immediately with a view to an operation at all costs no later than May."

It took some time for Wallis to take it in.

(The Chief of the Air Staff, as it happened, had sanctioned the project a week before, and Churchill and Merton were enthusiastic about it.)

CHAPTER IV

A SQUADRON IS BORN

AFTER battling for so long, Wallis, in the weeks that followed, sometimes ruefully thought he had got more action than he could stand. Life was work from dawn till midnight, planning, draughting, thinking and discussing, grabbing a sandwich with one hand while the work went on.

He told his workers briefly what he wanted them to do, but not what the bombs were to do, or when, or where. Only he, Harris and a selected few others knew that, and apart from them a curtain of secrecy came down. Each craftsman worked on one part and knew nothing of the others.

The team-work was excellent ; even the few formerly cautious ones forgot their reservations and everyone worked strenuously. By normal standards the job was impossible in the time, but the Chief of the Air Staff said it *had* to be done, and people conveniently ignored inconvenient regulations and cut whatever corners seemed necessary.

The full-size bomb was to be 7 feet in girth and of surprising length. Roy Chadwick, chief Avro designer, started taking the bomb doors off Lancasters and doing other strange things to them so they could carry it. Explosives experts, tactical authorities, secret service men and hundreds of others had a part in it, and over Germany every day a fast Mosquito flew 25,000 feet over the dams taking photographs. Deep in the underground vaults of Bomber Command men studied the photographs through thick magnifying glasses to check the level of the rising water and the defences. If the secret leaked out they would see the extra flak and the raid would have to be called off. It was going to be suicidal enough as it was. There seemed to be at least six gun positions around the Moehne alone, and that was no matter for comfort because the bombs would have to be dropped from very low level, so low that a pilot could lean out and almost dangle his fingers in the water. They would have to fly between two towers on top of the dam, and some of the guns were in these towers.

The Mosquitoes flew a devious way and crossed the dams as though by accident so the Germans would not be suspicious. An ugly sign appeared in the first few days : photographs showed the anti-torpedo boom in front of the Moehne was being repaired ; it had been loose and untidy, and now it was being tightened. Nothing else appeared to be happening though, and after a while it was reasonable to assume that it was only a periodical check. While the work pressed on in England, it seemed that the Germans were doing nothing significant.

And therein lies a story ! Barnes Wallis was not the only patriot to find that officialdom can be an immovable object to anything but irresistible force.

On August 29, 1939, a certain *Oberburgermeister* Dillgardt had written from his office in the Ruhr to the Wehrmacht chiefs in Muenster. " In view of the present military situation," he said delicately, he wanted to raise the question of the defence of large dams like the Moehne and the Eder. Dillgardt was an unusually perspicacious man and it is uncanny how his layman's mind worked along the same path as Wallis's.

Dillgardt said he was worried because he thought that a large bomb exploded deep in the water some 20 metres from the dam might conceivably blow a large hole in it owing to the compressive effects of the water. He admitted humbly that his experts did not agree with him, but he painted an ugly picture of what would happen if the dams were breached —almost identical with Wallis's conclusions. He submitted, with respect, that the dam defences be strengthened.

The military authorities wrote back politely. Dillgardt could " rest assured that the matter will receive the most careful and immediate consideration," and Dillgardt, presumably aware of the real meaning of this fatal phrase, wrote again, drawing their attention to a book called " The Curse of Bombing," in which the author, Camille Rougeron, spoke of the danger of bombing attacks on dams. The authorities thanked him again but the matter stayed " under consideration."

Over the next three years the files between Dillgardt and

the Wehrmacht grew to imposing fatness, a series of harrowing appeals sandwiched between dignified and adroit evasions. In a peacetime paper battle civilian officials can usually vanquish military officials, but in wartime the boot is on the other foot, and the military men in Muenster were impregnable.

Dillgardt even predicted that any attack would be made in May, when the dams were full. He pointed out the increasing size and power of British bombs, asked for heavier torpedo nets, for smoke screens, balloon barrages, searchlights and heavy flak, and every time he was fobbed off returned tenaciously to the attack. Now and then he tasted victory ; early in 1940 the Wehrmacht posted some heavy flak and searchlights around the Moehne, perhaps to keep Dillgardt quiet, and a few weeks later took them away again.

Twice more, when his persistence exasperated them into some concession, the Wehrmacht posted a little light flak there and then took them away again. And as Dillgardt pestered them anew a note of asperity crept into the answering letters ; the formal politeness deteriorated more and more. Sarcastically the generals expressed their gratitude for having their duty so generously explained to them by a civilian. Uncrushed, the dogged Dillgardt sent fresh reminders until one day a tormented general wrote tersely :

" *Sir,*
There is no further need for regular reports to be sent in to this office regarding storage level of these dams.
Heil Hitler ! "

Later on they threw him a last crumb by sending some 20 mm. guns.

At his headquarters in the wood Sir Arthur Harris (" Bert " to his friends and " Bomber " to the public) had been pondering how the attack should be made—and who should make it. On March 15 he sent for Air Vice-Marshal the Honourable Ralph Cochrane, who two days before had become Air Officer Commanding No. 5 (Bomber) Group.

" I've got a job for you, Cocky," Harris said and told him

about Wallis's weird bomb and what he proposed to do with
it.　At the end he said : " I know it sounds far-fetched, but
I think it has a good chance."

Cochrane said : " Well, sir, I've known Wallis for twenty-
five years.　He's a wonderful engineer and I've never known
him not to produce what he says he will."

" I hope he does it again now," Harris said.　" You know
how he works.　I want you to organise the raid.　Ask for
anything you want, as long as it's reasonable."

Cochrane thought for a moment.

" It's going to need some good aircrews," he said.　" I
think I'd better screen one of my squadrons right away and
start them on intensive training."

" I don't want to do that," Harris said.　" I don't want to
take a single squadron out of the line if I can help it, or interfere with any of the main force.　What I have in mind is a
new squadron, say, of experienced people who're just finishing
a tour.　Some of the keen chaps won't mind doing another
trip.　Can you find enough in your group ? "

" Yes, sir."　Cochrane asked Harris if he wanted anyone in
particular to command the new squadron, and Harris said :
" Yes, Gibson."

Cochrane nodded in satisfaction, and ten minutes later,
deep in thought, he was driving back to the old Victorian
mansion outside Grantham that was 5 Group Headquarters.
There could probably have been no better choice than
Cochrane for planning the raid.　A spare man with a lean
face, his manner was crisp and decisive, perfectly reflecting
his mind.　The third son of a noble Scottish family, he was
climbing to the top on his own ability ; he had perhaps the
most incisive brain in the R.A.F.—and that is no diplomatic
exaggeration.　His god was efficiency and he sought it
uncompromisingly—almost ruthlessly according to some of
his men, who were afraid of him, but his aircrews would
do anything he asked, knowing that it would be meticulously
planned.

Moreover, Cochrane knew Wallis well ; had worked with
him in the Royal Naval Air Service in World War I, flying
his experimental airships and testing the world's first airship

mooring mast, which Wallis had designed. Ever since then Cochrane had had a quick sympathy for the scientific approach.

That night a nuggetty little man with a square, handsome face, named Guy Gibson, took off on the last trip of his third tour. If he got back he was due for leave and a rest, having been on ops almost constantly since the war started. The target was Stuttgart and his Lancaster was laden with one of the new 8,000-lb. " blockbusters " (not the penetrating " earthquake " type that Wallis envisaged, but bombs had made startling strides in the past year).

An engine failed on the way to Stuttgart and the aircraft would not hold her height. Gibson eased her out of the stream, dropping towards the ground, but headed on. The last trip of a tour is an ordeal with its hopes of a six-months' reprieve. Before take-off the reprieve seems so near and yet so far, and waiting to get it over is not pleasant. Gibson took a chance rather than turn back and go through the waiting again.

Over Stuttgart he had the other three engines shaking the aircraft at full power and managed to drag up to a safe enough height to drop his bomb, then dived to the dark anonymity of earth and hugged the ground all the way back. That was Gibson's 173rd trip. He was a wing commander with the D.S.O. and D.F.C. Aged twenty-five.

He woke late, head still ringing with the engine noise, and lay curled up, half thinking, half dreaming of leave in Cornwall. That morning his leave was cancelled and, to his dismay, he was posted to 5 Group Headquarters.

A day or so later he was shown into Cochrane's office and saluted smartly.

" Ah, Gibson," Cochrane said. " Firstly, my congratulations on the bar to your D.S.O."

" Thank you, sir."

" Would you like to do one more trip ? "

Gibson gulped and said, a little warily :

" What kind of trip, sir ? "

" An important one. I can't tell you any more about it now except that you would command the operation."

Gibson said slowly, " Yes, I—I think so, sir," thinking of the flak and the fighters he hoped he had finished with for a time.

" Good ; that's fine. I'll let you know more as soon as I can," and a moment later Gibson was outside the door, wondering what it was all about. He waited two days before Cochrane sent for him again, and this time another man was with him, Group Captain Charles Whitworth, who commanded the bomber base at Scampton, a stocky, curly-haired man of about thirty, with a long list of operations behind him and a D.S.O. and D.F.C. on his tunic. Gibson knew him and liked him.

Cochrane was friendly. " Sit down," he said and held out a cigarette. " I asked you the other day if you'd care to do another raid and you said you would, but I want to warn you that this will be no ordinary sortie and it can't be done for at least two months."

Gibson thought : " Hell, it's the *Tirpitz*. Why did I say yes ! " The 45,000-ton " unsinkable " battleship was lying in a Norwegian fiord, a permanent menace to the Russia convoys and a lethal target to tackle.

Cochrane was still talking. " Training for this raid is so important that the Commander-in-Chief wants a special squadrom formed. I want you to form it. You'd better use Whitworth's main base at Scampton. As far as aircrews are concerned, you'll want good ones ; you'd better pick them yourself. I'm telling all the squadrons they'll have to give up some of their best crews. I'm afraid they won't like it, so try and take men who are near the end of their tours. There's a lot of urgency in this because you haven't got very long and training is going to be very important. Go to it as fast as you can and try and get your aircraft flying in four days."

" Well, er . . . what sort of training, sir ? " Gibson asked. " And . . . what sort of target ? "

" Low flying," Cochrane said. " You've got to be able to low-fly at night till it's second nature. No, I can't tell you the target yet. That's secret, but you've all got to be perfect at low flying. At night. It's going to be the only way, and I think you can do it. You're going to a place where it'd be

Above : Some of the Australians on the dams raid. L. to R. : Bob Hay, Lance Howard, David Shannon, Jack Leggo, Spam Spafford, Micky Martin, Les Knight and Bob Kellow.

Below : Gibson and his crew climbing into G for George just before they took off on the dams raid. L. to R. : Trevor-Roper, Pulford, Deering, Spafford, Hutchison, Gibson and Taerum.

Above : The Moehne Dam breached, photographed by our reconnaissance plane the morning after the attack.

Below : At dawn, five hours after the raid, the Germans took this picture of the Moehne Dam. By this time the lake had shrunk and the worst fury of the flood had subsided. The breach is 100 yards across.

wrong to send a single squadron at the normal height by itself.

Gibson knew what that meant. Germany ! A single squadron at 15,000 feet would get all the night fighters. It was not so bad for the main force, the stream of hundreds of bombers ; they confused the enemy radar, dispersed the fighters, and there was protection in numbers. Not so with a lone squadron. But low level, " on the deck," yes. Well, maybe ! Well, it was going to be low level anyway. Over Germany ! He knew a man named Martin who knew all about low flying over Germany. Gibson had met him when Martin was being decorated for it. Cochrane was still talking :

" I'm sorry I can't tell you any more for the moment, Gibson. The immediate problem is to get your crews and get them flying."

" How about aircraft, sir ? "

" The equipment staff have that in hand. The first will be flown in to-morrow." The interview was clearly over and Cochrane was already frowning at some papers on his desk. Gibson saluted, and as he turned the door handle Cochrane looked up again.

" One thing more," he said. " You'll have to watch security. As far as others are concerned this is just an ordinary new squadron. We'll think up a cover plan later."

Outside the door Whitworth said, " See you at Scampton in a couple of days. I'll get things fixed up for you. I imagine you'll be having about seven hundred men."

Somewhat bewildered, Gibson went off to the S.O.A. to see how one went about forming a new squadron, and half an hour later he was looking at a long list of things he had to do and people he had to see.

A staff officer helped him pick aircrew from the group lists. Gibson knew most of the pilots—he got the staff man to promise him Martin and help him pick the navigators, engineers, bomb aimers, wireless operators and gunners ; when they had finished they had 147 names—twenty-one complete crews, seven to a crew. Gibson had his own crew ; they were just finishing their tour too, but they all wanted to come with him.

The Staff Officer Personnel told him how many men of

different trades he wanted for his ground crews and promised to siphon off picked men from other squadrons and post them to Scampton in forty-eight hours.

The equipment officer promised to deliver ten Lancasters to Scampton within two days. Just for a start. More would follow. With them would come the spare spark plugs and tools, starter motors and drip trays, bomb dollies and winches, dope and paint and chocks and thermos flasks. Gibson was startled by the unending list. Another man promised the thousand and one items for the men : blankets and lorries and bootlaces, beer and socks, toilet paper and so on. He was two days on these details, helped by Cochrane's deputy, the S.A.S.O., Group Captain Harry Satterly, a big, smooth-faced man who was excellent at detail ; and then it was all done—except for one thing.

" What squadron are you ? " Satterly asked.

" What d'you mean, sir ? "

" What number ? You've got to have a number."

" Oh," said Gibson, " where d'you get that ? "

" Somewhere in Air Ministry," Satterly said, " but they probably don't work so fast there. I'll get on to them and fix it up. Meantime you'd better call yourselves ' X Squadron.' "

Just before dinner on March 21, Wing Commander Guy Gibson, D.S.O., D.F.C., commander of " X," the paper squadron, arrived at Scampton to take formal command. In the officers' mess he found some of his crews already arrived and the mess waiters looking curiously at them as they stood around with pints of beer in their fists. It was obvious they were not to be an ordinary squadron ; the average age was about twenty-two but they were clearly veterans. D.F.C. ribbons were everywhere ; they had all done at least one tour, and some had done two.

Gibson moved among them, followed by the faithful Nigger, his big black Labrador dog, who rarely left his heels. Someone laid a half pint of beer on the floor for Nigger, who stuck his muzzle noisily into it and did not look up till he had licked it dry.

From his old 106 Squadron, Gibson had brought three crews as well as his own—those of Hopgood, Shannon and Burpee. Hopgood was English, fair and good looking except for a long front tooth that stuck out at an angle. Dave Shannon, D.F.C., was a baby-faced twenty-year-old from Australia, but did not look any more than sixteen, so he was growing a large moustache to look older. He was slender, with long fingers and thick, fair hair, and moved gracefully.

Gibson spotted Micky Martin with satisfaction. They had met at Buckingham Palace when Gibson was getting his D.S.O. and the King was pinning on the first of Martin's D.F.Cs. Though he came from Sydney, Martin was in the R.A.F., slight but good looking, with a wild glint in his eyes and a monstrous moustache that ended raggedly out by his ears. At the Palace they had talked shop and Martin had explained his low-flying system.

He had worked it out that if you flew lower than most bombers you would avoid the fighters ; lower still and the heavy flak would all burst well above. And if you got right down to tree-top height you would be gone before the light flak could draw a bead on you. There was still the risk of balloons, but Martin reasoned there would not be any balloons along main roads or railways, so he followed those. He had had the same two gunners for two years, Toby Foxlee and Tammy Simpson, both fellow-Australians, and on their low-level junkets they had become expert at picking off searchlights. Simpson and Foxlee had both come with him ; he'd also brought an experienced navigator, a lean, long-chinned Australian called Jack Leggo, and his bomb aimer, Bob Hay, also Australian, had been a bombing expert at Group. Leggo was to be navigation officer of the new squadron, and Hay was to be bombing leader. It is unlikely that there was a finer crew in Bomber Command ; hence Gibson's pleasure.

He had chosen " Dinghy " Young as his senior flight commander. Young had already ditched twice in his two tours, and both times got back home in his rubber dinghy. Bred in California, educated at Cambridge, he was a large, calm

D 2

man whose favourite trick was to swallow a pint of beer without drawing breath.

Les Munro was a New Zealander, tall, blue-chinned and solemn, a little older than the others. He was standing by the bar looking into space when Gibson located him. " Glad to see you, Les," Gibson said. " I see you're setting a good example already, drinking a little and thinking a lot." Munro up-ended his pint and drained it. " No, sir," he said, " thinking a little and drinking a lot."

The other flight commander was Henry Maudslay, ex-50 Squadron, ex-Eton, an athlete, polished and quiet, not a heavy drinker. Towering above the rest was the blond head of a man who weighed nearly 15 stone, with a pink face and pale blue eyes ; good looking in a rugged way. Joe McCarthy, from Brooklyn, U.S.A., former life-guard at Coney Island, had joined the R.A.F. before America came into the war.

No one knew what they were there for but, looking at the men around them, realised something special was in the wind. Someone finally asked Gibson what " the form " was and Gibson simply said : " I know less than you, old boy, but I'll see you all in the morning to give you what gen I can."

The party broke up late and some of the crews were merry, though none so much as Nigger. Gibson's crew had been shoving cans of beer under Nigger's nose all the time, and Nigger, who had never been known to refuse one, staggered cheerfully out after Gibson, leaving a zigzag liquid trail down the corridor.

In the morning Gibson called all the crews to the long briefing room on top of station headquarters and said :

" I know you're wondering why you're here. Well, you're here as a crack squadron to do a special job which I'm told will have startling results and may shorten the war. I can't tell you what the target is or where it is. All I can tell you is you'll have to practise low flying day and night until you can do it with your eyes shut. . . ."

There was a little murmuring as they heard " low flying " and they started making rough guesses. A voice said distinctly.

" Christ ! The *Tirpitz* ! " Gibson said, " Don't jump to conclusions. Maybe it's the *Tirpitz*, maybe not. Whatever it is I want you to be ready. If I tell you to fly to a tree in the middle of England I want you to be able to do it. If I tell you to fly through a hangar that isn't wide enough for your wingtips I want you to have a go at that too. You've got to be able to do anything you're told without question." And there was a breathless silence.

" Discipline is going to be essential. So is security. You're going to be talked about. It's unusual to have a crowd like you forming a squadron. Rumours are flying round already, but "—and punching his fist at the air in emphasis—" you've got to keep your mouths shut. If you get stuck in a pub on the hops and someone asks you what it's all about, tell him to mind his own business. Your lives really depend on secrecy. If we can surprise them everything'll be fine. If they're ready for us . . . " He looked at them in silence.

He went on to talk about training and organisation, and when it was over the crews trooped out with little flutters in their stomachs, the sort of feeling you get before a raid. It goes once you get into the air.

Dinghy Young and Maudslay were busy dividing the crews into flights and Gibson walked over to No. 2 hangar, the great steel shed that was to be squadron headquarters. Along the sides were the little office rooms and outside one a queue of " erks." [1] Inside, a dapper little man with a toothbrush moustache broke off his interviewing and saluted smartly ; Flight Sergeant " Chiefy " Powell had just arrived to be the squadron's disciplinary N.C.O. The ground crews were arriving in scores and Powell already had half of them organised in their billets and sections. Discip. N.C.O's run a close second to service police for unpopularity, but Chiefy Powell was to become a sort of godfather to the squadron. He knew far more than Gibson about the detail that makes a squadron tick ; Gibson had been too busy flying. He gave Powell and Heveron, the orderly room sergeant, a free hand and " X " squadron rapidly took shape

[1] Ground crews.

but were still only a paper squadron, their entire equipment consisting of one trestle desk, one chair and one phone.

Cochrane rang Gibson : " I'm sending you over a list of lakes in England and Wales that I want photographed. Get someone on to it as soon as you can."

Gibson, who had learned not to ask questions, said, " Yes, sir," wondering when the fog of secrecy was going to lift. Lorries were rolling in with maps and Mae Wests, boots and more " erks " and envelopes and paper clips and spanners and all the other things.

Then the first crisis. A conscientious service policeman considered that the " erks " arriving for " X " Squadron were inexcusably scruffy and went eagle-eyed round the huts " lumbering " scores of men for dirty boots, tarnished buttons and crooked collars. Zealously he typed all the names on the regulation forms and dumped the wad in front of Chiefy Powell.

" I'm putting seventy-five of your men on a charge, Flight," he said primly. The snorting Powell took the charges in to Gibson, and Gibson riffled through them.

" God," he said, " the men didn't look too bad to me."

" They've been travelling to get here and some of them need new uniforms." Powell was like a hen guarding her chicks.

" Fair enough." Gibson ripped the charge forms into shreds and looked round the room. " We need a wastepaper basket."

He told Powell to arrange with the station equipment officer for a clothing parade in the morning, and Powell, holding the phone in his hand, called back through the door a couple of minutes later that the equipment officer said it could not be done.

" Give me that bloody phone," Gibson said, and five seconds later on the other end of the line a pilot officer (equipment) jumped with fright as the earphone seemed to erupt against his head. The squadron was re-outfitted next morning.

Gibson spent hours interviewing his aircrews, sizing up

the ones he didn't know, and found that some of the squadron commanders, told to send their best men, had played the age-old service game and got rid of a couple they did not want. Gibson told them to pack and go back.

Chiefy Powell found the same thing in the " erks " who were still arriving, among them being two outrageous duds from Gibson's old squadron, 106. A week before Gibson had been trying to get rid of them from 106. Now, with pleasure, he sent them back to 106. Some W.A.A.F. drivers and clerks had arrived and two of them were pregnant ; Gibson, more interested in the birth of a squadron, returned them too.

He walked into the mess bar just before dinner, tired but feeling they were getting somewhere, and Charles Whitworth buttonholed him :

" Well, Gibby," he said, " you're going to command 617 Squadron now."

The little man looked thunderstruck. " What the hell ! " he exploded. " 617? I thought . . . I . . . Who and where the hell are they ? "

" Here," said Whitworth peaceably. " You. Your new number. Someone in Air House has moved off his bottom. Your squadron marking letters are AJ."

He called for a pint each and they drank to 617 Squadron.

CHAPTER V

OVER THE HURDLES

HUMPHRIES, the new adjutant, arrived next afternoon; a little fair-haired man, only twenty-eight, he was keen on flying but his eyes had stopped him. Gibson told Humphries as much as he knew himself and as Humphries was leaving his office Gibson said :

"I don't know yet what it's all about, but I gather this squadron will either make history or be wiped out."

Humphries looked at him, not knowing whether he was joking.

"I beg your pardon, sir," he said, but Gibson was looking at maps on his desk and didn't answer.

In the morning the curtain lifted a little. Gibson got a call from Satterly, who told him to catch a certain train to Weybridge, where he would be met at the station.

"May I know who I'm meeting, sir?"

"He'll know you," Satterly said.

Gibson walked out of Weybridge Station at half-past two and a big man squeezed behind the wheel of a tiny Fiat said, "Hello, Guy!"

"Mutt," Gibson said, surprised. "God, are you the man I'm looking for?"

"If you're the man I'm waiting for, I am," Summers said. "Jump in." They drove down the winding tree-lined road that leads to Vickers and went past the main gates without turning in. "What's this all about, Mutt?" Gibson said, unable to hold back any longer.

"You'll find out." He turned off up a side road to the left. "You wanted to be a test pilot for me once. D'you remember?"

"I remember." That was when he had first met Summers. It must have been eight years ago now, back in 1935, when he was eighteen. He had wanted to fly, so he had got an introduction to Summers at Vickers and asked about becoming a

Vickers test pilot. " Go and join the Air Force and learn to fly first," Summers had advised.

" You'll be doing some testing soon," Summers said. " Not for me exactly, but quite a test." He turned in some double gates and they pulled up outside the house at Burhill. Summers led the way into a room with windows looking over the golf course, and a white-haired man got up from a desk.

" I'm glad you've come," Wallis said. " Now we can get down to it. There isn't a great deal of time left. I don't suppose you know much about the weapon ? "

" Weapon ? " Gibson said. " I don't know anything about anything. Group Captain Satterly said you'd tell me everything."

Wallis blinked. " Don't you even know the target ? "

" Not the faintest idea."

" My dear boy," Wallis said in a sighing and faintly horrified voice. " My dear boy." He wandered over to the window and looked out, pondering. " That makes it very awkward."

" Well," Gibson said, " the S.A.S.O. said . . ."

" I know," said Wallis, " but this is dreadfully secret and I can't tell anyone whose name isn't on this list." He waved a bit of paper in Gibson's direction and Gibson could see there were only about half a dozen names on it.

Summers said, " This is damn silly."

" I know," Wallis said gloomily. " Well, my dear boy . . . I'll tell you as much as I dare and hope the A.O.C. will tell you the rest when you get back." Gibson waited curiously, and finally Wallis went on : " There are certain objects in enemy territory which are very big and quite vital to his war effort. They're so big that ordinary bombs won't hurt them, but I got an idea for a special type of big bomb."

He told Gibson about the shock waves and his weird idea for dropping bombs exactly in the right spot. Gibson was looking baffled trying to follow the shock wave theory.

" You've seen it working in pubs, Guy," Summers said. " A dozen times. The shove-ha'penny board. Remember how you get two or three discs lying touching and flick another one in behind them. The shock waves go right through them but they all stay where they are except the front one, and that goes skidding off. That's the shock wave."

" Ah, now I get it."

" I thought you would."

" Come and I'll show you," Wallis said and led Gibson into a tiny projection room. Wallis thumbed the switches and a flickering screen lit up with the title " Most Secret Trial No. 1." A Wellington dived into view over water and a thing fell from it, seemed to drop slowly and then was hidden in spray as it hit ; the spray cleared and Gibson started in amazement at what he saw. The thing worked and he became conscious of Wallis's voice behind explaining why. The lights went up again.

" Well, that's my secret bomb," Wallis said. " That's how we . . . how *you're* going to put it in the right place."

" Over water ? " Gibson said, fishing for a clue.

" Yes," but Wallis avoided the subject of the target. " Over water at night or in the early morning when it's very flat, and maybe there will be fog. Now, can you fly to the limits I want, roughly a speed of two hundred and forty miles per hour, at sixty feet over smooth water, and be able to bomb accurately ? "

" It's terribly hard to judge your height over water," Gibson said, " particularly smooth water. How much margin of error is allowed ? "

" None. That's the catch. Sixty feet. Just that. No more. No less. So the aiming will be accurate."

" Well . . . we can try. I suppose we can find a way."

" There's so *much* to do." Wallis sighed.

On the way back to Scampton, Gibson puzzled over the target. The only likely ones, he decided, were either the *Tirpitz* or the U-boat pens, and he shuddered a little at the thought. They would be smothered in guns. At Scampton he found some Lancasters had arrived and ground crews checking them over. In the morning he told his senior men what height they would have to bomb at but nothing about the bomb itself.

Dinghy Young said : " We'll have to do all the training we

can by moonlight, and you don't get much reliable moonlight in this country."

" Could we fly around with dark glasses on ? " Maudslay asked.

" No, that's no good. You can't see your instruments properly."

Gibson said he'd heard of a new type of synthetic night training. They put transparent amber screens round the perspex and the pilot wore blue glasses ; it was like looking out on moonlight but you could still see your instruments. He would see if Satterly could get them some.

Leggo was worried about navigation. Low-flying navigation is different. You don't see much of the area when you're low, so they were going to need large-scale maps with plenty of detail. Large-scale maps meant constant changing and awkward unfolding. He suggested they use strip maps wound on rollers ; navigators could prepare their own. And if they were flying low, radio was not going to be much use for navigation. It would be mostly map reading.

Bill Astell, deputy A Flight commander, took off the first Lancaster and was away five hours, coming back with photographs of lakes all over the north country. Gibson laid out ten separate routes for the crews to practise over, and in the days that followed the Lancasters were nosing thunderously into the air all day and cruising at 100 feet over the flat fens of Lincolnshire, Suffolk and Norfolk.

Flying low seems faster and is more exciting, also more dangerous. There is the temptation to slip between chimneys or lift a wingtip just over a tree, and the R.A.F. was losing a lot of aircraft every month from fatal low-flying accidents. It was (naturally) strictly forbidden, and the pilots were delighted to be ordered to do it. Across several counties outraged service police reached for notebooks and took the big AJ aircraft letters as they roared over their heads ; the complaints came flooding into Gibson's office, and with smug rectitude he tore them up.

After a few days they came down to 50 feet and flew longer routes, stretching out to the north country, threading through the valleys of the Pennines, climbing and diving over the

Welsh mountains, then down to Cornwall and up to Scotland, eventually as far as the Hebrides, winging low over the white horses while the pilots flew steady courses and the rest of the crews gave a hand with the map reading.

Gibson took his own Lancaster, G. for George, and flew over to a lake in the Pennines, to test the business of flying accurately at 60 feet over water. Diving over the hills he flattened out over the lake, then pulled up over the hills at the far end ; tried it several times and found it fairly easy to keep his altimeter needle steady around 60 feet. But that trial meant little. Over Germany barometric pressures would be unpredictable, and altimeters work off barometric pressure. He had to find some way of judging his height without relying much on the altimeter. Practice might do it.

He tried again at dusk with fog drifting over the lake, and it was different. Not pleasantly. The smooth water merged with the gloom and he found he did not have much idea about judging height. They very nearly went into the lake and as he pulled sharply up there was a grunt over the intercom as Trevor-Roper in the rear turret saw the ripples on the water from their slipstream. Even Spam Spafford, Gibson's chunky bomb aimer, was shaken. " Christ," he said, " this is bloody dangerous." He had had a disconcerting vision of the looming water from the nose perspex. (The only one not perturbed was Nigger, dozing by the G-box. Nigger often flew with Gibson—though not on ops—and went everywhere with him on the ground.)

Gibson flew back and told Cochrane that if he could not find some way of judging height accurately there would be no chance of doing the raid.

" There's still time to worry about that," Cochrane said. " Just now I want you to have a look at models of your targets." He waved a hand at three packing cases in a corner of his office and Gibson eyed them curiously. " You can't train your men properly unless you know what they are, so I'm letting you know now, but you'll be the only man in the squadron to know. Keep it that way."

A corporal brought in a hammer, and Cochrane sent him

out of the room while Gibson gently prised the lids loose and lifted the battens. He stood looking down at the models, and his first reaction was a feeling of tremendous relief. Thank God, it wasn't the *Tirpitz* ! It took him a couple of seconds after that to realise they were dams. One was the Moehne, and the other two the Eder and the Sorpe, handsome models that showed not only the dams but the countryside in detail for miles around, as though photographs had taken on a third dimension. There were the flat surfaces of the lakes, the hills, winding rivers and the mosaic of fields and hedges. And in the middle the dams. Gibson stook looking for a long time and then Cochrane laid the lids back over them.

" Now you've seen what you've got to attack," he said. " Go and see Wallis again and come and see me when you get back."

The first thing Wallis said, eagerly, was :

" How did you get on ? "

" All right by day," Gibson said, " but not so good at night. In fact, flying level at night over water at sixty feet seems pretty nearly impossible."

" We'll work out some way of doing it. Now I'll tell you more about this Downwood business."

" Downwood ? "

" The code name for the raid." Wallis explained how the bombs were to explode deep against the dam walls.

" I've calculated that the first one ought at least to crack them, and then more bombs in the same place should shift the cracked wall back till it topples over . . . helped, of course, by the water pressure. The best times, of course, are when the dams are full. That will be in May. You'll need moonlight, and there's a full moon from the thirteenth to the nineteenth of May."

" About six weeks."

" Yes. You've *got* to be accurate or you might overshoot and the bomb will hit the parapet and go off there. That won't hurt the dam."

" Hurt us though," Gibson said as it dawned on him. " The aircraft would be just above it."

" Yes it would."

"Oh," Gibson said and went back thoughtfully to Scampton.

The synthetic night-flying gear arrived, transparent amber screens and blue glasses ; "two-stage amber," it was called. The screens were fitted in the cockpits, pilots donned their glasses and flying by day was exactly like flying in moonlight. They flew thousands of miles with them, first at 150 feet and then, as Gibson decided they were good enough, at 50 feet, the bomb aimers looking through the nose to warn of trees and hills.

Micky Martin lectured them on night low flying and there was little he had not learned about the pitfalls. One night he had hit a balloon cable low over Kassel, flying a Hampden, and should have crashed, but the cable carried away and they saw it in the moonlight dangling from the wing ; not a comforting sight, because when they had to come in slow to land at base with flaps and wheels down the cable would drag on the ground and almost surely catch in a hedge or fence and spin the Hampden in. On the way back Martin was wondering what to do about it when, to make things worse, a fighter jumped them. He dived to 50 feet to lose it and the cable caught on a tree and at diving speed it pulled itself free and they were all right—even lost the fighter.

Gibson took the screens and blue lenses away and sent the crews on low-level night cross-countries, first aircraft singly, and then, when the moon was right, in loose formations. Two crews were too keen and came back with branches and leaves in their radiators.

So far only Gibson knew what it was all about, but the rest of the people at Scampton were mighty curious. A pretty little W.A.A.F. driver called Doris Leeman summed up the general feeling when she entered in her diary : "Everyone speculating on the reason for the new gen squadron. So far nothing but training—most unusual as the crews have already done a tremendous amount of ops. They're evidently specially chosen." And a day or so later : "Have never seen Lancs fly so low as these boys fly them !"

The squadron did not know it, but security men were in the district to make sure that nothing leaked out. Phones were tapped and all mail censored. Security, as it happened, was good, though an " erk " said in a letter home : " The aircraft have been flying low with special night aids for some special op," and the letter was intercepted.

" Who is this fool ? " Gibson asked Chiefy Powell. He always asked Powell about any ground crew up on a charge. Powell knew them all, and Gibson knew Powell and trusted his opinions. " He's a good type, sir," Powell said, " and a good fitter."

Gibson had him brought to his office and tore a ferocious " strip " off him. All the ruthless side of his manner came out and the fitter broke down and cried. Gibson let him go with a reprimand.

One of the aircrews rang his girl friend and told her he could not see her that night because he was flying on special training. The phone had been tapped. Gibson called the whole squadron together and ordered the offender up on a table in the middle of them. He stood there miserable and pale.

" Look at him ! " Gibson bawled. " Look at the fool. Hundreds of men's lives in danger because one bloody fool can't keep his trap shut." And more in the same strain.

There were no more lapses.

Gibson was on the move from dawn to midnight every day, usually careering about on a little auto-bike from flights to armoury, to orderly room and so on. When he flew he kept his auto-bike in the hangar, apparently against some fiddling regulation because Scampton's zealous service policeman told Chiefy Powell the auto-bike would have to be moved.

Powell eyed him flintily. " You'd better see the owner," he said. " I don't think he'll move it."

" I'll see him all right," said the sergeant, " and he'll move it too."

So Chiefy took him in to see Gibson and shut the door behind him. There was a violent roaring behind the door and a white-faced sergeant came out.

The bike stayed where it was.

The crews were getting good at low night cross-countries and extended their trips out over the North Sea. Two of them were coming back in formation over Grimsby when the gunners of a couple of naval ships (who have itchy trigger fingers at sea) opened up on them, and as they darted in over the land the shore-based flak had a go too. They landed with little holes punched in the fuselage, complained to Martin and the wiry and diabolical Martin grinned and said, " Bloody good training. Make you flak-happy ! "

They practised low-level bombing on the range at Wainfleet, diving over the sand dropping 11½-lb. practice bombs with the low-level bombsight. The drops were not nearly accurate enough and Bob Hay said so disgustedly. Gibson took the problem to Cochrane.

Two days later a Wing Commander Dann, from the Ministry of Aircraft Production, called on Gibson.

" I hear you're having bombsight trouble for the dams raid."

" How the hell do you know about this ? " Gibson said.

" I've been let into it because I'm supposed to be a sighting expert," Dann explained. " I think I can solve your troubles. You may have noticed there are a couple of towers on top of each dam wall. We've measured them from the air and they're six hundred feet apart. Now this "—and he produced some drawings of a very elementary gadget—" is how we do it."

It was laughably simple ; a carpenter ran up one of the gadgets in five minutes out of bits of spare wood. The base was a small triangle of plywood with a peephole at one angle and two nails stuck in the other corners. " You look through the peephole," Dann said, " and when the two towers on the dams are in line with the nails, you press the tit. You'll find it'll drop in the right spot but you'll have to stick right on the speed."

Gibson shook his head in wonder. Workmen put two dummy towers on the dam across the neck of a midland lake, the bomb aimers knocked up their own sights and on his first try one of them dropped eight practice bombs with an average error of only 4 yards.

Still the problem of the height. Gibson tried repeatedly to see if practice made perfect, but it didn't. After his fifth

The Eder Dam breached, photographed by our reconnaissance plane the morning after the attack.

Gibson's crew tell their story at de-briefing after the dams raid. Standing at back : Sir Arthur Harris and A.V-M. Cochrane. Seated, L. to R. : Intelligence Officer, Spafford, Taerum and Trevor-Roper.

The moment in which H.M. King George VI selected 617 Squadron's badge. L. to R.: A.V-M. Cochrane, Gibson, H.M. King George VI and Charles Whitworth. Foreground : Model of the Moehne Dam.

try Dinghy Young landed and said, " It's no use. I can't see how we're going to do it. Why can't we use radio altimeters ? "

Gibson said he had thought of them a long time ago but they were not sensitive enough.

Time was getting short. Gibson got a call from Satterly. " They've finished the first two prototypes of the new bomb," Satterly said. " Fly down to Herne Bay to-morrow and watch the test drops. Take your bombing leader with you." That was April 15.

Wallis met them and next morning they drove out to a bare beach near Reculver. Half a mile back from the sea M.I.5 had cordoned the area off.

" I'm sorry to get you up so early," said the ever-courteous Wallis, " but the tide is up and that is the right time. We want to walk out at low tide and see how the bomb stands up to the shock of dropping."

In the east came two specks which grew into Lancasters, heading low over the shallows towards two white buoys bobbing on the water. " The other one's the camera air-craft," Wallis said as they watched them, and as the noise of engines filled the air Wallis was shouting above the roar, " He's high. He's too high." He sounded agitated. They swept up side by side and a great black thing dropped slowly away under the nearer one. It hit and vanished in a sheet of spray that hissed up towards the plane. For a moment there was nothing but the spray, and then out of it the fragments came flying.

" Broken," Wallis said and stood there very still. He took a deep breath. " They said it wouldn't work. Too big and heavy and the case too light. We've got another in the hangars. We'll try it this afternoon. The aircraft was too high."

Men worked hard that afternoon to strengthen the case of the second bomb while Wallis stripped to his underpants and waded to his neck in the freezing water, feeling with his feet for the fragments of the broken one. A launch took the broken bits on board and Wallis climbed in shivering, oblivious to everything but the ragged edges where the metal had burst.

They were on the dunes again as the sun was going down and the two aircraft came in sight, lower this time. Mutt Summers in the bomb plane was holding her steady at 50 feet. The suspense was painful. The black monster dropped away below, and again the water gushed skywards as it hit and out of the foaming cloud came the flying fragments as it broke.

Wallis said, " Oh, my God ! " And then as the spray cleared the incredible thing happened. They saw that the bomb had worked. Not as well as it should have, because some of the case had come away, but well enough for a start. In the cold dusk Wallis was sweating but happy.

(In the Lancaster, Summers was not happy. A lump of the casing had hit the elevators and one of them had jammed. The plane could just hold its height while Summers was holding his breath. He did a wide gentle turn and made a heart-stopping landing on the long runway at Manston with the trimmers.)

Wallis told Gibson : " We've still got a lot of work to do on the bomb ; but don't worry, it's going to be all right." Gibson and Hay took off in a little plane for Scampton and a few hundred feet up the engine coughed and died. There was only one way to go and that was down, but all the good fields were still covered with poles so the Germans could not land troops in an invasion. Gibson did his best to steer between them but a wingtip hit a pole, and as the aircraft slewed the other wing hit and they finished up sitting in a ball of crumpled duralumin, but were able to climb out and stand up, slightly bloody but unbowed.

A man came haring across the field, and when he saw they were not badly hurt he said severely, " I think they teach you young fellows to fly too early " ; and then a policeman arrived and said unemotionally, " I'm glad to see our landing devices work."

Gibson and Hay went back to Scampton by train, and on the way Gibson thought up a scheme to overcome the height problem : to dangle a long wire under the aircraft with a weight on it so it would skim the water when the aircraft was exactly at 60 feet. Full of hope, he tried it in G for George, but it didn't work. At speed the line trailed out almost straight behind.

Cochrane set the " back-room boys " to work on the problem and a day later Ben Lockspeiser, of the Ministry of Aircraft Production, arrived at Grantham with an idea. It was absurd to think how simple it was—and how effective. " Put a spotlight under the nose," he said, " and another one under the belly, both pointing down and inwards so they converge at sixty feet. When the two spots come together on the water, there you are ! "

Gibson joyfully told the crews, and when he had finished Spafford said casually, " I could have told you that. Last night Terry Taerum and I went to see the Ensa show, and when the girl there was doing her strip-tease there were these two spotlights shining on her. The idea crossed my mind then and I was going to tell you."

Gibson just looked at him.

Maudslay flew a Lancaster down to Farnborough and they fitted two spotlights on it the same day. Coming back he made test runs across the aerodrome and it worked beautifully. Maudslay said it was easy to get the circles of light together and keep them there. The idea was that they should touch each other, forming a figure " 8." He had Urquhart, his navigator, leaning his head out of the perspex observation blister behind the pilot, looking down at the ground and saying, " Down, down, down . . . up a bit . . . O.K.," and that was the procedure they adopted. They all tried it over Derwent Water using the same drill, and could fly to within 2 feet with wonderful consistency. Everyone was pleased but not exactly in ecstasy, because the same thought was in all their minds. An aircraft pelting up to a defended target at 60 feet did not make the crew very good insurance risks. And when it was showing lights too . . .

Down at Weybridge Wallis was still trying to strengthen the bomb and things were not going well. On April 22 they flew the first new model over to Reculver and dropped it ; it didn't break up, but it didn't work either and the tormented scientist was getting little sleep. Three weeks now to the time for the raid, and if they could not make it then it would have to be put off for another year ; probably, in view of official scepticism, for ever. The water in the dams was rising.

On April 29 they finished another modified bomb and Vickers test pilot Shorty Longbottom flew it to Reculver for the drop. It was pouring with rain and Wallis, out on the dunes, did not even notice it as he eyed the Lancaster diving out of the east towards the markers. Longbottom had her tucked down neatly to 60 feet at 258 indicated air speed, squinting through the rain squalls to hold his height and see the markers. The bomb fell slowly, hit cleanly—and worked. Down on the dunes, Longbottom, banking round, saw a white dot bobbing about. Wallis had taken his hat off and was waving it in the air, dancing and shouting while the rain ran down his face.

CHAPTER VI

TAKE-OFF

EARLY in May a strange-looking aircraft flew over Scampton. " God," Martin said, squinting up at it, " is that a Lanc, or isn't it ? What a monstrosity ! "

The aircraft dropped its wheels, landed and taxied to a hardstanding by 617's hangar, the first of the modified aircraft. It looked like a designer's nightmare ; the bomb doors were gone and the mid-upper turret and some of the armour, and there was a lot of queer junk sticking out underneath. It looked better for walking than flying. Avro's had done an unusually difficult and complicated job very quickly and quite brilliantly and the rest of the modified aircraft arrived in the next few days. " Capable " Caple, 617's " plumber," or engineering officer, checked them and the pilots found they flew all right, though they had lost a little performance.

A couple of days later, on May 8, Gibson, Martin and Hopgood flew three of them down to Manston, and Martin and Hopgood watched goggle-eyed while a bomb was loaded into each. Two dummy towers had been put up on the water at Reculver, and the three aircraft had a run at them. dropping the bombs with the quaint plywood bombsights. It was beautiful to watch. Three enchanting direct hits. Micky Martin came in a little low on his run and the spouting water hit his elevators and tore one of them loose. The big plane dipped towards the grey water but he had just enough control to get the nose up again and landed safely at Manston, where they fitted a new elevator.

" Good thing to check on," he said, unruffled. " Now we know what we *can't* do."

The worry and rush were telling on Gibson now ; he was irritable and a carbuncle was forming painfully on his face so that he could not get his oxygen mask on. Not that he was going to need oxygen on a low-level raid, but his microphone was in the mask. He went to the doctor, and in his detached professional way the doctor said, " This means you're over-worked. I'm afraid you'll have to take a couple of weeks off " ; and Gibson stared at him ludicrously and laughed in his face.

He planned to control the raid by plain-language radio, and Cochrane got them VHF fighter sets. Hutchison, squadron signals leader, wanted to set them up first in the crew room so they could have dummy practices on R/T procedure, and he and Chiefy Powell went to work on the sergeant carpenter to make screened benches for this, but the carpenter said he could not find any wood and was adamant till Gibson delivered him one of his blistering monologues over the phone, and the benches arrived that afternoon.

The stage was nearly set, but at Bomber Command and at Grantham there was secret dismay. For three days the Mosquito had been bringing back photographs that showed mysterious activity on top of the Moehne Dam. The dark shapes of some new structures had been appearing, growing from day to day. There were about five sets of them, visible as short black rectangles. The interpretive experts puzzled over them for hours, blowing up the photos as large as the grain would take, examining them under strong light and through magnifying glasses nearly as strong as microscopes. The structures threw shadows across the dam top, and they measured the shadows but still were baffled. There seemed to be only one answer—new gun positions. There must have been a security leak somewhere.

At midnight on May 13 a convoy of covered lorries rolled round the perimeter track to the bomb dump at Scampton ; a cordon of guards gathered round and the bombs were trollied into the dump and hidden under tarpaulins. They had only just been filled and were still warm to the touch.

Gibson drove off to see Satterly and plan the routes for the raid, taking with him Group Captain Pickard (of " F for Freddy ") because he was a " gen " man on German flak positions, and on a low-level raid there is nothing more important than plotting a track between the known flak. They spread their maps out on the floor and carefully pencilled in two separate tracks that wound in and out of the red blotches of the known flak.

The first one sneaked in between Walcheren and Schouwen, cut across Holland, delicately threaded between the night-fighter aerodromes at Gilze-Rijen and Eindhoven, snaked round the crimson blotches of the Ruhr, round Hamm, and south to the Moehne. The second one cut in up north over Vlieland, came in over the flak-free Zuyder Zee and joined route one north-west of Wesel. They plotted two more widely differing routes for the trip home so that any flak aroused on the way in would watch out in vain for the return.

The attack would be in three waves, Gibson leading nine aircraft on the southern route, Munro leading others on the northern, and five aircraft taking off a couple of hours later to act as a reserve. If the Moehne, Eder and Sorpe were not smashed by the first two waves, Gibson would call up the reserves. If they *were* smashed the reserves would bomb three smaller dams in the same area, the Schwelm, Ennerpe and Dieml.

Accurate navigation was going to be vital or there were going to be sudden deaths. The pencilled tracks had to go perilously near some of the red flak areas.

" Doc " Watson and his armourers were loading the bombs into the Lancasters. Martin watched Watson winching the bomb up into his aircraft, " P for Peter " (or, as Martin always insisted with a leer, " P for Popsie "). " Just exactly how *do* these bombs work, Doc ? " he asked.

" I know as much as you do, Micky," Watson said busily. " Sweet Fanny Adams."

" Ar, what do they pay you for ? " Half an hour later the bomb was in position and he and Boy Hay, Leggo, Foxlee, Simpson and Whittaker were crawling about inside the aircraft seeing that everything was in order when a fault developed in the bomb release circuit, the release snapped back and there was a crunch as the giant black thing fell and crashed through the concrete hardstanding, embedding itself 4 inches into the earth below. Relieved of the weight, " P for Popsie " kicked a little from the expanding oleo legs of the under-carriage.

Martin said, " Hell ! What's that ? " There was a startled

yell from an armourer outside and Martin yelled, " Hey, the bloody thing's fallen off ! "

" Release wiring must be faulty," Hay said professionally, and then it dawned on him and he said in a shocked voice, " It might have fused itself." He ran, yelling madly, out of the nose. " Get out of here. She'll go off in less than a minute." Bodies came tumbling out of the escape hatches, saw the tails of the armourers vanishing in the distance and set off after them. Martin jumped into the flight van near by and, with a grinding of gears, roared off to get Doc Watson. He had his foot hard down on the accelerator and swears that a terrified armourer passed him on a push-bike. He ran into Watson's office and panted out the news and Watson said philosophically, " Well, if she was going off she'd have gone off by this."

He got into the flight van and drove over to the deserted plane. Pale faces peeped out, watching him from the deep shelters round the perimeter track hundreds of yards away, and Watson turned and bellowed, " O.K. Flap's over. It's not fused."

The squadron was fused though ; painfully aware that something tremendous was about to happen. The aircraft were there, the bombs were there, both had been put together and crews were trained to the last gasp. Now was the time, Gibson knew, nerves would be tautening as they wondered whether there was going to be a reasonable chance of coming back or whether they would be dead in forty-eight hours. (And it was not only the aircrews who were tensed. Anne Fowler was too ; she was a dark, slim W.A.A.F. officer at Scampton, and in the past few weeks she and the boyish David Shannon had become a most noticeable twosome.)

Perhaps the least affected was the wiry and rambunctious Martin. Aged twenty-four, he had already decided that he was going to die, if not on this raid then on some other. Before the war was over anyway. During his first few " ops " he had often had sleepless nights or dreamed of burning aircraft. He saw all his friends on his squadron get " the chop " one after the other till they were all gone and knew it would only be a question of time before he would probably join them. So finally he had accepted the fact that in a fairly short time, barring miracles, he was going to die, not pleasantly. That was his strength and largely why he was so boisterous. Having accepted that, the next step was automatic : to fill every day with as many of the fruits of life as possible. He did so with vigour.

It was a corollary, more than a paradox, that he was not suicidal in the air but audacious in a calculating way, measuring every risk and if it were worth while, taking it, spinning it out as long as he could, but making every bomb tell. He did not believe in miracles.

One of the New Zealanders, painfully aware he might well be dead in forty-eight hours, had been getting his mind off it in the bar during the past few evenings, and after a few cans he always got a little homesick. He was only about twenty and home for him was about as far away as it was possible to get round the globe. He'd got into the habit, when the bar closed, of weaving over to the phone and saying gravely :

" Get me New Zealand."

The switch girl got to know the form well and she would answer, equally gravely :

" I'm sorry, sir, but the line to New Zealand is out of order. You'd better go to bed and I'll try in the morning."

" Oh ! Where's bed ? Give me course to steer to bed."

" You'd better get your batman to give you a course, sir. He'll show you where bed is."

" Oh, thank you very much." He was very young and always polite.

On the morning of May 15, you could clearly sense the tension, more so when word spread that the A.O.C. had arrived. Cochrane saw Gibson and Whitworth alone and was brief and businesslike.

" If the weather's right you go to-morrow night. Start briefing your crews this afternoon and see that your security is foolproof."

After lunch a little aeroplane landed and Wallis and Mutt Summers climbed out ; ten minutes later they were with

Gibson and Whitworth with a guard on the door. Gibson could not take his beloved Nigger on the raid but could not bear to leave him out altogether, so he gave him the greatest honour he could think of . . . when (or if) the Moehne Dam was breached he would radio back the one code word " Nigger."

In the hangars, messes and barracks the Tannoy came loudly and dramatically to life : " All pilots, navigators and bomb aimers of 617 report to the briefing room immediately." At three o'clock there were some sixty of them in the briefing room on the upper floor of the grey-and-black camouflaged station headquarters. They sat silently on the benches, eyeing the familiar maps, aircraft identification and air-sea rescue posters on the walls, waiting. Whitworth, Gibson and Wallis filed down the centre to the dais and Whitworth nodded to Gibson : " Go ahead, Guy." The room was still.

Gibson faced them, feet braced apart, flushed a little. He had a ruler in one hand, the other in his pocket, and his eyes were bright. He cleared his throat and said :

" You're going to have a chance to clobber the Hun harder than a small force has ever done before." Outside his voice, no sound. " Very soon we are going to attack the major dams in Western Germany." A rustle and murmuring broke the silence—and some deep breaths. They were going to have a sporting chance. Gibson turned to the map and pointed with his ruler.

" Here they are," he said. " Here is the Moehne, here the Eder and here is the Sorpe. As you can see, they are all just east of the Ruhr." He went on to explain the tactics, told each crew what wave they would be on and what dam they were to attack.

Wallis took over and described the dams and what the queer bombs were supposed to do, how success would cripple the Ruhr steel industry, how other factories would be affected and bridges and roads washed away.

Gibson stood up. " Any questions ? "

Hopgood said : " I notice, sir, that our route takes us pretty near a synthetic rubber factory at Huls. It's a hot spot. I nearly got the hammer there three months ago. If we go over there low I think it might . . . er . . . upset things."

Gibson looked thoughtfully at the map. Huls was a few miles north of the Ruhr. Satterly and he had known about the Huls flak when they were planning the route but had taken the track as far away from the Ruhr as they could. Better the flak at Huls than the Ruhr.

" If you think it's a bit too close to Huls we'll bring it down a bit," and he pencilled in a wider curve round the little dot. " You'd better all be bloody careful here. The gap isn't too wide. Err on the Huls side if you have to, but watch it you navigators."

Maltby got up. " What are the dams' defences like, sir ? "

" We've had extensive photo-recce over them for some time now," Gibson said, " and the defences seem to be confined to light flak. You'll be shown their position." He was uneasily wondering about those mysterious new structures on the top of the Moehne.

" Any balloons, sir ? " That was Maudslay.

" Up till yesterday the nearest ones were round a small factory twelve miles away. We don't expect any."

Someone asked if there were any nets on the lake and Gibson described the torpedo booms in front of the dam walls.

Leggo wanted to know how effective they would be against the bomb, and Gibson, with a sidelong glance at Wallis and a fierce grin, said :

" Not a sausage ! "

He crossed the room to a couple of trestle tables where three dust covers were hiding something, pulled the covers off, and there were the models of the dams.

" All of you come over and have a look at these," he commanded, and there was a scraping of forms as sixty young men got up and crowded round.

" Look at these till your eyes stick out and you've got every detail photographed on your minds, then go away and draw them from memory, come back and check your drawings, correct them, then go away and draw them again till you're perfect."

They were two hours doing that ; each crew concentrated

on its own target, working out the best ways in and the best ways out. The known flak guns were marked and they took *very* special note of them. Martin's crew were down for the Moehne with Gibson and Hopgood, and they stood gazing down at the model.

" What d'you reckon's the best way in ? " Leggo asked.

" First thing is to get the final line of attack," Martin said. " There's the spot ! " He put his finger on the tip of a spit of land running out into the Moehne Lake and ran his finger-tip in a straight line to the middle of the dam wall, right between the two towers. It met the wall at right angles. " A low wide circuit," he said ; " come in over the spit and we're jake."

It was eight o'clock before Gibson was satisfied they knew it all and said, " Now buzz off and get some grub. But keep your mouths shut. Not even a whisper to your own crews. They'll find out to-morrow. If there's one slip and the Hun gets an inkling you won't be coming back to-morrow night."

Back at the mess the gunners, engineers and wireless operators, who'd been waiting in a fever of speculation for five hours, were a little hard to convince.

" Well," demanded Toby Foxlee, Martin's gunner, his eager nose sniffing at the prospect, " what is it ? "

" Nothing," Martin said airily. " More training. That's all. You'll hear about it to-morrow."

" Training ? " Foxlee almost wailed. " I don't believe it. It can't be."

" It's true."

" Will you swear it ? "

" I swear it," Martin lied piously.

" Christ ! " Foxlee said. " I need a drink. What're you having ? "

" Shandy," said Martin, who drank little before a raid, and Foxlee gave him a long, cold look.

" Martin," he said, " you're a horrible bloody liar."

They all drank shandy and went to bed, taking little white pills that the doctor had doled out so they would sleep well. As Gibson was going along to his room Charles Whitworth came in looking worried and buttonholed him quietly.

" Guy," he said, " I'm awfully sorry, but Nigger's just been run over by a car outside the camp. He was killed instantaneously."

The car had not even bothered to stop.

Gibson sat a long time on his bed looking at the scratch marks that Nigger used to make on his door. Nigger and he had been together since before the war ; it seemed to be an omen.

The morning of May 16 was sunny. Considering the scurry that went on all day it was remarkable that so few people at Scampton realised what was happening. Even after the aircraft took off hours later the people watching nearly all thought it was a special training flight.

It was just after 9 a.m. that Gibson bounced into his office and told Humphries to draw up the flying programme.

" Training, sir ? "—more of a statement than a question.

" No. That is yes—to everyone else," and as Humphries looked bewildered he said quietly : " We're going to war to-night, but I don't want the world to know. Mark the list ' Night flying programme,' and don't mention the words ' battle order.' "

Watson, the armament chief, was dashing around busily, and so was Caple. The pilots were swinging their compasses. Trevor-Roper was seeing that all guns were loaded with full tracer that shot out of the guns at night like angry meteors and to people on the receiving end looked like cannon shells. That was the idea, to frighten the flak gunners and put them off their aim. Each aircraft had two ·303 Brownings in the front turret, and four in the tail turret. Each gun fired something like twelve rounds a *second* ; each rear turret alone could pump out what looked like forty-eight flaming cannon shells a second ; 96,000 rounds lay in the ammunition trays.

Towards noon a Mosquito touched down with the last photos of the dams. The water in the Moehne was 4 feet from the top. After lunch " Gremlin " Matthews, meteorological officer at Grantham, spoke to all the other group met. officers on a locked circuit of trunk lines for half an hour. Such conferences rarely found agreement but this time they did. The lively bespectacled figure of " The Gremlin " walked into Cochrane's office as soon as he had put the receiver down.

" It's all right for to-night, sir." He gave a definite prediction of clear weather over Germany.

" What ? " said Cochrane. " No ifs, buts and probablies ? " and " The Gremlin " looked mildly cautious just for a moment and took the plunge. " No, sir. It's going to be all right."

Cochrane went out to his car and drove off towards Scampton.

The Tannoy sounded about four o'clock, ordering *all* 617 crews to the briefing room, and soon there were 133 hushed young men sitting on the benches (two crews were out because of illness).

Gibson repeated what he had told the others the previous night, and Wallis, in his earnest, slightly pedantic way, told them about the dams and what their destruction would do. Cochrane finished with a short, crisp talk.

The final line-up was :

Formation 1 : Nine aircraft in three waves, taking off with ten minutes between waves :

> Gibson,
> Hopgood,
> Martin.
>
> Young,
> Astell,
> Maltby.
>
> Maudslay,
> Knight,
> Shannon.

They were to attack the Moehne, and after the Moehne was breached those who had not bombed would go on to the Eder.

Formation 2 : One wave in loose formation :

McCarthy,
Byers,
Barlow,
Rice,
Munro.

They were to attack the Sorpe, crossing the coast by the northern route as a diversion to split the German defences.
Formation 3 :

Townsend,
Brown,
Anderson,
Ottley,
Burpee.

They would take off later as the mobile reserve.

Supper in the mess was quiet, the calm before the storm. No one said much. The non-flying people thought it was to be a training flight, but the crews, who knew it was going to be business—probably sticky—could not say so and there was a faint atmosphere of strain.

With a woman's wit Anne Fowler realised it was to be the real thing. She noticed the crews were having eggs. They often had an egg before a raid, and always after they landed. Most of the others did not notice it, but she started worrying about Shannon.

Dinghy Young said to Gibson, " Can I have your next egg if you don't come back? " But that was the usual chestnut before an " op " and Gibson brushed it aside with a few amiably insulting remarks.

In twos and threes they drifted down to the hangar and started to change. It was not eight o'clock yet ; still an hour to take-off and still broad daylight. Martin stuffed his little koala bear into a pocket of his battle-dress jacket and buttoned the flap. It was a grey furry thing about 4 inches high with black button eyes, given to him by his mother as a mascot when the war started. It had as many operational hours as he had.

They drifted over to the grass by the apron and lay in the sun, smoking and quietly talking, waiting. Anne was with

Shannon. Fay, the other W.A.A.F. officer, was talking to Martin's crew. Dinghy Young was tidying up his office, just as a matter of course. He had no premonition. Munro seemed half asleep in a deck chair.

Gibson drove up and walked over to Powell.

" Chiefy, I want you to bury Nigger outside my office at midnight. Will you do that ? "

" Of course, sir." Powell was startled at the gesture from the hard-bitten Gibson. Gibson did not tell him that he would be about 50 feet over Germany then, not far from the Ruhr. He had it in his mind that he and Nigger might be going into the ground about the same time. He said to Hopgood : " To-morrow we get drunk, Hoppy."

Gibson found himself wishing to God it were time to go and knew they were all wishing the same. It would be all right once they were in the air. It always was. At ten to nine he said clearly, " Well, chaps, my watch says time to go." Bodies stirred on the grass with elaborate casualness, tossed their parachutes into the flight trucks, climbed in after them, and the trucks moved off round the perimeter track to the hardstandings. Shannon had gone back to the locker room for a moment and when he came out his crew, the only ones left, were waiting impatiently.

The bald-headed Yorkshireman, Jack Buckley, said like a father to his small son, " Have you cleaned your teeth, David ? " Shannon grinned, hoisted himself elegantly into the flight truck and then they had all gone. Shannon had one of the best crews. Buckley, older than most, of a wealthy family, was his rear gunner and a wild Yorkshireman. Danny Walker was an infallible navigator, a Canadian, dark, quiet and intensely likeable. Sumpter, the bomb aimer, had been a guardsman and was tougher than a prize-fighter. Brian Goodale, the wireless op., was so tall and thin and bent he was known universally as " Concave." And in the air the babyish Shannon was the absolute master, with a scorching tongue when he felt like it.

At exactly ten past nine a red Véry light curled up from Gibson's aircraft, the signal for McCarthy's five aircraft to start ; the northern route was longer and they were taking off ten minutes early. Seconds later there was a spurt of blue smoke behind Munro's aircraft as his port inner engine started. One by one the engines came to life. Geoff Rice's engines were turning ; Barlow's, then Byers'. The knot of people by the hangar saw a truck rushing at them across the field, and before it came to a stop big McCarthy jumped out and ran at them, roaring like a bull, his red face sweaty, the sandy hair falling over his forehead. In a murderous rage he yelled :

" Those sons of bitches. My aircraft's u/s and there's no deviation card in the spare. Where are those useless bloody instruments jerks ! "

The 15-stone Yank had found his own Lancaster, " Q for Queenie," out of action with leaking hydraulics, rushed his crew over to the spare plane, " T for Tom," and found the little card giving the compass deviations missing from it. No hope of accurate flying without it. If McCarthy had met one of the instrument people then he would probably have strangled him.

Chiefy Powell had gone running into the instrument section and found the missing card. He dashed up to McCarthy shouting, " Here it is, sir," and McCarthy grabbed it, well behind schedule now, and, turning to run back to the truck, scooped up his parachute from the tarmac where he'd thrown it, but his hand missed the canvas loop handle and he yanked it up by the D-ring of the rip-cord. The pack flaps sprang back in a white blossom as the silk billowed out and trailed after him, and he let out a roar of unbearable fury.

Powell was running for the crew room, but McCarthy snarled, " Goddamit, I'll go without one." He jumped into the truck but before the driver could move off Powell came running up with another parachute, and McCarthy grabbed it through the cabin and shot off across the field. There was a swelling roar from the south side ; Munro's Lancaster was rolling, picking up speed, and then it was low in the air, sliding over the north boundary, tucking its wheels up into the big inboard nacelles. Less than a minute later, as

McCarthy got to his aircraft, Rice was rolling too, followed by Barlow and Byers.

At precisely 9.25, Gibson in " G for George," Martin, in " P for Popsie," and Hopgood, in " M for Mother," punched the buttons of the booster coils and the wisps of blue smoke spurted as the engines whined and spun explosively, first the port inners, the starboard inners, the port outers and the starboard outers. They were going through their cockpit drill while the crews settled at take-off stations, running the engines up to zero boost and testing the magnetos. A photographer's flash-bulb went off by Gibson's aircraft ; Cochrane was there too, standing clear of the slipstream. Fay stood by " P Popsie," waggling her fingers encouragingly at the crew.

" G for George " waddled forward with the shapeless bulk under its belly (" like a pregnant duck," Gibson had said), taxied to the south fence, swung its long snout to the north and waited, engines turning quietly. " P Popsie " turned slowly in on the left, and " M Mother " on the right. Gibson rattled out the monotonous orders of his final check.

" Flaps thirty."

Pulford, the engineer, pumped down 30 degress of flap and repeated, " Flaps thirty."

" Radiators open."

" Radiators open."

" Throttles locked ? "

Pulford checked the nut on the throttle unit.

" Throttles locked."

" Prepare to take off," Gibson said and checked through to all the crew on the intercom. " O.K., rear gunner ? " " O.K." And then all the others. He leaned forward with his thumb up, looking to left and then to right, and Martin and Hopgood raised their thumbs back. Pulford closed his hand over the four throttles and pushed till the engines deepened their note and the aircraft was throbbing . . . straining ; then Gibson flicked his brakes off, there was the hiss of compressed air and they were rolling, all three of them, engineers sliding the throttles right forward.

The blare of twelve engines slammed over the field and echoed in the hangar, the tails slowly came up as they picked up speed in a loose vic, ungainly with nearly 5 tons of bomb and over 5 tons of petrol each. Gibson held her down for a long time and the a.s.i. was flicking on 110 m.p.h. before he tightened back on the wheel and let her come unstuck after a long, slow bounce. At 200 feet they turned slowly on course with the sun low behind.

McCarthy eased " T for Tom " off the runway twenty minutes late and set course on his own. At 9.47 Dinghy Young led Astell and Maltby off. Eight minutes after that Maudslay, Shannon and Knight were in the air. Anne waved them off. The final five, the reserve aircraft, did not take off till two hours later. By the time they arrived in the target area Gibson, if still alive, would know where to send them.

CHAPTER VII

ATTACK

GIBSON slid over the Wash at a hundred feet. The cockpit was hot and he was flying in his shirtsleeves with Mae West over the top ; after a while he yelled, " Hey, Hutch, turn the heat off."

" Thank God for that," the wireless operator said, screwing the valve shut. The heat in a Lancaster runs down the fuselage but comes out round the wireless operator's seat, so he is always too hot, while the rear gunner is always too cold.

The sun astern on the quarter threw long shadows on fields peaceful and fresh with spring crops ; dead ahead the moon was swimming out of the ground haze like a bullseye. Gibson flew automatically, eyes flicking from the horizon to the a.s.i., to the repeater compass in its rubber suspension.

The haze of Norfolk passed a few miles to port. In the nose, Spafford said, " There's the sea," and a minute later they were low over Southwold, the shingle was beneath them, and then they were over the water, flat and grey in the evening light. England faded behind. " G George " dropped down to 50 feet, and on each side Martin and Hopgood came down too, putting off the evil moment when German radar would pick them up. You couldn't put it off indefinitely ; about twenty miles from the Dutch coast the blips would be flicking on the radar screens and the orders would be going out to the flak batteries and fighter fields.

Martin ranged up alongside and there was a light winking as he flashed his Aldis lamp at them.

" What's he saying, Hutch? " Gibson asked.

" We're going to get screechers to-morrow night." Hutchison picked up his own Aldis and winked back, " You're damn right. Biggest binge of all time." Hutchison didn't drink.

Taerum spoke : " Our ground speed is exactly 203½ miles an hour. We will be there in exactly one hour, ten minutes and thirty seconds. We ought to cross the coast dead on track. Incidentally, you're one degree off course." The last part was the standing joke. The pilot who can fly without sometimes yawing a degree or so off course has yet to be born.

In the ops. room of 5 Group H.Q. at Grantham, Cochrane was walking Barnes Wallis up and down, trying to comfort him. Wallis was like an expectant father, fidgety and jittery, and Cochrane was talking of anything but the bomb, trying to get Wallis's mind off it, but Wallis could think of nothing else.

" Just think what a wonderful job you made of the Wellington," Cochrane said encouragingly. " It's a magnificent machine ; been our mainstay for over three years."

" Oh dear, no," lamented the disconcerting scientist. " Do you know, every time I pass one I wonder how I could ever have designed anything so crude."

A black Bentley rushed up the gravelled drive outside, pulled up by the door and the sentries snapped rigidly to attention as Harris himself jumped briskly out. He came into the ops. room. " How's it going, Cocky ? "

" All right so far, sir," Cochrane said. " Nothing to report yet." They walked up and down the long room between the wall where the aircraft blackboards were and the long desk that ran down the other side, where men were sitting. Satterly was there, " The Gremlin," the intelligence man and Dunn, chief signals officer, sitting by a telephone plugged in to the radio in the signals cabin outside. He would get all the Morse from the aircraft there ; it was too far for low-flying planes to get through by ordinary speech.

Harris and Cochrane talked quietly, and Wallis was walking miserably with them but not talking, breaking away every now and then to look at the big operations map on the end wall. The track lines had been pencilled in and he was counting off the miles they should be travelling. It was 10.35 when Cochrane looked at his watch and said, " They ought to be coming up to the Dutch coast now."

The sun had gone and the moon was inching higher into the dusk, lighting a road ahead across the water ; outside the dancing road the water was hardly visible, a dark mass with a couple of little flecks.

Taerum said, " Five minutes to the Dutch coast," and the crew snapped out of the wordless lull of the past half hour. " Good," Gibson said.   Martin and Hopgood eased their aircraft forward till the black snouts nosed alongside Gibson and veered out to make a wider target, their engines snarling thinly in gusts above the monotonous roar in " G George." Flying so low, just off the water, they seemed to be sliding very fast along the moonpath towards the waiting flak.

Spafford said, " There's the coast." It was a black line lying dim and low on the water, and then from a couple of miles out on the port side a chain of glowing little balls was climbing into the sky. " Flak ship," said Martin laconically. The shells were way off and he ignored them. The sparkling moonpath ended abruptly, they tore across the white line of surf and were over enemy territory. " New course 105 magnetic," Taerum called, and the three aircraft swung gently to the left as they started the game of threading their way through the flak.

The northern wave made landfall about the same time, sighting Vlieland and turning south-east to cut across the narrow part and down over the Zuyder Zee. Munro led them across the dark spit ; it was so narrow they would see the water again in about thirty seconds and have another seventy miles of comparatively safe water, but without warning there were flashes below and up came the fiery little balls. Munro felt the shock as they hit the aircraft, and then they were past and over the water again. Munro called on the intercom, to see if the crew were all right, but the earphones were dead.

Pigeon, the wireless op., was standing by his shoulder shouting into his ear, " No radio. No intercom. Flak's smashed it. I think everyone's O.K." Munro flew on several miles, trying to fool himself they could still carry on, but it was no good and he knew it. Without radio he could not direct the attack on the Sorpe ; could not even direct his own crew or get bombing instructions. Swearing, he turned for home.

Inside the Zuyder the water was dark and quite flat, treacherously deceptive for judging height. Geoff Rice slipped down a little to level at 60 feet by his belly lights, but the lights were not working properly and lured him lower as he tried to get a fix. A hammer seemed to hit the aircraft like a bolt and there was a tearing roar above the engines. Rice dragged her off the water, but the belly was torn out of her and the bomb had gone with it. The gutted fuselage had scooped up a couple of tons of water ; it was pouring out of her and the rear gunner was nearly drowning in his turret. Marvellously she still flew but was dropping back, and when they found the bomb was gone Rice turned her heavily back towards England.

The remaining two, Barlow and Byers, skirted their pin-point on the cape at Stavoren and ten minutes later crossed to the enemy land again at Harderwijk. No one knows exactly how soon it was that the flak came curling up at them again, but there is a report that as Barlow's aircraft hit the ground the bomb went off with a blinding flash, lighting the countryside like a rising sun for ten seconds before it died and left nothing. It was either then or soon after that Byers and his crew died too. Nothing more was heard from him. Only McCarthy was left of the Sorpe team, flying sixty miles behind, and perhaps that is what saved him.

Over Holland, Gibson, Martin and Hopgood were down as low as 40 feet, playing hide-and-seek with the ground, the bomb aimers calling terse warnings as houses and trees loomed up, and the aircraft skimmed over them. They were cruising fast and under the cowlings the exhaust manifolds were glowing. Once the three pulled up fast as the pylons of a power line rushed at them, and they just cleared the wires.

Four miles to port they saw the flare-path of Gilze-Rijen, German night-fighter field, and a few miles farther on they passed just to the left of the night-fighter aerodrome at Eindhoven. They could expect light fighters now ; the ops. rooms for miles around must be buzzing. Martin and Hopgood closed in on each side of Gibson for mutual pro-tection. They should be able to see any fighter coming in because he would be higher, while they, low against the dark ground, would be hard to see, and that was their strength. Also their weakness where the flak was concerned. Their aircraft were higher, outlined. Just past Eindhoven, Gibson led them in a gentle turn to the north-east on the new course that would take them round the bristling guns of the Ruhr.

A few miles back the other two vics of three were on course too. Dinghy Young pin-pointed over the canal at Rosendaal and turned delicately to take them between the fighter fields, but Bill Astell did not seem sure this was the exact turning point. He bore off a little to the south for a minute and then turned back, but had fallen half a mile behind and was a fraction off track. They did not see him again, and it must have been quite soon after that the flak or fighter, whatever it was, got him.

Fourteen left.

The leading three slid across the border into Germany and saw no light or movement anywhere, only darkness filled with the beat of engines. Taerum thought they were south of track, so they edged to the north, a little nervily because this was the treacherous leg ; they were coming up to the Rhine to sneak between the forewarned guns of Huls and the Ruhr. Just short of the river some twelve light flak guns opened up without warning ; the aircraft gunners squirted back at the roots of the tracer and then they were out of range. No one badly hit. The Rhine was rushing at them and up from a barge spat a thin line of tracer, but they were past before the bullets found them.

Two minutes later more guns opened up, and this time three searchlights lit on Gibson. Foxlee and Deering were shooting at the searchlights. One of them popped out but the two others held, and the air was full of tracer. The rear gunners came into action, the searchlights switched to Martin, blinding him, and Gibson could read the big P on the side of the Lancaster. Every gun was firing, the aircraft juddering with the recoil, and then they were through with throttles wide.

Ahead and just to the left another searchlight sprang to life and caught Gibson. Foxlee was firing instantly, holding his triggers in a long burst, his tracer whipping into the light. It flicked out, and as they went over in the dying glow they saw the gunners scattering. Tammy Simpson opened up from the rear turret till they were out of range. You can't take prisoners in an aircraft.

They were past and shook themselves back into formation. Hutchison tapped out a flak warning, giving the exact position, and way back in Grantham Dunn picked it up and the powerful group radio re-broadcast it at full strength to all other aircraft.

Gibson swung them north around Hamm, whose marshalling yards will for years be notorious. Taerum said, " New course, skipper, 165 magnetic," and then they were hugging the ground on the last leg, slicing between Soest and Werl. Now the moon was high enough to light the ground and ahead loomed the dark hills that cradled the water. They climbed to the ridge that rimmed the horizon, crossed into the valley, and down below lay the flat sheet of Moehne Lake.

It was like looking down on the model ; the same saucer of water, the same dim fields and across the neck of the lake the squat rampart hugging the water, crowned by the towers. In the half-light it looked like a battleship, but more impregnable. Reinforced concrete a hundred feet thick.

" God," Bob Hay said, " can *we* break that ? "

The dam came suddenly to life, prickling with sharp flashes, and the lines of angry red meteors were streaming into the sky and moving about blindly as the gunners hosed the area.

" Bit aggressive, aren't they ? " said Trevor-Roper. The pilots swung the aircraft away and headed in wide circles round the lake, keeping out of range and waiting for the others. There seemed to be about ten guns, some in the fields on each side of the lake near the dam, and some—a lot—in the towers on the dam.

Gibson started calling the other aircraft, and one by one they reported, except Astell. He called Astell again at the end, but Astell had been dead for an hour. After a while Gibson gave up and said soberly over the intercom., " Well, boys, I suppose we'd better start the ball rolling." It was

the end of the waiting and the start of action, when thought
is submerged. He flicked his transmitter switch :

" Hello all Cooler aircraft, I am going in to attack. Stand
by to come in in your order when I tell you. Hello ' M
Mother.' Stand by to take over if anything happens."

" O.K. Leader. Good luck." Hopgood's voice was a
careful monotone.

Gibson turned wide, hugging the hills at the eastern end
of the lake. Pulford had eased the throttles on and she was
roaring harshly, picking up speed and quivering, the nose
slowly coming round till three miles ahead they saw the
towers and the rampart of the dam, and in between, the
flat dark water. Spafford said, " Good show. This is
wizard. I can see everything." They came out of the hills
and slammed across the water, touching 240 now, and Gibson
rattled off the last orders :

" Check height, Terry ! Speed control, Pulford ! Gunners
ready ! Coming up, Spam ! " Taerum flicked the belly
lights on and, peering down from the blister, started droning :
" Down . . . down . . . down . . . up a bit . . . steady,
stead-y-y." The lights were touching each other, " G
George" was exactly at 60 feet and the flak gunners had seen
the lights. The streams of glowing shells were swivelling
and lowering, and then the shells were whipping towards
them, seeming to move slowly at first like all flak, and then
rushing madly at their eyes as the aircraft plunged into them.

Gibson held her steady, pointing between the towers.
Taerum was watching out of the blister, Pulford had a hand
on the throttles and his eyes on the a.s.i., Spafford held the
plywood sight to his eye and the towers were closing in on the
nails. Gibson shouted to Pulford, " Stand by to pull me out
of the seat if I get hit ! " There was a sudden snarling clatter
up in the nose ; Deering had opened up, his tracer spitting
at the towers.

The dam was a rushing giant, darkness split with flashes,
the cockpit stank of cordite and thought was nothing but a
cold alarm shouting, " In another minute we shall be dead,"
and then Spafford screamed, " Bomb gone ! " loud and
sharp, and they rocketed over the dam between the towers.

A red Véry light soared up as Hutchison pulled the trigger
to let the others know, and then the deeper snarling chatter
as Trevor-Roper opened up on the towers from the rear.

It was over and memory was confusion as they corkscrewed down the valley, hugging the dark earth sightless to
the flak. They were out of range and Gibson lifted her out
of the hills, turning steeply, and looked back. A voice in his
earphones said, " Good show, Leader, Nice work."

The black water between the towers suddenly rose and
split and a huge white core erupted through the middle and
climbed towards the sky. The lake was writhing, and as the
white column reached its peak and hung a thousand feet
high, like a ghost against the moon, the heavy explosion
reached the aircraft. They looked in awe as they flew back
to one side and saw sheets of water spilling over the dam and
thought for a wild moment it had burst. The fury of the
water passed and the dam was still there, the white column
slowly dying.

Round the lake they flew while Hutchison tapped out in
code to base. In a few minutes Gibson thought the lake
was calm enough for the next bomb and called :

" Hello ' M Mother.' You may attack now. Good luck."

" O.K. Leader. Attacking." Hopgood was still carefully
laconic. He was lost in the darkness over the hills at the end
of the lake while the others waited. They saw his bellylights
flick on and the two little yellow pools sliding over the water
closing and joining as he found his height. He was straight
and level on his run ; the flak saw him and the venomous
fireflies were darting at him. He plunged on ; the gap was
closing fast when the shells found him and someone said,
" Hell, he's been hit ! "

A red glow was blossoming round the inner port wing
tank, and then a long, long ribbon of flame trailed behind
" M Mother." The bomb aimer must have been hit,
because the bomb overshot the parapet on to the power house
below.

" M Mother " was past the dam, nose up, straining for
height so the crew could bale out, when the tanks blew up
with an orange flare, a wing ripped away and the bomber

spun to the ground in burning, bouncing pieces. The bomb went off near the power house like a brilliant sun. It was all over in seconds.

A voice said over the R/T, " Poor old Hoppy."

Gibson called up : " Hello ' P Popsie.' Are you ready ? "

" O.K. Leader. Going in."

" I'll fly across the dam as you make your run and try and draw the flak off you."

" O.K. Thanks Leader."

Martin was turning in from the hills and Gibson headed across the lake, parallel to the dams and just out of effective range of the guns. As Martin's spotlights merged and sped across the water Gibson back-tracked and Deering and Trevor-Roper opened up ; six lines of tracer converged on the towers, drawing their attention, so that for some seconds most of the guns did not notice Martin rocketing over the water. He held his height and Whittaker had the speed right. They were tracking straight for the middle of the dam between the moon-bathed towers when the gunners spotted them and threw a curtain of fire between the towers, spreading like a fan so they would have to fly through it. Martin drove straight ahead. Two guns swung at them, and as the shells whipped across the water sharp-eyed little Foxlee was yelling as he squirted back, his tracer lacing and tangling with the flak.

A sharp " Bomb gone ! " from Bob Hay, and in the same instant a shudder as two shells smacked into the starboard wing, one of them exploding in the inner petrol tank. A split second of flashes as they shot through the barrage. Tammy Simpson opened up from the rear turret, Chambers shot the Véry light and they were down the valley. Whittaker was looking fearfully at the hole in the starboard wing, but no fire was coming. He suddenly realised why and nudged Martin, yelling in his ear, " Thank Christ, the bloody starboard tank was empty ! "

Martin shouted, " Bomb gone, Leader."

" O.K. 'P Popsie.' Let me know when you're out of the flak. Hello 'A Apple.' Are you ready ? "

" O.K. Leader."

" Right. Go ahead. Let me know when you're in position and I'll draw the flak for you."

Martin called again, " ' P Popsie ' clear now, Leader."

" O.K. Are you hit? "

" Yeah. Starboard wing, but we're all right. We can make it."

The lake suddenly boiled again by the dam and spewed out the great white column that climbed again to a thousand feet. More water was cascading over the dam, but it cleared soon and the dam was still there.

Dinghy Young was on the air again. " ' A Apple ' making bombing run."

Gibson headed back over the lake where his gunners could play with fire, and this time Martin did the same. As Young came plunging across the lake Gibson and Martin came in on each side, higher up, and the flak did not know where to shoot. Young swept past the dam and reported he was all right. The great explosion was up against the dam wall again, beautifully accurate, but the dam was still there, and again Gibson waited till the plume of spray had cleared and the water was calm.

He called Maltby and ordered him in, and as Maltby came across the water Gibson and Martin came in with him, firing with every gun that could bear and flicking their navigation lights on this time to help the flak gunners shoot at the wrong target. The red cartridge soared up from Maltby's aircraft to signal " Attack successful."

In a few moments the mountain of water erupted skyward again under the dam wall. It was uncanny how accurate the bomb was. The spray from the explosions was misting up the whole valley now and it was hard to see what was happening by the dam. Gibson called Shannon to make his attack, and the words were barely out of his mouth when a sharp voice filled his earphones :

" Hell, it's gone ! It's gone ! Look at it for Christ's sake ! " Wheeling round the valley side Martin had seen the concrete face abruptly split and crumble under the weight of water. Gibson swung in close and was staggered. A ragged hole 100 yards across and 100 feet deep split the dam and the lake was pouring out of it, 134 million tons of water crashing into the valley in a jet 200 feet long, smooth on top, foaming at the sides where it tore at the rough edges of the breach and boiling over the scarred earth where the power house had been.

Gibson told Shannon to " skip it."

The others flew over and were awed into silence. In the moonglow they watched a wall of water rolling down the valley, 25 feet high, moving 20 feet a second. A gunner still on his feet in one of the towers opened up at them until lines of tracer converged on the root of the flak and it stopped abruptly. The awed silence was broken by a babble of intercom. chatter as they went mad with excitement ; the only man not looking being Hutchison, sitting at his keyboard tapping out " Nigger."

Soon the hissing stream and spray blurred the valley. Gibson called Martin and Maltby to set course for home, and told Young, Shannon, Maudslay and Knight to follow him east to the Eder. Young was to control if Gibson was shot down.

CHAPTER VIII

THE WRITHING LAKE

At Grantham a long silence had followed the flak warning at Huls, and then Dunn's phone rang sharply, and in the dead silence they all heard the Morse crackling in the receiver. It was quite slow and Cochrane, bending near, could read it. " Goner," he said. " From G George." " Goner " was the code word that meant Gibson had exploded his bomb in the right place.

" I'd hoped one bomb might do it," Wallis said gloomily.

" It's probably weakened it," Cochrane soothed him. Harris looked non-committal. There was no more from " G George," and they went on walking. A long silence. Nothing came through when Hopgood crashed. The phone rang, " Goner " from " P Popsie." Another dragging silence. " Goner " from " A Apple." Wallis swears even to-day that there was half an hour between each signal, but the log shows only about five minutes. " Goner " from " J Johnny." That was Maltby, and the aura of gloom settled deeper over Wallis.

A minute later the phone rang again and the Morse crackled so fast the others could not read it. Dunn printed it letter by letter on a signals pad and let out a cry, " Nigger. It's Nigger. It's gone."

Wallis threw his arms over his head and went dancing round the room. The austere face of Cochrane cracked into a grin, he grabbed one of Wallis's hands and started congratulating him. Harris, with the first grin on his face that Wallis had ever seen, grabbed the other hand and said :

" Wallis, I didn't believe a word you said about this damn bomb, but you could sell me a pink elephant now."

He said, a little later when some of the excitement had died down : " I must tell Portal immediately." Sir Charles Portal, Chief of the R.A.F., was in Washington that night on a mission, actually at that moment dining with Roosevelt. Harris picked up the nearest phone and said, " Get me the White House."

The little W.A.A.F. on the switchboard knew nothing of the highly secret raid. Even at Grantham, Cochrane's security had been perfect. She did not realise the importance of it all, or the identity of the great man who was speaking, and was caught off guard. " Yes, sir," she said automatically and, so they say, dialled the only White House she knew, a jolly little roadhouse a few miles out of Grantham.

Harris must have thought she was a very smart operator when the White House answered so quickly, and there are reported to have been moments of incredible and indescribable comedy as Harris asked for Portal, and the drowsy landlord, testy at being hauled out of bed after midnight, told him in well-chosen words he didn't have anyone called Portal staying at the place ; in fact, he didn't have anyone staying at all, because he didn't have room, and if he did have room he would not have anyone staying there who had people who called him up at that time of night. Not for long anyway.

Harris went red, and there were some explosive exchanges before one of them slammed the receiver down. Someone slipped down and had a word with the little W.A.A.F., and she tried in terror for the next hour to raise Washington, but without success.

Three kilometres down the valley from the Moehne lay the sleeping village of Himmelpforten, which means Gates of Heaven. The explosions had wakened the village priest, Father Berkenkopf, and he guessed instantly what was happening ; he had been afraid of it for three years. He ran to his small stone church, Porta Coeli (which also means Gates of Heaven—in Italian) and begun tugging grimly on the bell-rope, the signal he had arranged with his villagers. It is not certain how many were warned in time. In the darkness the clanging of the bell rolled ominously round the valley and then it was muffled in the thunder moving nearer. Berkenkopf must have heard it and known what it meant, but it seems that he was still pulling at the bell when the flood crushed the church and the village of the Gates of Heaven and rolled them down the valley.

It went for many miles and took more villages, a tumbling

maelstrom of water and splintered houses, beds and frying-pans, the chalice from Porta Coeli and the bell, the bodies of cattle and horses, pigs and dogs, and the bodies of Father Berkenkopf and other human beings.

War, as someone said, is a great leveller, but he did not mean it quite as literally or as bitterly as this.

The Eder was hard to find because fog was filling the valley. Gibson circled it for some time before he was certain he was there. One by one the others found it and soon they were all in a left-hand circuit round the lake. There was no flak ; probably the Germans thought the Eder did not need it. It lay deep in a fold of the hills ; the ridges around were a thousand feet high and it was no place to dive a heavy aircraft at night.

Gibson said, " O.K. Dave. Start your attack."

Shannon flew a wide circuit over the ridges and then put his nose right down, but the dive was not steep enough and he overshot. Sergeant Henderson slammed on full throttle, and Shannon hauled back on the stick and they just cleared the mountain on the far side.

" Sorry Leader," Shannon said a little breathlessly. " Made a mess of that. I'll try it again."

Five times more he dived into the dark valley but he failed every time to get into position and nearly stood the Lancaster on her tail to get out of the hills again. He called up finally, " I think I'd better circle and try to get to know this place."

" O.K. Dave. You hang around a bit and let someone else have a crack. Hullo ' Z Zebra.' You have a go now."

Maudslay acknowledged and a minute later was diving down the contour of the hills, only to overshoot and go rocketing up again like Shannon. He tried again but the same thing happened. Maudslay said he was going to try once more. He came slowly over the ridges, turned in the last moment and the nose dropped sharply into the gloom as he forced her down into the valley. They saw him level out very fast, and then the spotlights flicked on to the water and closed quickly and he was tracking for the dam.

His red Véry light curled up as Fuller called " Bombs

gone ! " but they must have been going too fast. The bomb hit the parapet of the dam and blew up on impact with a tremendous flash ; in the glare they saw " Z Zebra " for a moment just above the explosion. Then only blackness.

Gibson said painfully, knowing it was useless :

" Henry, Henry—hullo ' Z Zebra,' are you all right? " There was no answer. He called again and, incredibly, out of the darkness a very faint voice said, " I think so . . . stand by." They all heard it, Gibson and Shannon and Knight, and wondered that it was possible. After a while Gibson called again but there was no answer. Maudslay never came back.

Gibson called, " O.K., David, will you attack now? "

Shannon tried and missed again ; came round once more, plunged into the darkness and this time made it, curling out of the dive at the foot of the lake and tracking for the dam. He found his height quickly, the bomb dropped clear and Shannon roughly pulled his plane up over the shoulder of the mountain. Under the parapet the bomb spewed up the familiar plume of white water and as it drifted down Gibson, diving over the lake, saw that the dam was still there. There was only Knight left. He had the last bomb. Gibson ordered him in.

Knight tried once and couldn't make it. He tried again. Failed. " Come in down moon and dive for the point, Les," Shannon said. He gave more advice over the R/T, and Knight listened quietly. He was a young Australian who did not drink, his idea of a riotous evening being to write letters home and go to the pictures. He dived to try again, made a perfect run and they saw the splash as his bomb dropped in the right spot. Seconds later the water erupted, and as Gibson slanted down to have a look he saw the wall of the dam burst open and the torrent come crashing out.

Knight, more excited than he had ever been, was yelling over the R/T, and when he stopped he left his transmitter on for a few seconds by mistake ; the crew's remarks on the intercom. were broadcast, and they were very spectacular remarks indeed.

This was even more fantastic than the Moehne. The

breach in the dam was as big and there were over 200 million tons of water pouring through. The Eder Valley was steeper and they watched speechlessly as the flood foamed and tossed down the valley, lengthening like a snake. It must have been rolling at 30 feet a second. They saw a car in front racing to get clear ; only the lights they saw, like two frightened eyes spearing the dark, and the car was not fast enough. The foam crawled up on it, the headlights turned opalescent green as the water rolled over, and suddenly they flicked out.

Hutchison was tapping " Dinghy " in Morse ; that was the code to say that the Eder was destroyed. When he had finished Gibson called, " O.K. all Cooler aircraft. You've had your look. Let's go home," and the sound of their engines died over the hills as they flew west to fight their way back.

McCarthy had fought a lone way through to the Sorpe, tucked down in rolling hills south of the Moehne. The valleys were full of mist, so it was a long time before he pin-pointed himself over the lake, dimly seeing through the haze a shape he recognised from the model.

He tried a dummy run and found, as the others found before at the Eder, that there was a hill at each end so that he would have to dive steeply, find his aiming point quickly and pull up in a hurry. He tried twice more but was not satisfied and came in a third time, plunging through the mist trying to see through the suffused moonlight. He nearly hit the water and levelled out very low. Johnson picked up the aiming point and seconds later yelled, " Bomb gone ! " and they were climbing up over the far hills when the bomb exploded by the dam wall. McCarthy dived back over the dam and they saw that the crest had crumbled for 50 yards. As they turned on course for England, Eaton tapped out the code word that told of their successful drop.

Wallis's joy was complete. Cochrane radioed " G George," asking if he had any aircraft left to divert to the Sorpe, and Hutchison answered, " None." Satterly, who had been plotting the path of the reserve force by dead reckoning, radioed orders to them.

Burpee, in " S Sugar," was directed to the Sorpe, but he did not answer. They called again and again, but there was only silence. He was dead.

Brown, in " F Freddy," was sent to the Sorpe and reached it after McCarthy had left; the mist was swirling thicker and, though he dived low over the dam, Oancia, the bomb aimer, could not pick it up in time.

Brown dived back on a second run but Oancia still found the mist foiled him. They tried eight times, and then Brown pulled up and they had a conference over the intercom. On the next run Oancia dropped a cluster of incendiaries in the woods to the side of the dam. They burned dazzlingly and the trees caught too, so that on the tenth run Oancia picked up the glare a long way back, knew exactly where the target was and dropped his load accurately.

They pulled round in a climbing turn and a jet of water and rubble climbed out of the mist and hung against the moon; down in the mist itself they saw a shock wave of air like a giant smoke ring circling the base of the spout.

Anderson, in " Y Yorker," was also sent to the Sorpe, but he was still later than Brown, and now the valley was completely under mist so that the lake and the dam were hidden and he had to turn back with his bomb.

Ottley, in " C Charlie," was ordered to the Lister Dam, one of the secondary targets. He acknowledged " Message received," but that was the last anyone ever heard from him.

The last man was Townsend, in " O Orange," and his target was the Ennerpe. He searched a long time before he found it in the mist, and made three runs before he was satisfied and dropped the bomb. It was accurate.

Ten out of the nineteen were coming home, hugging the ground, 8 tons lighter now in bomb and petrol load and travelling at maximum cruising, about 245, not worrying about petrol; only about getting home. The coast was an hour away and the sun less than that. They knew the fighters were overhead waiting for a lightening sky in the east.

Harris had driven Cochrane and Wallis to Scampton to meet the survivors, and in the ops. room at Scampton he picked up the phone to try and get Portal again. This time he prepared the ground for smart service by telling the girl that the speaker was Air Chief Marshal Sir Arthur Harris, Commander-in-Chief of Bomber Command.

" Yes, of course," said the indulgent girl, who knew the absurd things that plastered New Zealand flight lieutenants were liable to say, " you've been on it again, sir. Now you go and get your batman to put you to bed. He'll give you your course to steer."

There was an explosion in the ops. room and an unusually intelligent intelligence officer hared down the stairs and told the girl the frightful thing she had done. Someone soothed the irate man in the ops. room while the girl beseeched the G.P.O. to get Washington faster than ever before. This time the lines were clear and before long a mollified Harris had the pleasure of telling Portal, " Operation Downwood successful . . . yes, successful ! "

Gibson saw the dark blotch of Hamm ahead and swung to the east. To the left he saw another aircraft ; it was going too near Hamm, he thought, whoever it was, and then the flak came up and something was burning in the sky where the aircraft had been. It was falling, hit like a shooting star and blew up. It may have been Burpee. Or Ottley.

Townsend was the last away from the dams area. He flew back over the Moehne and could not recognise it at first ; the lake had changed shape. Already there were mudbanks with little boats stranded on them, and bridges stood long-legged out of the shrinking water. The torpedo net had vanished, and below the dam the country was different. There was a new lake where no lake had been ; a strange lake, writhing down the valley.

Miraculously most of them dodged the flak on the way back ; lucky this, because dawn was coming, the sky was paler in the east and at 50 feet the aircraft were sitting ducks. In Gibson's aircraft Trevor-Roper called on the intercom., " Unidentified enemy aircraft behind."

" O.K., Trev." " G George " sank till it was scraping the fields and they could see the startled cattle running in panic. Trevor-Roper said, " O.K., we've lost him," but Gibson still kept down on the deck.

Over Holland he called Dinghy Young, but there was no answer and he wondered what had happened to him. (Group knew ! They had got a brief message from Young. He had come over the coast a little high and the last squirts of flak had hit him. He had struggled on a few more miles, losing height, and then ditched in the water.)

Coming to the West Wall, Gibson climbed to about 300 feet, Pulford slid the throttles right forward and they dived to the ground again, picking up speed, and at 270 m.p.h. they roared over the tank traps and the naked sand and then they were over the grey morning water and beyond the flak.

Ten minutes later it was daylight over Holland, and Townsend was still picking his way out. He was lucky and went between the guns.

Maltby was first back, landing in the dawn and finding the whole station had been waiting up since dusk. Harris, Cochrane and Wallis met him at the hardstanding and he told them what he had seen. Martin landed. Mutt Summers went out to meet him and found Martin under the aircraft looking at a ragged hole in his wing. " Hullo, Mutt," he said. " Look what some bastard's done to Popsie."

One by one they landed and were driven to the ops. room, where Harris, Cochrane and Wallis listened intently. Gibson came in, his hair pressed flat from eight hours under his helmet. " It was a wizard party, sir," he said. " Went like a bomb, but we couldn't quieten some of the flak. I'm afraid some of the boys got the hammer. Don't know how many yet. Hopgood and Maudslay for certain."

They had bacon and egg and stood round the bar with pints, drinking and waiting for the others. It was an hour since the last aircraft had landed. Shannon said Dinghy Young had ditched, and someone said, " What, is the old soak going to paddle back again ? That's the third time he's done it. He'll do it once too often." Young *had* done it once too often. He was not in his dinghy this time.

Wallis was asking anxiously, " Where are they ? Where are all the others ? "

Summers said, " Oh, they'll be along. Give 'em time. They've probably landed somewhere else " ; but after a while it was impossible to cover up any longer and Wallis knew they were all standing round getting drunk for the ones who were not coming back. Except himself ; he didn't drink. Martin made him take a half pint but he only held it and stood there blinking back tears and said, " Oh, if I'd only known, I'd never have started this ! " Mutt and Charles Whitworth tried to take his mind off it.

The party was getting wound up. Someone said, " This shouldn't be only a stag show," and a couple of minutes later an Australian and three others were invading the sacrosanct W.A.A.F. officers' room. One girl sat up in bed and pulled the clothes high over her.

" You can't come in here ! " she shrieked.

" Yes I can," one of them said, grabbing up two tennis balls from the dressing-table and stowing them in his tunic. He strutted round showing off his new bust line. " All girls together," he yelled. " Come and join the party."

The girl said she never went to parties before breakfast, so they grabbed the bed and started tossing it up towards the ceiling until she squealed, " All right, but get out while I dress."

Gibson left the party early, but not for bed ; he went over to the hangar to give Humphries and Chiefy Powell a hand with the casualty telegrams to the next of kin. Fifty-six beardless men out of 133 were missing, and only three had got out by parachute at a perilously low height to spend the rest of the war miserably in prison camp. Gibson had expected to lose several over the Moehne, where those sinister installations had been spotted by the recce aircraft, but they had lost only one there. (It was not till after the war that they discovered that those dark shapes on top of the Moehne had been—trees . . . ornamental pine trees. In the middle of the war the Germans would not send extra guns but had gone to the trouble of decorating it.)

Around lunchtime the party survivors transferred to

Whitworth's house and Whitworth's best port. Wallis came tiredly downstairs in a dressing-gown, distressed about the losses, and after a while he left to fly back to Weybridge with Summers. Martin gave him a sleeping-pill as he was leaving so he would sleep that night. He slept all right. The weary scientist swallowed the pill sitting up in bed at home and went out like a light.

About two o'clock even the durable Martin and Whittaker were ready for bed, but they were all up again at five o'clock and drove over in buses to a party at Woodhall Spa. On the way back David Shannon and Anne were sitting close together, and Shannon leaned closer so the others couldn't hear and asked her to marry him.

" Oh, David," she said, and there was a pause, " n-n-not with that moustache."

Shannon fingered the growth defensively. It was a dear possession ; made him look years older—at least twenty-two. He groaned. " What is it ? " he said. " My moustache or you ? " There was only silence and he sighed, " All right, I'll whip it off."

In the morning 617 Squadron went on leave, three days for the ground crew, seven days for the aircrew survivors— except Gibson, who stayed on two days to write to the mothers of the dead. He refused to let Heveron type the usual form letter but wrote them all out in his own hand, different ones each time, fifty-six of them.

In London and in their homes the crews found they were famous, though the headlines in Germany were not so flattering. A recce Mosquito arrived back from over Germany with the first pictures of the damage, and they were breathtaking. The Moehne and Eder lakes were empty and 330 million tons of water were spreading like a cancer through the western Ruhr valleys, the bones of towns and villages showing lifeless in the wilderness.

The Ruhr, which had been enduring its ordeal by fire, was having it now by water. For fifty miles from the Moehne and fifty miles from the Eder coal mines were flooded and factories collapsed. At Fritzlar one of Hitler's largest military aerodromes was under water, the aircraft, the landing ground, hangars, barracks and bomb dump. Roads, railways and bridges had disappeared. The Unterneustadt industrial suburb of Kassel, forty miles from the Eder, was under water, and the flood ran miles on down the Fulda Valley. Canal banks were washed away, power stations had disappeared, the Ruhr foundries were without water for making steel. A dozen waterworks were destroyed as far away as Gelsenkirchen, Dortmund, Hamm and Bochum. The communications system feeding raw materials to the Ruhr and taking away the finished weapons was disrupted. Some factories were not swept away but still could not work because there was no electricity. Or no water.

In the small town of Neheim alone 2,000 men, including 1,250 soldiers, were diverted to repair damage. Another 2,000 men were trying to repair the dams. And in the months ahead, in the Battle of the Ruhr, there was not enough water to put the fires out.

The official German report said it was " a dark picture of destruction." By the next autumn they might know how much industrial production would be ultimately affected, but estimated it was going to mean the equivalent of the loss of production of 100,000 men for several months.

A hundred and twenty-five factories were either destroyed or badly damaged, nearly 3,000 hectares of arable land were ruined, 25 bridges had vanished, and 21 more were badly damaged. The livestock losses were 6,500 cattle and pigs.

There was a moral price to pay too ; there always is. 1,294 people drowned in the floods, and most were civilians. Most were not Germans—there were 749 slaves and prisoners among the dead. There had been a Russian P.o.W. camp in the valley below the Eder.

After the raid the Germans diverted hundreds of soldiers with flak guns to guard all the other dams in Germany. While they were working like beavers to repair the Moehne they also built two tall pylons 2,000 yards back from the dam wall and strung between them a heavy cable across the lake. From this other cables dangled to the water, and lashed to them were contact grenades to catch low-flying aircraft.

They strung two heavy anti-torpedo nets near the dam wall, and another one a thousand yards away. On the dry side of the dam they strung a steel mesh curtain on posts sunk into the sloping wall.

Oberburgermeister Dillgardt was vindicated, but it was too late. The stable door was shut, but the horse had gone.

Gibson spent his leave quietly with his wife, Eve, who had had a shock when she had opened the papers and found Guy's name and photographs splashed over the front pages. All the time he had been at 617 he had told her he was having a rest at a flying training school.

Micky Martin was summoned to Australian Air Force Headquarters, where a dark, pretty girl called Wendy tried her damnedest to get him to talk about the raid for a story for Australia, but all the incorrigible Martin would say was, " Come and have lunch with me," and kept it up until she did.

Back at Scampton. Gibson found a letter for him addressed from a country vicarage. It enclosed, for his information, a copy of a letter which the writer had sent to *The Times* :

" *Sir,*
In international bird-watching circles, the bombing of the Moehne Dam has caused grave concern. For three years previous to the outbreak of war a pair of ring-necked whooper swans nested regularly on the lake. They are almost the rarest of Europe's great birds. The only other pair known to have raised a brood during recent years were a pair of the Arctic sub-species which were photographed by the aunt of the late Professor Olssen, of Reykjavik, on their nest on the shore of Lake Thongvallavatn, Iceland, in 1927.

Has anything been heard of the fate of the Moehne pair, probably the last in Europe? And, in view of the rarity of these beautiful birds, why was the bombing of their home permitted? Furthermore, assuming that this operation was necessary, could it not have been deferred until the cygnets (if any) were full grown?

Yours faithfully, etc., etc."

The Times must have smelt a rat and did not publish it, which was just as well because Gibson found later it had been written by two intelligence officers at Scampton.

Micky Martin got a letter too. The Australians wrote saying they were collecting souvenirs for a war museum, and could he send them a souvenir of the dams raid. Martin, irreverent where headquarters were concerned, wrote back :

" *Sir,*
I am very interested in your museum and am sending you, enclosed, the Moehne Dam.
                                                Yours faithfully."

And under his signature he got Toby Foxlee to scrawl in red ink : " *Opened by censors and contents confiscated by the Metropolitan Water Board.*"

Then the decorations came through—thirty-three of them. Gibson was awarded the Victoria Cross. Martin, McCarthy, Maltby, Shannon and Knight got D.S.Os. Bob Hay, Hutchison, Leggo and Danny Walker got bars to their D.F.Cs. There were ten D.F.Cs., among them Trevor-Roper, Buckley, Deering, Spafford and Taerum. Brown and Townsend got the Conspicuous Gallantry Medal, and there were twelve D.F.Ms., among them being Tammy Simpson, Sumpter, Oancia and Pulford.

When he heard the news Gibson rang for Flight Sergeant Powell.

" Chiefy," he said quietly, " if I ever change, tell me."

On May 27 the King and Queen visited the newly famous squadron, and the crews pressed their uniforms and stood in front of their aircraft to be presented, though one noted pilot overlooked one point and was standing there smartly to attention with an orange sticking out of his pocket. That day was Shannon's twenty-first birthday, and Gibson had primed the King beforehand, so that when Shannon was presented the King shook him warmly by the hand and said jokingly, " You seem to be a very well preserved twenty-one, Shannon. You must have a party to-night."

Gibson had had a competition for a design for a squadron

badge, and after the parade he showed the King the roughs and asked if he would choose one. The King called the Queen, and unanimously they picked a drawing showing a dam breached in the middle with water flowing out and bolts of lightning above. Underneath, the motto was "*Après nous le deluge* "; most apt, particularly as it had a royal background —Marie Antoinette had used it.

That night, when the royal party had left, Shannon had his party. Towards the end an apparition came leaping into the mess. Charles Whitworth had robed himself in hunting kit, red coat and white breeches, and pranced around tootling on a hunting horn, hurdling the furniture till there was a bellow from the doorway: " What the devil's going on here ! " In the frame of the door stood an obviously senior officer, rows of braid up his sleeve, gold oak leaves on his cap and ribbons plastered across his chest. A hush fell, and then slightly glazed eyes focused and a chorus of catcalls burst the silence.

" Shannon ! "

Shannon had slipped away and put Whitworth's tunic and hat on. He stalked in, stopped in front of Whitworth and boomed, " Who is this wretched fellow in fancy dress ? "

Whitworth blew him a raspberry on his hunting horn.

" Whip him off to the guard-room ! " Shannon shouted. " Clap him in irons ! "

He turned to his wireless operator, the lanky Concave Goodale, and roared, " Stand to attention when you look at me ! "

" You're not standing so well yourself," Goodale said rudely.

Buckley padded forward, eyeing his skipper indulgently, and said, " Let's have his pants."

Bodies closed in menacingly, but Gibson said, " No. Give him grace. It's his twenty-first birthday."

Someone, patently insober, said, " Shannon, I think you're drunk," and Shannon said with hauteur:

" Sir, if so, it is by Royal Command."

CHAPTER IX

THE BLACKEST HOUR

WEEKS passed placidly. Gibson wrote and asked the Chester Herald to approve the chosen badge. The squadron got new aircraft and did a lot of training flying, both high and low level, finding it boring, and to give them something to think about Gibson laid on compulsory P.T. for all aircrew. On the second morning three men did not turn up for it, so Gibson made them run round the perimeter track, four and a half miles, and to make sure they ran the whole way he sent the dismayed Chiefy Powell with them. Powell came in a reluctant fourth. A few days later a couple more decided to chance it and stay in bed; Gibson made them do an extra half hour P.T. in gas masks and there were no more absentees.

All those decorated were to attend an investiture at Buckingham Palace on June 22, and on the 21st they went up to London in two special carriages. The staider ones and those with wives were mostly in one carriage, and the bloods gathered in the other, pockets bulging with bottles, and settled down to pontoon and poker.

An hour later Humphries was chatting in the respectable carriage to a few of the wives and W.A.A.F. officers when a wireless operator appeared in the doorway, immaculately dressed except that he had no pants. Long shirt tails kept him technically decent.

" Losht my pantsh," he mumbled. " Very awkward. Can't see King without pantsh."

Humphries jumped up and screened him from the giggling W.A.A.Fs., pushed him into a toilet and walked along to the compartment where Trevor-Roper and Maltby were noisily playing cards. He tried the casual approach:

" I say, have any of you chaps by any chance seen Brian's pants ? "

Screams of mirth.

" Why, Adj., has he lost them ? "

" You know he has," Humphries said severely. " It's not

really so funny. He just walked into a compartment where there were a couple of ladies."

Louder screams of mirth. They were crying with laughter.

" Quite well made, isn't he ? " gasped Jack Fort and the compartment rocked with laughter again.

Trevor-Roper was eyeing Humphries' pants sinisterly, but Humphries held his ground. " You wouldn't think it was funny if it had been your girl friends."

" Ah well," Maltby said, " I suppose not." He pulled a pair of crumpled pants from under the seat and tossed them over.

" Have a Scotch before you go, Adj.," Trevor-Roper said. He whipped the cap off a bottle and poured till the top of the vacuum flask was nearly full. He was grinning ; it was clearly a case of sinking the neat spirit or losing his own pants, and Humphries chose the spirit, downing it in one gulp, so that for a fearful instant, through the tears, he thought the top of his head was coming off.

" I'm proud of you, Adj.," Trevor-Roper said. " Have another." But Humphries had retreated with the pants.

They got safely to London, a tribute to Humphries' tireless and tactful shepherding, but that evening he fell into bad company again, finding himself in a suite at the Savoy with the mountain of man from Brooklyn, Joe McCarthy, and Toby Foxlee. He does not remember where he went that night but at some hour in the morning he found himself back at the Savoy. Trevor-Roper walked in and said, " Let's have a drink. The party hasn't started yet."

In the morning, when he tried to open his eyes, Humphries thought the ceiling had fallen on him, but the investiture was at 10.15 a.m. and he just *had* to get up. They were nearly all in the same boat but they all made it, pale and heavy-eyed.

617 Squadron was decorated *en masse* first, taking precedence over the other V.Cs. and high orders, a historical precedent that may never be repeated. And when the band struck up the Anthem it was not the King who emerged but the Queen ; the first time a queen had taken an investiture since the days of Victoria.

Gibson went up first to get his V.C., and one by one the

others. The Queen took Joe McCarthy's great paw and stood chatting with him for a long time, asking him questions about America, while the big blond tough from Brooklyn turned pink and stammered out answers.

That night A. V. Roe's gave them a celebration dinner. The only mistake all night tickled everyone ; the printers had labelled the menu " The Damn Busters."

More weeks of training, high and low level, and the crews, who were supposed to be the pick of Bomber Command, became " browned off." Men of other squadrons who were doing several ops. a week took to ragging them as the " One op. squadron," and one of the 617 bomb aimers, Jimmy Watson, a droll little Yorkshireman, composed a lament on the subject. Sung to the tune of " Come and join us," the first verse ran :

" *The Moehne and the Eder dams were standing in the Ruhr,*
  But six one seven Squadron went and knocked them to the floor.
  Now since that operation six one seven's been a flop
  And we've got the reputation of the squadron with one op."

Cochrane told Gibson he had done enough operations and would not let him fly again. Squadron Leader George Holden, D.S.O., D.F.C., arrived to take over, but Gibson stayed on for a few days. Holden was slight and youthful with fair wavy hair but a brusque manner. Before the war he had worn a bowler and carried a rolled umbrella, but was a very tough young man. He had felt very sick once but kept flying on ops. for over a week till he nearly collapsed after landing one night and went to the doctor, who examined him and said, a little startled, " Well, I think you've had pleurisy, but you seem to be nearly all right now."

617 went to war again on July 15, against power stations in Northern Italy, at San Polo D'Enza, near Bologna, and Aquata Scrivia, near Genoa. Mussolini was toppling, the battle of Sicily was raging, and supplies for the Germans were streaming down Italy on the electrified railways. They hoped to cripple the railways by striking at the power. It was a long way, the aircraft would arrive with tanks two-thirds empty

and there was no hope of flying back to England. Yells of
joy when they were told they would fly on to Blida, an airfield
in North Africa, near Algiers. The only glum one was
Gibson, categorically forbidden to go. Holden was to lead
six aircraft to Aquata Scrivia, and Maltby to lead the other
six to San Polo D'Enza. Gibson sadly waved them off from
the end of the runway.

It was a " cissy " trip ; no opposition on the way, but
they found the targets cloaked in haze and bombed largely
by guesswork. Several aircraft were hit and Allsebrook lost
an engine, but they all landed safely at Blida. At the de-
briefing McCarthy threw his parachute down disgustedly and
said, " You know, if we'd only carried flares to-night we
could've seen what we were doing." No one took much
notice just then, but it was that remark, remembered later,
that was partly responsible for the history they made.

North Africa was a novelty for about two days. The
airfield was a plain of baked earth, and the crews, sweating
in wooden barracks, lay about sipping red wine and sun-
bathing. The weather closed in and they were stranded for
ten days, getting browned off by boredom instead.

On the flight home they called at Leghorn to deliver some
bombs over the docks, but again there was haze and they were
not pleased with the bombing.

Martin flew back over the Alps at 19,000 feet, to the dismay
of Tammy Simpson in the rear turret, who had thought they
were returning low over France and had worn only his light
tropical kit. Back at Scampton they thawed him out with
rum.

The squadron greeted them most warmly as they clambered
out of the aircraft with bottles of benedictine and wine, and
dragging crates of oranges, figs and dates. Martin jumped
out wearing a fez.

Gibson was not there to meet them. He had gone. Harris
and Cochrane had put a definite stop to his flying by asking
Winston Churchill to take him with him to America for a
" show the flag " tour, and Gibson had had no option. He'd
been so upset he had not been able to face the farewells.

On July 29 the squadron dropped leaflets on Milan to

persuade the wavering Italians that the war was profitless. It was singularly unstimulating, and McCarthy summed up the feeling by grumbling, " It's no better than selling goddam newspapers." The only bright feature was that they went on to Blida again and re-stocked with benedictine and oranges.

One aircraft had been commissioned to bring back a keg of wine for a senior group captain. They brought it back all right, but it vanished from the aircraft after landing and there was a great deal of care-free laughter in the ground-crew barracks that night. Also an explosion from the group captain. Chiefy Powell was told to catch the culprits, but after a decent interval of about three days he reported it was a complete mystery, feeling somewhat disgruntled because he was the only man who had been noble enough to refuse a beaker.

In August they were back to boredom. No ops., but training all and every day.

It was about this time that disturbing reports were coming out of Germany about a mysterious new weapon. Apparently Hitler's notorious " secret weapon." Agents could not say what it was but sensed it was something special. A couple of escaped prisoners of war reached England with information that hinted at rockets and indicated an area north-east of Luebeck. In the Pas de Calais area thousands of workmen were swarming about monstrous new concrete works. A recce aircraft brought back a photograph of a strange new factory at Peenemunde, north-east of Luebeck. Lying on the ground were pencil-shaped objects that baffled the interpretive men, but little by little they began to connect the rocket reports with the pencil-shaped objects and the concrete structures, which would obviously be impervious to any R.A.F. bombs. The 12,000-pounder thin-case bomb was nearly ready, but it was purely a blast bomb, to explode on the ground and knock over buildings. It would not dent masses of concrete half embedded in the earth.

The spies were right. Sixty miles from London, just behind Calais, Hitler was building his secret-weapon blockhouses, fantastic structures which would bombard London and the invasion ports non-stop in spite of anything we could do. They were all of reinforced concrete, walls of 16 feet thick and roofs 20 feet thick ! No known bomb would affect them. The Todt Organisation promised Hitler that.

At Watton, Wizernes and Siracourt the blockhouses were to be assembly, storage and launching sites for rockets and flying bombs. Twelve thousand slaves were working on them, and deep under the concrete they were carving tunnels and chambers in the chalk and rock where Germans could live and fire their rockets without interruption.

But greatest nightmare of all was the grotesque underworld being burrowed under a 20-foot thick slab of ferro-concrete near Mimoyecques. Here Hitler was preparing his V.3. Little has ever been told about V.3, probably because we never found out much about it. V.3 was the most secret and sinister of all— long-range guns with barrels 500 feet long !

The muzzles would never appear above earth ; the entire barrels would be sunk in shafts that dived at 50 degrees 500 feet into the ground. Hitler was putting fifteen of these guns in at Mimoyecques, five guns, side by side, in each of three shafts. They were smooth-bore barrels, and a huge slow-burning charge would fire a 10-inch shell with a long, steady acceleration, so there would be no destructive heat and pressure in the barrel. In that way the barrels would not quickly wear out as Big Bertha did in World War I. These were more monstrous in every way than Big Bertha ; they fired a bigger shell, could go on firing for a long time and, more important than that, they had a rapid rate of fire. Thick armour-plate doors in the concrete would slide back when they were ready, and then the nest of nightmare guns would pour out six shells a minute on London, 600 tons of explosives a day. They would keep that up accurately day after day, so that in a fortnight London would receive as much high explosive as Berlin received during the whole war. But that fortnight would be only the start of it.

The War Cabinet did not know this, but they *did* know enough to be extremely worried. There were anxious (and very secret) conferences (which coincided with the fact that

Cochrane was strongly pressing for renewed interest in Wallis's shock-wave bomb—he wanted to use it on the Rothensee ship-lift). Soon the Chief Executive of the Ministry of Aircraft Production, Air Chief Marshal Sir Wilfred Freeman, sent for Barnes Wallis, who was now held in esteem and some awe. Freeman said :

" Wallis, do you remember that crazy idea of yours back in 1940 about a bomb ? "

" I seem to have had a lot of crazy ideas then," Wallis said wryly.

" I mean about a *big* bomb, a ten-tonner and a six-tonner. You wrote a paper about it. To penetrate deep into the earth and cause an earthquake."

" Ah, yes," said Wallis, his eyes lighting up.

" How soon can you let me have some ? "

It was so sudden that Wallis was staggered. He thought a while.

" About four or five months," and he added quickly, " that is, if I get facilities. There's a lot of work to it, you know."

" Right. Will you go and see Craven right away, please. I'll ring him and tell him you're coming over."

Sir Charles Craven, head of Vickers, was also a Controller of the Ministry of Aircraft Production. Wallis was shown into his office near Whitehall ten minutes later, and before he could say a word Craven was booming at him :

" What the hell d'you want the services of twenty thousand men in Sheffield for ? " Apparently Freeman had already been on the phone.

Wallis explained and got a promise of full support. He had little time to relax in the next few weeks. First he held a " Dutch auction " with Roy Chadwick the Avro designer.

" Roy," he said, " can your Lancs carry seventeen thousand pounds for two hundred and fifty miles ? "

" Oh yes," Chadwick said. " Easily."

" Could they carry nineteen thousand ? "

" Oh . . . er . . . I think so."

" Well now, Roy," Wallis said persuasively, " how about going to the full ten tons ? "

" Oh good Lord, I don't know about that."

H 2

" Now come on . . . if you tried more powerful engines and strengthened the undercarts."

" Well . . . Oh, I suppose it *could* be done."

" Thanks," said Wallis and went off to Sheffield to iron out more of the problems that seemed endless. The bomb had to be made from a *very* special steel; there were only two foundries in the country capable of casting the casings, and both were fully occupied on other vital work.

New methods of casting had to be evolved, new forms of heat treatment for hardening so the bombs could plough into hard ground faster than sound and not break up. The fuses had to stand up to the same shock. There were not enough firms capable of machining the finished bombs. It was a question of finding firms throughout England who might be able to machine one each month. There had to be special machines designed and built to fill them with explosive, and new methods of testing. The Lancasters would have to be extensively modified to carry them; special trucks and dollies designed and built to handle them, and special winches to get them into the aircraft.

On August 30, 617 Squadron moved to Coningsby, another bomber airfield in Lincolnshire. Scampton had been a grass field, but Coningsby had long bitumen runways, more suitable for aircraft carrying very heavy loads. Flying was still confined to training, high and low level, aimlessly it seemed, and suddenly they were switched to low level. Cochrane told Holden that they had to be as good as they had been for the dams raid, and there were some new crews to train.

Cochrane and Satterly had long conferences with Holden and Group Captain Sam Patch, the station commander at Coningsby. There was a new verve about the squadron, a feeling of expectancy. At nights the aircraft hurtled low over the flat country and heavy lorries drove in to the bomb dump, their loads hidden under heavy tarpaulins. But it was not to be quite like the dams raid: that was obvious because they were still using the orthodox Lancasters. A flight of Mosquito night fighters arrived at Coningsby, and stayed. Apparently they were going to have fighter escort.

On September 14, Holden drew up a battle order for that night ; a short one, eight crews, the pilots being Holden, Maltby, Knight, Shannon, Wilson, Allsebrook, Rice and Divall. Target was the Dortmund Ems Canal, the freight link between the Ruhr and central and eastern Germany, including the North Sea. At that time 33 million tons a year passed along it, of which only a small fraction could be diverted to the railways. Near Ladbergen the fields fell away below the level of the canal and earth banks guided the water across the lowlands. One bomb breaching the bank would flood the countryside and there would be no canal. At least, no water in it ; and that would starve the Ruhr of coal—and do many other things. Pre-fabricated U-boats were made in the Ruhr, for instance, and they could only be taken to the sea along the canal.

It was to be another very low-level raid, partly for bombing accuracy and partly because they thought the flak low down was less of a risk than fighters high up, concentrating on eight lonely aircraft. Cochrane saw that it was one of the most carefully planned raids of the war. As in the dams raid, the route curled delicately between the known flak. A specially designed beacon would be dropped near the canal as a pin-point and night fighters would engage the flak which guarded the most vulnerable points on the canal, although not the point chosen for the attack, which was some two miles from the nearest guns. A weather recce plane would check the visibility in the canal area before the Lancasters arrived. Most important of all they were going to drop the new 12,000-lb. light-case bombs for the first time. (Not to be confused with Wallis's developing earthquake bomb.)

They took off at dusk with no illusions ; memories of the dams losses were too fresh and they had a human yearning for the placid if less stimulating days of the Italian trips.

They were an hour out, low over the North Sea, when the weather Mosquito found the target hidden under fog and radioed back. Group recalled the Lancasters and as the big aircraft turned for home weighed down by nearly 6 tons of bomb David Maltby seemed to hit someone's slipstream ;

a wing flicked down, the nose dipped and before Maltby could correct it the wing-tip had caught the water and the Lancaster cartwheeled, dug her nose in and vanished in spray. Shannon swung out of formation and circled the spot, sending out radio fixes and staying till an air sea rescue flying boat touched down beneath. They waited up at Coningsby till the flying boat radioed that it had found nothing but oil slicks.

Maltby's wife lived near the airfield, and in the morning Holden went over to break the news, dreading it because it had been an ideally happy marriage. Maltby was only twenty-one. The girl met him at the door and guessed his news from his face.

" It was quick," said Holden, who did not know it was his own last day on earth. " He wouldn't have known a thing."

Too stunned to cry, the girl said, " I think we both expected it. He's been waking up in the night lately shouting something about the bomb not coming off."

Holden came back looking tired and got out another battle order. If the weather was right the raid was on again. Martin came back from leave that morning and demanded to take Maltby's place. Tammy Simpson, who had been flying with Martin for two years now, noted philosophically and a little querulously in his diary : " Mick's a bloody fool volunteering. This is going to be dangerous." Shannon was hoping the weather would be right this time. Moustacheless, he was to marry Anne in a week and was supposed to have left for London that morning to arrange the wedding. Anne had already wangled a posting for herself to Dunholme Lodge, an airfield near Coningsby.

At dusk in the control tower McCarthy watched the heavy aircraft lift off the runway and head east. Also watching was a languid W.A.A.F. who said as the aircraft merged with the darkness. " My God, I only hope they get there to-night ! The trouble the A.O.C.'s gone to over this . . ."

McCarthy turned on her and snarled, " The hell with you and all the A.O.Cs. What about the seven lives in every kite ! " The building vibrated as the door slammed behind him.

Over the North Sea the Lancasters kept loose formation

in two boxes of four. It felt like the dams raid all over
again ; they were down to 50 feet to fox the radar and on
strict radio silence. The faster Mosquitoes would be taking
off now to pass them somewhere on the way in and set about
the flak as the bombers arrived. Over the canal itself the
weather Mosquito radioed back that it was perfectly clear.

The bombers crossed the Dutch coast and there was no
sign of flak. Holden seemed to be flying a perfect course,
which was just as well because the moon was up and it was
full, throwing soft light over the fields as they moved towards
Germany and Ladbergen.

Ahead of them a small town loomed up and high chimneys
and a church steeple seemed to be rushing at them. Martin
waited for Holden to swing to one side, but Holden elected to
bore straight across and climbed to clear the steeple till he
was about 300 feet. The more low-flying-wise Martin
dropped right down to roof-top height and, on the other side
of Holden, Knight and Wilson did the same, till even from the
ground they were nearly invisible against the horizon. Holden
was limned against the moonlight.

There was one light gun in Nordhoorn and its crew had
been alerted. Holden was halfway across when a procession
of glowing red balls streamed up, and in a shaven fraction of
a second Toby Foxlee was firing back, so that only about
five shells pumped up before Foxlee's tracer was squirting
down and the gun abruptly stopped.

One of the five shells punched into Holden's inner starboard
wing tank. There was a long streamer of flame trailing back
beyond the tailplane ; the aircraft showed clearly in the
glow and they could see it was going down. The port wing
was dropping and then the nose ; she was falling faster,
slewing to the left, right under Wilson and Knight with a
12,000-pounder on board ! Martin yelled sharply over the
R/T : " Break outwards ! "

Wilson was just turning away when Holden's aircraft hit
on the edge of the town almost under him ; the 12,000-
pounder went off and the town and the sky were like day.

Martin called the other two anxiously. Knight came right
back and said he was all right, but it was twenty seconds

before Wilson answered, a little shakily, saying they were jarred by the explosion but he thought nothing serious was broken. A little later they were back in formation, Martin leading. They swept into Germany, grimmer now. Gibson's crew had been in Holden's aircraft. Spafford, Taerum, Pulford, Hutchison ; they were all gone.

One by one they picked up pin-points and the canal was only five minutes away when a blanket seemed to come down in front and they found themselves in mist. It was unbelievable. The area had been clear and moonlit half an hour before, no trace of trouble, and now the ground was a smudge, and they edged up to over a hundred feet to be clear of obstacles. The fog had moved in from the east without warning, almost without precedent. Some of the experts said later that Allsebrook, the deputy controller, should have called it off then, told everyone to go home and forget it till next time, but that is debatable. As it was they pushed on.

There were locks along the canal and every one was armed with flak. The trouble was that the Lancasters could not see the canal until they were right on it, and then it was too late to bomb. They would have to bomb from 150 feet—because they could not see the canal if they went any higher—and hope the flak would miss, which at that height was unlikely.

All of them tried flying across the canal to pick it up, hoping they could swing sharply on to it, but found it was nearly impossible. Split up now, they searched the area but kept blundering into the flak, and then they turned away and tried again, refusing to bomb till they were certain they were in position. The Mosquitoes had arrived and, with their greater speed and smaller size, were charging back and forth trying to silence the gunners, but could not pick them up in the fog.

Allsebrook is believed to have bombed eventually but where his bomb went is not known. They never found the wreckage of his aircraft either. Wilson was heard briefly over the R/T saying something about going in to attack. The bomb was still aboard when the aircraft hit the ground about 200 yards beyond the canal and made a crater 200 feet across.

Divall was heard briefly over the R/T, but that was the last anyone ever heard from him.

The gentle little Les Knight shouted over the intercom. that he could see the water, and then flak was coming at them and they were weaving. Johnson, the bomb aimer, yelled that he could see trees looming ahead and *above* them, and as Knight pulled up hard the bomber shuddered as she hit the tree-tops, and then they were clear with branches stuffed in the radiators, both port engines stopped and the tailplane damaged.

With the two starboard engines roaring at full power the Lancaster, with the bomb still aboard, was just able to hold her height. No chance of bombing in that condition, and Knight called up Martin : " Two port engines gone. May I have permission to jettison bomb, sir ? " It was the " sir " that got Martin. Quiet little Knight was following the copy-book procedure, asking respectful permission to do the only thing that might get him home.

Martin said, " For God's sake, Les, yes," and as the bomb was not fused Knight told Johnson to let it go. Relieved of the weight they started to climb very slowly.

After the gunners had thrown out all the guns and fittings they could, Knight got her up to about 1,400 feet and headed towards England, the aircraft waffling soggily at 110 m.p.h. The controls were getting worse all the time until, though he had full opposite rudder and aileron on, Knight could not stop her turning to port and it was obvious he could never fly her home. He ordered his crew to bale out and held the plane steady while they did. When the last man had gone he must have tried to do the same himself, and must have known all the time what would happen when he slipped out of his seat. There was perhaps a slight chance of getting clear in time, but as soon as he took pressure off stick and rudder the aircraft flicked on her back and plunged to the ground. Knight did not get to the hatch in time.

Geoff Rice tried for an hour to find the canal, was badly holed by flak and finally had to swing his winged aircraft out of the area, jettison the bomb and head for home. Shannon was seventy minutes before he got a quick sight of the high

banks of the canal, wheeled the Lancaster along the water
and Sumpter called, " Bomb gone ! " There was an eleven-
second delay on the fuse, so they only dimly saw the explosion.
The bomb hit the tow-path. If it had been a few feet to
one side, in the water, it would have breached the canal wall.

Martin spent an hour and a half plunging at 150 feet in
the fog around the canal trying to give Bob Hay a good
enough sight on the few spots where the high earth bank was
vulnerable. Now and then he caught a brief glimpse of the
water, but it was either at a spot where the banks were low
and solid or the flak was too murderous to give them a chance.
It squirted at them when they were right on top of it and they
had to wheel away into the fog. The aircraft jolted twice as
shells punched into it, and once a sudden burst of tracer
ripped through under the cockpit so that Martin jumped
with shock, one foot slipped off the rudder bar and the big
Lancaster swung so crazily he thought it was all over.

The gunners had been firing whenever they got a chance
and Tammy Simpson reported his ammunition was getting
low. Martin told him to forget the flak and save what he
had left in case they got a chance to fight their way home.

Once or twice he was able to come up to the canal diagonally
so that it was easier to turn along it, but each time the glimpse
of water came too late or the flak was coming point blank at
them and they had to pull away.

On the thirteenth run Hay got a glimpse of water in the
swirling fog and called, " There it is ! " Martin turned away
in a slow and regular 360 degrees circle, opening his bomb
doors and calculating the exact moment he should come over
the water again so the straighten-up would be gentle. It
was a beautifully timed turn ; they were low over the sliver
of water with no flak, just long enough for Hay to call, " Left,
left, a shade right . . . bomb gone ! " and then Whittaker
slammed the throttles hard on and Martin pulled her steeply
round in a " splitarse " turn as the flak opened up.

A little later they hurtled back across the canal and saw
the water boiling where the bomb had exploded, a few feet
from the bank, just a few feet too far, because the bank was
still there.

They were still over Germany and dawn was breaking as they came out of the fog. On full throttle, " P Popsie " was shaking at 267 m.p.h., the fastest she had ever travelled at low level. As they slid round the end of Sylt two last guns sent shells after them and then they were over the sea.

They landed two hours overdue and found Cochrane still waiting. He had heard of the losses from Shannon, who was first back, and his face was leaner and grimmer than ever. Martin was the third back, out of eight. Cochrane knew there would not be any more. He said :

" How was it ? "

" I'm terribly sorry, sir," Martin said. " It didn't breach. The mist beat us, and the flak." He told what had happened. Cochrane listened keenly and at the end he was staggered when Martin said, " I'm very disappointed, sir, but if the weather's clear to-morrow—I mean, that is, to-night now— I think we can get it, if you'll let us have another crack."

" How many crews have you got left ? "

Martin thought for a while and said, " Well, there are three of us in my flight, and three more in Shannon's flight. That ought to be enough, sir."

" Six ! " Cochrane said. " Out of your original twenty-one ! "

" It ought to be enough, sir. I'm just sorry about last night."

Cochrane said gently, " I don't think you have to apologise for anything, Martin. I'll let you know later about to-night. Meantime you'd better go and get some sleep." He took Sam Patch by the arm and led him over to the corner and Patch for the first time sensed that Cochrane had let slip the mask of his reserve. There was no mistaking it, and almost no defining it, an intensity about his eyes, his whole face and his voice as he said :

" Patch, I'd like to make Martin a wing commander on the spot and put him in command of the squadron. You know the boy better than I do. Would you recommend him ? "

Patch thought for a moment before he made the answer for which he has been kicking himself ever since : " It's two jumps up the ladder, sir; I'm not sure he's ready for it. He's had no experience in administration."

" Well, I'll at least get him made a squadron leader and give him temporary command." Cochrane caught Martin as he finished stowing his kit away and said in his sudden-death way, " You're a squadron leader now, Martin, and for the time being you're in command of the squadron."

Martin looked after the retreating back and said, " Christ! " A moment before he hadn't even been a flight commander. Patch said, " Well, you've got responsibilities now, Mick. Come and have a walk and talk till you relax." Martin was too exhilarated to sleep. They paced slowly across the air-field, right to the blast walls of the bomb dump, lonely in its isolation on the far side of the field.

" I didn't think anything could have gone wrong," Patch was saying. " I thought we had the perfect plan this time."

" Oh, we should've pranged the thing," Martin said disgustedly. " That bloody mist. You couldn't see a thing."

There was a long silence; the air was fresh, the grass soft and springy under their feet, and Martin, after eight hours in the air, was far from sleep with the light-headed exhilaration you get after you're so tired you can hardly stand and then get your second wind. He had been awake over twenty-four hours. He said suddenly: " Well, there it is, sir. Two real ops. and six crews left. Maybe this is the end. They'll make us an ordinary line squadron . . . or disband us altogether."

" Probably *will* be the end if you try that canal again to-night," Patch said drily. " You were silly to volunteer again. You're not immortal."

" No, sir."

" D'you think you'd get away with it again to-night ? "

" Couldn't be any worse."

" I suppose it occurs to you the flak will be expecting you." Martin said soberly, " I suppose so."

" Forget it a while, Mick," Patch said. " I don't think the A.O.C.'ll let you try again for a while anyway. He doesn't like losing crews, and you lost five out of eight last night . . . six including Maltby the night before. You'll lose the rest if you go again to-night. We've got to think out a cleverer way of doing it."

There was another silence and Patch broke it by saying tentatively:

" What d'you think about 617 taking a rest for a while ? You've taken an awful beating and you've got to fill up with new crews and train them. What d'you think ? "

Martin said, " No. Let's do another one right away and get the taste out of our mouths. Otherwise we're going to get scared of going back."

" The A.O.C.'ll decide that anyway," Patch said. " Maybe you've had your day on special duty."

They called at the office on the way back to see about the casualty reports, but Chiefy Powell and Heveron were already attending to them. Patch took Martin over to the mess for breakfast and sat and talked to him. Patch had not been to sleep for nearly thirty hours himself but he never changed his routine when a raid was on. He never failed to visit every aircraft before it took off; always waited up till the last crew had landed and then went over to the mess with them for bacon and eggs and yarned as long as they wanted him to. He never went to bed himself till he'd seen the last of the boys off to bed. He was a round-faced, heavy-set, youngish man, direct and honest. If you did a good job, Patch would go to tremendous trouble to let you know. If you did a bad job he would tell you how and why, so you would do better next time. If you failed to mend your ways he would crack down hard, and then in the mess that night he would be normal and friendly to the punished one.

As Martin was finishing breakfast McCarthy and the laconic Munro came in, clicked their heels and peeled off sizzling salutes. " Good morning, *sir*," they chorused, and Martin had the grace to blush. They congratulated him and, in grimmer mood, paid their respects to the dead. Martin gave his first orders. " Will you get cracking on making what aircraft we've got left ready for to-night. I'm thinking we'll be on again. Let me know when the target comes through." He added, almost as an after-thought, " May be the same target to-night."

"All right," said McCarthy. "Push off to bed and grab some shuteye."

Shannon had only got to bed himself about half an hour before. He had written a little note to Anne, apologising for not being able to go up to London. Anne got it over at Dunholme Lodge that afternoon. Quite a short note : "Sorry, darling. Couldn't make it. Been up two nights. Lost six out of nine. Please forgive. I'm rather tired." For the first time she saw the writing was shaky.

She had been up all night herself in the ops. room at Dunholme Lodge. About dawn they got a report that five out of the eight were shot down and she was crying when someone ran over and said, "David's all right. He's back." But the tears only fell faster.

Martin got nearly five hours' sleep. McCarthy regretfully woke him at two o'clock, shaking his shoulder and saying, "Target's through, Mick," until the tired boy shook the sleep out of his head and said, "Where ? "

"Somewhere in the south of France. Bridge or something."

Martin pulled some clothes on and saw Patch over in the planning room. Patch said, "You're not going back to the canal yet. You're going with 619 Squadron to have a go at the Antheor Viaduct. It's on the Riviera, near the Eytie border, and carries the only good railway into Italy from France. If you prang it you'll stop half the Hun reinforcements to Sicily."

Martin said, "I'm sorry it isn't the canal," and he so obviously meant it that Patch just looked at him.

They found the viaduct without trouble fifteen miles west of Cannes, seeing in the moonlight the 90-foot stone arches curving across the beach at the foot of a ravine. The idea was to dive to 300 feet and stab 1,000-lb. bombs into the stone with delayed fuses. It was like a cocoa-nut shy ; bang on and the cocoa-nut is yours, miss by an inch and lose your money. They missed by inches. The bombs went through the arches and exploded on the ground all around ; the viaduct was pitted by splinters but that was all. The only real result was that it woke the Germans up to the vulnerability of the railway, and soon after that the flak batteries moved in.

Shannon scrounged a few days' leave, went up to London and married Anne. They spent part of their honeymoon in a hotel, and when they walked into the bar one night Anne heard someone say, " Good God, that boy looks too young to be in the Air Force." Shannon turned round and the man saw he was wearing a D.S.O. and D.F.C. and his eyes stuck out like organ stops.

The Chester Herald answered Gibson's letter about the squadron badge, questioning the motto. It was true Marie Antoinette had said, " *Après nous le deluge*," but she had used it in an irresponsible connection. Martin chewed it over with Patch, and Patch said, " Well, change it to ' Après *moi* le deluge.' That ought to fix it." Martin wrote back accordingly.

A day or so later Cochrane sent for him. " I think we might be able to use this dams bomb of Wallis's against the *Tirpitz*," the A.O.C. said. The *Tirpitz* was still sheltering in Alten Fiord. " You can't fly up the fiord to get her ; that'd be death, but she's moored only about half a mile from the shore where the land rises steeply. You might do it by surprise, hurdle the hill, dive and bomb before they wake up." There was a hill near Bangor, he said, about the same height and gradient. Martin was to go and practise over it to see if he could level out soon enough on the water at the right height and speed.

Martin flew " P Popsie " over to North Wales and spent an afternoon diving over the coast, climbing and trying again. It called for most delicate judgment, but towards the end he found he could do it with 40 degrees of flap down. It meant diving 60 m.p.h. faster than permitted with 40 degrees of flap and that meant the flap was likely to collapse on one side. If that happened at low level the aircraft would spin straight in. He reported to Cochrane that he was willing to chance that. He knew what the *Tirpitz* defences would be like at low level but thought the raid would be possible.

" We wouldn't need too many aircraft, sir. Myself, McCarthy and Shannon would go. I don't imagine there will be much chance of a second run. but we know the form of attack well and we could practise over the Bangor hills so we get it right the first time." He suggested they do the raid by moonlight or at dusk or dawn, so there would be some gloom for cover but enough light to see the ship. Matter-of-factly he added : " I think you should be prepared to lose the three aircraft, sir, but we'll have a go and probably get her."

Cochrane, who had not met anyone quite like Martin before, looked at him for some time and finally said, " Well, I'll let you know about it. Meantime start building up the squadron again with new crews. I'll have some picked ones sent to you."

(Actually it was not the *Tirpitz* that Cochrane was after at this time. " Tirpitz " was the " cover plan " to camouflage the real plan. He was, in fact, scheming to smash the big dam at Modane, in Italy, and the hills round Bangor resembled the hills round Modane Dam. Martin discovered that seven years later.)

Martin was interviewing new pilots and crews for the next week, and it was not easy. 617's fame—or notoriety—had spread and it was known as a suicide squadron. Some quite brave men were posted to it but told Martin openly they did not want to stay. Martin did not argue. They were quite willing to fly with their own squadrons, where perhaps one crew in ten finished a tour ; in 617 it seemed that no crew had a chance. He did not press anyone who was not willing —they would be no good to him—but sent them back to their old squadrons, and after a week had found only four crews willing to join him : O'Shaughnessy, Willsher, Weedon and Bull. He was doubtful about accepting Willsher because Willsher looked younger even than Shannon, only nineteen, a thin, fair boy a year out of school.

Willsher had trouble finding a crew until a red-faced, broken-nosed, tough-looking Londoner called Gerry Witherick insisted on being his rear gunner. Witherick was unkillable. He had flown nearly a hundred missions and was a hard case with a soft heart and a riotous wit.

Group at the dams raid dinner given to the survivors by A. V. Roe and Co. Numbered figures are : (1) R. K. Pierson ; (2) Sir Hew Kilner ; (3) Charles Whitworth ; (4) Les Munro ; (5) test pilot Sam Brown ; (6) "Capable" Caple ; (7) Sgt. Heveron ; (8) Harold Wilson ; (9) "Chiefy" Powell ; (10) Trevor-Roper ; (11) "Johnnie" Johnson ; (12) "Hobbie" Hobday ; (13) H. R. Humphries ; (14) MacLean ; (15) "Mutt" Summers ; (16) Barnes Wallis ; (17) Sir Roy Dobson ; (18) Lance Howard ; (19) Micky Martin ; (20) Jack Leggo ; (21) Nicholson ; (22) David Maltby ; (23) Joe McCarthy ; (24) Guy Gibson ; (25) Len Sumpter ; (26) Toby Foxlee ; (27) Bob Hay ; (28) Tammy Simpson ; (29) Roy Chadwick.

Above : One of the most remarkable photos of the war—the moment at which Cheshire dropped his incendiary markers on the factory at Limoges. The incendiaries are showering over the factory roofs and, top-left centre, is the tailwheel of Cheshire's Lancaster.

Below : The remarkable bombing of the Michelin factory at Clermont-Ferrand, when they were told to hit the two factory workshops and leave the canteen. Centre : the two factory buildings destroyed, and lower right, the large canteen, undamaged.

A letter came for Martin from the Chester Herald regretting that " Après *moi* le deluge " was questionable too. An aged Greek had used it to show selfishness.

" Why couldn't the damn Greek stick to his own language ? " Martin growled to Sam Patch. " What d'we do now ? "

" Write back politely and explain that the badge had already been chosen by the King," Patch said. " Just say how sorry you are that the King's prerogative should be overlooked."

CHAPTER X

SNIPER SQUADRON

THE fate of 617 was decided at high level. " We'll make 'em a special duties squadron," said Sir Arthur Harris. " They needn't do ordinary ops., but whenever the Army or Navy want a dam or a ship or something clouted we'll put 617 on to it. They'll like that—keep the Army and Navy happy too. And we'll put all the old lags in 617. That's just the thing for them. Make 'em the old lags' squadron."

" The old lags " was Harris's affectionate and respectful name for the really hard-bitten aircrews who only wanted to do operations. Every now and then there would be a crew who, after finishing their tour, would stubbornly boggle at taking their six months' rest training new aircrews. They insisted on staying on operations and were dearest of all to Harris, probably because they had the same volcanic temperament as himself.

Harris said 617 could stay in 5 Group with Cochrane, and Cochrane had it in his mind to make them a " sniper " squadron for super-accurate bombing with Wallis's 10-tonner. Ordinary bombing, he knew, would waste most of the 10-tonners, and there would be none to waste. He was well aware (it is no great secret now) that bombing had sometimes been almost primitively inaccurate.

They had started the war bombing by moonlight, but as German night fighters multiplied they had had to use dark nights because of losses, and now they were even having to stick to " dirty " dark nights when heavy cloud gave added cover (and obscured targets).

British people who had endured the Blitz read with under-standable satisfaction of R.A.F. bombers over Cologne or Essen or Hamburg, or of the Hamm sidings being pounded. They did not know (they would have been shaken to know, and the propaganda people did not dare tell them) that many of these raids did little damage. Some did none at all, and many people still do not know that. Harris, people like

Cochrane, " Pathfinder " Bennett and the " back room boys " were trying to find how to hit targets in blind weather and it was about this time that the main force was starting to produce really good results.

Up to this time a little more than one out of three raids were really effective. The Germans built dummy targets outside cities, spread camouflage nets over tell-tale lakes and rivers in the towns, decoyed the bombers in every way they could, and even lit fires in fields so the bombers would think they were hitting their target. Often the crews bombed open fields instead. A pilot once came back from Mannheim and said he was the only aircraft that had found the city. They barked at him for getting lost himself until he produced his aiming point photograph, which showed he was right. The other bombers had dropped their loads on fields or some other town. By 1943 there had been over a hundred attacks on Essen, anything from eighteen to a thousand aircraft dropping a huge weight of bombs against Krupps, but most bombs fell elsewhere and significant damage was quite limited.

That was why the Pathfinder Force had been formed, and now that they were in action bombing was becoming more effective. P.F.F. found and marked the target areas with coloured flares, and the main force bombed these markers. It stopped them bombing open fields, but it was still " carpet bombing," hateful, and yet, it seemed, necessary.

And losses still mounted. Now they were about 4 per cent.; one bomber in twenty-five failed to return. Or average it another way—a squadron of twenty aircraft would lose every one in twenty-five raids. A tour of operations was thirty raids; then, if you were still alive, you had six months' rest and went back for another tour. In lives and labour and for the minor damage done, bombing was not economical enough for Harris.

At Farnborough, in 1941, a man named Richards had invented a piece of intricate mechanism he called the Stabilising Automatic Bomb Sight. It incorporated a gyro ; in perfect conditions it could aim a bomb uncannily, but Harris thought it was too complicated for the hellish conditions of actual bombing. For one thing, a bomber using it had to run perfectly straight and level up to the target for ten miles, a perfect mark for flak, searchlights and fighters. Harris said it would mean death for too many of his boys, who had little enough chance as it was, and Bomber Command could not take much heavier losses.

Another school of thought said the S.A.B.S. *could* be used economically by a small force. Cochrane was one of them. He argued that from high level the S.A.B.S. could hit a well-marked target so accurately that they would not have to send the squadrons back to the same place again and again. In the long run they would lose less. He wanted to train 617 till they could use the S.A.B.S. in battle and deliver Wallis's 10-tonners, when they arrived, in the right spots.

There were many conferences and then Harris agreed.

Patch called Martin to his office. " The *Tirpitz* is off for the time being," he said and Martin sighed gently with relief. " The A.O.C. has something new for you. From now on your squadron role is changed to ultra-accurate high-level bombing and you're going to be practising till your eyes drop out. You've got to get down to an *average* of *under* a hundred yards from twenty thousand feet." Martin's eyes almost dropped out on the spot. " The reasons," Patch went on, " are that there's a new bomb coming up . . . a big one. You'll only be able to carry one and they're so expensive every one will have to be spot on." He said they were getting a new bomb sight at once.

A day later a tall, thin man with lively eyes walked into Martin's office carrying a bundle wrapped in oilskin and announced that he was Squadron Leader Richardson come to help 617 convert to the S.A.B.S.

" This is it," he said, carefully unwrapping the bundle. " It's the loveliest thing in the world." The S.A.B.S. looked like an ordinary bomb sight except that a bulky gyro was encased in it. Richardson handled it lovingly, and in the next few days the squadron found out why. He was not a bomb-aiming enthusiast, he was a fanatic who started talking bomb-aiming at breakfast and was still on the subject at bedtime. If he talked in his sleep no one doubted what the subject would be. He lectured the crews, flew with them, experimented with them and after a time no one had any chance of not knowing everything about the S.A.B.S. Bob Hay, haunted now by his own profession, christened him " Talking Bomb." Much of the credit for what happened belongs to " Talking Bomb," who had been a pilot in World War I and managed in due course to fly on fifteen raids with 617 to watch his beloved bomb sight in action.

617 did no ops. for weeks, but night and day the aircraft were 20,000 feet over the bombing range at Wainfleet aiming practice bombs at the white dots on the sands with the S.A.B.S. It needed far more than a hawk-eyed bomb aimer ; it called for teamwork. The gunners took drifts to help the navigator work out precise wind direction and speed, and navigator and bomb aimer calculated obscure instrument corrections. An error of a few feet at 20,000 feet would throw a bomb hopelessly off. Altimeters work off barometric pressure, but that is always changing, so they used a compli- cated system of getting ground-level pressures over target and correcting altimeters by pressure lapse rates (with temperature complications). A small speed error will also throw a bomb off, and air speed indicators read falsely according to height and the attitude of the aircraft. They had to compute and correct this, and when it was all set on the S.A.B.S. the pilot had to hold his exact course and height for miles while the engineer juggled the throttles to keep the speed precise. That, over-simplified, expresses about a tenth of the complications. When the bomb aimer had the cross-wires on the target he clicked a switch and the S.A.B.S. kept itself tracking on the aiming point by its gyros, transmitting corrections to the pilot by flicking an indicator in the cockpit. The bomb aimer did not have to press the bomb button ; when it was ready the S.A.B.S. did that, and even told the pilot by switching off a red light in the cockpit.

First results were only fair, average errors being about 180 yards, but the crews soon started to get the hang of it. " Talking Bomb " flew with them all, the only way of check- ing. A good bomb aimer might get poor results because of pilot inaccuracy, so " Talking Bomb " switched pilots and bomb aimers and coached the weak ones. There was plenty of scope for error.   At 20,000 feet the bombs left the aircraft two miles short of the target and dropped for forty-five seconds before they hit, throwing up the little puffs that were plotted from the sandbagged quadrant stations.   Results were phoned to Coningsby and the crews got them as soon as they landed so they could see what had gone wrong.

" Talking Bomb " himself was very accurate with the S.A.B.S., and before long a couple of crews could emulate him.   Martin's was one.   Within three weeks Hay set an example with an average of 64 yards.   Some of the others, however, were still well over a hundred yards and Cochrane drove over to look into it, got " Talking Bomb " to give him an hour's instruction on the S.A.B.S. and took off as bomb aimer in " P Popsie " to try it.   On the ground one or two people indulged in a little anticipatory lip-smacking.

Martin flew sedately and when Cochrane had called his last " Bombs gone ! " brought him straight back.   " Talking Bomb " met them with the results and an expression of great respect.   Cochrane had achieved the extraordinary average of 38 yards.   For a moment the A.O.C.'s face loosened into a faint grin but he froze it off and said crisply, " Well, if I can do it you people ought to be able to."

Someone muttered in the background, " If we all could we'd all be A.O.Cs.," and that time Cochrane had to laugh.

After he went Hay said darkly to the other bomb aimers, " Well, you're going to have to pull your fingers out now." He turned to Martin : " Hell, Mick, why didn't you kick the rudder as he was going to bomb ? "

A letter came to Martin from the Chester Herald, gracefully yielding in the matter of the squadron badge.   He had not realised it had been chosen by the King and by no means would he interfere with His Majesty's prerogative.   The badge was therefore approved, with the motto " Après moi le deluge."   He enclosed an imposing piece of prose with the official description :

" *On a roundel, a wall in fesse, fracted by three flashes of lightning in pile and issuant from the breach, water proper.*"

There was a session in the mess that night to celebrate it. Concave Goodale had a bad smoker's cough and had been sitting in a chair coughing to clear his throat for a couple of hours when someone said, " Poor old Concave. He's nearly dead. He's got a foot in the grave." Ivan Whittaker said, " Oh, he *is* dead. Let's bury him." He and Martin slipped away and got a sheet from someone's bed, but Concave saw them come in with it and retreated into the lavatory. There was another door on the other side of it, and Whittaker slipped round and caught Concave coming out, throwing the sheet over his head. They carried him back kicking, wrapped him like a cocoon in the sheet and laid him on a trestle table in the kitchen. Someone brought in the padre, a cheerful grey-haired man with a broad Irish brogue who gazed, startled, on the shrouded victim and said, " What's all this about? "

" Goodale's coughed himself to death," Whittaker said lugubriously. " We're going to bury him." Concave raised his head with a sickly grin. Eight volunteer pall-bearers lifted the table to their shoulders and set off in a wavering slow march, followed by an entourage banging on tin plates, singing " Abide with him " and moaning the " Volga Boatman." In the ante-room they set the table on its trestles again and Concave lay in state in front of the fireplace, the others standing around in a solemn circle. The padre grinned but declined to read the burial service, so someone grabbed a paper-backed novel and chanted an improvised service.

As he intoned " Dust to dust and ashes to ashes " the elderly local defence officer sprinkled ash from the fireplace on Concave and bawled, " Slack away." He nudged one of the trestles, the table-end lurched and Concave rolled off and landed in a half-sitting position on his bottom vertebræ. He let out a groan, his head dropped back with a bump and his eyes rolled up so the whites were visible. He lay still and everyone saluted him. They unwrapped him and said, " O.K., Concave, you're in hell now," but Goodale did not move and the laughter became uncertain and died. Someone said, " He's really out." They carried him away and laid him on his bed ; the doctor arrived and found a lump on Concave's spine as big as an egg.

The elderly defence officer ran contritely in with one of his dearest possessions, a bottle of very old brandy, pulled the cork, put the bottle to Concave's lips and up-ended it. Concave spluttered and coughed, brandy running down his chin ; his eyes opened, he licked his lips and a soft smile dawned. He closed his eyes again, opened his mouth and the defence officer poured in more brandy.

" He'll be all right," said the doctor. They stayed a while encouraging him to absorb more medicine and then softly retreated, all happy (particularly Concave) except the defence officer, who could not find his bottle of brandy.

There are some who solemnly lament that wartime flying men were known on occasion to drink more than was seemly. That not-always-tactful man Arthur Harris called the worst examples of disapproval " unctuous rectitude." Perhaps the rigidly virtuous might acquire a more flexible understanding if they followed the young pilot to the airfield and watched his face in its hood when the chocks were pulled away. Better still, follow him into the air, strapped to a seat and deafened by noise, held precariously aloft by wings relying on in-constant engines and petrol tanks, highly vulnerable to the assaults of flak and fighters, fog and ice-cloud. Follow him up there not once but sixty times till violent death is a threefold statistical certainty.

They played hard because they had little time to play, and more often than not it was high rather than potent spirits which affected them.

Higher circles were satisfied now that in Peenemunde lay the heart of Germany's secret weapon, rockets or whatever they were, and Harris sent 600 heavy bombers to dissect the spot. Pathfinders lobbed their markers in the middle, and for the first time the main force used the " master bomber " technique that Gibson had started over the Moehne Dam ; a " master of ceremonies " circled low directing the bombers by radiophone on to the choicest markers, and Peenemunde rocket centre was almost wiped off the map, putting the advent of rockets over England back by six months. Having failed to protect it, Hans Jeschonnek, Hitler's night-fighter chief, suicided. The Germans learnt anew the virtues of dispersal.

617's bombing kept slowly improving. Three more crews arrived : Bill Suggitt, a Canadian squadron leader, to take over A Flight, Clayton and Ted Youseman, an Englishman, who never stopped talking flying. There were the usual incidents—two aircraft hit trees low flying and were written off (though no one was killed), Martin had an engine catch fire in the air but doused it with the extinguishers. Shannon's aileron cables snapped over the North Sea, but he made an emergency landing, using trimmers to keep his wing-tips level and making a wide, flat turn on rudder alone. He claimed it was better than his usual landing, which, Sumpter said rudely, was nothing to boast about.

Spurred on by Cochrane, Sam Patch and Martin tried to find a way of minimising the danger of the ten-mile run-up to the target using the S.A.B.S. " Talking Bomb " was a fertile source of ideas.

" This is what you ought to do," he said. " You all fly round the target in a great big circle like Red Indians, see ? and then someone gives the word and you all turn inwards and come in like the spokes of a wheel. The Hun won't know who to shoot at."

" That's O.K., Talking Bomb," Martin said, " but what happens when they all get into the middle ? "

" Oh, put 'em at different heights."

" What about the bombs falling on the lower aircraft ? "

" There must be a way over that," " Talking Bomb " muttered.

It was a somewhat similar idea that they adopted, and it depended on immaculate timing and navigation. The aircraft, at different heights, would circle a spot in sight of the target but outside the defences, and when the markers were down the leader would assess their accuracy, give the order to bomb and they would all come in, converging slightly. If

there were twenty guns below, for instance, and only one
aircraft coming in, the twenty guns would all be firing at it,
but with twenty planes coming in at the same time, too
widely scattered for a box barrage, there would be only one gun
against each aircraft—twenty times less chance of being hit.

New troubles kept cropping up with the S.A.B.S. For
instance, the thermometers (necessary in getting outside
temperatures for computing precise height from the altimeters) were showing errors up to 5 degrees, enough to
throw a bomb over a hundred feet the wrong way. Farnborough put in new type thermometers, but two more
corrections were still necessary. Airflow against the bulb
caused friction and heat, and this had to be corrected by a
table based on the indicated air speed at the time. Then
cockpit heating affected part of the thermometer which was
inside the aircraft and that, too, had to be calculated and
allowed for, but by early November the squadron had an
average bombing error of only 90 yards.

Good enough, Cochrane thought, and at dusk on November
12, Martin led the squadron off to try out the S.A.B.S. in
battle. The target was the Antheor Viaduct again, an easy
one so that they could give the S.A.B.S. fair trial. In the
bomb bays hung 12,000-lb. light-case " blast " bombs.

They found the viaduct in half-moonlight, but this time it
was different . . . four searchlights and half a dozen guns
round it. Running up, the viaduct was hard to pick up in
the glare of the searchlights ; the next little bay looked
exactly the same and several crews bombed the wrong bay.
Some of them got the right bay in their graticules but could
not distinguish the viaduct. Rice, O'Shaughnessy and one
other got near misses, 50 yards away, but the blast was not
enough to damage the viaduct.

They flew disgustedly on to Blida again and it was then that
Martin recalled what McCarthy had said about flares after
San Polo. Everyone agreed that if they had had flares to
mark the viaduct they could have hit it. Two days later
they flew back to England, but Youseman never arrived. No
one ever found out what happened to him and his crew but
a German fighter probably got them over the sea.

Martin reported to Cochrane the need for target marking, and Cochrane sent him and Patch to Pathfinder Headquarters to talk it over with the experts. Pathfinders promised to mark their next target, and Martin put the crews back on training to perfect their S.A.B.S. technique.

Martin's time as temporary commander was up. Cochrane would not replace him with any ordinary squadron commander (none of whom, in any case, was eager to take on the suicide squadron), but he had found the man he wanted. Leonard Cheshire, at twenty-five, was the youngest group captain in the R.A.F., and was not only willing to return to operations but actually asked Cochrane to drop him back to wing commander so he could take over the squadron. He did not look the part at all. Gibson had looked the part ; Gibson and glamour were indivisible, but Cheshire looked more like a theological student thinly disguised as a senior officer ; yet he had done two tours and won a D.S.O. and bar and D.F.C. He was tall, thin and dark, a strange blend of brilliance (sometimes erratic), self-consciousness, confidence and soft-spoken charm. Highly sensitive and introspective, he yet lacked, quite illogically, the foreboding imagination that makes some sensitive men sweat with fear before a raid. Once he had walked from Oxford to Paris without a penny in his pockets to win half a pint of beer. He liked a suite at the Ritz on leave and to bask in a Mayfair cocktail bar. At twenty he had an Honours degree in Law at Oxford (where his father was Vinerian Professor of Law—England's highest such appointment), and at twenty-four, in a few weeks' joyous leave in New York, he had met and married Constance Binney, who had been America's top film star, successor to Mary Pickford, in 1922. She was a bride of forty-one.

He had a gentle consideration for other people and a Puckish sense of humour, but in the air he was cool, efficient and calculating. In a way he had a mind like Barnes Wallis, liable to get ideas that horrified people but turned out to be right. He had been flying a certain type of heavy bomber at a time when losses of that type were inexplicably heavy. They had acquired too much extra equipment, so that fully loaded, at operational height, they were slow, flew soggily and were inclined to yaw and drop into a fatal spiral with the rudders locked over. Then they added kidney cowls to blanket the exhaust flames from night fighters, and that, for Cheshire, was the last straw. He considered it made the aircraft more dangerous than the enemy and asked permission to take the cowls off his squadron's aircraft.

Everyone flatly disagreed except his A.O.C., Air Vice-Marshal Carr, who let Cheshire do so, with the result that his losses fell. It was the first step to taking off a lot more : front turret, mid-upper turret and armour-plate ; freed of the excessive drag and weight the plane flew more comfortably, the engines were not overworked and losses fell further.

For two days after Cheshire joined 617 little Doris Leeman, his W.A.A.F. driver, sat in the shooting brake outside his office with nothing to do. She watched Cheshire walk away several times, and at last she could stand it no longer and went in to Chiefy Powell. " Doesn't he *know* I'm waiting for him ? " she asked, with the anger of a woman kept waiting inexcusably. " You'd better tell him," Powell said, so she knocked at his office door and told him, and was staggered when he confessed he didn't know he had a car at his disposal. It was fairly typical of the man ; never taking for granted what lesser men demanded.

The destruction at Peenemunde had put Germany's rocket programme back six months, and they stopped work on the monster rocket blockhouses to go ahead with the more dispersed flying-bomb sites. Recce aircraft were bringing back to England photographs showing mysterious new activity in the same areas, the erection of many low, curved buildings in clearings in woods, and next to them short sets of rails that seemed to start and end in nothingness. Intelligence men christened them " ski sites " because the long buildings were the same shape as skis, and bit by bit they connected them more definitely with secret-weapon reports.

It was clear that these and other satellite launching sites could be put up very quickly and were more or less mobile. They were springing up all over the place and ordinary blast bombs could smash them, but after Peenemunde, Hitler seemed to be relying for protection on dispersal—numbers, camouflage and mobility—instead of three or four centralised targets.

In Whitehall, Churchill, the Air Council, Harris, Sir Stafford Cripps (now Minister for Aircraft Production) and Sir Wilfred Freeman discussed the situation uncomfortably, and one day Freeman sent for Wallis.

" We're stopping work on the ten-ton bomb," he said. " The big targets we had for them aren't so important now, and Sir Stafford doesn't think the ten-tonner justifies all that work."

Wallis could not dispute the logic of it. The biggest bombers would have a very short range with a ten-tonner— little more than across the Channel, and in that area there seemed no other targets important enough. There were plenty in Germany, of course, but the Lancasters could not carry the 10-tonner as far as that.

Wallis pleaded with Freeman to let him go ahead with the 12,000-lb. scaled-down version of the 10-tonner, to penetrate deeply in the same way and cause an earthquake shock. The Lancasters could drop them deep inside Germany on the kind of targets he had originally had in mind. Freeman thought for a long time, and in the end he said yes—a bold decision to make on his own. He knew that neither the Air Council nor the Ministry of Supply liked the idea of either the 10-tonner or the scaled-down version, because they were designed to be dropped at 40,000 feet for proper penetration. The Lancaster could not drop them from higher than 20,000, and the Council and Ministry considered they would not thus penetrate deeply enough for the proper earthquake effect.

Freeman made the decision so much on his own initiative that no Requirement Order was issued for the bombs, which meant that the Air Force did not have to accept them— or pay for them. He gave the scaled-down bomb the code name of " Tallboy," and Wallis hoped to have one ready for trial by March.

Cochrane had his eye on the mobile launching sites as targets for 617 but left them in peace while Cheshire kept his crews perfecting the S.A.B.S. technique, and for some

weeks the squadron did no operations until, on December 10,
Cheshire got a call from Tempsford for the loan of four crews.
Tempsford was the hush-hush airfield where planes took
off to land agents in occupied countries and drop arms
to Resistance fighters. Cheshire chose McCarthy, Clayton,
Bull and Weedon, and they flew their aircraft to Tempsford.

McCarthy landed back at Coningsby two days later, walked
into Humphries' office and dumped two kitbags on the floor.
" Bull and Weedon's kit," he said. " They've had it."

" Oh God ! When ? "

" Last night. We did a special low-level thing, dropping
arms and ammunition. They must have hit trouble." He
added disgustedly, " I didn't even find the damn target area."

He went back to Tempsford that afternoon, and he and
Clayton tried again that night—successfully.

Cheshire, meantime, had had one of his more spectacular
ideas. His brother had recently been shot down and captured and Cheshire had been thinking a lot about prisoners
of war. He sent for Martin, and Martin found him in the
planning room huddled over maps spread out on the table.
Cheshire greeted him with bright eyes and a pleased grin.
" Mick," he said, " we're going to drop Christmas parcels to
the prisoners of war on Christmas Day."

" Oh," Martin said. " Sounds interesting, sir. Whereabouts ? "

" Stalag Luft III. Here." Cheshire stabbed his pencil at
a spot on the map, and Martin leaned over and saw the point
was resting on a small town called Sagan, between Berlin and
Breslau, up near the Polish border. They had never flown
so far as that over Germany and Martin said cautiously, " It's
a long way."

" We've got the range all right."

" How're we going to find a little thing like that at night ? "

" Won't have to, old boy. Going by day. Christmas
morning."

" By day ! "

" Yes."

" By DAY ! "

" Don't worry. We can do it. Nip in over the Baltic low
level and surprise 'em. We'll get away with it."

" How many aircraft ? "

" Three ought to be enough."

" Who ? " Martin felt that his ears were laid back and the
whites of his eyes showing.

" Me, you and either Shannon or Munro."

" Uh ! " Martin looked at the map silently. " What sort
of food were you thinking of taking, sir ? "

" Oh, things like chickens and raisins and chocolate. It
ought to give them a hell of a lift."

Martin said, trying to keep the edge out of his voice,
" D'you think we could drop some parcels addressed to our-
selves ? We'll still be there on Boxing Day, you know, either
on the ground or under it."

" Oh, I don't think it'll be that bad, Mick. We'll paint the
aircraft white, put red crosses over them and take the guns
out."

" Oh ! No guns ! "

" We can do the trip in by night," Cheshire said, " arrive
about dawn so we'll have no trouble pin-pointing it, drop the
stuff about a hundred feet to make sure it gets into the compounds and nip out across the Baltic. That's the shortest
way out, and I'll get Pickard to meet us with his Mossies and
take us home."

Martin said : " If there's any cloud we could try and make
our retreat in them, if there's any retreat."

" O.K.," Cheshire said cheerfully. " That sounds good
enough."

He called the others to the briefing room and told them :
they listened in startled silence, but had acquired such faith
in him that he soon had them planning a fund to buy chickens
and hams and volunteering to give up their sweet and cigarette
rations. They went round surrounding farms, bargaining for
chickens, cheeses and bacon ; and Cheshire, Martin and
Shannon practised low-level formation. Cheshire had warned
everyone to keep quiet about it because if Cochrane got to
hear there would be no chickens for the prisoners, but probably bread and water for Cheshire.

CHAPTER XI

DIRECT HIT

HARRIS had been sending bombers by day to smash at the mysterious " ski sites " in the Pas de Calais, but too many German fighters swarmed up to protect them. It left him with a pretty problem . . . the targets were so small and well hidden that the squadrons would not be able to pinpoint and bomb them accurately by night ; what was good enough for a big industrial area was not precise enough now. Cochrane asked permission for 617 to try their precision bombing with P.F.F. (Pathfinder Force) to mark the pinpoint with incendiaries, and Harris agreed.

Night after night 617 was briefed, but the target was smothered under low stratus cloud until, on December 16, Cheshire led nine Lancasters off. A Pathfinder " oboe " Mosquito flew with them to mark the target. " Oboe " was a new way of radar pin-pointing ; two beams went out from England and crossed exactly over the target to let the pilot know when he was there. This night the " oboe " plane dropped a casket of incendiaries, and they cascaded into the wood that hid the " ski site." At 10,000 feet 617 saw them winking among the trees like tiny glow-worms, swung in together according to the drill, nicely scattered so that the flak was ineffective, and all the 12,000-pounder " blast " bombs went down within a couple of minutes. Around the incendiaries the wood erupted in flame.

Back at Coningsby they developed the aiming-point photos (taken by photo-flash) and a groan went up. The markers had been 350 yards from the target ; the bombs were all round the markers with an average error of only 94 yards, but that meant that the bombing was so good that the ski site was untouched. It was the most accurate high-level night bombing of the war, but that made it all the more bitter.

It confirmed a suspicion both Cheshire and Cochrane had had . . . Pathfinders were fine for area marking but not precise enough for pin-point targets. Martin suggested they

Micky Martin's durable Lancaster, P for Popsie. Inset left, Martin, and right, Arthur Kell, who took over P for Popsie from him.

Above : The extraordinary direct hit on the Saumur tunnel obtained on the first "earthquake bomb" raid, showing how the bomb blew out the mountain over the tunnel. The tiny figures give an idea of the size of the crater.

Below : Shot from inside the Saumur tunnel after the Germans had cleared up the mess in time for the invading armies to take over.

drop parachute flares over the target, lighting up the area so that a couple of aircraft could dive to low level and drop incendiary markers " spot on " the target. Cheshire agreed, but Cochrane, with the memory of the Dortmund Ems painfully fresh in his mind, would not hear of more low-level work.

Cheshire and Martin went off quietly and tried low-level marking on the ranges in the hope that they could get Cochrane to change his mind. They dropped practice bombs from about 200 feet using the low-level bomb sight and were only mildly satisfied with the results. They found they could land a bomb accurately but the trajectory was so flat that the bomb tended to bounce and skid 200 yards beyond the target. And at night-time they found in the Lancasters that they were shooting past the range target before they saw it.

On December 20 they tried P.F.F. " oboe " marking again on an armament factory near Liège but found the town hopelessly cloaked under low cloud. On the way back (with their bombs) Martin saw a Lancaster going down in flames with one of the gunners still firing at the fighter. Back at Coningsby they waited up, more out of conscience than hope, but Geoff Rice, one of the five survivors of the original squadron, did not return.

They tried again with the " oboe " Mosquito on a ski site, but again cloud defeated them.

Cheshire called on an intelligence officer in London for a final check on his P.o.W. " chicken run." The intelligence man listened to the plan with horror and said, " My God, you can't do that ! If you drop things in the compounds the Germans'll think you're dropping them arms, and as the prisoners rush out to pick them up they'll be mown down."

Cheshire said, " I didn't think of that," went back and told Martin and Shannon sadly that they would have to call it off, but it didn't sadden the other two at all.

The weather closed in until the night of December 30, when they went with an " oboe " plane to another ski site. Three bombs were direct hits on the " oboe " markers, but the markers were again a couple of hundred yards off the target and the ski site escaped.

Cheshire pleaded with Cochrane for permission to mark at

low level.   His idea was that P.F.F. should drop flares by
" oboe " to illuminate the area, and he and Martin should fly
low enough to put a marker right on the spot.

Cochrane replied with a flat no, and added, " Try and find
another way.   Try marking with the S.A.B.S. from about five
thousand feet.   If you can light the area enough with flares to
get a sight, you ought to be able to do it accurately."

Cheshire suggested in that case that 617 might as well carry
their own flares and dispense with the Pathfinders.   Cochrane
agreed and on January 4 they flew back to the Pas de Calais
without the " oboe " plane.   From 12,000 feet the squadron
dropped floating flares, but cloud foiled Cheshire and Martin
at 5,000 feet, so they both dived to 400 feet (pre-arranged and
strictly off the record) and skimmed over the dim clearing
from different directions.   The markers landed in the clearing
but both sets bounced and skidded 100 yards into the woods,
so that the clearing was straddled by them.

The squadron managed to put most of their bombs between
the markers, badly damaging the ski site ; Cheshire thought
it was fairly successful but was not exactly delighted . . .
skidding markers were too uncertain to rely on.   In the next
few days he, Martin and " Talking Bomb " kept experimenting to find a permissible way of marking.

Between 3,000 and 6,000 feet on a clear aiming point by
day they found they could put down a marker within 40 yards
of a target—near enough for Cochrane—but could not do it
on a hazy target, and there was little chance of getting a
clear enough aiming point at night.   Moonlight and flares
would help, but any important target was going to be
camouflaged.

That was the week the squadron moved from Coningsby
to Woodhall Spa, about ten miles away.   Woodhall was a
one-squadron station and that was the reason for the move.
As a " special duties " squadron on new and rather hush-hush
projects, Cochrane wanted them to go on working in somewhat exclusive isolation.

Snowstorms had mantled the field and the runways were
under a 6-inch carpet.   Everyone on the squadron, officers
and aircrew too, turned out to shovel the snow off the runways

so the planes could get off the ground. They worked from dawn till midnight for two days, long lines of men shovelling at the white acres while W.A.A.Fs. brought them coffee and sandwiches and rewarded them with a rum ration when they finished work at night.

About this time a Military Brain conceived that, if a large dam just north of Rome could be breached, the flood would tangle German communications in Italy and help the imminent break-out from the Anzio beach-head. 617 was the logical squadron for the job, and Cochrane—a little reluctantly—put them on to intensive dams-type training . . . low flying. It would have to be Wallis's dams bomb again, dropped from 60 feet, but the Italian dam lay in a lake surrounded by high hills, a worse proposition even than the Eder. It meant sliding over a hill and losing 1,800 feet in 3,000 yards to be at 60 feet over the water in time to bomb, a frighteningly steep dive in a heavy aircraft at night. It was going to need a lot of skill. They measured 3,000 yards out over the air-field, marked the extremities, and Martin stood off from one mark with a theodolite to measure height while each pilot came over the far mark at 1,900 feet and tried to cross the next mark at 60 feet. Pilots who could not do it after a couple of trial runs got the benefit of Martin's salty vocabulary and were spurred on to achieve success next time.

One other complication was that they would have to take off for it from North Africa because the all-up weight would be too great from England ; and if the Germans got an inkling that the Dam Busters' Squadron was flying to Africa for a raid they would very likely put two and two together, put balloons and guns by the dam and save their dam as well as kill most of the crews.

Cochrane and Cheshire hit on the solution. Cochrane sent in lorry loads of enough arctic equipment and clothing to outfit the whole squadron, and Cheshire stored it under guard in a locked hangar, then dropped a hint that they were going to North Africa. From that moment the whole squadron was convinced they were going to Russia. The more they were told it was to be Africa the surer they were that it was Russia.

K 2

The pilots practised low flying constantly over Lincolnshire and Norfolk. On January 20, O'Shaughnessy was practising diving over the sea by the Wash and levelling out at 60 feet, but he was concentrating so hard on his altimeter that he did not notice the land looming up. The Lancaster smacked her belly on a hill rising off the beach, bounced, charged into another rise in the ground and rolled into a flaming ball, cremating the crew except for Arthur Ward, the wireless operator, who was thrown clear with a broken leg. That was the day the Authorities decided that if the dam were breached it might kill many civilians and perhaps disrupt the Allied advance more than the Germans, and so they called it off. Such is war.

In between low flying Cheshire and Martin had kept experimenting to find a way of marking, and one day, flying back from the range, Martin saw a patch of seaweed in the water that took his fancy. Always ready to spice his flying with a little variety he peeled off in one of his usual spectacular turns, dived steeply and dropped a bomb. It was a direct hit.

When he landed he jumped out of " P Popsie " quivering with excitement. " That's it, sir," he said jauntily to Cheshire. " We've got it. I didn't use the bomb sight when I dropped that thing over the seaweed and it was a piece of cake. If we can dive-bomb markers point-blank over a target we can put 'em right on the button without the bomb sight and they won't skid off. What's more, we could see the target much better from above than coming up to it down low."

Cheshire went out and tried it that afternoon and it worked like a charm, almost without practice.

Next night they went back to the Pas de Calais. Munro dropped flares and Martin, turning a blandly blind eye to orders, tried his new method, peeling off, sticking his nose steeply down and aiming his whole aircraft at the ski site. He found that dive-bombing low at night in a four-engined plane was a slightly hair-raising business but dropped his markers in the dive and pulled out at about 400 feet. They were a new type of marker, red and green flares known as " spot fires," and as he pulled up and levelled off Martin saw the two lights like red and green eyes winking in the middle of the clearing. It was a clear night ; from 12,000 feet they were plainly visible, and the rest of the squadron plastered the rocket site out of existence.

A couple of nights later they went to another flying-bomb site ; Martin dived low again, laid his spot fires accurately and a few minutes later the target was littered about a few smoking craters.

Cheshire went to Cochrane and told him of the new method (that is, told him of the seaweed and the trials over the range, not of Martin's actual dives over the targets). Knowing that Cochrane approved of low-level marking on every count except the risk, Cheshire assured him that the diving attack, straight down, up and away, with only a few fleeting seconds near the ground, was reasonably safe. He added earnestly : " Sir, if we're going to mark accurately we *must* be low enough to see exactly what we're doing, and I'm sure that Martin is right when he says that right low down we're actually safer. I can't find any way of marking accurately from medium level. Will you let us try this new way on some lightly defended target ? "

Cochrane considered for a moment, looked up and said, " All right, we'll give it a trial."

The target he chose was the Gnome-Rhone aero-engine factory at Limoges, 200 miles south-west of Paris. The Germans had taken it over but there was hardly any flak for miles.

There was an immediate complication. War Cabinet vetoed the target because the Germans had 300 French girls working in the factory on night shift and there were French homes nearby. Churchill would not have French people killed if he could possibly avoid it, particularly as this was not a vital target.

Cheshire replied that as far as the homes were concerned he would guarantee they would put all bombs on the target itself. To protect the girls in the factory he offered to make several dummy runs over the factory to give everyone plenty of time to get clear. Cochrane backed him up and, after a silence from Whitehall, permission came through for the raid.

on the understanding that if one Frenchman was killed there would be no more. Cochrane told Cheshire : " Our future stands or falls on this one. If anyone slips you won't get another chance. Not in France or Belgium anyway, and I won't let you make guinea-pigs of yourselves over Germany." Cheshire, at briefing, told the crews the same thing, Cochrane and he planned it with fanatical care.

Twelve aircraft took off into bright moonlight and reached Limoges just before midnight. The town was evidently not expecting bombs because the blackout was bad. Lights showed all over the place and in the factory itself all the workshop lights were on and it was obvious that the Germans had them working hard. Pat Kelly, Cheshire's gay, chunky little navigator, looked down on the lighted streets, making wistful comments about the bistros and French girls he imagined he could see.

Cheshire dived low and hurtled over the factory at a hundred feet, and as he climbed and turned he saw all the lights vanish. He dived back over it again, and Astbury, his bomb aimer, could see people running below and throwing themselves flat. A third time he dived in warning, and on his fourth run held her down to 50 feet till he was practically scraping the workshop roofs. Astbury called " Bombs gone ! " and a cluster of brilliantly glowing incendiaries cascaded into the exact centre of the workshops. In the Lancaster the cameraman filmed it.

Martin dived in the same way and two red spot fires joined the incendiaries. Cheshire called, " Markers dead centre. Bomb as ordered."

At " Zero plus 1 " (one minute past midnight) Shannon dropped the first 12,000-pounder from 10,000 feet. It exploded in the middle of the incendiaries and blew them to smithereens but started a big fire that was just as good. In the next eight minutes nine more bombs fell right on the factory, and one fell just outside in the river. The last man, Nicky Ross, had a " hang-up " ; his bomb did not release, so he went away and came in on another run. At " Zero plus 18 " his 12,000-pounder lobbed in the crater that Shannon's bomb had made.

Cheshire cruised overhead for a while, but there was nothing to see but flames and smoke and soon he turned for home. Apart from two machine guns there was no opposition and none of the Lancasters was holed, not even Cheshire's.

In the morning a recce aircraft brought back pictures which showed that of the factory's forty-eight bays half were scars on the ground and the rest were only shells. A target had never been more completely expunged, and Cheshire knew that, on undefended targets at least, he had proved his point. Cochrane was delighted.

(A message reached England from Limoges not long after. The girls of the Gnome-Rhone factory wished to thank the R.A.F. for their considerate warning and would be pleased to welcome the people concerned after the war.)

Bob Hay also deserved credit for the bombing at Limoges. He and "Talking Bomb" had the bomb aimers so well trained in the S.A.B.S. that from 15,000 feet *at night* they could guarantee two direct hits on any target, 15 per cent. of bombs within 25 yards of the centre and 75 per cent. within 80 yards, a remarkable feat when it is considered that the crack Pathfinders were never called upon to mark with more than 150 yards accuracy.

CHAPTER XII
GALLANT FAILURE

In Italy the Allies were preparing to break out from Anzio and the Germans were preparing to stop them. Trains carrying 15,000 tons of supplies a day were passing over the Antheor Viaduct, and for the third time 617 was ordered to smash it.

Cochrane thought a 12,000-lb. " blockbuster " within 10 yards of the viaduct might knock a span down but this time he warned Cheshire that he must not try " deck-level " marking unless it were absolutely necessary. There were twelve heavy guns and several lighter guns around the viaduct, plus searchlights.

With heavy bombs the range was dangerously far from Woodhall Spa, so they refuelled at Ford in the south, Cheshire flying McCarthy's " Q Queenie " as his own aeroplane was being overhauled and McCarthy was on leave.

They found the bay at midnight but it was so dark they could not see the viaduct from above 3,000 feet, and as soon as Cheshire and Martin slipped down to that height the flak opened up terrifyingly, nearly twenty guns predicting and concentrating on the two of them. Cheshire made a run to drop his markers, but the searchlights caught him long before he was in position and shells were bursting all round him, so that he had to turn away. Martin tried a run but the same thing happened. Cheshire came in again and Martin flew parallel, higher and about a mile out, to draw the flak. It took some of the flak off Cheshire, but not enough ; his aircraft shuddered in the blast of near misses and jagged lumps of flak ripped holes in his wings and fuselage. He slid out to sea and swung in again, but as he straightened up for the run Martin's voice sounded in his earphones : " Hold off a minute, Leader. I think I'm in position for a low run. I can see everything."

He had dived over the hills inland, was hugging the ridges so that the flak could not see him against the dark mass, and turning down the long ravine that cut down to the viaduct across the bay. When they had looked at the maps at briefing it did not seem possible that an aircraft could get down that way but Martin, who could land a Lancaster out of a steep turn, had his nose dipping into the ravine and could see the viaduct dead ahead, limned against the phosphorescence of the surf on the beach.

Cheshire called back, " O.K. Mick, go ahead."

" Try and draw the flak as long as you can," Martin said. He was deep into the ravine ; the viaduct was about a mile in front and some 1,500 feet lower ; he throttled his engines back to keep the sound from the guns and at 230 m.p.h. opened his bomb doors and knew he was making the best bombing run he ever had. The guns down by the viaduct were all firing, but their target was Cheshire weaving in towards them from the other side at 4,000 feet.

In the nose of " P Popsie " Bob Hay said over the intercom., " Target markers selected and fused."

" Right," said Martin. " I'm going to level out in the last second."

" O.K." The bomb sight was no use in a dive. Hay relied on Martin for the signal.

The ravine ridges were towering on each side and the viaduct was rushing at them, growing hugely. One gun on the eastern end suddenly swung and out of its muzzle-flashes a chain of shells was swirling at them. Hay called, " Now ? " and Martin yelled, " No ! No ! " He eased the nose up, a second dragged into eternity, he shouted, " Now ! " And as he shouted a shell smashed through the nose and exploded in the ammunition trays under the front turret. The aircraft rocked in the crashing din and jagged steel and exploding bullets shot back into the fuselage, hitting flesh and ploughing through hydraulic and pneumatic pipes, control rods and fuse boxes.

Hay must have pressed the button as the bomb-release contacts parted, and then they shot a bare couple of feet over the viaduct and dipped towards the water as half a dozen more guns swivelled and spat at them. Foxlee was still alive ; for the first time in months he was in the mid-upper turret instead of the nose, and now he was cursing and shooting back, and so was Simpson in the rear. Martin pulled the nose off the water and Whittaker rammed the throttles forward but there was almost no response from the engines.

" P Popsie " was bathed in glare but Simpson and Foxlee put three of the searchlights out with long bursts. They were practically in the water now, and in the glow of the last light Simpson saw the spray hissing up from the prop-wash and thought for a moment it was smoke from a burning engine. Then they were out of range and Martin lifted " P Popsie " a few feet off the water, praying with thankfulness as he found she still had flying speed.

Whittaker leaned over and yelled in his ear, " Port inner and starb'd outer throttles gone and pitch controls for the other two gone." That meant two engines would stay throttled back as they had been for the run down the ravine, and the other two, in fully fine pitch, were straining themselves at maximum revs. on extreme power to keep the aircraft flying.

Martin became conscious of Cheshire's voice : " Are you all right, 'P Popsie '? Are you all right? Can you hear me? " Nearly a mile above he had seen the Lancaster rocket over the viaduct, caught by the searchlights and with all the guns pounding her.

Martin called back : " Still airborne, Leader. Hit badly I think. Two engines gone and crew hurt." He had felt the sting in his own leg as the shell went off in the nose and knew he had been hit. Whittaker was doubled up now, holding his legs.

Cheshire's voice came back : " Can you make it back home, Mick? "

" Not a hope, sir. We'll try and make for the nearest friendly land."

" All right, boy. Good luck ! "

Martin was calling the roll round his crew. The tough little Foxlee was all right. Bob Hay did not answer. Whittaker gave him a twisted grin, swearing and hunched, holding his legs. The rest were all right. He called Hay twice more but there was only silence, so he said, " Toby, see if Bob's all

right. His intercom. must be busted." Foxlee swung out of
his turret and wormed down towards the nose. He lifted
his head towards Martin. " He's lying on the floor. Not
moving."

Over the viaduct Cheshire was trying to drop his markers
but again was coned by searchlights and hit by flak, so he had
to stand the Lancaster on a wing-tip and pull her round to the
safe darkness at sea. It meant several miles for another run.
He came in again about 3,000 but again he was battered
and had to pull away. He climbed to 5,000 but the flak
caught him once more, and now there was another worry
on his mind. Out to sea the squadron had been circling for
half an hour waiting for the markers and he knew they were
getting short of petrol. Met. had radioed that England was
under fog and only two fields were suitable for landing. They
would need plenty of petrol to search and land through the
fog . . . or risk losing the whole squadron.

On his sixth run he dived to upset the predicted flak and
was able to drop flares that lit the viaduct. He turned back
for another run and this time the searchlights did not find
him. The guns predicted on him but he threaded through
them and soon his markers sprang to glowing life as they hit ;
he saw in the light of the flares that they were on the beach
about a hundred yards from the viaduct.

He swung in again with his last two markers, but four
second short of release point two shells hit " Q Queenie "
and she almost stood on her head in the blast. It threw
Astbury off his bombing aim, but Cheshire got her back
under control and found she would still fly and there was no
fire.

The squadron headed in, unable at 10,000 feet to pick
up the viaduct from the flares but trying to allow for the
error of the markers. The gap was fiendishly hard to judge
in the darkness. One 12,000-pounder went off brilliantly
15 yards from the side of the viaduct, but that was 5 yards too
far and the viaduct shook but was not damaged beyond
chipping from fragments. Six more exploded a few yards
further on and pitted the great stone piers a little more. It

was good bombing, but not quite good enough. Long after they were supposed to, they turned for home.

Whittaker had taken his tie off and wrapped it round his thigh as a tourniquet. There were a dozen pieces of flak in his legs but the pain was passing into numbness now. He grabbed one of the roof longerons, pulled himself up and found he could stand. Foxlee stuck his head up from the nose and said, " Bob's unconscious. Get a first-aid kit, will you ? " Whittaker pulled one of the little canvas bags out of its stowage and eased himself down into the nose. Hay was lying on his side, his head pillowed on the perspex right up in the nose. " Give him some morphia," Foxlee shouted, and Whittaker nodded, unclipped the canvas pack and took out one of the tiny morphia hypodermic tubes. Foxlee unzipped Hay's Irvin jacket sleeve and rolled the battledress sleeve up till Whittaker could see the soft flesh of the forearm, pale in the gloom. He felt the flesh was still warm, jabbed in the needle and squeezed till the tube was empty.

" Let's get him over and see where he's hit," he shouted. Together in the cramped space they edged him over on to his back and Whittaker crawled up and gently turned the head over. He saw the great hole in the side of the head and felt the stickiness in the same moment. He said, " Oh, my God ! " and felt he was going to be sick, looked up at Foxlee, but Foxlee was looking down. He had lifted his hand off Hay's chest and the blood showed darkly on his fingers. " He's got it in the chest," he said, and Whittaker said, " Yes, the poor devil's had it."

He crawled back up into the cockpit to his seat beside Martin, leaned over and said, " Bob's dead." Martin looked at him a moment, then looked ahead again and gave a little nod.

Whittaker noticed Kenny Stott, the new navigator, standing by Martin's seat. " Where're we going ? " Whittaker said, and Martin gave him a wry little grin. " Somewhere friendly, I hope," he said. " Just been talking it over with Kenny. Got any ideas ? "

" Whatever's nearest. How 'bout Gib. ? Or Sicily ? Or North Africa ? "

Stott said, " What about Sardinia ? Or Corsica ? Aren't
they closer ? "

" Is Corsica ours ? " Martin asked, and Whittaker cut in,
not sensing then the unconscious humour of it : " Yeah. I
saw we got Corsica in the *News of the World* last Sunday."

" O.K.   Fair enough.   Kenny, give me a course for North
Corsica."

Stott went back to his charts and Whittaker said he would
try and assess the damage.   Martin found " Popsie " had just
enough power to claim a little more height, very slowly, so he
edged the nose up a little, and soggily, not far from stalling
speed, the Lancaster started climbing laboriously.   In the
darkness she was full of noise, the high-pitched screaming of
the two good engines battering at the ears in waves because
they would not synchronise properly.

He felt his right foot in the flying boot was wet and
remembered he had been hit in the calf.   He had enough
sense not to strip his leg to investigate because the trouser
leg and high flying boot would help staunch the blood.   The
trouble was, if he lost too much blood, he would pass out
and they would all die because no one else could fly " Popsie,"
particularly the way she was.   Against the ragged thrust of
the engines the trim would not hold her either straight or
level and he was working all the time to keep her flying.
With one hand he pulled his tie loose and wrapped it round
the calf over the spot where the shrapnel had hit him, knotting
it tightly so that it would press the trouser leg against the
wound with the effect of half bandage, half tourniquet.

Whittaker came back.   " Not too good," he said.   " The
floor's all smothered in grease.   It's from the hydraulics, so
you can count them out.   Air pressure's gone too."

" I know," Martin said.   " I can't get the bomb doors up."

" The CO_2 bottle seems all right," Whittaker said, " so
you'll probably be able to get your undercart and flaps down
but you won't have any brakes to pull up with."

" Oh Christ ! "

" I've kept the best bit to the last," Whittaker said morbidly.
" The bomb-release fuses have gone for a Burton and we've
still got the bombs on board."

" I thought so. That's why she's flying like a bloody brick."

Stott came up with a course for North Corsica, and Martin swung on to the new heading. They were about 2,000 feet now.

" We'll have to get rid of the bombs," Stott said. " The fusing circuit's bashed in too, so they must still be fused. We can't unfuse 'em. If you can get high enough I might be able to prod the grips through the floor with a ruler and trip them."

Martin was trying to coax more height out of the stricken plane. He had a 4,000-pounder and several 1,000-pounders in the bomb bays, and the minimum safety height for dropping a 4,000-pounder was 4,000 feet.

Curtis was tapping out a " Mayday " (S.O.S.) and excitedly reported, after a while, he had made contact with Ajaccio in Northern Corsica. An advanced R.A.F. fighter unit had just moved in there and the airfield and flarepath were serviceable.

Foxlee came up from the nose and said in a puzzled voice, " Bob's still warm. His body's quite warm. I think he might be alive." Whittaker went down to investigate and came back up again, a little excited. " He *is* warm," he said, " He *must* be alive still." Martin told Curtis to warn Ajaccio to have a doctor meet them. Curtis made contact again and came back to the cockpit. " They say they haven't got a doctor with any facilities to look after a bad head wound. They say if the kite'll hold together we ought to make for Cagliari. That's in South Sardinia. There's an American bomber base at Elmas Field there, and they've got everything, but it's another one hundred and fifty miles."

Martin said feelingly, " Christ, what a party ! Give me a new course, Kenny." The aircraft was still full of numbing noise ; a gale was howling through the shell-hole in the nose and the two good engines still screamed in high pitch. Whittaker was watching his gauges nervously, waiting for the engines to crack under the strain.

They were about 2,700 feet when the stars blotted out and they were in heavy rain, followed soon after by hail. Water was sweeping in through the nose, and then darkness swallowed them as they ran into heavy cloud. It was ice cloud. Martin saw supercooled water droplets filming over the leading edge of the wings, forming the dangerous glazed ice that altered the aerodynamic shape and robbed the wings of lift. He had no spare speed to give him lift, and then the propeller of one of the two good engines slipped right back into coarse pitch and could not be budged out of it. The revs. dropped down to about 1,800 ; the engine was still giving power but the propeller could not use it all. Martin felt the controls getting soggy ; he held on to her, correcting the waffling with great coarse movements, trying to coax her to stay up because Stott was shoving a ruler down through the floor into the bomb bay against the bomb grips. He got a 1,000-pounder away and then the aircraft stalled. Martin couldn't hold her ; the nose fell, she squashed down and the starboard wing-tip dropped and they were diving and turning, on the verge of a spin. He had hard left rudder on and the rudder caught her, the spin checked and she was diving, picking up speed. He eased her out but they were down to 1,800 feet. That was clear of the cloud, and soon the thin ice cracked and flicked off the wings. He started climbing again. They still needed 4,000 feet to drop the 4,000-pounder.

It took a long time. At 2,500 feet they were in the ice-cloud again, but Stott prodded two more 1,000-pounders free before the ice started to make " Popsie " soggy again, and this time Martin eased her down out of the cloud before she stalled. He started climbing again and found they were running clear of the worst of the cloud. It was still there, but higher and thinner, and only the barest film of ice seemed to be shining on the wings. " Popsie " slowly gained height, passed the 3,000 mark, but then progress was terribly slow and when at last they reached 3,200 she could not drag herself any higher. She was still at the climbing angle but moving no higher, like an old man trying to climb a fence and not being able to pull himself up.

" She's only squashing along," Martin said. " Can't make the safety height, Kenny. What're our chances if we drop the big one here ? "

" Better than trying to land with the bloody thing," Stott said. " Let's give it a go."

He went back to the winch slits in the floor and probed. Martin felt the aircraft jump weakly in the same moment that Storr yelled, " She's gone ! " Martin tried to turn away but knew he could not get far enough for safety. The 4,000-pounder took fourteen seconds to fall and it felt like fourteen minutes. The sea below and a little to one side opened up like a crimson rose and almost in the same moment the shock wave hit the aircraft. She jumped like a startled horse and a wing flicked, but Martin caught her smartly with rudder and they were all right.

Curtis came up a couple of minutes later. " Elmas Field says the best way in is over the mountains in the middle of Sardinia."

" How high are they ? " Martin asked. Stott said they were 8,000 feet and Martin showed his teeth sardonically.

They got a landfall on Sardinia about 3.30 a.m. and turned to follow the coast all the way round the south tip, and on e.t.a. Martin let down through light cloud and they came out about 1,000 feet and saw the flarepath.

" Thank God for that," he breathed, and a minute later changed his mind. Elmas was on a narrow spit of land. It had one runway only, a dangerously short one for an emergency landing. Martin steered low over it to see what the overshoot areas were like because they were probably going to need them, and felt a chill as he saw that some genius of an airfield designer had had the fabulous idea of building the runway *across* the spit of land, so that the runway started very abruptly at the beach and stopped just as abruptly and dismayingly quickly at the cliff, where the sea started again. No overshoot.

He still had two 1,000-lb. bombs that Stott could not reach and they were almost certainly fused, so a belly landing was out of the question. With the emergency CO_2 bottle the undercarriage might go down, or it might not ; the tyres might be all right or they might have been punctured, and if they were the aircraft stood a good chance of ground-looping so that the undercart would collapse on to the fused bombs. If his first approach was not perfect the aircraft, without brakes, would certainly run over the far cliff. There was not enough power to go round for a second approach.

Whittaker yanked down the handle of the CO_2 bottle, and the undercart swung down and seemed to lock. In the gloom they could not see the tyres. There was just enough pressure left to get some flap down. Martin headed in on a long, low approach, dragging in from miles back, while the crew snugged down at emergency stations. Coming up to the runway he was dangerously low, deliberately, and in the last moment he cut all engines and pulled up the nose to clear the dunes. The speed fell and at about 85 m.p.h. she squashed on the runway about 30 yards from the end, not even bouncing. The undercart held, and as she rumbled on Martin started fish-tailing his rudders. The far cliff was running towards them and he pushed on full port rudder. " Popsie " swung and jolted over the grass verge, slowing more appreciably. She started to slew, tyres skidding just short of a ground-loop, and came to a halt 50 yards from the cliff-top.

Foxlee said, " Well, you old bastard, I'll never bitch about your landings any more."

An ambulance and fire truck had been chasing them along the runway, and a young doctor swung up into the fuselage and they directed him up to the nose. He was out a minute later and said, " I'm sorry, but your buddy's gone. He was dead as soon as it happened."

He went over to Whittaker, lying on the grass, and cut his trouser legs away, exposing the legs messy with blood and torn flesh, and where there was no blood they had a distinct blue tinge. He worked for quarter of an hour on them, dabbing, cleaning and bandaging, while Martin gingerly pulled up his own trouser leg to inspect the damage to himself. The doctor finished bandaging Whittaker and as they loaded him into the ambulance told him, " That's a close call, boy. You nearly lost a leg." He turned to Martin. " Now let's have a look at you," but Martin said as off-handedly as he could, " Don't bother about me, Doc. I'm quite all right."

When he had uncovered his leg he had found one tiny spot of blood on a tiny puncture where a tiny piece of flak, at its last gasp, had just managed to break the skin. It had stung at the time, and imagination had done the rest. The wetness he had felt round his foot was not blood gushing into his flying boot but sweat !

About the same time the rest of the squadron was landing at Ford in thick weather. Tommy Lloyd, Woodhall intelligence officer, had flown to Ford and de-briefed them, and then the weather worsened and it looked as though they were stranded for a while. Suggitt thought he could make it to Woodhall Spa all right and offered a seat in his aircraft to Lloyd, a gallant and revered World War I veteran. The immaculate Lloyd accepted but insisted on having a shave before take-off. A little later, spruce and monocled, he climbed into " J Jug " with Suggitt, and five minutes later the aircraft flew into a hill and everyone was killed instantly except Bill Suggitt, who lingered a couple of days before he died.

The rest flew back later, and Cheshire's " erks " found 150 holes in " Q Queenie." The port wing had to be scrapped. McCarthy, back from leave, was outraged to find his beloved " Queenie " so battered and a comic but slightly acid note edged his Brooklyn accent when he said loudly and meaningly in the mess (Cheshire was standing near) : " It's a remarkable coincidence that the wingco has been flying his own aircraft for three months without getting a spot on it, and then sends me on leave and takes mine and does this to it."

They buried Bob Hay in Sardinia. Whittaker stayed in hospital while the rest made rough repairs, flew " Popsie " on to Blida, where R.A.F. " erks " did a thorough overhaul, and then filled her up with benedictine, wine, fruit and eggs and flew back to Woodhall Spa, where Cheshire met them with the news that Cochrane had vetoed any more operations for them. " It's no use arguing, Mick," Cheshire said. " He means it. He says you'll only kill yourself if he lets you go on." Martin *did* argue, but Cochrane posted him to 100 Group Headquarters, where he immediately wangled himself on to a Mosquito night-fighter squadron doing " intruder " work over Germany.

[I have a letter which Cheshire wrote to a friend some four years after this, talking about the old days. He said : " The backbone of the squadron were Martin, Munro, McCarthy and Shannon, and of these by far the greatest was Martin. He was not a man to worry about administration then (though I think he is now), but as an operational pilot I consider him greater than Gibson, and indeed the greatest that the Air Force ever produced. I have seen him do things that I, for one, would never have looked at."]

It is not a bad tribute from a man who has himself often been labelled one of the world's greatest bomber pilots. I have these words of Cheshire's in my notes : " I learned all I knew of this low-flying game from Mick. He showed me what you could do by coming in straight and hard and low, and I never saw him make a mistake."

Cheshire himself, in fact, was undoubtedly the most out-standing of the 617 pilots, though if one suggested this he would decry it with a gently and faintly derisive smile. Always he had a talent for self-effacement, a soft-spoken modesty, and many qualities not usual in hearty men of action and courage. His courage could match any man's, and in addition he was always a strange blend of leader, intellectual, man of action and man of ideas and ideals (some-times eccentric and seldom conformist). Inevitably he has an awareness of this and balances it by a deprecating intro-spection. He has never quite rid himself of the idea that he lost his nerve at Antheor, that he should have tried to go in low like Martin, and does himself no justice, because he and his crew would almost surely have died, probably before being able to lay their markers, and that would have de-stroyed any chance of success for the raid.

As it was, the raid was within 5 yards of success, but that is a sore point with 617. Antheor seemed to have a hoodoo on them.

CHAPTER XIII

THE MOSQUITO PLAN

CHESHIRE reported to Cochrane that the Antheor raid had convinced him of three things :

(a) Accurate marking was essential for accurate bombing of small specific targets.

(b) Accurate marking could only be done reliably at low level.

(c) Low-level marking was *very* dangerous on defended targets with a big aircraft like the Lancaster.

Cochrane was not yet convinced that low-level marking was practicable, but he told Cheshire he would lay on more lightly defended targets so the experiment could go on. He wanted the system perfected by the time Wallis's " tallboy " was ready ; the first one was nearly ready for testing, and after that they would be some time building up stocks. Meantime the squadron needed some re-forming. With Martin and Suggitt gone there were no flight commanders.

It was Cochrane's idea to split 617 into three flights for easier organisation and training ; a happy idea, because it gave Cheshire a chance to promote Shannon, McCarthy and Munro, now the only three of the original squadron left, and all battle-tested, reliable and ideal in temperament and training for 617's unique role. Shannon was an old-young man now, venom-tongued on occasion, highly strung on the ground (though not the slightest neurotic), but calm and detached as an iceberg in the air. McCarthy, strong as an ox and even-tempered, stood no trifling—his way with a young fool who forgot himself was swift and vigorous. Munro, the slow-speaking, taciturn New Zealander, so earnest and dour that he was known as " Happy," did most of the tedious routine work in the squadron and never even suspected that the W.A.A.F.s on the station adored him as a strong, silent man. The Australian, the American and the New Zealander, each in some way typifying their national characters, led by the subtle and audacious Englishman, a strong combination of leaders in a squadron that ever was an oligarchy, but a respected and revered one.

McCarthy, incidentally, now that he was a squadron leader, let himself take on a little of the colour of his surroundings. With a touch of Brooklyn wit, he bought himself a pipe, a walking stick and a dog, and took the dog for long walks in the countryside, claiming that, as he had to be pretty much of a gentleman officially, he was goddamned if he wasn't going to have a crack at looking the part too.

The squadron had several new pilots now, including another American, Nicky Knilans, a droll youngster from Madison, Wisconsin, with precisely the quality of nervelessness that Cheshire wanted in 617. Knilans had already done about twenty trips with 619 Squadron and been in strife on nearly every one of them. Several times on the way to the target he had had engines shot out, and more shells had ripped chunks out of his aircraft, but he had always pressed on and bombed and had a D.S.O. to commemorate that laudable habit. Once his rear gunner had been cut in two by a night fighter, and it was such a terrible mess that, when they landed back at base, the ambulance driver who met them had had hysterics and largely left it to the nerveless Knilans to get the remains out of the turret.

Knilans had joined the Canadian Air Force before America came into the war and had just recently been transferred. Now a " lootenant " in the U.S. Air Force, he wanted to stay and finish his tour in the R.A.F., and had a row with his crew when he had them posted with him (without telling them) to 617. They claimed it was a suicide squadron, but, as Knilans pointed out, few people on 619 had ever finished a tour either, so it didn't make much difference. The crew was even more unhappy when Knilans suddenly seemed to develop into an exceedingly ham-fisted pilot. He was given a new aircraft, " R Roger," when he joined 617 and could not make his usual three-point landings any more ; even the take-offs were frightening, as " R Roger " seemed most reluctant to leave the ground, and when she did leave climbed like a tired brick. " Give the game away, Nicky," one of his

gunners said. " You're getting flak-happy. You can't even
fly any more."

" Doggone, it's not me," said the badgered American.
" It's this bloody-minded aircraft. You don't have to fly it,
you have to understand the son of a bitch."

In the next few weeks 617 was busy training new crews
and settling down with the new flight commanders. Cheshire
and " Talking Bomb " kept flying around at 5,000 feet trying
medium-level marking, but could find no way of lining-up an
indistinct target. Cochrane told them to keep trying.

The first couple of prototype " tallboys " were finished,
and at Ashley Walk range, in the New Forest, the complicated
process of testing them started. They were sinister objects,
21 feet long, shining blue-black steel, slim and perfectly
streamlined, weighing 12,030 lb. A Lancaster dropped one
on test from 20,000 feet, and it sliced through the air like
a bullet till it was falling faster than a bomb had ever fallen
before. Long before it hit it passed the speed of sound, and
as the compressed waves of the sonic barrier piled up round
it the bomb vibrated in flight so that it almost toppled and
was deflected slightly from its even course, just enough to
interfere with the fanatical accuracy that Wallis wanted.

He overcame it with a brilliant idea, offsetting the tail fins
so that, as the next bomb dropped and gathered speed, the
offset fins began to revolve it. Faster and faster it whirled
till by the time it reached the speed of sound it was spinning
like a high-speed top, and the gyroscopic action held it
perfectly steady as it plunged through the sonic barrier. At
Shoeburyness the blind Air Commodore Huskinson put
other prototypes through heat and cold and rough-usage
tests, dragging them over rough ground on bomb dollies
and throwing them against concrete walls. They filled one
with RDX, stood it on its nose and exploded it. Instruments
scattered for hundreds of yards registered the effects, and in
a concrete shelter a very high-speed camera took a slow-
motion film of it. It was obviously impossible to point the
camera at the bomb ; they shielded the camera behind a
shelter pointing at a mirror so placed that it reflected the

explosion into the lens, and got some extraordinary photographs showing the bomb slowly swelling under the tremendous pressure within, like a balloon blown to bursting point, till it was nearly twice its normal size, and then the casing burst with deeply satisfying results.

At Ashley Walk they dropped a " tallboy " with dummy filling from 20,000 feet and it sank 90 feet into the earth, almost enough for the maximum camouflet that Wallis had planned from 40,000 feet, and certainly enough to make a respectable earthquake.

Came the day of dropping the first " live " one, and they buried a movie camera in the earth to film it. There was some discussion as to where the camera should go, and perhaps it was logical (if a little cynical) that they decided to bury it right in the centre of the white circle that was the target, on the assumption that it was the safest spot.

The result was a lesson for anyone who doubted Wallis's genius. Peering over the edge of the sandbagged dug-out half a mile away, they saw the slim shape streak down and hit the centre of the target, right on the camera ! The dug-out trembled, and where the camera had been was a smoking, stinking crater eighty feet deep and a hundred feet across.

Cochrane called Cheshire to Group H.Q., told him the earthquake bomb had passed its tests with honours and they were now building up stocks for " a big operation " in the spring and summer. 617 was still the only squadron good enough to drop it with the S.A.B.S. but they still had not perfected their marking technique.

On March 2 Cheshire led fifteen 617 Lancasters to an aircraft factory at Albert, in France. Over it the Germans had spread enormous camouflage nets painted with dummy roads and buildings. Cheshire identified the factory from surrounding landmarks, dived low through flak, but his bomb sight was out of order. Munro dived and planted incendiaries and two red spot fires, and a few minutes later the blockbusters crashed down. One toppled and fell outside but the rest, with 617's uncanny accuracy, were direct hits. No more aircraft were made at Albert for the Germans.

Next night to La Ricamerie needle-bearing works at St. Etienne, near Lyons, smallest and hardest target yet. It lay in a narrow valley with 4,000-ft. hills on each side, and the actual target, in the middle of a built-up area, was only 40 yards by 70 yards. Cochrane warned Cheshire again that on no account was a single Frenchman to be hurt.

Met. forecast good weather but the squadron found the target blanketed under unbroken cloud and brought their bombs back. The attempt, however, was notable for two incidents that illustrate the remarkable spirit of the squadron.

Les Munro lost an engine on take-off but got into the air safely and, instead of turning back, which would have been normal, flew on with three engines, arriving only a minute late.

The second concerned a Warrant Officer Rushton, a gunner in Duffy's crew, a hard-boiled bunch of Canadians. Duffy was ill that night and could not fly, so Rushton begged Cheshire to take him along with him. No particular reason, except that he did not want to be left out of an operation. That sort of thing happened often on 617. A navigator broke his collar-bone in a football game one day and sneaked out of sick quarters next night to fly with his crew.

Duffy's crew had made themselves notorious the night they had arrived on the squadron. When they went upstairs to bed they could not find the toilets but, being resourceful men from the backwoods, had relieved themselves out of the window. In the morning they were brought before the group captain, who eyed them coldly and said : " If you fellows do your job properly you can get away with almost anything on this squadron, but one thing you *can't* do is piddle on the group captain."

He had been walking below at the wrong moment. The rest of the squadron thought it wonderful that a crowd of new boys should do that to a senior officer from a great height.

The weather cleared and they tried La Ricamerie again, finding the valley dark under broken cloud. Cheshire dived low between the hills and made six risky runs up and down trying to mark but found he could only see the factory at the last moment. On the sixth run he judged his distance, shoved his nose down and let go his incendiaries ; they lobbed on the main factory building but had such a low trajectory that they bounced a hundred yards beyond. Munro dived and undershot. Shannon came in ; his markers hit a workshop roof and bounced. Arthur Kell, a lanky Australian who had been a champion amateur boxer and taken over Micky Martin's " P Popsie," came in at roof-top height, and his incendiaries stayed in the middle of the factory.

Cheshire told the bombers above to aim at the last marker, and soon the darkness was lit by flashing explosions and flames. Morning revealed that only the wall round the factory remained ; the rest had disappeared and there was no damage outside.

More nights of waiting for the weather ; it had been snowing for days and they turned out every day to try and shovel the drifts off the runways and crack the ice off the wings, but as soon as they had finished the snow was coming down again. One night they got off in freezing cold to plaster an aero-engine factory at Woippy, near Metz, but flew through ten-tenths cloud the whole way and found the cloud just as thick over the target. No hope of bombing.

On the way home Duffy's plane was " jumped " by two JU88s and a F.W.190. The first burst sent a bullet through the hand of McLean, the rear gunner, but McLean, after a few salty comments, found his hand was still working and more than evened the score by shooting down both 88s, and possibly the F.W.190 as well.

It was so cold in the rear turrets that the oxygen mask studs on Gerry Witherick's, helmet had stuck to his face. He did not know it till he dragged his helmet off and a couple of square inches of skin came away with the studs. The M.O. consoled him with a rum ration.

Next night to the Michelin rubber factory at Clermont Ferrand, partly sabotaged but still making the Germans 24,000 tyres a month. This was an amazing raid. The factory consisted of four large buildings—three workshops, and the fourth was the workers' canteen, just beside them. War Cabinet was still worried about the risk of killing French people, and from a high level the startling instruction came down that they were to smash the three workshops but on no account damage the canteen. It would be such a fine gesture and such good propaganda ! (It would also be, a high officer remarked, " a bloody miracle.") To make it more difficult it was a black, moonless night.

Cochrane drew up a most detailed plan and also sent six Lancasters from 106 Squadron with a special new radar navigation aid to drop flares. McLean, his hand swathed in bandages, wanted to fly as usual with Duffy but Cheshire flatly forbade him.

The flares brightly revealed the factory, and Cheshire made three low runs over it at a hundred feet to warn the workers, and on the third run his markers fell short. He called on Munro, Shannon and McCarthy to mark, and they all dive-bombed their spot fires on the workshop buildings.

Seven minutes later the bombing was over and the factory was smothered in flame and smoke. Cheshire radioed back, " Michelin's complexion seems a trifle red."

In the morning a Mosquito took a picture of the smoking ruins. Six of the 617 aircraft had been carrying 12,000-lb. " blockbusters " and every one was a direct hit on the work-shops, which could work no more. Just beside them the workers' canteen was untouched. Cochrane sent the picture off to War Cabinet.

Cheshire had been pondering some new marking ideas. Remembering Martin's experiences at Antheor and his own and Munro's troubles marking the needle-bearing factory up and down the dark valley, it seemed to him that Lancasters were too big and clumsy for marking ; too big a target for the flak and too clumsy for manœuvring low over rough ground on pin-point targets. He went to Cochrane and suggested that he try marking in a Mosquito, and Cochrane liked the idea. The twin-engined Mosquito was much faster as well as smaller and " nippier." Provided Mosquitoes could be used, Cochrane for the first time began to feel more comfort-able about the idea of sending crews out to mark at low level.

A new idea was already growing in Cochrane's mind : to have 617 mark for the whole of his 5 Group, about twelve squadrons, instead of the Pathfinders. He did not consider

the Pathfinders accurate enough for his purposes and a polite
" cold war " had, in fact, been developing between 5 Group
and the Pathfinders, aggravated a little by 617, who were
already tending to consider themselves " Pathfinders to the
Pathfinders." Cochrane had already sounded out Harris on
his new idea and Harris had reacted favourably. Cochrane
reasoned that if they could show that low marking in Mosquitoes was reasonably safe, Harris would probably give
5 Group its chance. He said to Cheshire :

" Well, I'll see if I can get you a couple of Mosquitoes,
and then I'd like you to try them first on easy targets. If
it seems all right, you could have a go at a tough one."

A bond was developing between the two men. Cochrane
did not have an easy personality and few of the hundreds
who were daunted by him ever realised that underneath the
crisp and almost ruthless front he was shy, with rigid control
over his emotions. His precise brain dwelt on operational
efficiency. He watched his men from close quarters and
visited them constantly. He never, for instance, missed
attending a squadron dance, so that he could know them and
gauge their temper (and so that they could gauge him). Yet
the reserve that covered his shyness made him wary of the
embarrassments of easy-going familiarity that might lessen
his unswerving concentration. Cheshire was brilliant in a
more erratic way, and Cochrane's relentless logic was a brake
on this occasional waywardness. They were an ideal combination. Cheshire was a natural tactician in personal
relationships, gentle and unobtrusive but with a quiet confidence and the charm that comes from treating everyone.
high or low, as a real person and not as a Thing.

It was not easy for Cochrane to get hold of Mosquitoes for
617. They were in short supply and great demand ; Pathfinders and other squadrons had priorities for them, and the
idea of a heavy-bomber squadron using some experimentally
evoked sturdy protests in some high places. While Cochrane
was working on this, 617 went ahead perfecting their technique
with Lancasters on several small French targets. On March
18 they visited the explosives factory at Bergerac, on the
banks of the Dordogne, under rigid orders that there was to

be *no* low flying. Cochrane would not risk his choice crews before the Mosquitoes arrived.

For once, in the light of flares, Cheshire's bomb aimer, Astbury, got a good sight at 5,000 feet and put his markers on the factory. Munro did the same. Shannon and McCarthy branded the explosives dump nearby, and Bunny Clayton put a 12,000-pounder in the middle of the dump. For fifteen seconds it looked as though the sun was coming up underneath ; the ground was one great orange flash that Cheshire described as " fantastic." It lit the sky for miles so clearly that Cheshire looked up and saw the remaining ten aircraft of his squadron heading in to bomb, and five minutes later the factory as well as the dump was a sea of flame. Cheshire radioed back, " The powder works would seem to have outlived their usefulness." No bomb fell outside the works.

The Germans had another explosives works in France near a town called Angouleme, in a bend of the Charente. Cheshire led fourteen aircraft there the following night, put his spot fires in the centre and ten minutes later was able to radio back, " In accordance with tradition." The factory had ceased to exist. Again no damage outside.

A pleased Cochrane rang Cheshire next day. " Pack your over-night bag," he said. " You're coming down with me to see Air Chief Marshal Harris about a couple of Mosquitoes."

That night they dined with Harris in his house near High Wycombe, Cheshire for all his urbanity feeling uneasy in the company of the two most terrifying commanders in the R.A.F. He needn't have worried ; the fire-cracker and the meticulous planner chatted nostalgically about their days in Iraq when they were both young flight lieutenants not fanatically addicted to administration.

Over the port Harris suddenly said, " Cheshire, what makes you think you can mark from nought feet in a Mosquito and get away with it ? "

" There's no question that we can mark accurately, sir. The only thing is having a reasonable chance in the face of heavy opposition. Air Vice-Marshal Cochrane thinks a Lancaster is too big and slow. Against heavy opposition I'm inclined to think now he is right, but I believe he agrees with me that the chances in a Mosquito are good. I believe in a Mosquito we can have a go at any target under the sun and mark with under twenty yards accuracy."

" I've always wanted to bomb Munich properly, and I've never succeeded," Harris said. " It's got four hundred guns. D'you think you could mark that on the deck and get away with it ? "

" Yes, sir. I do."

Cochrane cut in, saying that they should practise first with the Mosquito on less lethal targets so they would know precisely what was possible.

" All right," Harris said, " I'll see if I can get you two Mosquitoes . . . just on loan for a month. If by that time you can mark Munich accurately for me, you can keep them."

Just behind Calais the Germans had started work again on the bomb-proof rocket and long-range gun bases. Thousands of slaves were crawling over the massive blockhouses and it was obvious that the secret-weapon project was nearing completion again. Whitehall knew now that the weapon was to fall on London and the invasion ports, but kept it very secret. (They still knew nothing of the long-range guns, the 500-ft barrels of which were then being brought up through Belgium.) If the secret weapons started up before the invasion and the R.A.F. could not destroy the blockhouses, London would be destroyed and it was likely that the invasion would also be wrecked.

Churchill was insisting on twice-daily Intelligence reports. Some reports put the weight of the secret-weapon warhead as high as 10 tons of explosive and suggested they might fall at a rate of thousands a week. Churchill ordered the preparation of plans for the evacuation of London and told Sir Arthur Harris that the blockhouses were to be destroyed without fail before they were ready for action.

Wallis's " tallboy " was the only weapon Harris knew of that might smash them, but the " tallboys " would not be ready for some time. They would have to be dropped from at least 18,000 feet to get enough speed for penetration, and only one squadron could drop them accurately enough. But the sites would be so well camouflaged in the bomb-pocked earth that a bomb aimer would have trouble getting them in his bomb sight from 18,000 feet even by day. Though the sites were fairly plastered with flak, they would have to be marked clearly and with unprecedented accuracy because there would be no " tallboys " to waste. It was a pretty problem, and Harris called the Pathfinder chief, Bennett, and Cochrane and Cheshire to a conference at his headquarters.

Bennett said frankly that the Pathfinders were not equipped to mark with such accuracy, and Cochrane suggested that 617 might be able to do the marking as well as the bombing.

Cheshire said : " I doubt if it could be marked accurately at medium level. You'd have to run-up straight and level, and at that height the searchlights would blind you so you couldn't see the target, and the flak would pretty surely get you anyway. I should think, sir, we could mark it at very low level in a diving attack."

Cochrane said warningly, " Not in a Lancaster."

" No, sir. In a Mosquito, as we discussed before. She's so fast we could be in and out before the defences could nail us."

Bennett said, " I don't think you'd find the Mosquito fast enough to dodge the defences . . . you'll have enormous casualties."

Cheshire held stubbornly to his own viewpoint and added, " In any case, sir, I can't see that there is any other way."

The conference was virtually stalemated. Harris said grimly, " Well, the job's got to be done. If P.F.F. aren't equipped for it, how about your boys, Cochrane ? "

Cochrane accepted the challenge. " We'll get down to it, sir," he promised.

A day later Cochrane phoned Cheshire : " I've got two Mosquitoes for you. They're over at Colby Grange. Go and learn to fly them and be quick about it. Let me know as soon as you're ready to use them."

Cheshire was delighted with the Mosquitoes, and within two days felt at home in them. The only possible fault he could find was that, carrying a load of heavy markers, their

range might be a little short for some of the more distant
targets. Munich, for instance, would be barely within range,
so he asked Group to get him some long-range drop tanks as
soon as possible.

A gratifying indication that their bombing success was
spreading to the outside world came when the two American
Air Force generals, Spaatz and Doolittle, flew over to
Woodhall to inspect them and inquire about the marking
technique. Cheshire explained it with pride, and Spaatz
wanted to know if there was any particular problem they had
not solved yet.

" Well," said Cheshire, straight-faced, " there is still one
problem actually, and that's to find some way of de-calibrating
the bomb sights, because the damn bomb aimers are lobbing
all their bombs in the same hole."

" Oh, is that so," Spaatz said with a fierce grin. " Well,
how's about you and us having a bombing contest, and we'll
show you how to land a bomb in a pickle barrel ? "

Cheshire accepted the challenge eagerly, but it never came
off because there were sterner things to do, which was a
pity because it would have settled a lot of arguments. 617
was confident of the result, and probably with justification.
With the S.A.B.S., the direction of Cochrane and the skill
of Cheshire and Martin, they were showing that bombing—
and night bombing at that—could be confined almost completely to military targets and that there need be no slaughter
of the innocents. 617 was entitled to feel proud of themselves.
Morale had climbed far above the grimness of the " suicide "
days, and in the past month they had flown 149 sorties and
dropped 473 tons of bombs without, as far as they knew,
hurting any civilians.

Significant peaks are seldom seen through the smoke of
battle ; it is only when time moves the beholder to a clearer
perspective that the peaks stand out. No one on 617 at this
time realised that they were already a workshop of tradition.
Still only a fledgling squadron, they had a spirit probably
unequalled by any other unit. Achievement lay behind them
already ; that was one reason, but only a part of it. More
subtle factors invoked the rest.

First, the aircrews were volunteers. They were where they wanted to be ; not square pegs in round holes. They could leave whenever they wanted to, and none of them ever wanted to. They had pride in their special competence and purpose and were honoured for it.

Secondly, there was Cochrane, dedicated to his job. His lively little personal assistant, Carol Durrant, deftly warded off all distractions from him and left him free to concentrate on his precise work. Having carefully chosen his squadron commander, he briefed and guided him and then shrewdly left him to choose his own team and run it.

Cheshire had the perception to recognise the peculiar character of a bomber squadron. The Air Force is the only fighting service where one section of the same unit does the most dangerous job of the war and the other the safest. With an expectation of death far higher than the Navy or Army, the aircrews had to face action day after day, week after week, virtually alone, with only their consciences as monitors. The ground crews, on the other hand, were liable to frustrations which could only be soothed if they could be assured of their value, and Cheshire delicately gave them those assurances.

When he landed in the early morning after a raid his driver usually found him under the wing sharing cocoa and sandwiches with his ground crew. As anxiously as they asked him how he had got on he would be asking them if they had managed to get any sleep while he was away, or thanking them for the performance of the aircraft, all with a friendly touch and a few jokes thrown in.

With flying or ground crew he was a leader and never a driver, never bullying, overbearing or petty, though his tongue could be quietly devastating if you merited it. His aircrews almost worshipped him, and the ground crews' feelings were probably deeper because he treated them with warm consideration, and they were not used to it.

Incompetence was never tolerated on the squadron but high spirits were, and the result was what Cochrane had aimed at : a unit of functional quality. He had long thought that one good performer was worth ten bad ones, and with

617 he proved it. The intriguing thing was that, so long as
they were completely efficient, the rather punctilious Cochrane
never unduly interfered with their somewhat spirited attitude
towards life, and so in the intrinsic lunacy of war they found
a purposeful comradeship.

Signs of their growing prestige were not lacking.   March
brought them nine more decorations ; popular ones.   Among
them were a Bar for Martin's D.S.O., a second Bar for
Cheshire's D.S.O., a Bar for Whittaker's D.F.C., and the
D.F.C. to add to Foxlee's D.F.M.

Cheshire flew down to Weybridge to see Wallis about tactics
for dropping the " tallboys."

" I haven't really designed this thing for concrete," Wallis
said, " so I think, my dear boy, it might not be a good thing
to drop them right on the roofs of those wretched concrete
affairs ; they might bounce out again like corks.   However,
you needn't worry ; just drop them down at the side in the
earth and they'll bore down and blow them up from underneath."   He stuck pins in a diagram to show the vulnerable
points and added disapprovingly, " The Germans are very
silly not to put twenty feet of concrete *under* these things,
not on top."

Cheshire suggested as tactfully as he could that, though he
had enormous faith in his squadron, it was one thing to stick
pins in a diagram and another to drop a bomb in that spot
from 20,000 feet.

" Oh well," Wallis said huffily, " if I'd known you propose
to scatter the bombs around the countryside like grass seed
I'd never have bothered to design them."

CHAPTER XIV

THE UNAPPEASING OF MUNICH

On April 4 Cheshire reported to Cochrane that he was ready with the Mosquito. Cochrane rang Harris and asked permission for his whole group to operate by themselves, led by 617 to mark the target, which was to be a large aircraft factory just outside Toulouse. Harris agreed, and next night they took off.

Cheshire found his Mosquito handled delightfully. A flare force lit up the factory and Cheshire dived fast and low over it, but, not satisfied with his positioning, pulled up sharply without dropping his markers. Heavy flak opened up on him as he corkscrewed away. He would almost certainly have been hit in a Lancaster, but the shells did not even scratch the Mosquito's paint. He dived again, once more was not satisfied and pulled up in a hail of shells. The third time his markers fell in the centre of the buildings, and again he climbed steeply away, unscathed. At 10,000 feet the squadrons moved in. Munro put an 8,000-pounder right on the markers and the rest of the bombs slathered the spot.

In the morning a recce aircraft found the factory flattened and only an occasional crater in the fields beyond.

Four days later 617 continued the experiment, going alone, led by Cheshire in the Mosquito, to attack the biggest German air park and signals depot in France, at St. Cyr, some two miles west of Versailles. Cheshire put his nose nearly straight down from 5,000 feet, let his markers go from 700, and they lobbed on the western corner of the target. He ordered the bombers in and soon rolling coils of smoke hid the target.

Cheshire landed as dawn was breaking and found Cochrane in the de-briefing room ; he had been waiting up all night to see how the raid went and took Cheshire aside.

" That's the end of the experiment, Cheshire. I'm satisfied you can do it low in Mosquitoes now, and we're going to start thinking of the big targets. I'm getting you four new

Mosquitoes. Train three or four picked pilots to use them and be quick about it."

The four Mosquitoes arrived that afternoon, and in the next six days McCarthy, Shannon, Kearns and Fawke spent their waking hours flying them. They were to fly Mosquitoes exclusively from now on and their crews were split up. Shannon kept the tough Sumpter as his navigator. Danny Walker stayed as squadron navigation officer, Goodale went off for a well-deserved rest, and Buckley joined another crew. The lanky and good-natured Concave had won a D.F.C. and Bar as a wireless operator, which is not far short of a miracle, because decorations for good work by a crew usually went first to the pilot, then to the navigator and bomb aimer. Or to a gunner who shot enemy aircraft down, or an engineer who had a chance to keep battered engines going in the air. A wireless operator had little chance.

Decorations were a vexed question because there was no way of equitable distribution. Cheshire had strong views on the subject ; as usual, unorthodox views but extraordinarily perceptive. Generally he divided courageous aircrews into two categories : (*a*) men with acute imagination who realised they would probably die and who forced themselves to go on, and (*b*) men who, though intelligent, could shut their minds off from imagination and carry on without acute forebodings of the future. Cheshire puts himself in the second group and, typically, regards the first group as the braver men.

" That's the highest form of courage," he said once. " They have a hell of a time but keep going. Usually they're not the spectacular types and they don't win the flash awards, but they're the bravest.

" Actually, as far as I could, I tried to get men of the second type, like me. Not thinkers. We didn't have the hard inward struggle and weren't in danger of being deflected by imagination."

The peculiar thing is that Cheshire *is* a thinker, a highly imaginative one, but with that queer capacity for ignoring the probabilities of personal catastrophe. I don't believe it is escapism either, because he is too coldly perceptive and introspective for that. He examines himself so closely that he would realise in a second if he were trying to delude himself. There is something deeper in it, some sort of fatalism. Most aircrew men had a mental defence mechanism that led them to believe, " This can't happen to me," even when they knew it *could* and probably would. Cheshire must have had some of that. Somewhat baffled, I have tried to classify him as a practical mystic, whatever that means.

He told me once : " Decorations are not particularly a test of courage but a test of success. There aren't many awards for failure ; a few, but not many, no matter what bravery was shown."

It is not a bad comment from a man with his decorations. There is a clash in Cheshire between self-conscious ego and honesty, and the honesty is the stronger.

On April 18 Cheshire reported to Cochrane that the Mosquito crews were all ready, and that night 617 marked for 5 Group against Juvisy marshalling yards, eleven miles south of Paris.

Munro's flares lit the area beautifully ; Cheshire, Fawke, Shannon and Kearns dived to 400 feet and lobbed their spot fires into the middle of the web of rails, though one bounced outside. It all went like clockwork. 617 bombed the spot fires accurately, as usual, and then the rest of 5 Group, 200 Lancasters, surged in and excelled themselves. They were used only to area bombing and not precision bombing, but this time, with the bright aiming points of the markers, they put nearly all their bombs in the target area. Some fell outside on the marker that bounced but morning reconnaissance showed the ragged end of rails in acres of erupted earth where a thousand craters overlapped each other. (It was eighteen months after the war before the yard was again in action.)

From the spot fire that bounced, Cheshire learned the importance of releasing the markers before the Mosquitoes started to flatten out of the dive, and that was another step towards perfection of the technique.

Next night they led 5 Group to the other important Paris marshalling yards, La Chappelle, a very ticklish target because these yards lay just outside the Gare du Nord and were fringed by high tenement buildings. Light and heavy flak hosed up at them, but the Mosquitoes plunged through it and laid all their spot fires except one in the centre of the rails ; the one that missed fell on the tenements. The bombing that followed was as accurate as ever, but inevitably some of the bombs fell on the inaccurate marker and the whole tenement buildings were flattened. (For a year Cochrane worried about the French people who he thought must have died in them, until he discovered that the tenements had been occupied by a regiment of the Luftwaffe.)

Once again 617 lost no aircraft and the Mosquitoes did not have a single hole among them. To Cheshire and Cochrane —and to Harris too—it was further confirmation of their ideas.

Cochrane flew to Woodhall that morning after the raid, saw Cheshire privately in Cheshire's office and, as usual, wasted no words :

" Now you can have a crack at Germany. To-morrow you're going to Brunswick . . . One Group as well as Five Group, so you'll be leading about four hundred aircraft. Pathfinders will drop flares and you'll mark with red spots."

There was one alternative, he said. If cloud hid the target, special radar Pathfinders would mark " blind " with green spots instead.

The first P.F.F. flares went down over Brunswick, but Cheshire could see no target (rail yards) by their light. More flares went down seven miles north, and over that spot Kearns and Fawke saw the target and dropped their red spots " on the button." Cheshire gave the order to bomb, and the first bombs were just exploding when the reserve radar Pathfinders ran into cloud nearby and dropped their green spots on fields three miles away. Most of the main force, according to orders, turned for them.

Cheshire called till he was blue in the face, but the radio was jammed and only a few aircraft picked up his message. Nearly all the bombs fell on the wrong markers out in the fields.

After they landed back at Woodhall, Cochrane flew over in

his Proctor and Cheshire started apologising for the mix-up. Cochrane cut in :

" All right, Cheshire. Don't you worry about that. You did your part perfectly. We've learned a bit more from it and we'll see the trouble doesn't happen again. How do you feel about Munich ? "

" As soon as you like, sir. We're ready."

" I've been on to Air Chief Marshal Harris. If the weather is all right you're going to-morrow night, leading the whole group again. You'll go for the rail yards."

Together they planned it, and this time it looked as though it could not miss. Bomber Command was to raid Karlsruhe half an hour before to draw the fighters. 617 was to lead 5 Group towards Switzerland as a feint ; six Lancasters were to swerve south towards Milan dropping bundles of " window " (thin strips of metal foil) to delude German radar into thinking 5 Group was heading for Italy. Just before the Group reached Munich, radar Pathfinders were to drop flares, and Cheshire and the Mosquitoes were to mark, the rest of 617 were to drop more markers from medium level with the S.A.B.S. in case the early markers were blown out, and then the 200 Lancasters were to bomb.

One point worried Cheshire. " Munich is about as far as a Mosquito can get without overload tanks," he said. " I've asked for them but they haven't come yet. We're not going to have enough margin for bad winds or upset timing without them."

" Give Group a sharp nudge about them," Cochrane said. " I'm going down to the C.-in-C. with the plan."

Cheshire phoned Group, and they said they would do all they could. He phoned them again next morning and was dismayed when they told him the tanks were in acutely short supply and other Mosquito units had priorities. It seemed that one or two people still tended to regard 617's Mosquitoes as an unorthodox and slightly reprehensible novelty.

Cheshire got hold of Pat Kelly, his navigator, and they worked out a new plan for the Mosquitoes : to fly first to Manston, in Kent, a hundred miles nearer the target, pour in all the petrol they could and fly straight to Munich across all the defences. Kelly plotted the distance, worked out their range from Manston and looked up grimly.

" If everything goes dead to time—which I've seldom seen —and if the winds are all in our favour—which I've never seen—we might just get back, but probably won't."

Cheshire went to a high officer at base and explained respectfully that, even taking off from Manston, he doubted if the four marking Mosquitoes would get back. It was usual to have a couple of hours' petrol in reserve—at least—to allow for contingencies. With the very best conditions they might arrive back with a few minutes' petrol. Personally he had never had to fly on a raid in such conditions. Nor did he know anyone who did. What should he do ?

The answer was not inspiring.

" If you can't do this marking in Mosquitoes," the high officer said, " you'll have to do it in a Lancaster. Whatever you do the raid has to go on."

Cheshire said, " Yes, sir."

He went back and collected the four Mosquito crews. They got a preliminary Met. report : heavy cloud—possible ice cloud—over the western half of Germany ; perhaps clear over Munich. At 14,000 feet the winds might be reasonably favourable. The four navigators bent over their calculations and looked up grimly.

Kelly said, " If everything goes perfectly we might get back to Manston." They all knew that a raid rarely went perfectly.

One of them exploded : " Hell sir, we don't mind sticking our necks out over the defences. That's just part of the job, but we can't see any point in such a bloody unnecessary risk. What sort of fools are we supposed to be ? "

Cheshire said, " I'm sorry, but we've got to go." There was a brief silence and one of them said, " All right."

The four Mosquitoes flew down to Manston and were refuelled and parked at take-off point so they would waste no fuel taxi-ing. Sitting silently over dinner with the others, Cheshire got a phone call from Cochrane.

" I'm deeply sorry about the overload tanks," Cochrane said. " Can you make it ? "

" We'll have a go, sir. I think it will be all right."

" I just want to let you know," Cochrane said, " I've had a word with the C.-in-C. When you get back he's giving the whole squadron a week's leave."

Cheshire went and told the others, and Kelly said acidly, " Fat lot of good that's going to do *us*." Cheshire had never seen them like that. They seemed almost on the verge of mutiny, not because they were too scared (they were scared all right, but so is nearly every airman before a raid), but this time it *was* unnecessary.

Around dusk Cheshire said, " Well, let's get it over." They walked out silently ; it was clear over England, the sun dipping under the horizon and the sky above flaming orange. Cheshire said, " What a glorious sunset ! " From the others a sullen silence, and then Shannon, without even lifting his eyes towards the west, said, " Damn the sunset. I'm only interested in the sun*rise*."

They took off without warming up, climbed straight on course to 14,000 feet and over the North Sea ran into heavy cloud.

They were coming up to the Rhine. Or hoped they were. Cloud lay on the earth like a deep, drifting ocean, rolling up unbroken to 17,000 feet, and in the hooded glow of the cockpits each pilot found comfort in the dim shape of his navigator beside him, feeling they were outcasts sealed in a small world. Beyond the numbing thunder of engines lay nothing but blackness and they only sensed that somewhere in a few square miles of sky they were together, unseen. Cheshire broke radio silence to ask Shannon how he was finding the weather and felt his scalp prickle as a voice out of the past spoke in his earphones, " Is that you, sir ? " He recognised it instantly, through the static and the careful anonymity . . . Micky Martin.

He called back, " Is that you, Mick ? "

" Yessir."

" Where on earth *are* you ? "

" Oh, I'm around."

" What the hell are you doing ? "

" Sticking my neck out for you types."

(Martin was a hundred miles away in another Mosquito, a night fighter, his job being to " beat up " German night-fighter fields, encouraging the fighters to stay on the ground while the bombers plastered Karlsruhe and Munich ; another part of Cochrane's planning.)

One wastes no time in radio chatter over enemy soil. Plotting stations need few seconds for a " fix." Cheshire said, " Good luck to you, Mick," and Martin answered laconically, " Good luck to you too. Be seeing you."

The other Mosquitoes heard it and flew on a little more cheerfully. It seemed an omen somehow, but whether for good or bad they were not quite sure.

Apparently it was for good ! The clouds thinned, winds stayed kind and exactly on zero hour they came out over Munich. No mistaking it ; the flare force had arrived and massed guns were vomiting upwards. At 14,000 feet the flashes of bursts split the night and lines of red balls were marching up from the lighter guns. There must have been a hundred searchlights ; pale fingers probing the dark, lighting now and then on aircraft which glinted like ants and turned to burrow into the crevices of the night. Mostly they vanished, but one was caught in a second beam, and a third. They saw it coned and held as it dived and turned and climbed, a trapped little ant. The flak hunted it ; in the glare they saw the brighter flashes all round and then the ribbon of flame as the Lancaster dived again ; this time the nose never lifted.

A flare abruptly glowed in the darkness, then another, a third—five . . . one by one they lit till thirty hung flaming in the sky over the naked city, so that Cheshire recognised from the photographs the kidney-shaped park, the long lake, drilled streets of pygmy houses and the lined acres of the rail yards. He shouted over the R/T, " Marker Leader going in " and peeled off from 10,000 feet, holding the nose down till the little Mosquito was moving into the flak faster than she had ever travelled. Sliding past 5,000 feet he lined her up on the rail yards, focused his mind on them, still aware in a curiously detached way of shells, balloon cables and searchlight dazzle, hoped he would miss them and coldly shut his mind to them. The little plane was shivering with the headlong surge and the busy fury of the engines ; Cheshire barely heard the screaming noise : she was twisting in the rising speed against the trim and he was coaxing her to arrow dead straight in the dive, forcing himself to wait for the dragging seconds till he suddenly jabbed the bomb button and eased back on the stick. He felt her lifting out instantly, the mounting " g " ramming him hard down into his seat, a phantom load dragging at his lips, his cheeks, his eyeballs and his blood, heavier and heavier, till his vision was greying out as the Mosquito flattened low over the roof-tops, curved up and climbed nimbly away. He let her lift into the darkness over the flares before he rolled her out on one wing, looked over the side and saw his markers, two red eyes glowing in the rail yards.

Shannon dived in the same way and put his markers within a hundred yards of Cheshire's. Kearns did likewise. Cheshire called the 617 Lancasters, told them to back up, and minutes later their clusters of incendiaries splashed into brightness on the rail yards.

It was the spearhead that Bomber Command had never had over Munich ; even the giant flashes from the 8,000-pounders and the coils of smoke soon rolling over the rail yards did not hide the pin-points of the markers, and the bomb aimers made the most of it.

The destruction was not all on one side. Cheshire several times saw the trails of flame, like shooting stars, streaking for the ground and the explosions when they hit. It was the flak that caused most of them. Nearly all the fighters had been sent to Karlsruhe or down to Milan, and few had enough petrol to fly back to Munich.

Petrol shortage or not, Cheshire flew full throttle round and round the inner city at 1,000 feet, checking the accuracy and ready to call up with new instructions if the bombing looked like moving off the target area. The gunners below could hear him and the searchlights and flak chased him, but the Mosquito was too fleet. Once a beam held him for a second and destroyed his night vision, but he was too fast to hold low down and passed into darkness again. Light flak ex-

ploded around him ; he heard the crack of the shells and the
aircraft shook from near misses. A dozen lumps of shrapnel
gashed it and hit the engines but hurt no vital spot.

Satisfied he could do no more he turned for home ; the
other Mosquitoes were already on their way. It was not a
happy trip back ; no flak or fighters to speak of, but Kelly
doing intricate petrol calculations, thumbing the fuel gauge,
plotting his track and e.t.a., and trying to look philosophical.
It seemed the longest trip they had ever made, and then they
came in over Manston with ten minutes' petrol on the
gauges. Some gauges on low tanks are as reliable as a woman's
intuition. They might have petrol for ten minutes, or fifteen
minutes, or ten seconds, and were going to need at least five
minutes for approach, circuit and landing.

Throttled right back in coarse pitch, Cheshire flicked his
navigation lights on and dipped his nose towards the long
runway, where the flarepath shone like a stolid but comforting
guard of honour. Kelly said : " What's wrong with their
runway ? Look at those funny lights down there." Cheshire
looked . . . puzzled. There *were* lights blinking in and out
of the flarepath. " Funny," he said. It hit him suddenly
and he shouted to Kelly, " Turn those bloody navigation
lights off. It's a Jerry fighter."

The target, they found out later, was Gerry Fawke, just
settling down on the runway. The fighter had stalked him
round the circuit and gone for the kill when Fawke had his
flaps, undercart and speed right down and was helpless, unable
to turn sharply—unless he wanted to stall and spin in. Luck,
it seemed, stayed with 617 that night. The German fighter,
with a " sitter " in front of his guns, missed completely.
Fawke rolled to a stop and the flarepath flicked off. Cheshire
made a careful approach, took a quick sight at the last moment
with his landing lights and set his aircraft down safely. In
the briefing room he found the other Mosquito crews. None
had got down with more than fifteen minutes' petrol to spare
(a terrifyingly small margin).

Shannon said, " Wake me at sunrise. I want to see it."

Back at Woodhall later in the morning, they found the
617 Lancasters all back except Cooper. No one ever found

out where Cooper went down. Cochrane flew over, showing
what was, for him, extravagant delight, a wide but faintly
embarrassed smile, as he congratulated and thanked them.
He said to Cheshire, " You might like to look at this." It
was an aerial photograph of Munich, brought back by recce
Mosquito an hour earlier. Round a couple of scars on the
outskirts were circles of ink, and Cochrane tapped the spots
with his finger. " That's how it was up to yesterday afternoon
after all the other raids." He put his finger on the cratered
rail yards. " Last night," Cochrane said. " It seems to
justify us."

The photograph staggered even Cheshire, who knew what
the bombing had been like. There must have been a hundred
times more damage in that one raid than the dozen previous
ones, especially as the previous damage had been on no
significant target. This time they had struck an effective
blow.

It proved Cheshire's contention that he could mark a
heavily defended target at low level without undue risk, but
the photograph also showed that one solitary marker from
the high force had fallen outside the target area and drawn
some of the bombs, so that a lot of houses were either gutted
shells or mounds of rubble. Unfortunate though that was,
it led to further improvement in the marking technique.
Cochrane and Cheshire had both thought it too dangerous
to rely on one marker only, since it might be obscured by
smoke or hit by a bomb. Now they realised that dropping
too many markers could also be risky, and thereafter they
tended to cut the number of markers down to try and eliminate
such accidents as the one stray marker at Munich.

Many ordinary people probably died in those crumbled
houses, and the post-war domestic moralists, whose virtue
increases as the memories of Nazism recede, are likely to
point the accusing finger. Most will probably keep pointing
it until, Heaven help us, another war starts and their virtue
will become tempered by the slightly more powerful instinct
of self-survival. A few will continue to point the finger with
wistful idealism until one day, perhaps, morals and the
practical affairs of man become compatible.

On the strength of Munich, Cochrane drove down to see Harris and asked for four extra Mosquitoes so that another of his squadrons could learn the 617 way of target marking.

Harris, who never did things by halves, said, " Not four Mosquitoes, Cocky " ; and almost before Cochrane could feel his disappointment Harris went on, " I'm sending you a squadron of Mosquitoes from Pathfinders and two Pathfinder Lancaster squadrons. You can operate as a group by yourselves now. Get 617 to teach the new Mosquitoes low marking, and then they can mark for your group, with the two Lanc. squadrons as flare force. That'll release 617 for some special jobs."

CHAPTER XV

EARTHQUAKE BOMB

COCHRANE sent for Cheshire and took him walking in the grounds of headquarters away from listening ears.

" You'll be doing no more operations for a month," he said, " and then you'll be doing a very special one. You'll spend the next month training for it. I warn you now it's going to be dull training, but it may be the most important job you've done. You will have to fly more accurately and carefully than you've ever imagined."

He would say no more, but next day a scientist, Dr. Cockburn, arrived at Woodhall from London and also took Cheshire walking. They lay alone on the grass by the airfield, obviously for privacy, and the imaginative Cheshire was highly intrigued by the " cloak and dagger " atmosphere. Cockburn said : " I understand you can be trusted to keep your mouth shut, so I'm going to tell you something a lot of Cabinet Ministers and generals don't know yet. You know by now an invasion is coming off very soon. If the weather is right it will be in about a month, and landings will be made west of Le Havre. We want to fool the Germans we're going in somewhere else."

Cheshire waited.

" On that night," Cockburn went on, " there's going to be a big convoy fourteen miles wide passing across the Channel at seven knots.

" Sounds a pretty big invasion," Cheshire said.

" That isn't the invasion. They'll be heading towards Cap d'Antifer, on the other side of Le Havre."

" A diversion ! "

" Yes."

" I must say," Cheshire said, " it sounds a pretty big diversion. Have they got all those ships to spare ? "

" No. They won't be ships. They'll be you and your boys."

Cheshire rolled over and looked at him. " Us ! " he said

blankly and then got the glimmerings of an idea. " Dropping window ? "

" That's it," said Cockburn. " It's going to need the most precise flying you've ever done. Can you do this . . . can you all fly in a very wide formation, invisible to each other, and do a lot of intricate manœuvring, keeping within three seconds of all your e.t.a.'s and within twenty feet of your height."

" My god ! I don't know. Doesn't sound very possible."

" It'll have to go on for hours and hours," Cockburn said, " so you'll do it in two waves. Eight aircraft for a few hours and then the second eight taking over from them." He went on to explain the technique : lines of aircraft a set distance apart, flying precise courses at precise speeds and height, throwing out window at intervals of a precise number of seconds. The planes would fly thirty-five seconds on course, turn evenly, fly a reverse course for thirty-two seconds, a slow turn again back to the first course and start throwing out more window. They would thus start the original course again at a point slightly ahead of where the previous one started and the first of the new lot of window would drop from the aircraft at the moment that the first bundle dropped on the previous leg hit the water, so there would be no interruption of the steady blips on German radar. It would go on like that for eight hours, timed to give an effect of a large convoy several rows of ships deep moving at seven knots towards the French coast.

" We've got the theory worked out," Cockburn said at the end. " Are you good enough to do it ? "

Cheshire said, " I think my crews are good enough for anything, but I don't think they're going to be happy doing a stooge job on invasion night."

" It so happens," Cockburn said, " that there'll be no flying job more important than this on that night. You might tell them that. The fact that they may not be fired at is beside the point."

The training never let up except for one day when the weather closed in. Otherwise there was no moment, night or day, in the next month when some 617 aircraft were not flying, particularly by night, cruising at a steady 200 m.p.h.

on a steady course and height, curving in even turns to reverse courses, turning back on the stop watch, unspectacular, tedious and demanding meticulous care and skill. Understandably the crews, with the uninhibited sap of youth running in them, became restless, and Cheshire, bubbling as ever with ideas, evolved schemes to occupy them. The first was a route march that left them limp and protesting.

Next, from the Commandos, he got the idea of an escape exercise so that, if they were ever shot down and got away with their lives, they would have a few clues about getting back through hostile territory. It was a Sunday afternoon when he lined up all the crews who were not flying, took away their hats and all their money, packed them in covered vans so they could not see outside and drove them to different spots twenty miles from the airfield. He warned them that the Home Guard and police had turned out with orders to nab any airmen without hats, and promised every one who got back safely a bottle of beer. So the game started.

Some cut across the fields to walk, some stole bikes to pedal, some hitched lifts in lorries. The police and Home Guard nailed at least half of them and there were some thrilling chases across country. One man, running from the Home Guard, fell into a canal ; another, caught by a policeman, entered a little too warmly into the spirit of the thing and laid the constable out with a sizzling punch. After that the police entered more warmly into the spirit of things too, and locked six of them up for the night.

Nicky Knilans and his team had the best idea ; they hitched a lift to the White Horse pub., where they were known to the point of affectionate notoriety, borrowed money from the publican and drank ale till closing time, whereupon they borrowed their bus fare home. Police stopped the bus, so they jumped off the back, took to the woods and straggled home hours later to demand their prize beer.

With only monotonous training instead of ops. at night the tension had relaxed and the mess became almost a home from home. Cheshire's ex-film star wife, Constance Binney, was a cheerful influence ; she played the piano beautifully, and after dinner the crews clustered round and sang.

Several dogs haunted the mess, and one Scottie used to jump out from dark doorways and snap at passing ankles. It became a favourite trick among the boys to imitate the Scottie. Nicky Knilans saw McCarthy coming up the stairs one day, so he got down on his knees in a dark doorway and waited. He heard the footsteps clumping along the hall and as the legs appeared leapt out with a growl and grabbed the nearest ankle in his teeth, looked up with a grin . . . and the grin faded. McCarthy had turned off into a room and Knilans saw a strange wing commander looking down at him blankly. The wing commander shook his head and walked on, all his views on Americans fully confirmed.

They all sensed the invasion was drawing near; Cheshire had the idea that the Germans might drop paratroops on British airfields on D-Day, so he persuaded Doc Watson's armament section to issue as many aircrew as they could with either a revolver, Sten gun, rifle or hand grenade. It was one of his few sad mistakes. For three days life was a precarious possession at Woodhall. First they set dinner plates up on the lawn near the mess and loosed off at them with Sten guns from the second-floor windows. That palled after a while, so they started lobbing hand grenades in the general direction of the sergeants' mess. At night time Buckley became a terrible menace, keeping a vigil by his bedroom window and loosing off clips from his Sten gun over the heads of late home-comers so that they had to crawl to bed over the back lawn on their bellies.

Even Witherick, who was known to be too durable for death by any of the known methods of war, commented uncomfortably, " Hell, the only time you're safe on this damn squadron is when you're in the air ! " It became obvious that German paratroops were less of a menace than the local aircrew army, so Cheshire collected all the weapons and returned them to the armoury. Peace descended once more on the mess, to the regret of Shannon and McCarthy. Shannon and McCarthy were rarely seen apart ; they drank together and dined together and it was logical, therefore, that they should act together to revive the reign of terror, climbing to the roof of squadron headquarters to drop a Véry cartridge down the adjutant's chimney. They knew the innocent Humphries had a fire in the grate.

A Véry cartridge in artful hands is like a semi-lethal firework ; exploding in a confined space it resembles a small but concentrated bombing raid, providing a monstrous crash, sheets of coloured flame and clouds of choking smoke. Half the beauty of the thing is that it goes on for about fifteen seconds. They dropped it down the chimney and started laughing as the waves of sound came rocking up from below.

Unfortunately it was not Humphries' chimney, but the commanding officer's. Cheshire scuttled out, pursued by flashes and rolling fumes, ran on to the tarmac and spotted his two flight commanders hiding behind a chimney. With aristocratic dignity he said nothing but for several nights Shannon and McCarthy found themselves doing duty officer together, an irksome task which kept them out of their beds and abstemiously patrolling the station buildings.

Throwing Véry cartridges into the mess fire had long been a favourite sport, so Cheshire thought it time to issue a stern order that no firearms, cartridges or pyrotechnics of any kind be brought into the mess building.

He was woken that night by a scuttling outside his window, threw it wide open and saw a rat running across the roof. Quick as lightning he grabbed his own .38 revolver from his dressing-table and took a pot-shot that bowled the rat over and echoed through the quiet night like a small cannon. Cheshire was still leaning out of his window, revolver in hand, when the next window shot open and the head of Danny Walker poked out. " Got the dirty rat that time," Cheshire said triumphantly and became conscious of Walker's eyes staring coldly, focusing on the hand that held the gun. He felt his face going red and ducked inside, laying the pistol down, and heard Walker's voice next door, talking loudly to a mythical room-mate, " But I tell you, old boy, I distinctly heard the man say that *no* one under *any* circumstances was to have a firearm inside the mess."

On June 1 Avro experts fitted new automatic pilots in the Lancasters for the D-Day operation, and Nicky Knilans at last found out why his much-cursed " R Roger " flew like a lump of lead. They found it needed longer elevator cables than the others, inspected to find out why and discovered that the elevators had been put on upside down at the factory.

Knilans had been flying it for months like that and, as Cheshire said, " Only you and God, Nicky, know how you stayed up."

" Not me, sirrrr," Knilans said in his American drawl . . . " Only God. I didn't know."

At any rate he was very relieved, but not so much as his crew. " R Roger " had so often frightened them.

On June 5 everyone was confined to camp, and at dusk, with guards on the doors of the briefing room, Cheshire told the crews that the invasion was about to start. The first wave of eight planes took off about 11 p.m. with twelve men in each aircraft, an extra pilot, extra navigator and three men to drop the bundles of window out.

They made absolutely no mistakes that night, though it would have taken an error of only four seconds in timing to make the convoy suspiciously change position on the German radar. Hour after hour they flew in the blackness over the Channel, turning on stop-watches up and down on reversed courses while the window was tossed out at four-second intervals. Round 3 a.m. the second wave of eight aircraft took over, the trickiest part of all because they had to come in directly behind with split-second timing to carry on. They saw nothing of the invasion.

They were to break away just before dawn, before the light was good enough for the Germans to see from the shore that they had been tricked. By that time they should be within seven miles of the French coast, and that is exactly where they were. Farther north another squadron was doing a similar task with at least as much success.

They had their reward as they turned for home ; the German coastal batteries opened up . . . not the flak but the big guns, aiming 12-inch shells by radar prediction at the ghost armada. German E-boats came out from Calais and Boulogne but they would have needed aerial torpedoes to do any damage.

It is history now that the Germans really thought the main invasion was aiming at that area. (In prison camp in the heart of Germany that day, I heard the German radio announcing two huge armadas heading in towards Cap d'Antifer and Calais. It gave us great joy, but we wondered for months what had happened to those convoys.)

Inland from Boulogne and Dieppe the bulk of the German Army, which should have been hurrying to the real invasion area on the other side of Le Havre, waited . . . and waited, poised to swoop on the armadas that were not there. By the time the Germans woke up to it other squadrons had blasted bridges over the Seine between them and the invasion and the Allied troops were consolidating their landings with greater freedom from counter-attack than they had dreamed possible.

Cheshire was driving round the perimeter track with Munro that evening for no particular reason that he can remember, and just past the A Flight hardstandings they passed a huge tarpaulin-covered lorry cruising slowly along.

" What's that doing here ? " Munro murmured, not very curiously, and Cheshire, his head still full of D-Day precautions, said, " Lord knows. Let's find out."

They drove across the lorry's bows ; it stopped and they climbed out of their jeep and went back to the lorry driver. " What have you got in there ? " Cheshire asked.

" Boilers for the cookhouse, sir," the driver said.

" Aren't you going the wrong way? The cookhouse is over there," Cheshire waved a hand to the rear.

" Well I dunno, sir. They told me to deliver them over there." The driver pointed to the far side of the field.

" The bomb dump ! That's the bomb dump. Who told you that? " A suspicious edge had crept into Cheshire's voice.

" That's what they told me, sir."

Cheshire said, " Let's have a look at this, Les. Something funny here." He heaved himself over the tailboard of the lorry. Another tarpaulin covered a shapeless bulk in the back ; he tugged a corner clear and, unbidden, a grunt of surprise came out of him. " My God," he said, " look at these ! "

Lashed to the floor were two shining steel monsters. They were like sharks, slim, streamlined and with sharp noses. " Bombs," Cheshire said, almost in awe. " Wallis's ' tall-boys '."

They followed the lorry to the bomb dump and were staggered to find the dump nearly full of " tallboys," snugged down under tarpaulins. An armament officer said apologetically, " They've been coming in at night time for the past week, sir. I was told to keep quiet about them."

Cheshire tore back to his office, got Cochrane at Group on the secret scrambled phone and told him he had just been inspecting " the new boilers for the cookhouse in the bomb dump." He heard what sounded like the ghost of muted amusement in Cochrane's voice :

" Just see they're safely in storage, Cheshire. You'll be using them soon."

The call came without warning forty-eight hours later. Intelligence had reported a German panzer division moving up from Bordeaux by rail to attack the invasion. The trains would have to pass through the Saumur Tunnel, near the Loire, over a hundred miles inland, and in the late afternoon Harris suggested to Cochrane that they might have a chance of blocking the tunnel before the trains reached it. They would have to move fast ; it would be nightfall before bombers could reach the spot, and a tunnel on a dark night would be an elusive pin-point of a target. Only one squadron could do it ; that was obvious. And probably only one type of bomb !

Cheshire got the order about 5 p.m. to take off as soon as they could, and there was a mad rush to collect everyone (Shannon and Munro, for instance, were playing cricket at Metheringham), trolley the " tallboys " out of the dump and winch them up into the bomb bays. They were airborne soon after dusk, and it was shortly after midnight that Cheshire, in his Mosquito, dropped flares by a bend of the river and saw where the rails vanished into the tunnel that led under the Saumur hill.

He dive-bombed from 3,000 feet, aimed his red spots

point blank, and as he pulled up from about a hundred feet saw them lying beautifully in the tunnel mouth. Ninety seconds later the Lancasters were steady on their bombing runs, and a couple of minutes later the first earthquake bombs ever dropped on business were streaking down.

Ten thousand feet above, the crews felt disappointed. The "tallboys" did not make a splash of brilliant light like the blockbusters but showed only momentary red pin-points as they speared into the earth and exploded nearly a hundred feet deep. The little flashes they made were all round the markers but the crews turned for home with a feeling of anti-climax, and it was not till the recce Mosquito landed next morning with photographs that the impact of what they had done hit them. With one exception the fantastic craters were round the tunnel mouth, two of them in a line along the rails as though giant bites a hundred feet across and seventy feet deep had been torn out of the track bed.

But what really staggered everyone was the bomb that had fallen on the hill 60 yards from the tunnel mouth. No one ever found out whose bomb it was, which is a pity, because some bomb aimer would have received an instant decoration (though the credit should really go to Barnes Wallis). The hill rose steeply from the tunnel mouth, and under the spot where this bomb hit lay 70 feet of solid earth and chalk down to the tunnel. The bomb had bored straight through it into the tunnel itself and exploded there. Something like 10,000 tons of earth and chalk were blown sky-high and the mountain collapsed into the tunnel. It was one of the most startling direct hits of all time.

The panzer division did not get through. It was several days before dribs and drabs of them started to reach the invasion front on other transport, but by then it was too late for the decisive counter-attack they were supposed to have made. The morning after the raid the Germans collected all the excavation gear in the district and slaved for weeks clearing the tunnel, filling in the craters and laying new rails. They just had it nicely finished when the Allies broke out of their bridgehead and took it over. (They found then that only one "tallboy" had fallen outside the target area . . . it had exploded among a group of very old Frenchmen and blown them to smithereens, but no one else was upset, because they had been there a long time, lying several feet deep in a cemetery.)

The morning after the Saumur raid a high officer from Bomber Command burst into Sir Wilfred Freeman's office waving a recce photograph of the smashed tunnel.

" My God," he yelled, " why haven't we been able to use this incredible thing before? How many more of them have we got? "

" None for you, I'm afraid," said a Vicker's executive who happened to be in the room, and the high officer looked at him open-mouthed.

" What'd you mean? "

" Well, we've got some more, but they're all ours. None for you."

" What *are* you talking about? "

" Your boys have never given us a Requirement Order for them, so we had to make them on spec. They all belong to us."

" I see," said the High Bomber Officer. " We'll fix this Requirement Order business right away." He crossed to the desk, picked up the phone and the Requirement Order was delivered that afternoon.

In the nights that followed the invasion, German E-boats sneaking out of Le Havre caused death and destruction among the convoys ferrying men and guns over to Normandy. The darkness that covered the convoys from the Luftwaffe also hid the speeding E-boats that weaved among the landing craft, loosed their torpedoes and vanished. By day they sheltered in the concrete pens at Le Havre, and around dusk they slid out of the pens and gathered in the harbour, preparing for the night's forays. Cochrane thought that, if the " tallboys " could make an earthquake on land, they might just as easily make a tidal wave in water. Wallis promised him they would, and so as soon as the weather cleared, on June 14, 617 flew over at dusk to Le Havre on the second 'tallboy" raid. Some 400 more Lancasters of 1 and 5 Groups followed them, loaded up with 1,000-lb. bombs.

Cheshire, in his Mosquito, whipped round the harbour area at 3,000 feet, saw the dozens of E-boats lined up, and as he peeled off in a dive-bombing attack the flak came up in streams. He'd never seen flak like it. In the dusk it looked like green and red bubbles rising in shaken soda-water. The air was full of rushing tracer and he knew that that was not even the half of it . . . only a quarter. One in four of the light flak shells were tracer ; the rest were rushing with them, but not visible. Two miles outside the harbour the other Mosquitoes saw him diving into the beaded curtain of red and green and thought he had no chance. At about 700 feet (as he let his markers go) they saw the nose start to come up. The little Mosquito flattened low over the water, holed half a dozen times already, and Cheshire held her straight, heading out to sea, relying on speed alone to beat the guns. A minute later he was back to 3,000 feet and out of range. On the quay, by the lines of E-boats, the red markers were winking clearly.

Shannon, deputy marker, who had seen the flak like a wall of flame, called up : " Hello, Leader, shall I go in and back up ? "

Sitting beside and slightly behind him, Sumpter picked a heavy torch out of its stowage, held it over Shannon's head and muttered, " God, David, if he says yes, I'll brain you ! We can die more peacefully out here."

A few seconds dragged while Cheshire looked again at his markers and called back, " No, David ; they'll do," and ordered the Lancasters circling a few miles away, at 12,000 feet, to head in.

Fifteen " tallboys " dropped almost together into the water by the pens and then the 400 other Lancasters moved in and the harbour vanished under smoke.

When the recce photographs came back in the morning even Wallis was staggered. Not one E-boat was left afloat in Le Havre. Two were still visible, thrown bodily up on to the quay, and the rest were swallowed in the maelstrom of water torn apart by the " tallboys " and then by the smaller bombs. (For a time they thought that some may have slunk out of the harbour that night to a safer port, but weeks after, when the British took Le Havre, they found that none had escaped.) The crashing water had even smashed through the doors of the pens and destroyed any chance of shelter in them. In fact, three of the " tallboys " had been direct hits on the pens, bored through the concrete and wrecked the neat little quays inside.

Next night the squadron went to repeat the dose at Boulogne, also a troublesome E-boat base. Thick cloud hung over the port with heavy flak bursting through it. Cheshire marked alone (his Mosquito newly patched from last night's damage), but the crews above found it nearly impossible to draw a bead on them. About ten were able to drop their " tallboys " without being able to see results, and the remaining ten brought their bombs back. (Cochrane had made a strict order that no " tallboys " were to be wasted. Crews were never to jettison them except in extreme emergency. If they could not see their target reasonably clearly they must bring their " tallboys " back. Landing an aircraft with a 6-ton bomb on board is not as difficult as it sounds.)

We know now that in these two raids on Le Havre and Boulogne 133 small ships (mostly E-boats) were sunk. As Harris said the morning after Boulogne in his message of thanks to Cheshire and his squadron, " If the Navy had done what you have done it would have been a major naval victory."

That was the morning the V1 " buzz-bombs " started to fall on London. The V2 rockets would follow soon. . . . Intelligence was sure of that.

CHAPTER XVI

SMASHING THE SECRET WEAPON

CHESHIRE had only tumbled into bed at 5 a.m. after the Boulogne raid, and was dragged out of sleep at 9 a.m. to find his batman tugging at his shoulder.

" Phone, sir."

He took up the phone and heard the Base Intelligence Officer's voice : " Can you please come over to the ops. room right away. It's urgent, sir."

He was there in ten minutes, and the intelligence officer greeted him with a few words that shook the last of the tiredness out of him : " The secret weapon has started, sir. They're landing missiles on London and the invasion ports. Don't know how serious it is yet, but you're to stand by to take off as soon as the weather clears. This is your target," he passed over an aerial photograph, an enlargement that showed an enormous square concrete building. " We don't know how thick the concrete is," the intelligence officer was saying, " but as far as we can gather from agents over there it might be up to twenty feet thick . . . roof as well as the walls. It's near a place called Watten, just behind the Pas de Calais."

Air Commodore Sharp, the base commander, bustled in. " You know about these from the A.O.C.," he said. " I gather the rest of Bomber Command is cracking at the mobile sites, but they think the worst trouble will come from these four blockhouses, and your " tallboys " are the only things with a hope of touching them. You'll have to go in daylight to see your aiming points properly and mark them with smoke bombs. We'll give you fighter cover."

Cochrane had a word with him over the phone a little later, brief and to the point : " We've got to knock these out somehow, and we'll have to go on until we do. Whitehall is all set for the evacuation of London and we don't know yet whether these things might wreck the invasion. You'll have to work hard."

To lay on a raid, plan it, brief the crew, bomb and fuel the aircraft took at least two hours. This time it was more difficult, because the " tallboys " needed special handling, but they did it inside two hours that morning. The crews were briefed and they all went down to the flights, pulled on their flying kit and waited. Over the Pas de Calais a sheet of ten-tenths stratus stretched for miles at 2,000 feet, making it impossible to bomb. They could not have seen any aiming point from above, and they would have to bomb from at least 15,000 feet for penetration. The idea was to get near misses as much as direct hits. A direct hit might not pierce the concrete roof, but near misses would bore into the earth by the foundations and shake the structure with earthquakes. Wallis thought that a near miss up to 40 yards away would do more damage than a direct hit. The concrete monster at Watten was not the great primary source of power that Wallis had at first visualised for his earthquake bomb, but, fortuitously, it was an even more important target.

The crews stood by all day at the flights. Lorries brought food and coffee from the mess for them, and over the radio they heard the grim reports of the flying bombs falling on London. But the cloud stayed over the Pas de Calais, over Watten and the other concrete rocket sites.

At eleven o'clock they were released but no sooner had they climbed into bed than they were called up again, pulled on their clothes and rushed down to the flights. Before they had their kit on the raid was cancelled once more. Back to bed . . . and at 4 a.m. called out again. A cup of tea and down to the flights and then it was cancelled again. They went back to bed and were called at 7 a.m. Down to the flights once more. Met. thought the cloud might be clearing.

It did not clear but the crews stood by all day, lying on the grass by the tarmac waiting for the call, but the call never came. It went on for three days like that till bed was only a memory. They lived down on the flights while the low cloud lingered over France and the buzz-bombs kept falling, ate cold food brought from the mess and tried to sleep curled up in blankets on the floors.

The eighteen Lancasters bombed-up on the hardstandings

brought another complication. Under the load of petrol and bombs the undercarriages began to sink. The bombs would have to come off, at least temporarily. But it would take hours to bomb up again and they could not afford the time if the weather cleared briefly. Cheshire had them de-bombed on a rota system so that at any one time only two or three aircraft were without bombs. As soon as their undercarts had been relieved they winched the bombs up into them again and gave temporary relief to other aircraft.

On the morning of the third day, exhausted, they were stood down and went off to bed, and in the early afternoon the clouds over France rolled away. From Group came the instant call ordering a " time on target " which gave them a bare ninety minutes to get airborne.

No one at Woodhall will easily forget that hour and a half of mad rush. In the middle of it Cheshire was in the ops. room settling the hundred and one final details inseparable from a raid—time and place of fighter rendezvous, bomber marshalling point, codes and so on—when a young pilot officer rushed in and said that a headquarters group captain wanted to see him immediately outside. " Ask him if he'll please excuse me just now. I'm terribly busy," Cheshire said. The P/O. rushed outside and was back again in a few seconds. " He says he's sorry, sir, but it's most important. You *must* come."

Cheshire groaned, " What the hell's happened now ? " and dashed out, thinking it was another cancellation.

The group captain was waiting on the grass verge. He had just arrived and had not heard about the raid. Cheshire saluted and the group captain looked a little severely at him. " Do you realise, Cheshire, that your squadron is last in the Group war savings scheme ? " he said. " I'm very concerned and you've got to do something about it immediately."

Cheshire looked blankly at him.

" Yes, sir, I'll do something right away," saluted and was running back to the ops. room before the group captain could stop him. By some sort of miracle the eighteen Lancasters, headed by two Mosquitoes, were climbing away from Woodhall on the scheduled minute.

Cheshire flew over Calais at 8,000 feet and searched the area for several minutes before he was able to pin-point the camouflaged mass of concrete in the ground haze. The earth for a mile around was torn up by the fruitless bombs of other raids, so that nothing stood out clearly. As he flew over it seventy guns opened up and black puffs stained the air all round him. He felt reluctantly that there was only one thing to do : ten miles away he peeled off, held the nose steeply down and came in straight and fast on high power, so the engines were screaming in his ears and the plane shaking like a live thing. He let his smoke bombs go at 2,000 feet (as it was daylight the smoke would show more clearly than red flares), pulled steeply out of the hail of fire, marvellously untouched, looked back and saw no sign of smoke. The markers had failed to ignite.

Shannon dived the other Mosquito in the same way, and as he pulled up smoke puffed on the ground near the target. In the haze it seemed near enough, and there were no markers left anyway, so Cheshire called the Lancasters and saw them wheel in at 18,000 feet, open bomb doors and track stolidly through the flak. Fascinated, he saw the " tallboys " for the first time falling in daylight, the sun glinting off them as they streaked down, picking up speed till they were moving faster than sound, and then they vanished in a wisp of dust in the moment of impact. They had eleven-second delayed fuses and the seconds dragged till the ground burst in the shadow of the concrete and tens of thousands of tons of earth reared up in a climbing mushroom. Cheshire gaped, and beside him, dumbfounded, Kelly muttered, " God help the Jerries ! " The target was hidden.

Recce photos later showed the bombs had circled Shannon's smoke markers, but also showed the markers had been about 70 yards wide. Some of the " tallboys " had fallen some 50 yards from the concrete target and, in the hopes that they had done the job, Cochrane sent 617 next day to Wizernes, where a huge concrete dome, 20 feet thick, lay on the edge of a chalk quarry, protecting rocket stores and launching tunnels that led out of the face of the quarry, pointing towards London.

The squadron reached the spot but found it hidden under cloud and brought their " tallboys " back. Cheshire landed with a new idea forming in his mind. If a Mosquito was better for marking than a Lancaster, then an even smaller and faster aircraft should be better still. He took his idea to Sharp, and the base commander said : " The American fighters have got the range you want. How about a Mustang or a P.38 ? " Cheshire said he thought that either would be ideal, and Sharp promised to try and get one through Air Ministry. He tried for the next two days but Air Ministry did not seem to be able to help, so Sharp said he would fly over to an American base himself and try " off his own bat." He had worked with the Americans before and appreciated their methods of direct action.

Meantime Cheshire took 617 to Wizernes again but once more the cloud hid it. On the 24th they tried again and this time located the camouflaged dome dimly in the ground haze. Cheshire dived through brisk flak but his smoke bombs " hung up," so Fawke dived and laid his markers on the edge of the dome and the bombs fell spectacularly round the markers. Three of them exploded next to the tunnels in the side of the quarry, one sliced deep under the edge of the dome, and Dicky Willsher, who had just had his twentieth birthday, sent one right into the mouth of one of the tunnels. The face of the quarry seemed to burst open.

The flak got Edward's plane on the run-up. A shell exploded in the port wing and the tanks caught fire. The others saw the Lancaster lose height slowly for a few seconds and then the nose dropped into a steep dive and she went over on her back. Two parachutes came out before she hit and the " tallboy " blew up. It was the first crew the squadron had lost for several weeks. Several men had been wounded in the air and a few aircraft written off, but for some weeks death had taken a holiday, the longest holiday it ever took in the squadron.

Though they were on daylight raids now the squadron did not fly close shoulder-to-shoulder formation as the Americans did. The S.A.B.S. was one reason ; having to fly undeviatingly for ten miles on the run-up would make a close formation a sitting target for the flak. On the run-ups they flew what Cheshire called a " gaggle "—lines of five aircraft abreast, each 200 yards apart and each rank 300 yards behind the one ahead.   Every plane flew at a different height as well, so that, while they were a most dispersed target for the flak, they could converge on the target and bomb almost together.

That had another advantage.   Smoke from the first bombs had often obscured the target from later bomb aimers, but with the gaggle formation the last bombs were on the way down before the first bombs hit.

When he landed back at Woodhall, Cheshire found a Mustang waiting.   Sharp's American friends had promptly said, " Sure," and an American pilot had flown one over. The pilot explained the cockpit to Cheshire, bade him a cheerful farewell and left him inspecting his new toy.   It was only then he began to realise fully what he had taken on.   He had never flown an American aircraft before ; in fact, had not flown a single-engined aircraft since his early training days five years before.   He had never flown a single-engined fighter at all, nor had he had to do his own navigation for years.   The ground crews had their problems too.   For a long time they could not even find where to fill the petrol tanks.

Cheshire decided that before he took it for a practice flip he would try and learn a little more about it, but those prudent hopes crashed in the morning when Cochrane ordered the squadron off for the Siracourt rocket site.   They found then that the smoke markers would not fit in the racks under the Mustang's wings, and the armourers worked like furies rigging a makeshift wire contraption to hold the markers on. One of the navigators helped Cheshire work out his courses, and he wrote them on a piece of paper and strapped it to his knee.   He took off in the Mustang half an hour early to get the feel of it, but did not try any practice landings ; there was too much chance of breaking it on his first landing, and if he was going to do that he preferred it to be after the raid had been done.

It is unlikely that a pilot has ever before or since done an operation—particularly such a specialist one—on his first flight in a new type of plane.   The change in his case from multi-engined to single-engined fighter makes the feat all the more remarkable. It bristled with difficulties. His timing had to be within thirty seconds over the target to co-ordinate with the bombers, and the Mustang cruised about 90 m.p.h. faster than the Lancasters. He could not very well work out changes of wind as well as map-read and fly. He had to be his own navigator, bomb aimer, gunner and wireless operator as well as learn to fly a new type well enough in an hour to be able to dive-bomb through thick flak.

From the start the Mustang delighted him and inside half an hour he felt he had the " feel " of it. She was lighter than the Mosquito and there was no comparison at all with a Lancaster. From 7,000 feet he spotted the concrete slab that protected the underground Siracourt rocket dump, and when the bombers reached marshalling point he dived to 500 feet, revelling in the way the Mustang picked up speed, and put his smoke bombs within a few feet of the concrete. Someone put a " tallboy " through the middle of the slab, and it pierced 16 feet of ferro-concrete before it exploded. Another hit the western wall and blew it in, and another erupted deep under the rim of the slab.

Night had fallen when they got back from Siracourt, and Cheshire's first Mustang landing had to be a night landing, which makes it about twice as difficult. He remembers little about it (in the same way that a man who bales out never remembers pulling the rip-cord) except that suddenly the little fighter was rolling smoothly on the runway, to his mild surprise and relief.

(If 617's bombing seems monotonously " dead-eye " remember that they dropped them at nearly 200 m.p.h., 18,000 feet up and several miles back from the little squares of concrete that merged with the earth and were usually unseen by the bomb aimer. From that height and distance even the white square on a bombing range looks the size of a pin-head. Cheshire's smoke bombs were as good an aiming point as possible, but usually the ground haze veiled the smoke. No other squadron could have done it.)

Grey cloud still hung over the Pas de Calais ; it was forming over the North Sea and blowing over the land, and

The *Tirpitz* lying capsized in Tromso Fiord.   Alongside her are salvage vessels.

Above : A ten-ton " Grand Slam " being taken from the bomb dump.

Below : The Bielefeld Viaduct, showing the flooded craters made by the months of
futile bombing and, in the shadow of the viaduct, the huge crater made by
the first " Grand Slam," which brought it down.

617 stood by at dawn every day waiting for it to lift while the buzz-bombs fell on London. To the south the invasion was locked in the bridgehead, and even if they broke out the Seine still barred the way to the rocket sites. In London the nation's leaders (though not the unaware people) waited anxiously in case the mystery sites should start up. They guessed they must be nearly ready.

Several times the crews ran to the aircraft, and once actually took off, but the cancellation came instantly. The raids a squadron did never reflected the ordeal behind them, the nerve-fraying sequence of briefing every morning about 5 a.m., followed by postponement, by stand-by, ready to take off when the order came, never knowing if one would still be alive by nightfall. And then the dusk would come, bringing release till 5 o'clock the next morning. It went on like that day after day, not only at this time but all through the war for every squadron. Often they took off and battled through the flak and fighters only to find the target lost under cloud, so that they had to bring their bombs back, to be ready at dawn next day.

Cheshire had done ninety-eight raids now. At the ruling casualty rate he was living strictly on borrowed time. Statistically he should have been killed for certain four times. Arthur Pollen, the Woodhall intelligence officer, asked him how he felt about it, and Cheshire answered, " You don't feel the strain, Arthur. You keep on going more or less automatically and don't worry." Pollen noticed as he was talking that Cheshire's right eye was twitching, but Cheshire was not aware of it.

At last, on July 4, the weather cleared. Not a moment too soon. London was taking a beating. As the clouds rolled away over France 617 took off to hit back, target this time being the big store of rockets and buzz-bombs hidden in a cave at Creil, near Paris. It ran deep under a hill—at least 25 feet of chalk and clay over it—and the idea was both to collapse it and seal it up. Fawke went ahead in a Mosquito to get weather and wind information in advance. Cheshire flew his now beloved Mustang, and seventeen Lancasters carried the " tallboys."

Cheshire dived to 200 feet and aimed his markers so accurately that Fawke did not have to back up. Several " tallboys " then smashed through the cave roof with great ease ; others collapsed the entrance and wrecked the railway that brought the rockets into the cave.

Next afternoon to Mimoyecques, where the Germans were sinking the fantastic gun barrels 500 feet into the ground to fire 600 tons of explosive a day on London. War Cabinet still did not know this ; they only knew it was one of Hitler's secret-weapon sites. From above it was nearly invisible, a 30 by 20 yards square of camouflaged concrete shielding the gun tunnels beneath.

An hour before dusk Cheshire, in the Mustang, found the spot in the chalk hills behind Calais, dived and lobbed his markers on it. When the " tallboys " came down he saw one direct hit, and four were " very near misses," which were probably more effective.

A message summoning him to Cochrane met him when he landed and he drove straight over to Group. Cochrane said when he walked in : " I've been looking at the records and I see you've done a hundred trips now. That's enough ; it's time you had a rest. I've got hold of Tait to take over." Cheshire opened his mouth to argue and Cochrane said, " It's no use arguing. . . . Sorry, but there it is. A hundred is a good number to stop at.". He went on and thanked him, quietly and with no flowery nonsense, and dropped another bombshell : " Shannon, Munro and McCarthy will come off too. They've been going continuously for about two years and it's time they had a rest as well."

There were, as Cheshire expected, protests from Shannon, Munro and McCarthy, but from that moment they were changed men, gayer, but in a less violent way, and only then he realised that the strain had been telling on his three durable flight commanders. Munro, known so long as " Happy " because he never smiled, became like a small boy, running round the mess cracking puns and laughing at anything.

They had earned a rest ; all of them had D.S.Os., D.F.Cs. and Bars. The squadron gave them a send-off at which one or two (prodded perhaps by alcohol) were near tears, but before the hangovers had subsided Wing Commander Willie Tait had arrived to take over. He put Fawke up to flight commander and brought two veteran pilots, Cockshott and Iveson, as his other lieutenants. Tait was a Welshman, belonging to no recognisable type but with a unique Celtic streak of his own. Smoothly brown-skinned and slim, with straight black hair, he had his own brand of introspection and dry wit. He had a habit sometimes, when he was with you, of saying nothing at all for long stretches of time, standing with his mouth primly pursed, a half can of beer held in extraordinary fashion under his armpit, his arm curled round and the glass caught between his hand and wrist. If he opened his mouth at all it was to stick a large pipe in it and hold it tightly to his mouth with his whole hand clenched over the stem, as though he were trying to hold thoughts inside himself. He was twenty-six, had two D.S.Os. and a D.F.C.

The cloud was back over France, so that for ten days there was no bombing ; a lucky reprieve for the rocket sites, but at least it gave the squadron a chance to settle down under the new leaders, and Tait a chance to learn the marking technique in the Mustang.

On July 17 Met. reported the clouds rolling away, and a couple of hours later 617 was on the way to Wizernes. For this, his first marking effort, Tait flew one of the Mosquitoes with Danny Walker as navigator. Thick haze lay over the ground and they circled a long time in the flak before they could faintly pick up the great blockhouse merging with the torn earth. Tait dived from 7,000 to 500 feet before he let his smoke marker go accurately, and Fawke backed up. A few minutes later both Knights and Kearns got direct hits with " tallboys," and several more " tallboys " sent up awe-inspiring eruptions 40 to 50 yards away, more or less where Wallis preferred them.

More days of waiting for the weather, and on the 20th they went back to Wizernes. Tait, flying the Mustang for the first time on business, found wisps of broken cloud drifting over the area and thick haze on the ground. A lot of flak was coming up ; he dived through it and lobbed his smoke markers, pulled steeply up to 4,000 feet, looked down and could only just see the smoke drifts. Obviously the bombers, miles back at 18,000 feet, would never see it, and so he did an unheard-of thing . . . called up the bombers and said, " Try and aim at me," then dived into the bursting flak directly over the blockhouse and circled it at 1,000 feet, hoping the glinting of his wings would draw the eyes of the bomb aimers to the spot.

The Mustang shook in the shell blasts, and little holes were suddenly appearing in the wings and fuselage as machine-gun bullets and shrapnel punched through. Two bullets went through the petrol tank (which was self-sealing) and just missed the glycol coolant tank (which was not), and even then the bomb aimers did not see him.

They called up on their bombing runs and said they could not identify a thing, and Tait at last swung away out of the flak, an extremely lucky young man to be still airborne and personally unpunctured. The squadron turned and brought their " tallboys " back home.

They waited five more days for the cloud to clear and on the 25th went to Watten, Tait again in the Mustang. Murderous flak came spitting up all round the blockhouse, but this time, for the first time in weeks, there was neither haze nor cloud and in the crystal-clear air the target stood out so clearly that the bomb aimers reported they could see it from miles back, and Tait did not have to mark.

They had half-hour delay fuses on the " tallboys " that day, so they saw no explosions, but as the bombs sliced into the earth puffs of dust shot into the air from the shadow of the blockhouses.

Fawke lingered half an hour near the spot with a camera in his Mosquito and brought back beautiful photographs of the explosions . . . five direct hits and half a dozen very-*very* near misses. The squadron did not escape scot-free. Three aircraft were badly hit by flak, one gunner died, his throat cut by flak, and one aircraft had to jettison its " tallboy " to stay in the air. Harris sent them special congratulations.

Again they waited for the weather and on July 31 flew to deal with a flying-bomb storage dump in a railway tunnel near Rilly La Montagne. Once more the air was crystal clear, no marking was needed and they caved in each entrance to the tunnel with their uncanny accuracy. They lost one of their most distinguished crews this day. F/Lt. Jock Reid had won a V.C. on a previous tour ; a quiet young man, bashful about the red ribbon under his wings. Flak got his Lancaster as they were driving up to the target and only two parachutes came out.

Next day they tried to go back to Siracourt but once more the cloud beat them and they brought their bombs back. Actually it did not matter. The battle of the rocket sites was over. The liberating armies burst out and reached the Pas de Calais area and, as it happened, there was nothing for them to do about the rocket sites except stare in wonder. 617 had destroyed them.

At Watten they found that " tallboys " had smashed the roof and wrecked the building inside so badly that the Germans had abandoned it.

The great rocket assembly and launching site at Wizernes was reduced to rubble. The 10,000-ton dome on top was knocked off its foundations, the launching tunnels below had caved in, and so had most of the maze of galleries where men were to have lived and stored and fired their rockets.

At Creil they found that the deep limestone caves which were to have protected their rockets and buzz-bombs had collapsed for hundreds of yards and buried them instead. Much the same at Rilly La Montagne.

A " tallboy " had gone right through the 16-ft. concrete roof at Siracourt site, exploded beneath it and wrecked it. Near misses had shaken two of the four sides of the lower walls to pieces. The Germans had stopped work on the site to dig deep air-raid trenches and then abandoned the lot.

Most spectacular was the wreckage at Mimoyecques, where the fabulous guns of V3 were to have fired on London. One " tallboy " had ripped a corner off the 20-foot thick concrete roof and completely blocked the left-hand gun shaft. A near miss had collapsed the right-hand shaft and shaken the remaining shaft out of plumb. Five hundred feet down when the bombers came, 300 workers had been sheltering in what they must have thought was complete safety. They are still there, entombed.

Hitler had squandered men and materials to shield his "impregnable" rocket sites, only to find, too late, that for all the fabulous concrete on top his *Festung Europa* had no roof . . . all because a stubborn, white-haired old scientist in 1939 would not believe that the world's experts were right about bombing.

When the first cannon-ball smashed a breach in a castle wall it was not only the stonework that fell ; it also burst the bulwarks of the powerful isolationist barons and was the beginning of the end of the feudal system. And when the first "tallboy" fell on Watten it not only pierced the shield of the secret weapons, but stripped another layer of protection from Germany. Hitler could not, or would not, believe it and tried to build more protection on top. He sent nearly 10,000 workmen to the great U-boat pens at Hamburg, Bremen, Ijmuiden and Bergen to pile more concrete on top. They already had ferro-concrete roofs 16 feet thick, but the Germans wanted to increase this up to 30 feet. After the waste of work on the rocket sites it was an enormous diversion of his war effort.

It was logical that Churchill, Freeman and Harris should send Wallis over to France to see what his "tallboys" had done, with an eye to what they might do in the future. After Churchill, Wallis was probably the first man to go over there as a civilian. He refused to wear uniform. "What's the use of uniform to an old man with white hair like me ? " he said. " Good heavens, I couldn't even stand being tortured ! " So he went in a dirty old raincoat and grey slacks, and an American major wanted to arrest him in France as a spy.

The Calais area had not yet been properly cleared, but Wallis was so fascinated by the great blockhouses and the damage that he pottered about abstractedly, oblivious of the guns going off all round. When he flew home they took him to Harris's office in the trees near High Wycombe, and Harris silently showed him photographs of the workmen swarming over the U-boat pens at Hamburg, Bremen and Ijmuiden. They were enormous pens, some of them 300 feet square and 70 feet high.   It was obvious that they were being further strengthened.   Agents' reports confirmed this.

" Looks as though we're going to have some more substantial targets," Harris said.   " After what you've seen of the rocket sites, do you think a 'tallboy' could cope with these ? "

" I think one or two ' tallboys ' broke up on the concrete," Wallis said.   " If we're going to have something still bigger to deal with, I think we should throw something bigger at them."   He added artlessly, " Something like a ten-tonner. I've been suggesting a ten-tonner for some time now, and I believe the Lancaster has developed enough to carry it into Germany."

Harris looked at him.   He said after a while, " Mr. Wallis, I said once you could sell me a pink elephant.   I think perhaps this time you might at last sell your ten-tonner."

That was a *very* satisfying day in Wallis's life.

CHAPTER XVII

VICTORIA CROSS

617 was a delighted squadron ; not because of the coming 10-ton bomb (they were not told about that yet) but because Leonard Cheshire had just been awarded the V.C. It was the second V.C. to the credit of the newest squadron in the R.A.F., and one of the most remarkable V.Cs. ever awarded.

The citation specified no one act of superb gallantry but listed some of the things he had done : the time a shell had burst inside his aircraft and he had continued on to the target, his volunteering for a second tour as soon as he had finished his first, his third tour, and then his insistence on dropping rank to do a fourth in a " suicide squadron." There was a piece on his part in the Munich raid, when he cruised through the flak over the roof-tops, and it noted that he had done a hundred raids.

A V.C. is often won in a moment of exalted heroism, but there can be no tougher way of winning it than by four years of persistent bravery. It was Cochrane who put Cheshire up for the medal. High commanders sometimes lose touch with the men under them, but the brusque Cochrane, who was always round the Group, never did that, and his crews sensed it. He won their utter faith not by geniality but by hard work and clear thinking to avoid tactical blunders that would have wasted their lives.

The perceptive Cheshire probably saw that more clearly than anyone. I quoted a letter of Cheshire's earlier paying tribute to Micky Martin. There is another part of the letter that reads : " In tracing the evolution of our low-level bombing technique don't under-estimate the contribution of Cochrane. He is the only senior officer with a really clear, unbiased brain that I have met. He followed our course with great attention to detail, was remarkably quick to grasp the fundamentals and was seldom hoodwinked. If I ever asked for anything and he refused, he always gave me clearly his reasons.

" If we ever needed anything we usually got it immediately. I used to think that if I asked him for an elephant I'd get it by return of post. As a matter of fact I once *did* ask him for an elephant because the tractors kept getting bogged in the mud, but the mud dried up and he said we didn't need the elephant then.

" One day I asked him for two Lancasters fitted with nitrogen tanks (a guard against fire) for the leading high-level crews. He hadn't a hope on earth of getting them officially because they were all booked up months in advance by the Pathfinders, who, though they didn't need them as badly as we did, had the highest priority of all. Cochrane merely called up the makers, asked them to let us have the first two that came off the line without letting anyone know, and we got them three days later.

" It was much the same with everything else, and we should have been lost without someone as strong and critical as Cochrane behind us. He is, of course, a strict disciplinarian, ruthless in dealing with inefficiency, and there is no doubt that he was the key figure behind all that 617 achieved."

617 had lost its priority targets now and Cochrane was busy finding new ones of sufficient importance and diminutiveness to merit the " tallboys' " and 617's specialist attention. Tait had been completely accepted by the squadron. An *élite* corps, they had regarded him a little aloofly (after Cheshire and Martin) until he had gone down to circle Wizernes in his Mustang as a personal aiming point for the bombs as well as the flak ; then they went so far as to chide him with fond concern for sticking his neck out so imprudently. Tait, on the other hand, had completely accepted 617, finding in it a rare spirit he had not seen since the first year of the war, before the full impact of it had hit the squadrons. In this fifth year of the war there were few volunteers for rugged ventures. 617 was different. They were all volunteers liable for any dangerous but profitable task.

They bombed a bridge at Etaples with 1,000-pounders (the rocket sites had drawn heavily on " tallboy " supplies), but though they hit the bridge the bombs did little damage to it.

Cut-off German garrisons were fiercely defending the French Atlantic ports of Brest, Lorient and La Pallice, while the Kriegsmarine used the ports as U-boat bases. Cochrane switched 617 on to the massive concrete U-boat pens in those ports, and on June 5 the squadrons bombed the Brest pens in daylight, battling through the heaviest flak they had met for some time to score six direct " tallboy " hits before smoke covered the target.

On the bomb run a salvo of three flak shells slammed into Cheney's Lancaster. The last one exploded in the bomb bay, badly wounded the navigator and wireless operator, and fire broke out in the starboard outer engine. Cheney feathered, pulled the extinguisher and got the aircraft back under control. He asked for a new course, and the navigator, unable to speak, crawled up and pointed out the figures in his log book. Both wounded had lost their oxygen masks, and Cheney pushed the nose down to lose height so they could breathe, and then fire broke out all along the starboard wing. The aircraft was riddled with holes and the end was near. Cheney shouted, " Bale out ! " and held the plane steady while all the crew except himself and the wireless operator got out.

The wireless operator could not move and Cheney tried to trim the aircraft in a slow climb while he went back to help him. Several times he had to scramble back to the controls as the Lancaster fell into a dive, but he finally got the wounded man to the escape hatch, saw that he was conscious and able to pull the rip-cord and pushed him clear. The hatch jammed then, and he sweated and tugged at it while the aircraft plunged down till he forced it open and slipped through himself.

He landed in the sea and after a couple of hours a French fishing boat picked up him and two others, and later they got back to the squadron. No one ever found out what happened to the others.

The day after Brest they went to the U-boat pens at Lorient and scored at least two direct " tallboy " hits and several near misses before smoke blotted them out.

Duffy and his crew of tough Canadians did not go on that

trip. Tait had told them the previous night that they had
finished their tour and were to go on rest, so Duffy took up
his navigator in one of the Mosquitoes for a final local flip.
It was the one that Cheshire had flown to mark on the Munich
raid and it may have been that he strained the mainspar on
that mad dive, because when Duffy was pulling out of a dive
over Wainfleet Sands the starboard wing folded and at about
400 m.p.h. they went many feet deep into the mud.

Duffy's D.F.C. and promotion to flight lieutenant came
through that afternoon.

The weather stayed fine and the squadron worked hard,
averaging a " job " every couple of days. They went back
to plaster the pens at Brest a couple of times and made several
visits to similar targets at Lorient, Bordeaux and La Pallice.

On most of these raids the bombers took off independently
to rendezvous over Hastings and form up into their " gaggle "
at about 18,000 feet. " Baby-face " Willsher had been living
there peacefully a year or so before and used to pick out his
mother's house, stand up in the cockpit and wave out of the
window, yelling, " Hi Mum ! Hullo Mum ! " His mother
must have seen them go over a dozen times, blissfully unaware
that her favourite young man was on his way to the flak and
fighters.

They lost two or three on the raids but morale was high.
Some old crews went (or, rather, were sent) on rest ; new
crews came in, and between raids they all practised hard with
the S.A.B.S. on the bombing range.

Sometimes there were not enough " tallboys " and they
carried 2,000-lb. armour-piercing bombs, but these hardly
chipped the pens. Sir Arthur Harris was constantly demanding more " tallboys," sending for his armament staff officer
and saying to him : " Can you scrape up enough ' tallboys '
by to-morrow for a go at Brest ? " (Or Lorient, or La Pallice,
or wherever it might happen to be.)

The answer too often was : " No. I'm afraid not, sir."

" That's no damn good to me. Go and see Freeman."

Off the armament officer would go to Sir Wilfred Freeman,
who would usually end up by saying, " Tell Bert he can't
have the moon." Back he would go and deliver the message

in diplomatic language, to which Harris would reply with a ferocious grunt.

For one of the raids on La Pallice they could scrape up only seven " tallboys," and the squadron lobbed six of them as direct hits on the pens, getting more congratulations from Cochrane, who said, " You've broken all records."

Wallis had not designed the " tallboy " to go through thick ferro-concrete, but it was such an extraordinary weapon that time and again it did so, even though it never had time to reach its prescribed speed. They usually dropped it from around 18,000 feet instead of 40,000 because the Lancasters could not carry it higher.

The Brest pens had concrete roofs 16 feet thick. One or two of the " tallboys " split on them, but the rest penetrated deep and exploded the rest of the way through, creating chaos in the shelters. After the first raid the Germans tried to repair and strengthen them but a couple more raids taught them that it was no good. The " impregnable " concrete monsters were vulnerable, and that made their French ports too hot for U-boats. Agents sent word to Britain that the U-boats were fleeing from these ports and were not expected back.

The agents also suspected that the Germans planned to sink the old battleship hulk *Gueydon* in the mouth of Brest Harbour so the Allies could never use the port. 617 flew over and dropped 1,000-pounders on her at her old anchorage from three miles up and by evening the old battleship was many fathoms deep.

Wallis's new 10-tonner was coming along as fast as possible, but that was not very fast because it was a far more complicated job, even, than the " tallboy." Freeman had christened it with the code name of " Grand Slam " and delivery date for the first one was roughly February, 1945. Meantime the Americans were starting to produce " tallboys " and were evolving a new (and very efficient) method of making " grand slams."

CHAPTER XVIII

TO RUSSIA

IT might be said that the fate of the battleship was finally sealed in the bath of Air Vice-Marshal the Honourable Ralph Cochrane. In his waking moments work was rarely absent from his mind ; he had been thinking of the *Tirpitz* for a long time, and it was in his bath one morning that he finally made up his mind to get permission for 617 to sink her. He climbed out, dried, dressed and flew down to see Harris, and Harris said yes.

Tirpitz was still in Alten Fiord, in the Arctic Circle, by the northern tip of Norway. Merely lying inside her girdle of torpedo nets she forced the Allies to divert three battleships, badly needed elsewhere, to guard the Russia convoys. The Allies had been trying to " get " her for over two years. First a Russian submarine damaged her ; then British midget submarines put her out of action for six months. Next the Fleet Air Arm hit her, but now she was ready for sea again.

Cochrane flew to Woodhall. " Tait," he said (typical of the man), " you're going to sink the *Tirpitz*." For a while they discussed ways and means. One problem, Cochrane warned, would be the smoke screen round the ship. The Germans had run a pipeline round the shores of the narrow fiord and could pour out smoke by turning a tap. Also there were scores of smoke pots round the ship, and they could smother the fiord under smoke in eight minutes. There would be no time to waste manoeuvring for a bomb run. Tait went over to the mess to have a glass of beer and think about it.

He spread maps on his office floor and measured the distance there and back. It was formidable ; something like 3,000 miles . . . probably beyond range. He loaded three Lancasters with bombs and full petrol and sent off three of the youngest crews (because the maximum range is what the least experienced can do) to fly round England a distance equal to the distance to the target. He sent another plane with half petrol to fly similarly, representing the distance back with a lighter load. When they landed he measured the petrol they had used, and the two ends of the string did not meet. He reported to Cochrane that the *Tirpitz* was just outside their range.

Two days later Cochrane flew over and said, " You can do it from Russia." He put a finger on the map. . . . " Here. Yagodnik." Yagodnik was a Russian airfield on an island in the Dvina River, about twenty miles from Archangel . . . only 600 miles from Alten Fiord. " Fly to Yagodnik from northern Scotland with your bombs," Cochrane said. " Refuel there, do the job, return to Yagodnik to refuel again and come home."

He said there were enough " tallboys " now to send 9 Squadron with them. 9 Squadron could not use the S.A.B.S. but had become nearly as accurate with the Mark XIV bomb sight. Two Liberators would carry ground crews and spares.

The planners worked fast and three days later, on a good weather report, the squadron (carrying their " tallboys ") flew to Lossiemouth, refuelled and in bright sunshine on September 10 took off heavily on the long haul to Russia, laden a ton overweight with petrol and bombs.

At dusk they crossed the Norwegian coast, and as they droned steadily north, nearer the Pole, the magnetic compasses started to play tricks, but luckily the night stayed clear and they were able to pin-point themselves over the fiords and check with the sextants. They crossed the Gulf of Finland and flew on through the night till, in the half-light of an Arctic dawn they turned east for Yagodnik.

Long separated from the others in the night, each plane found itself drifting alone through pale grey cloud. Some Russian had said the cloud had never been below 1,000 feet in twenty-five years, but Tait was at 1,000 feet and could see nothing.

He eased her down gently, but at 500 feet still saw nothing but greyness. They should be over the steppes now ; if so the ground would be flat with no treacherous hills rising in their path. He hoped they were over the steppes.

At 400 feet they saw trees like ghosts through the drifts and some of the strain lifted from the little huddle in the cockpit. They had been sitting there ten hours, silent in the glow of the instruments.

On and on they flew over a flat sea of trees, endless, desolate and remote ; no roads, no towns, not even a track, here and there a small pool of grey water. Otherwise only trees with mist twisting round their trunks. Drizzle blurred the windscreen ; they were flitting in and out of cloud even at 300 feet, and Arthur Ward, the wireless operator, could not raise the Yagodnik radio beacon (none of the others raised it either. It was the wrong kind of beacon).

E.T.A. was up. They should be there now, but still only the trees and less than an hour's petrol. Tait turned south to search. Knowing the compasses and weather might play tricks, they had been relying on that beacon. Worry was hammering at him ; not so much on his own account but for all his other aircraft.

Daniels, the bomb aimer, suddenly shouted that he could see a river through a break in the cloud and Tait slanted the nose down ; they broke into clear air and below was an airfield with a Lancaster landing and two more circling. Five minutes later they were thankfully on the ground and found that only a handful of aircraft had arrived. Including 9 Squadron, there were over twenty more to account for. They walked over to a ramshackle hut on the field, Tait feeling the dread rising in him. None of the missing planes could have more than half-an-hour's petrol. It looked like disaster.

In the next half-hour seven more Lancasters and the two Liberators arrived, the crews dog-tired after twelve hours in the air and marvelling at having made it safely after the past hours of taut nerves.

The moment came when none of the aircraft could still be in the air, and thirteen were still missing. A Russian interpreter came over and said that a Lancaster had landed on an airfield on another island in the river. Five minutes later he reported that four Lancasters were safely there. Then word started coming in from all over the place of Lancasters in various fields a hundred miles around, and in three hours they knew the location of every aircraft.

It was unbelievable. In the wilderness the Russians had traced the aircraft as fast as could be done in England and dropped parachute medical teams and guides to isolated ones. (One parachute guide reached a stranded crew all right, but it was a case of the blind leading the blind because the guide himself got lost for twenty-four hours !) It was equally incredible that there were no casualties, though two 617 aircraft and four of 9 Squadron were written off because they were irretrievable in marshes.

Knilans had been getting ready to crash-land when he came to a small field, and the petrol gauges were on " Zero " when he dropped the plane low over a fence and, with brakes hard on, pulled up inches short of the trees. Minutes later Iveson droned into sight and landed safely in the same field. Wyness and Ross crash-landed in marshland. Flak hit Carey's plane badly over Finland, but Gerry Witherick nailed one of the gunners before they were out of range and they reached Yagodnik, where they riveted patches over the holes.

The Russians lodged all the sergeants in underground huts and escorted the officers over a gangplank to a houseboat where a banner flapped, bearing the words, " Welcome to the glorious flyers of the R.A.F." " Cor," said Witherick, " what a line ! " Otherwise there were no social distinctions. Both huts and houseboat crawled with bugs and had the same musty smell of drains and lavatories. While the well-warned crews sprayed their quarters with Keatings and tried to prise the windows open, Tait stood by to fly to Iveson and Knilans. A Russian pilot took him to an antique biplane, and Tait flinched when he saw two mongoloid Russians hitting the engine with a hammer ; they stopped, he climbed reluctantly in and the cabin lid closed over him like a coffin top.

To his faint surprise, the Thing flew and half an hour later the Russian pilot landed next to the two Lancasters. Tait found his two crews held in a tumbledown wooden house set in a sea of mud. The Russians had fed them well but were not allowing them out. Some Russian girls were there but the crews were behaving impeccably, not even ogling the girls, partly

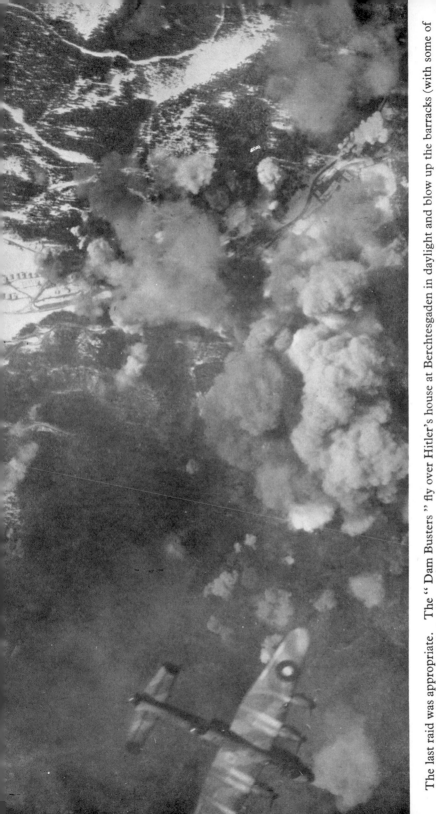

The last raid was appropriate. The "Dam Busters" fly over Hitler's house at Berchtesgaden in daylight and blow up the barracks (with some of the occupants) of Hitler's S.S. bodyguard.

Barnes Wallis, still working, after the war, on the drawing board where his ideas took shape.

because the girls were not attractive and partly because one of them had entertained them by lifting a burly Russian guard off the floor with one hand. Paddy Blanche, Knilans' gunner, was recovering. He hadn't been injured, but at lunch-time they had set a tumbler of vodka in front of him, and he had thought it was water and drunk it straight off before his face had turned white then crimson and purple as he fought for breath.

Iveson had just enough petrol to get to Yagodnik and took off at full throttle, barely clearing the trees. The Russians brought more petrol for Knilans ; he roared over the grass to take-off but his spark plugs were fouled and the engines were sluggish. Feeling the power lacking (she would have lifted easily enough but for the 6-ton bomb) Knilans shoved the throttles through the " gate," hauled her off the ground and she lunged into the tree-tops and cut a swathe through the foliage for a hundred yards. Boughs shot up all round, twigs and leaves scooped into the radiators, a lopped branch knifed through the nose and shot into the cockpit beside Knilans, and then the engines hauled her clear. Wind howled through the smashed nose into Knilans' face so that he could hardly see and flew with a hand over his face, peeking between two fingers. One engine cut out because of overheating from the blocked radiator, but they made it safely to Yagodnik and the ground crews set about repairs.

Rain poured on Yagodnik and for three days they waited for it to lift. Friendly Russians tried hard to amuse them, but outside the huts lay a sea of mud and the crews relaxed indoors, chasing bugs and eating sour black bread, borscht and half-cooked bacon . . . when the last of the breakfasters rose the head of the lunch queue sat down. They washed it down with vodka, which (said Willie Tait) was the secret of Russian survival in that climate. His opinion was respected because he was the only one the bugs refused to bite. Tait claimed it was because they were capitalist bugs and respected his rank, but Witherick said that even Russian bugs had to draw the line somewhere.

A Russian interpreter, who grinned all the time (showing steel false teeth) and smelled of perfume, took them at night to an underground cellar to see an unnerving film that went on for hours, all about battles . . . mostly Russian tanks, planes and cheering soldiers rushing forward in a continuous pandemonium of crashing explosions . . . dead Germans everywhere.

Next day a team of bullet-headed little men (imported for the occasion) played them football. Whenever Russian players tired they went off and on came reserves, among them the local Russian commander and the airfield commander, who were fed assiduously with passes by their men until a glancing blow off the senior man's knee went into the goal, whereupon the band struck up triumphantly and the rest of the team, duty done, went back to playing normally. The Russians won easily, 7—0.

On September 15 the sun crawled out of the horizon low to the south and shone in a clear sky. The crews were out in their aircraft, running up the engines hopefully, when the weather plane darted over the airfield like a blue kingfisher and landed with the report that the sky over Alten Fiord was clear. Minutes later twenty-eight Lancasters of the two squadrons were lifting off the bumpy grass and turning west. Tait flew slowly, the rest of his squadron picking up station behind till they were in their gaggle low over the White Sea, and on strict radio silence to delay detection. Grey water close below muffled the thunder of the engines till they crossed the barren shore of Lapland and the echoes came up from the ice-worn rocks. The land was lifeless but for odd stunted trees ; it rose a little and the aircraft lifted their noses gently over the contours.

Tait had an engine running rough, shaking the plane like a rolling-mill, but he headed on worrying about having enough power for the bombing climb. Ninety miles from Alten Fiord the mountains reared ahead and, on full throttle and revs., Tait's rough engine cleared and he climbed easily over the last ridge. They were dead on track.

Ahead Alten Fiord lay quietly in the sun like a map ; they raced for it at 11,000 feet to beat the smoke screen, but as they picked out the black shape at her anchorage under the cliff, white plumes started vomiting out of the smoke pots and streaming across the water.

The bombers were quivering on full power five minutes from bombing point as the white veils started wreathing her. There must have been a hundred pots pouring smoke. Flak was firing from the heights now ; the gaggle ran steadily through the black puffs, and then the *Tirpitz's* guns opened up. Two minutes from release point the drifting veils were fast smothering her. Daniels, in the nose of Tait's aircraft, took a long bead and called, " Bomb sight on ! "

The black hull finally vanished in its shroud but the masttops stood clear a few seconds later, and then they too were gone. Daniels tried to hold his graticule on the spot but found no mark in the drifting smoke and guessed as the seconds dragged that he must be wandering off. The Lancaster leapt as the bomb clattered away and Tait swung the wheel hard over, swerving out of the flak.

Behind him the others had all lost their mark in that agonising last minute. Howard, Watts and Sanders bombed on dim gun flashes through the smoke. Kell and Knilans bombed on the spot last seen, and the others, in frustration, did not bomb at all. Pale flickers in the smoke showed bombs exploding, and after one of them a plume of black smoke spurted through the whiteness. Tait felt a moment of hope but judged it was only a " tallboy " striking the shore. Some of the Lancasters swung back through the flak for a second run, but the screen was thicker than ever and they turned for Yagodnik.

When they landed, Woods, one of the bomb aimers, said he had seen Daniels' " tallboy " hit the ship, but no one believed him. The Russians did not try to hide their displeasure at the failure. Some of the bombers still had their " tallboys " and they wanted to go back and try again, but the weather broke once more, rain drizzled down, winter's cloud hung over the north, and disconsolately they gave up the idea and took off for home. Levy's aircraft never arrived. Somewhere over Norway they wandered off track—probably through a flabby compass—and flew into the mountains. They were an all-Jewish crew, a quiet, unobtrusive team, utterly reliable. With Levy were four of Wyness's crew.

It was the nearness to success that hurt Cochrane most. He

said wryly, " Another minute's sight and you'd have got her. I was afraid those smoke pots might balk you." He did not tell Tait at the time but he had no intention of leaving the *Tirpitz* in peace.

A couple of nights later the squadron joined 5 Group to bomb the Dortmund Ems Canal, scene, a year earlier, of 617's blackest night. Mosquitoes marked at low level in the way they had learned from Cheshire and the bombs that followed split the canal embankment. The group bombed more accurately now than a year earlier. After his experiment with 617, Cochrane had seen that the rest of his squadrons trained hard in the same direction.

Tait had lost an engine on take-off that night but had feathered and kept going hard on the other three ; slower, of course. He came out of cloud over the target and saw the water that was the artery of Germany's northern transport system pouring through the gaps into the countryside. There was a price on it that night ; fighters got among the returning bomber stream, and Tait saw the path back littered with burning Lancasters. 617 was lucky and lost only one. Stout's plane went down somewhere ; they never found out where

The canal had a bad time after that. The water drained for miles between lock gates, and scores of barges were stranded on the mud with coal, prefabricated U-boats and other essentials. Hitler drove 4,000 slaves to rebuild the breached walls, and when they had nearly finished, 5 Group knocked them down again. Back to work went the reluctant slaves, and this time they finished it. The Germans opened the lock gates to let the water through again, and two hours later the Lancasters were over and away went the walls again. They never did get the canal working again.

Knilans was told he had " finished." After two straight tours without rest he had " operational fatigue " ; his mind still registered mistakes in the air but his muscles would not respond. He had another disappointment too. His D.S.O. medal arrived—in the post. Knilans had set his heart on having it pinned on at an investiture.

Humphries kept it for him in the squadron safe while

Knilans miserably waited for his posting, and whenever the inactivity got a little too much for him he used to wander down to the squadron office, moon around bashfully for a while and then say, " Humph, can I have a look at my medal? " Humphries would solemnly take it out of the safe, and Knilans would hold it in his hand and sigh, " Heck, I guess that King never will get to meet me now."

He was entitled to several medal ribbons, including some American ones, but for a long time the only one he would wear was the D.S.O. ribbon. (Later he added to it when his D.F.C. came through.)

Recce aircraft reported the *Tirpitz* was missing from Alten Fiord and there was a great " flap " (particularly among the nautical people) till a message came through from a Mr. Egil Lindberg. Lindberg was a Norwegian who operated a secret transmitter from a room above the morgue in Tromso. The *Tirpitz* had arrived in Tromso, he reported, with a great hole in her for'd deck. She had been hit by a very heavy bomb (Daniels's " tallboy " *had* hit the ship. He was probably the most " hawk-eyed " bomb aimer of the war). Lindberg thought the *Tirpitz* had come to Tromso because the repair facilities were better there. Cochrane got the news and did not care a hoot about the repair facilities. The important thing to him was that Tromso was 200 miles south of Alten Fiord—it shortened the return trip by 400 miles . . . and that put the *Tirpitz* just within range of Lossiemouth.

He called Wing Commander Brown, his engineering staff officer, and said, " Brown, we've got to get three hundred more gallons in 617's Lancasters."

" Yes sir. We can fit overload tanks in the bomb bays."

" No, we shall want the ' tallboys ' there. Come on, come on, you're versatile. Is there anything in the depots that would do? We haven't time to get anything made."

Brown was miserably without a glimmer of an idea till he remembered some Wellingtons had once carried long pencil-shaped overload tanks. If they could find some of those they could slide them into the Lancaster fuselages. Cochrane grunted approval, and Brown scoured England by telephone, locating tanks one by one and sending trucks to collect them.

A new consideration interrupted Cochrane's *Tirpitz* plans. The right flank of the American dash across France into Germany had been halted at the Belfort Gap ; ahead the Rhine barred the way into Germany, and on the Rhine by the Swiss frontier lay the Kembs Dam. It was obvious that when the Americans stormed the river the Germans would blow up the flood-gates, releasing a massive head of water that would sweep the assault forces to destruction in mid-river or isolate those who got across. There was only one way out—smash the flood-gates first, let the water spend itself and then drive at the river. Only a heavy charge, deep in the water and pressed against the sluice gates, would burst them ; the ideal target for the freak bomb 617 had used on the Moehne and Eder but the modified aircraft to carry that bomb had long been re-modified to normality. It would take weeks to adapt more aircraft for the bomb and train the crews in the delicate technique ; more weeks than they could afford.

It was no good trying to bomb it from high level. The chance of a heavy bomb landing in exactly the right spot, within a foot of the dam wall on the upstream side, was far too slim. A direct hit on the top would do no good. There was only one way . . . Cochrane decided that a " tallboy " dropped low over the water just short of the flood-gates would slide cleanly into the water till it hit a gate and stick in the concrete. They would give it a delayed fuse so the low-flying bombers would not be blown up as well.

It would have to be done very accurately ; that meant doing it in full daylight, and the dam was circled with guns. The bombers would have to fly very low, straight and level, and run the gauntlet. No question as to who should do it !

Cochrane planned it craftily. They would split in two formations ; one would come in and bomb from the west at 8,000 feet, drawing the flak ; and in the precise moment their bombs were hitting, six Lancasters would sneak in low from the east for the real assault. At the same instant a Mustang squadron would dive on the flak-pits with guns and rockets so the flak might not notice the low-level force, at least till the bombs were gone. It was going to need split-second timing, and 617 practised every day for a week till their final rehearsal

over Wainfleet went perfectly. Tait was insisting on leading
the low-level force.

They knew, or sensed, that the Kembs might be a " shaky
do," though that did not much affect their thinking or living.
They were used to it and the mind makes its own defences.
After battle they always flew home to the island fortress and
lived among fields and placid villages, which rather insulated
them in the mess from the sharper realities of battle, just
enough to take some of the edge off the fear that lived in
them like a raw little nerve.

617's mess at Woodhall was in the Petwood Hotel for
instance ; stockbroker's tudor if you like but a pleasant place,
agreeably panelled and set in gardens. The beer was good,
Waafs in white coats served your meals and you slept in a
bed with sheets, remote from battle. You lived like a normal
human and it fortified that deceitful little thought, " It
can't happen to me," until the weather cleared and you got
a time on target : then the transition was always brutally
swift—four hours later you would be a few hundred miles
away, tight-lipped and sweating it out in the noise, the
ugliness, the fear and the death.

Sometimes, if the time on target were a few hours away,
some of the insulation stayed a while round the little nerve,
as on October 7, the day of the Kembs raid. Take-off was
in the afternoon and after morning briefing and testing the
planes the crews read in the mess or walked in the garden
and two of the flight commanders, Tony Iveson and " Duke "
Wyness, even went over to a nearby army mess to lunch with
their friend the lieutenant-colonel, commander of the local
regiment.

Among the waiters, white linen and conversation the war
shrank ; it was not forgotten but you observed it through the
wrong end of a telescope and talked of it as if it were almost
abstract. Wyness, for instance, talked during lunch not of
the raid but in philosophical terms of courage and cowardice
in the face of the enemy, saying with the earnest assurance
of twenty-three years that a man's duty lay along the path
of the utmost endurance in the face of the enemy's efforts.

That very neatly expressed the distinctive quality of the

squadron and it was apt enough coming from Wyness because he himself was quite typical of the new types who made the squadron. He already had a D.F.C. when he came to 617 and a reputation as a " press on " type, a handsome young man, a six-footer, slim, with blue eyes, a somewhat classical nose and really golden, curly hair.

One of the pilots under him was Kit Howard and the orderly room had a story that Wyness came from the estate of Howard's family, though neither Howard nor Wyness seemed to notice it. In both of them, as in Tait, Iveson and the others, was the continuity of the early, chosen types like Gibson, Cheshire, Martin and Shannon. They maintained the quality and buttressed the tradition.

And then, after lunch, they accepted the transition and went to battle. The colonel drove them to their planes in his jeep, asked them both to dine with him that evening when they got back, and waved them off.

They all took-off into light haze and ran into a pall of cloud over Manston, where they were to meet the fighters. It is dangerous to break radio silence on the outward journey but this time it was less of a risk than missing the fighter escort, so Tait made two short transmissions ; the first to 617 : " Four thousand feet. Don't acknowledge." They recognised his voice, climbed blind through the cloud and at 4,000 feet came into the sunshine. Tait called the fighter leader and told him they were overhead ; two minutes later the Mustangs lifted out of the white carpet, shook themselves into formation and they were on their way.

It was clear over France, and strange to be flying peacefully over the land that had been hostile so soon before. Bomb craters still studded the fields but the scars were already softening as rain and sun mellowed the torn earth and the grass crept in.

The scars vanished over Champagne and they flew over green and yellow meadows and towns by gleaming rivers. Tait, for the first time, felt an intruder, finding it hard, this day, to adjust himself to the sharp transition. Raiding at night they were alone in darkness filled with unknown danger, and inside the cockpit it was tense and appropriate to war, but this peaceful sunshine made it somehow unreal and the task ahead repugnant. He found himself thinking of wine and clear river water, lost in introspection while a separate part of his brain and his arms and feet were part of the aeroplane, flying on undeviatingly.

Patches of cloud brought him back to reality. Cloud over the Rhine would hide the high force and leave him and the " suicide squad " open to the flak. The cloud thinned again ; the high force swung behind Fawke and started climbing ; Tait slid to the right and nosed down till he was hugging the ground under the radar waves, and the other five Lancasters trailed after him. They skirted the Swiss frontier, clearly marked with red and white crosses on the ground, but Watts must have swung his plane a shade too close and the Swiss flak opened up on him, smashing his starboard outer engine. He feathered quickly, hauled over to the left and kept going. From a rear turret a voice said, " It's O.K. I'm here." Gerry Witherick was riding with Watts this day, and everyone knew he always got back unscratched.

They slid past Basle on the right and turned down the river, opening bomb doors. Three miles ahead Tait saw flashes round the low parapet of the Kembs, but the guns were aiming high at Fawkes' formation. Great flashes and columns of spray rushed up round the dam ; the timing of the high-force bombs was perfect. Tait's aeroplane was rock-steady on, course and no word was spoken, except once, a terse " O.K." from Daniels. They were committed to it now, sliding over the smooth water with taut nerves and dry mouths. Tait saw Mustangs diving out of the sun over the dam and dared to hope the flak would not see him, but abruptly the white-hot balls came darting at them. He felt the plane jump as the bomb slid away, slammed the throttles on, did not see the bomb knife cleanly into the water 10 yards from the right-hand sluice-gate, but heard the vibrant rattle as the rear gunner opened up and they hurtled over the dam.

Behind him Castagnola's plane lurched in Tait's slipstream and threw the bomb wide. Tait hauled hard over to the right for the shelter of the hills, climbing on full power, engines blaring in fine pitch as they dragged her up. He turned abeam and saw a Lancaster rocking over the dam on fire, flame and smoke streaming in her wake. She dropped a wing and plunged into the river bank, rolling over in a ball of fire. When it is quick it is a good way to die.

Tait heard a voice in his earphones—Howard's, he thought —saying, " Had a hang-up. Going round again." Howard, of the noble family, was rather a formal boy, but brave. Perhaps foolhardy. This time the gunners were wary, not distracted. Howard came alone down the river and all the guns saw him. They got him a long way back and he blew up in mid-air with the bomb on board.

The surviving bombers turned for home ; in five minutes the sound of their engines had died away and the dam lay quietly in the sun as though nothing had happened, except for the two columns of greasy smoke pouring from the spots where Howard and Wyness and their crews had died.

There had been half-hour delay fuses on the low-force " tallboys." Twenty minutes after the raid a Mosquito droned high over the dam and circled it, the pilot watching till he saw the water beside the right-hand sluice-gate burst and mushroom into the air. A massive torrent plunged through the gate, and in twenty-four hours the banked head-waters of the Rhine had dropped so much that barges far into Switzerland grounded on the mud.

Tait had made a " dicy " landing with a flak shell in one wing-root and a tyre shot away. Several of the others were badly holed. Iveson, without changing, walked over to the army mess to tell the colonel that his other dinner guest, the boy who had lunched with him, was lying several hundred miles away in another country, cremated in his plane. He found the colonel (who was a Scottish rugby international) in the bar, took him aside and they sat on the stairs while Iveson told him about it. The hurt was gathering in the colonel's face and then, very quietly, he was crying : you could, I suppose, call it crying ; no noise, no sobs, no shaking shoulders but the tears starting to glisten in his eyes till they spilled and kept wetting his cheeks.

When he was able to, he said, a little unsteadily and with humility, how futile he felt his own efforts were in comparison to the Air Force. He said he had never had much chance for action but now he felt the impact of the war more than ever before.

So did Iveson when he saw the tears. They had got so used to seeing planes beside them with their friends fall smoking out of the sky that the familiar expression they all used, " got the chop," had almost a humorous quality about it, but that was just part of the insulation, the old mental defence mechanism.

(Three weeks later, in the landing on Walcheren, the colonel won a D.S.O. for some act of inspired bravery.)

The squadron never knew for certain whether the raid helped the advance, whether their fourteen room-mates died in saving hundreds or whether it was just one of the premiums paid in war, a precaution which, after all, was not needed. So many valiant deeds in war are sterile. The monstrous rocket sites they bombed in the Pas de Calais may never have been finished in time, whether they had bombed them or not. It was a part of war. Tait was well aware that most of the effort of war was spent against an enemy who was not there ; that for every shell which hit a target, hundreds were fired that missed, and for every bullet, thousands.

The next days were a fever of activity getting ready for the *Tirpitz*. The brunt of it fell on Cochrane, Tait, Brown and the ground crews. With tests and graphs Tait worked it out that from Lossiemouth they could just reach the *Tirpitz* in Tromso with a bare—a very bare—safety margin in case of adverse winds, but it meant loading in so much petrol they would be taking off nearly 2 tons over the maximum permissible weight. He agreed to try that if they could have Merlin 24 engines . . . they were more powerful than the engines in the 617 Lancasters. There were some of these engines in 5 Group, scattered among odd aircraft in various squadrons at other airfields. For three days and nights the ground crews worked non-stop in shifts, taking the Merlin 24's out of aircraft all over Lincolnshire, bringing them back to Woodhall, taking out the 617 engines, putting in the new ones and taking the 617 engines to be put in the other aircraft they had " robbed." It would have been so simple if they could merely have exchanged planes, but only the 617 Lancasters had the specially big bomb bays to carry the " tallboys." The weather was dense fog continuously, and at night the bright hangar lights gleamed like will-o'-the-wisps across the streaming tarmac.

Brown had collected the long, thin overload tanks from all over England. The erks had to take the rear turrets off every plane to slide the tanks in, then put the turrets back on again. They took the mid-upper turrets off completely, also the pilot's armour plate and any equipment not vitally necessary, so as to save weight.

(The same things were done on 9 Squadron aircraft too. Cochrane was sending them as well.)

That done they waited on the weather, and that was the worst time of all. In October and November a prevailing westerly blows continuous stratus cloud from the sea over Tromso . . . except for perhaps three days a month, when the wind briefly changes to the east and the sky is clear for a few hours. They would have to be in position at Lossiemouth to take off when one of these clear periods existed, and hope it would last till they got there. But neither Harris nor Cochrane could let them stay at Lossiemouth indefinitely " on spec." They needed them down south in case of emergency targets. The only way was for the squadron to fly to Lossiemouth when a break seemed possible. At the most they had six weeks left for the attack. After November 26 the sun does not rise above the horizon at Tromso, though for a few days after that there would be just enough twilight at midday for bombing. After that no light till spring. A nice problem in long-range weather forecasting.

The word came on October 28, and thirty-six Lancasters of 617 and 9 Squadrons flew north to a bleak field near Lossiemouth. At midnight a Mosquito over Tromso radioed that the wind was veering to the east, and in drizzling rain, at the deathly hour of 1 a.m., the Merlin 24's straining on emergency power, dragged the overburdened Lancasters off the ground.

They flew low as usual, in sight of the caps on the dark water ; hours later crossed the Norwegian coast and turned inland towards Sweden to keep the mountains between them and the Tromso radar. They wheeled left in a long climb, topped the ridges and saw Tromso Fiord and the ship . . . and saw in the same moment, moving in from the sea, towering drifts of cloud. The wind had changed.

It was a race again, like those sickening moments over Alten Fiord, but this time the white screens were higher and thicker. At 230 m.p.h. the bombers charged towards the ship and the cloud. A minute from release point they still saw the ship, but with thirty seconds to go the cloud slid between them !

They couldn't dive under it to bomb ; lower down the " tallboys " would not have penetrated the armoured decks. Daniels tried to keep his bomb sight on the spot where he last saw the ship. Flak was bursting through the cloud among them now. Daniels called " Bombs gone ! " and Tait dived into the cloud to try and see where it fell. Fawke, Iveson, Knights and one or two more bombed on vague glimpses and dived too. Others swung away to try another run. Through gaps in the cloud at about 13,000 feet Tait saw flashes as bombs exploded in the water round the ship. One or two others said they thought they saw a direct hit or near miss. Martin (a different Martin) made two more runs, got a glimpse on the third run and bombed half blindly. Gumbley made four runs but got no sight at all.

Carey's Lancaster had been hit by flak on the first run ; the starboard outer engine stopped and petrol streamed out of a riven tank, luckily without catching fire. He turned back on three engines for another run and the cloud foiled him. He tried again and again, ploughing steadfastly through the flak till, on the sixth run, an almost desperate bomb aimer let his " tallboy " go with faint hope.

Tait had ordered everyone to dive to 1,000 feet to pick up speed and steer for home. As Carey screamed down he passed over a small island ; a single gun on it pumped a shell into another engine, which died instantly ; petrol was streaming out of another burst tank (miraculously no fire again), and then the hydraulics burst and the bomb doors and undercarriage flopped down. The two good engines on full power just held her in the air against the drag ; the engineer thumbed his gauges, scribbled a few calculations and said, " Sorry, Skip. Not enough gas to get home."

From the rear turret came a protesting, grimly flippant voice : " Hell, this can't happen to me." Witherick was flying with Carey this time. He had a habit of switching crews.

" Christ ! " said Carey. " Can't it? You watch ! "

He turned the winged plane back towards the land and, staggering through the air a few hundred feet up, they threaded through a mountain pass and slowly crossed the barren country. Half an hour later the navigator said they were over Sweden. The two engines were dangerously hot and Carey crash-landed in a bog near Porjus. The Lancaster tilted frighteningly on her nose, poised a moment and settled back, and they climbed out.

The rest of the squadron landed at Lossiemouth and heard that a recce plane radioed that the *Tirpitz* was untouched. They flew down to Woodhall, where Tait found a message from Cochrane : " Congratulations on your splendid flight and perseverance. The luck won't always favour the *Tirpitz*. One day you'll get her."

On November 4 they flew up to Lossiemouth again. A gale warning came through that night and in the morning the weather was dreadful. It stayed dreadful ; they flew back to Woodhall and waited, practising bombing whenever they could. Five days later they were still getting gale and frost warnings and time was getting short.

Arthur Kell's bomb aimer tripped on the stairs and fractured his skull, and Tait told Kell he would have to miss the next *Tirpitz* trip unless he could find a S.A.B.S.-experienced bomb aimer. Kell rang Astbury, now twice tour-expired, waiting at Brighton for a ship home to Australia. Astbury went A.W.L. from his draft and turned up at Woodhall, a misdemeanour to which Tait turned a blandly Nelsonian blind eye.

CHAPTER XIX

THE NAKED BATTLESHIP

A NEW complication jolted Cochrane. Intelligence reported that twenty to thirty German fighters had moved in to Bardufoss airfield, thirty miles from Tromso. No doubting why! Two strong attacks had been made on the *Tirpitz* ; the Germans would give the next one a lethal reception. For accuracy the squadron would have to bomb by day spread out in the gaggle so they could not give each other protection, and the R.A.F.'s ·303 guns were no match for the cannon of fighters. If the fighters fell on them—and that seemed likely—there was every chance of slaughter. Few bombers, if any, would return.

Cochrane found himself in the old position of the commander forced to stay at his desk and decide whether to send his men into an ambush. Some commanders grow too detached to be particularly conscious of the problem. Cochrane was acutely conscious of it. There had been two unlucky failures, and he spent troubled hours trying to equate the chance of a " third time lucky" success with the probable losses. For all his coldness there was a personal factor this time that he tried to eliminate. 617 never knew (and would never have guessed) that they were the apple of his eye ; he had a respect for them amounting to affection.

But it was an operational war. That was the clinching factor. He decided they would have to go if the cloud let them.

Next day the weather was improving. Tait was playing football with his crews on the airfield, surrounded by the circle of silent cloaked Lancasters, when he was summoned to the operations room, and there, still in striped jersey and studded boots, he got his orders. In a few hours they were flying up to Northern Scotland.

That was about the afternoon a paper was dumped in an " In " tray in Whitehall, and a senior officer with a lot of braid round his sleeve picked it out and groaned when he read the rather peremptory suggestion from High Circles that instead of " tallboys " on the *Tirpitz* raid they should drop 2,000-lb. armour-piercing bombs. In the room at the time was an airman who had done a lot of work in developing the " tallboy." " Oh God," he said, " the two-thousand-pounders'll never do it ! What do we do now ? " The high officer pondered, his fingers relaxed and the slip of paper floated back into the " In " tray. " Have lunch," he said, and added a moment later, piously, " I'll look into this to-morrow. I *do* hope I'm in time."

Some time after midnight the weather Mosquito, sliding through darkness on the way back from Tromso, reported fog in the fiords and cloud half-way up Norway. There was a possibility Tromso might be clear by dawn, but there were distinct icing conditions (a real bogy for heavy-laden aircraft). It was not encouraging. Tait discussed it with the Met. men, and at the end he said, " All right. We'll give it a go."

Over Lossiemouth stars were glinting in a clear sky and the air was frosty. Tait drove out to his aeroplane and found the dangerous rime ice already forming on his wings in spite of the glycol the ground crew had poured on the leading edge. One by one round the field the engines were whining and coughing explosively, bringing the big bombers to quivering life. When Tait started his starboard inner it let out a high-pitched scream as the starter motor stuck in engagement. He hoped it would clear before the engine seized—in much the same way as he hoped the rime ice would clear. With 7 tons of fuel and 6 tons of bomb, each plane was grossly overweight at 32 tons. No margin for any trouble on take-off.

At 3 a.m. the straining engines dragged them into the air, the great wheels slowly retracted and locked, the engines relaxed and they turned slowly on course at 1,000 feet. (Tait's engine chewed the gears off the starter motor and was all right. He was flying his own aircraft again, " D Dog," for the first time since she was crippled over the Kembs Dam. He always had luck in her.)

They flew slowly to save petrol, flame floats bobbing on the water in their wake as they checked for drift. Tait had slipped in the automatic pilot and tried to doze, as he always did on outward trips over water ; he believed in taking sleep when he could get it, but seldom got it.

The sky was paling in the east as they reached the Norwegian coast, turned right, climbed over the mountains and dipped into the inland valleys. The sun lifted over the horizon and the valleys lay soft under snow, flecked with bare rocks. Snow crests surrounded them, tops laced with pink like vast wedding cakes, except to the south, where the sun splintered on the ice-peaks and sparkled with the colours of the spectrum like a diamond necklace, radiantly lovely. Fog-filled lakes passed slowly below but there was no cloud. Rendezvous was a narrow lake cradled between steep hills a hundred miles south-east of Tromso, and Tait flew slowly towards it, saw no water but recognised it as a long pool of fog in the trough and over it saw aircraft circling like black flies.

He flew across it firing Véry lights to draw them, and they turned in behind and started the climb towards Tromso. That was the moment the radar picked them up, and within a minute the fighter operations room at Bardufoss knew that enemy bombers were closing on the *Tirpitz*. At 14,000 feet the bombers were all at battle stations. One last mountain shouldered up, and as they lifted over the peak it lowered like a screen and there again, folded in the cliffs, lay Tromso Fiord and the black ship, squat in the distance, like a spider in her web of torpedo nets. It was like looking down from the " gods " on a Wagnerian stage, a beetle in green water cupped in the snowy hills, all coral and flame. There was no cloud. And no smoke screen. *Tirpitz* lay naked to the bomb sights.

Even the air was still. On the flanks of the gaggle Tait saw the front rank riding steadily. They seemed suspended ; motionless but for the sublime hills falling slowly behind, immaculate and glowing with the beauty of sunrise and the indifference of a million years to the ugliness of the intrusion. So must many an Arctic coast burn unseen.

Far below the basin seemed to sleep in the shadow, but *Tirpitz* broke the spell with a salvo, sparkling from stem to stern with flashes as billows of smoke from the guns wreathed her and drifted up. Her captain had just radioed urgently to Bardufoss to hurry the fighters.

Tait opened the bomb doors and slid the pitch levers up to high revs. ; the engines bellowed and the exhausts glowed even in that cold light. Black puffs stained the sky among the gaggle as the flak reached them, and then the guns round the fiord opened fire. Tait watched anxiously for the smoke pots, but the smoke never came (the pots were there all right, just brought down from Alten, but the Germans had not yet primed them). The bomb sight was on and the ship drawing nearer while the gunners in the rear turrets watched the ridges anxiously for the first fighters. It was all up to the rear gunners when the fighters came ; there were no mid-upper gunners.

Now it was water, far below, sliding under the nose. Tait felt his hands on the wheel were clammy, and Daniels's breathing rasped over the intercom. The bomber was unswerving, shaking in the engines' thunder, and out of the cockpit Tait could see the bomb doors quivering as the airflow battered at them. The red light came on—ten seconds to go . . . seconds that dragged till " D Dog " leapt as the grips snapped back and the bomb lurched away. Tait hauled hard over to the left and on either side saw others of the front rank doing likewise.

One by one the gaggle wheeled as the bombs went. They watched, wordless, through the perspex for thirty seconds till a great yellow flash burst on the battleship's foredeck. From 14,000 feet they saw her tremble. Another bomb hit the shore ; two more in close succession hit the ship, one on the starboard side, by the bridge, and another abaft the funnel (one of them was Astbury's). Another one split the sea 5 feet from her bows, and then the smoke pall covered her and only dimly through it they saw the other bursts all inside the crinoline of nets.

One constant glare shone through the smoke. She was burning. There came another flash and a plume of steam jetted 500 feet into the air through the smoke as a magazine went up.

Three minutes later 9 Squadron bombed the dark shroud

over her, and then the black flies crawling in the sky turned south-west and curved down towards the sea, picking up speed for the run home. They never saw a fighter. The last thing they saw as the smoke lifted was the *Tirpitz* starting to list.

The cloud they had feared closed in on the long slog home, and Tait was driving blindly through it when his artificial horizon collapsed in a mess of ball bearings and mechanism. After eleven hours in the air his eyes felt like hot coals as he focused rigidly on the other instruments ; then the aerial iced up and they could not get a homing for a long time, and when they did it was a diversion. Lossiemouth was cloaked in rain, and Tait turned east and found a small Coastal Command field, where he touched down smoothly.

At the control tower a young pilot officer asked if they had been on a cross-country, and Tait primly pursed his mouth, looked in aloof shyness at the ground and said, " Yes." A torpedo-bomber squadron lived on the field, and later he told the C.O. where they had been.

" Did you get her ? " the C.O. asked.

" I think so. Gave her a hell of a nudge anyway."

" Thanks," the C.O. said. " *We* might have had to do it. Low level. I shouldn't have liked it."

They drove over to Lossiemouth, where they met the rest of the squadron, and were drinking in the bar when the recce plane radioed that *Tirpitz* was upside down in Tromso Fiord, her bottom humped over the water like a stranded whale.

In his room in Tromso, Lindberg, the Norwegian agent, was tapping out the Morse signals that confirmed it. Under his floor, in the morgue, the Germans were laying out their dead.

Not all of the dead. A thousand men were trapped below when she rolled over. The Germans tried to cut holes in the hull to reach them but did not get any out. They had spent the war miserably, lying in the bleak fiords of Norway, never venturing out. They fought the ship to the last, died without honour when the war was nearly over, and after the war still lay rotting in her hull.

The fighter commander at Bardufoss was facing court martial. Radar had warned him forty-five minutes before the bombers reached the ship, and all that time the *Tirpitz's* captain had been sending him urgent messages. He was still asking for the fighters when the bombs blotted out his radio, but the fighters never came.

Just after *Tirpitz* saw the bombers come over the mountain, a message came from Bardufoss that an enemy formation was over the air-field and the fighters could not take off, but there were no Allied fighters for a thousand miles. No one seems to know quite what happened. Some of the fighters are said to have taken off, but by some miracle they did not intercept.

The squadron flew back to Woodhall and were greeted outside the control by an Army band playing " See the conquering heroes come." In the mess they found messages from the King, War Cabinet, Harris, Cochrane, Wallis, the Navy, Prince Olav of Norway, and even one from the Russians, congratulating them.

(It was not till after the war they found it had all been unnecessary. The bomb Tait and Daniels had dropped six weeks earlier at Alten Fiord had damaged *Tirpitz* beyond repair.) The Germans towed her to Tromso, not to repair her but to moor her in shallow water as an unsinkable fortress. Powerful German forces in Northern Norway meant to hold out there. They blundered and moored her in 50 feet of water and tried to repair the mistake by filling in the sea-bed beneath her with dredges, but did not have time. There was still enough water below to let her down.

Someone at the Admiralty apparently did not *quite* agree and said (a little huffily, according to the story) that they could not mark her as definitely sunk because her bottom was still showing ; but that did not deter a certain dynamic personality at Bomber Command from grunting with deep satisfaction to one of his subordinates when he heard the *Tirpitz* was sunk, " That's one in the eye for the Nautics ! "

The incredible Cochrane took it all in his stride. At least on the surface. They held a conference every morning at

5 Group to discuss the previous night's operations, and the coming night's plans. Cochrane presided over them, looking flintily over his half-moon glasses like Harris, and the morning after the raid, when he sat down, his staff officers thought that this time they would see a break in the iron exterior. Cochrane glanced at his minutes and said, " Er . . . last night's raid. . . . Successful ! *Tirpitz* sunk ! Now, about to-night's operations . . ."

CHAPTER XX

BACK FROM THE DEAD

AFTER the excitement of the *Tirpitz* came anti-climax. Unbroken cloud lay over Europe for weeks, making high precision bombing impossible. 617 stood by constantly, were briefed hopefully a dozen times and then the cancellations came. Once they got into the air but were recalled.

Carey, Witherick and company arrived back, gloating over their taste of peacetime flesh-pots in Sweden but furious at missing the end of the *Tirpitz*. " You might have waited for us, sir," Witherick said aggrievedly to Tait. " You *know* I always come back."

Increasing sea losses testified to the fact that Germany's fleet of " schnorkel " U-boats was increasing. For all the main force bombing, the U-boats found shelter in the massive pens and Cochrane switched 617 on to them again. They battered the pens at Ijmuiden (the port of Amsterdam) with six direct hits. Calder's Lancaster was badly hit by flak and he made an emergency landing at a nearer base. A fair-haired, keen-faced young Englishman, Calder was making a name for himself as a determined pilot. Joplin was hit in Knilans's old " R Roger," struggled back to England but crashed near Woodhall, killing two of the crew. Calder led them on the next trip and they slammed some more " tall-boys " on top of the Ijmuiden pens, leaving a huge hole in the massive concrete roof.

Cochrane decided that Tait had done enough. Tait had four D.S.Os. now and two D.F.Cs.—a record—and Cochrane did not want him to strain his luck too far. Shopping round for a new commander, he found no one with all the qualities he wanted till an air commodore heard the position was vacant and asked to be dropped in rank and given the job—a laudable request, as it meant stepping down from a highly-prized rank. This was Johnnie Fauquier, a Canadian, and a tough one, a thick-set, ex-bush pilot, who did not smile much (nor say much. With his curt voice he did not have to say much).

Ten years older than most of them, he was as forceful as a steam-roller. The night he arrived there was a party to farewell the revered Tait and welcome the new man.

To put it mildly, 617's welcome to a new commander was exacting. They were, perhaps, a little above themselves, conscious of their lustre and jealous of trespass on it. It is a trait common to an elect corps, an inseparable if less tractable facet of the unique ardour that leads men to the corps and drives them on to the heights. It is the hand-maiden of achievement and often the mainspring of it. You find it among commandos, business tycoons, geniuses, and sometimes in child delinquents. It is invaluable in a soldier and some-times indecorous in a civilian. 617 had it. That was the first thing Fauquier found out.

Someone said, " Sing a song or take your pants off " . . . their favourite way of puncturing the dignity of a high officer. Fauquier unhitched his pants imperturbably, and Witherick, secure in the legend of his immortality, cooled him off with a can of beer strategically aimed from the rear. Fauquier philosophically hitched up his pants and thus passed the test.

He had his revenge. Cochrane had told him when he took over, " You've got to see 617 is kept up to the mark and stays as good as ever." Fauquier saw to that. Feeling that the war was almost over, the crews had been in a mood to relax and were scandalised when Fauquier got them out of bed in the frosty early mornings for P.T. Storms were sweeping over Europe and the runways were snowed up, so there was no flying. Fauquier gave them lectures instead, and then made them shovel snow off the runways.

On the last day of the year the weather eased and he led them on more serious work. Convoys had been streaming out of Oslo under cover of night as the Germans tried to move troops back from Norway to reinforce the crumbling fronts. Cochrane told them to unmask a convoy with flares and set about it. It was a bleak, black night, but they found the convoy and, lit by the floating flares, the convoy fanned out and scattered. The bombers chased them, but the ships zig-zagged all over the sea. 617 had never dealt with mobile targets before and cursed eloquently as they found they had not mastered the technique of positioning the flares. Fauquier and a couple of others found a cruiser and hunted her, only to see their bombs fall just too wide to be effective. The others all missed too and flew home in chastened mood, but cheered up considerably when they heard that the cruiser in her efforts to dodge the bombs had run on the rocks.

More days waiting for weather ; more briefings, more cancellations, till January 12, when they went to Bergen, in Norway, on the old campaign against U-boats. For the first time Fauquier flew a Mosquito to direct them and for the first time in months German fighters fell on them like a swarm of hornets. They got Pryor on their first strike and he went straight into the sea. Three of them lunged at Nicky Ross on the flank of the gaggle. Watts, next to him, saw the tracer flicking into the Lancaster and lumps flying off her. He wheeled to help him, but Ross was going down, slewing into a spiral with three engines smashed. Near the water he seemed to recover ; the spiral stopped, the mad dive eased and the plane had almost flattened out when it abruptly vanished in a sheet of spray.

The fighters hammered Iveson too, set his port inner on fire and riddled his tailplane and rudder so that he had almost no fore-and-aft control. He was fighting to keep her flying, while his two gunners and the wireless operator baled-out, and suddenly the fighters broke off the attack and vanished. They were not very resolute.

Heavy flak over Bergen crippled Castagnola and he had to jettison and turn for home. The rest took vengeance. Someone put a " tallboy " squarely on the stern of a large ship and in two minutes she had blown up, rolled over and sunk. The rest got several direct hits on the pens.

Next morning Chiefy Powell was sadly typing out the casualty report on Nicky Ross (who had been on the squadron nearly a year—longer than any other pilot) when the door swung open and in walked Ross himself.

Powell gaped.

" Wotcher, Chiefy," quoth the ghost. " Home again ! "

" Good God, sir ! Where've you come from ? "

" Air sea rescue picked us up. Bloody cold in that dinghy."

He sat on a corner of the desk and rattled on amiably about the details.

After some splutters Powell found speech. " D'you know what I was doing when you walked in, sir? Typing your death notice ! "

" Ar, hold it for a while, Chiefy," said the cheerful Ross. " You're a bit premature."

Bad weather again. Weeks of it, with stand-by, briefings, cancellations, training and more training—and P.T.

Meantime the first " grand slam " was nearly ready. A thousand craftsmen had been working for months on the top-secret project and only a bare dozen of them knew what it was all about. In Sheffield the English Steel Corporation had spent weeks trying to find a steel that would stand up to the shock. They forged shells from all the steels they knew and fired them into concrete and steel till they found one that stood up to it, a secret formula of their own. Two firms in the country could cast the complicated casing, and for each bomb they had to build an individual concrete covered core to the most precise ten-thousandth of an inch, position it meticulously inside a sand-surfaced mould, pour the molten steel in and wait two days for it to cool before they could chip the core away. The 10-ton casting travelled then a hundred miles for machining.

It puzzled the workmen. One man watching the shining brute said he thought it was a midget submarine. The executives labelled it officially as a " boiler," but that fooled no one. Around the Sheffield pubs the men sometimes referred to it surreptitiously as " the big bastard." It was a devil to handle. The Army had nearly all the cranes, and the firms had to make special trailers for it because the railways did not have the facilities to handle it. At the filling factory they built a special cradle for it, stood it inside on its nose and built a high platform so they could pour in the tons of explosive a bucketful at a time. They tried thirty different types of fuse before they picked on one they thought would stand up to the shock of impact.

Like the " tallboy," " grand slam's " tail had offset aerodynamic fins to make it spin so fast in falling that the gyroscopic effect would stop it toppling as it shuddered through the sonic barrier. When the tail was put on " grand slam " would be 25 feet 6 inches long. At its thickest part it was 3 feet 10 inches in diameter, and the finished bomb was to weigh just over 22,000 lb. It was such a difficult undertaking that they could produce no dummies for normal tests ; they hoped to have one prototype to drop before they used it on business.

But that was a few weeks ahead yet.

The German fighter force was nearly spent now, making it possible for 617's inadequately armed Lancasters to penetrate deeper and deeper against the enemy by day. They carried on with " tallboys " against the U-boat pens, slathering the concrete strongholds at Poortershaven, Ijmuiden, Hamburg and the monster at Farge, near Bremen, losing two or three crews but getting literally dozens of direct hits on the massive roofs.

Designed for earth penetration and dropped from less than half the prescribed height, the " tallboys " never did quite penetrate the thickest of the concrete before exploding, but did almost as well. As on the Brest pens, they knifed deeply in and then blew right through the ceiling.

At Hamburg they brought down a thousand tons of concrete that crushed two U-boats inside and crippled six others. They smashed servicing gear, killed dozens of men and created panic.

At Ijmuiden they brought down 13,000 tons of concrete over hundreds of feet of roof and wall (near misses did a lot of that by shock wave). Much the same things happened at Bergen and Poortershaven. At Bergen a near miss sank two U-boats and lofted another one on to the dock wall.

Congestion in these ports and pens had been growing steadily worse as the Allies overran Germany's other bases. Now, after the bombing, it was lapsing into chaos, U-boat raids were dwindling and the morale of the men who built, serviced and sailed them was decaying.

His armies poised for the jump over the Rhine, Eisenhower asked the Air Forces for an all-out assault on German communications to sever the front from the rest of Germany. Now that the Dortmund Ems Canal was permanently drained the vulnerable points were the railway bridges, and most vital of these was the Bielefeld Viaduct, not far from Bremen, main link between the Wehrmacht defending the arsenal of the Ruhr and the great centres of north-west Germany. The idea was to starve the front of men and materials and split the country into " islands " that could be taken one by one.

Three thousand tons of bombs had already been aimed at the Bielefeld Viaduct ; the earth for a mile around it was torn into overlapping craters, but the 75-foot arches of the viaduct still firmly bridged the marshes for the trains running south. The light-case bombs of the main bomber forces were not powerful enough to do more than chip it. Cochrane turned 617 on to it, and so began the battle of Bielefeld.

They took off with their " tallboys " one morning, but found the viaduct under ten-tenths cloud and brought them back. Next day they tried once more but again found unbroken cloud. Days later the cloud had cleared ; they flew back to Bielefeld, found it reasonably clear and a few minutes later the viaduct was hidden under smoke as the " tallboys " crashed round it. Half an hour later, when the smoke lifted, a recce aircraft found the viaduct still there. " Tallboy " craters lay in its shadow, but the viaduct was no rotund target like a bull's-eye or a U-boat pen. From 18,000 feet it was almost indistinguishably threadlike. It was like trying to stick a dart in a line.

They waited on the weather and tried again a few days later, but once more found it under cloud. Doggedly they went back a fifth time and turned away in fuming frustration once more. There seemed to be something diabolical about the persistence of the cloud that shielded it.

That night two heavy trailers rolled round the perimeter track to the bomb dump carrying the first two " grand slams." In the morning armourers trollied them out and slowly winched them up into Fauquier's and Calder's Lancasters, specially modified in readiness for this day. They had the most powerful Merlin engines, the fuselages, undercarriages and main beams of the bomb bays had been strengthened and the bomb doors taken off (they could not have closed round the great girth of " Grand Slam ").

" Grand Slam " had never been tested. There had not been time. Only one other " grand slam " existed, and that very morning a Lancaster was going to drop it over the range in the New Forest. Group was waiting for that, and also for the cloud to clear.

Just before noon Met. reported the cloud over Germany rolling away. As Fauquier was briefing his crews a phone message reached Group from the New Forest : " The beast went off all right ! "

CHAPTER XXI

"GRAND SLAM"

AT one o'clock 617's engines were bursting into life round the field. Fauquier was running up his engines, testing his magnetos, when there was a crash from the starboard inner and the propeller jerked to a grinding halt as it seized. Fauquier, muttering with frustration, knew the aircraft would never get off the ground on three engines. There was only one thing to do . . . borrow Calder's aircraft. The fact that he might then be shot down instead of Calder never even occurred to him, and would not have worried him if it had. He scuttled out of his plane and went haring across the field.

Calder saw the running figure, shouting and waving hands in urgent signals, guessed what had happened and cracked his throttles open. The Lancaster lurched forward and, with the small figure sprinting despairingly in the rear, rolled thunderously down the runway, picking up speed till it lifted heavily over the far fence on the way to drop the world's biggest bomb.

The "tallboy"-armed gaggle fell in behind, watching Calder's wings in wonder and alarm. On the ground a Lancaster has no perceptible dihedral, the wings spread in a flat, straight line, but Calder's wings now were a graceful arc, curving up at the tips as they took the strain of the 10-tonner. Those underneath could see the great missile hanging in the bomb bays where the bomb doors used to be.

The sky was clear of cloud ; they skirted the flak at Bremen and ten minutes later picked up the line of the viaduct threading across the marshes. Calder headed in, the laden bomber thrusting smoothly through the bumps till Calder felt her bound up as the "grand slam" slipped away from the grips.

Wheeling away, they watched it drop like a silver shark, slowly starting to spin as its nose dipped lower and it picked up speed, lunging towards the viaduct. It fell for some thirty-five seconds and from far above the sharpest eyes picked up the squirt of mud as it speared into the marsh 30 yards from the foot of one of the arches.

Eleven seconds later the marsh seemed to split and a vast core of mud and smoke vomited up, blotting out 500 feet of the viaduct.   In the next seconds " tallboy " explosions erupted along both sides of the viaduct. Calder peeled off to try and see what had happened ; slowly the mud settled, the wind wafted the smoke away, and as the target appeared through the veils Calder saw that the viaduct looked like a Roman ruin. Seven massive arches over a hundred yards were missing.

He could see almost no collapsed masonry underneath and thought for a moment that the bomb had blasted the arches into dust, but could not believe that possible.

Later they found that the one " grand slam " had com-pletely vindicated Barnes Wallis's theory that a near miss could be more effective than a direct hit. It had penetrated about a hundred feet, and the shock wave had shivered the arches to cracking point ; the explosion had produced a near " camouflet," blasting an enormous subterranean cavity underneath, and, robbed of their foundation in the mud, the weakened arches had collapsed into the abyss. It was the perfect trapdoor effect, the " hangman's drop " that Wallis had planned in 1939.

A recce photograph showed an enormous crater which Wallis described as " exquisite."   Cochrane wired 617 : " You certainly made a proper mess of it this time and incidentally added another page to your history by being the first squadron to drop the biggest bomb on Germany. Good work. Keep up the training. We can't afford to put them in the wrong place."

In the next few days trailers delivered several more " grand slams " to the bomb dump, and on March 19 Fauquier got his delayed chance to drop one. The target was in historic territory for 617, the Arnsberg Bridge, a long masonry viaduct a few miles north of the Moehne Dam. Five Lan-casters carried " grand slams," and the other fourteen had " tallboys." The first bomb was a direct hit on the viaduct and the rest, including Fauquier's " grand slam," went down into the centre of the smoke that gushed up. When the smoke lifted, the central spans were a pile of rubble in the river bed.

Two days later they went to the Arbergen Bridge, near Bremen. Flak got a direct hit on Gumbley's aircraft on the run-up and he went straight down in flames. Price had to swerve out of the way of the falling aircraft, marring his bombing run, but he straightened up and his bomb aimer, Pilot Officer Chance—by a very good chance indeed—lobbed his " tallboy " a direct hit on the viaduct. There was one more direct hit and a lot of near misses. Two piers collapsed, another one was thrown 15 feet out of alignment and earthquake shock threw a span off another pier. Target destroyed.

Next day they went to the Nienburg Bridge, near Bremen, over which the Germans were taking oil to the front. It was not heavily defended, so Fauquier evolved a new plan to try and save some of the precious earthquake bombs. On the way up to the target he ordered four aircraft to start their bombing runs and told the others to circle nearby and wait for orders in case the first four missed. It was an unprecedented idea, and the very fact that Fauquier considered it possible speaks eloquently of their phenomenal accuracy. He himself dived low to one side of the target to watch.

The results were fantastic. The four Lancasters made a steady run in loose formation and bombed almost in the same second. Fauquier saw the first two bombs hit simultaneously (one of them a " grand slam ") on each end of the bridge. The bridge span lifted bodily and still intact into the air, seemed to hang there a second, and in that very moment a third bomb hit it fair and square in the middle. When the smoke had cleared there was no visible sign of the bridge whatsoever and the squadron turned for home, taking their fifteen remaining bombs with them.

Fauquier said when he landed, " Hell, I'd hate to have to do *that* again to prove it."

The Germans had one last railway bridge still serving the Ruhr ; it was also near Bremen, and 617 went there early next morning. The first three bombs (from 16,000 feet) hit almost in the same second, all direct hits (including Fauquier's and Calder's " grand slams "). The next two were very near misses, followed by what seemed to be one more direct hit before smoke smothered the ruins.

(Kehrl, head of the German planning office, said later that chaotic communications were responsible for 90 per cent. of the decline in German war production in the last three months of the war.)

If Wallis's big bombs had been available earlier (with the aircraft to carry them) the Germans would probably not have lasted as long as they did. Their industry and transport would have been disrupted earlier, just as Wallis had forecast in 1939, though the R.A.F. might have suffered sore losses battling through the fighters by day deep into Germany in the earlier stages, as the Americans did.

As there were no worthwhile bridges left, 617 went back on the U-boat pens. At Farge, near Bremen, 7,000 slaves had sweated for two years to build the biggest concrete structure in the world, 1,450 feet long, over 300 feet wide and 75 feet high, a staggering monument to Hitler's ruthless obstinacy. The first design was for a roof 16 feet thick, but after 617 had visited the Brest pens Hitler had put on another thousand slaves, and in March, 1945, the roof was 23 feet of solid reinforced concrete and the pens were just ready for use.

617 paid their call on March 27 and sank two " grand slams " deep in the roof which exploded right through, making holes 20 feet across and bringing down thousands of tons of concrete. Several " tallboys," direct hits and near misses, cracked the monster and undermined it and the pens were never used.

It was hard to find good targets now till a recce plane brought a report that Germany's last pocket battleship, the *Lutzow*, was sheltering in Swinemunde, in the Baltic, deep into enemy territory towards the Russian Front, where fighters could be expected. 617 slogged up there on April 13 (not an encouraging date) only to find it smothered under cloud. They went back two days later ; ten-tenths cloud again. By this it was obvious they were after the *Lutzow*. Fauquier guessed the German fighters would be alerted and he asked for, and got, an escort of long-range fighters. Next day they went back with the fighters and found the target clear but the flak waiting for them.

They picked out the *Lutzow* far below, a microbe on the water beside the quay, and as they turned on her the flak burst among them savagely, predicting deadly accurately on the unwavering formation. Clusters of puffs blotched the patch of sky in which they moved, so that nearly every one of the eighteen bombers was hit and holes opened in wings and fuselages as shrapnel ripped through. Gordon and Gavin both lost engines and started to lag. A heavy shell got a direct hit on Powell ; his port wing folded up and the big plane spun down dragging a tail of flame like a comet. One parachute came out.

Then the gaggle was peeling off out of the flak as the bombs went down. Three bombs hit close together, straddling the ship, one in the alley between the bows and the quay. Other bombs vanished into the spray and smoke that enveloped her.

They flew back unmolested and next morning were stood down completely. After the flak only two of their aircraft were serviceable, and the ground crews were toiling over the others, riveting on patches. The aircrews were content to relax and await news of the *Lutzow*. The recce aircraft landed with photographs, and such was the squadron's self-confidence that a howl of incredulity went up as they saw the *Lutzow* still by the quay, apparently untouched. The recce pilot swore there was no mistake. He had flown right over her, and there, indubitably, she lay, decks clearly visible.

It was not for another two days they found out that *Lutzow* had sunk as far as the sea-bed would let her. The near miss by the bows had torn out her bottom ; the dock was not very deep, but *Lutzow* was finished, lying on the mud.

(Someone in the Navy claimed she was not *really* sunk because her decks were still above water.)

As soon as their aircraft were repaired 617 took some " grand slams " and " tallboys " to Heligoland and plastered half the island's fortress's big guns. Next day they went back and plastered the other half, ending Germany's mastery of the approaches to the north-west ports.

Cochrane went to take over Transport Command, which,

now the shooting was nearly over, was coming into its own. The new 5 Group A.O.C. told Fauquier he was grounded because he did not want him killed in the last moments. The tough Canadian had just finished his third tour and had won three D.S.Os. and a D.F.C.

The remnants of the Wehrmacht were said to be pulling back into Hitler's " Southern Redoubt " in Bavaria, where Berchtesgaden lay. It seemed that there was no more work for 617 till someone remembered that Hitler had recently told his Party chiefs, " I have read these days in the British Press that they intend to destroy my country house. I almost regret that this has not been done, for what I call my own is not more valuable than my compatriots possess."

Eager to ease his conscience, 617 flew to Berchtesgaden, hoping that if Hitler was there they might bury him in his house. As the world knows, Hitler was in Berlin, but it made no difference because the land was deep under snow and Berchtesgaden merged with the white hills and low cloud so that the squadron could not pick it out. However, they identified the nearby S.S. barracks, home of Hitler's bodyguard, and flattened them with four " tallboys " and a selection of 1,000-pounders, and that, with Hitler away, was probably more useful than laying their eggs on the Eagle's Nest.

That was 617's last operation, or perhaps not quite the last. Fauquier went to Germany on his own and by chance received from a beaten enemy a somehow symbolic surrender in the name of the squadron.

The Admiralty, while admitting 617's accuracy on the U-boat pens, would not believe that their big bombs had gone through the concrete roofs. Harris told Fauquier to go over and see, and he flew to a Tactical Air Force base just south of Hamburg. In the morning, with another group captain and an interpreter, he drove off in a jeep for the Hamburg dock area on the understanding that Hamburg was to surrender at ten o'clock that morning.

Driving through Hamburg they wondered why they saw no signs of Allied troops and why German soldiers stared at them, but it never occurred to them that Hamburg had not, in fact, surrendered and no British troops, apart from themselves, had reached the city.

They pulled up in the shadow of the great pens, walked through a side door and stood fascinated by the cavernous ruin inside. Several of the big bombs had punched through the roof, and twisted metal and the rubble of fallen concrete littered the place. They were looking soberly down on two crushed U-boats sunk in one of the docks when they became aware that they were not alone. A Nazi sailor stood behind them. He saluted. Would the officers be good enough to come and see his commanding officer? They followed him to the other side of the pens and stopped in surprise to see 200 German sailors lined up. Their commanding officer marched up, clicked his heels and saluted. He would like, he said, to surrender the Hamburg dock area.

Fauquier was most embarrassed. He still did not know that Hamburg was still in German hands. Neither, as it happened, did the German officer. The pens were out of touch by phone with Hamburg city, and that is the only reason he was surrendering to Fauquier instead of Fauquier to him.

The interpreter rather tactlessly told the German that Fauquier had led the raid which had smashed the pens, a most disconcerting *gaffe*. Fauquier waited warily for the avenging wrath and was astonished when the German clicked his heels, bowed to him and said cordially, " My congratulations on a very good raid."

Fauquier, not knowing quite what to do, clicked his own heels, bowed back and said, " Thank you."

The German said that he had been in the pens at the time with a lot of his men and everyone had been killed except him. He was the sole survivor because he had happened to be in the steel-enclosed overhead crane. He invited them to lunch in his mess. The mess was a literal " mess " in a crazily-tilted cabin of a half-sunken cargo ship. They followed him on board and lunched on dry biscuits spread with sausage meat while the German told them their bombs were rocket-propelled to break through the concrete roof of the pens. Fauquier did not enlighten him.

Totally unaware of the protocol of surrender, Fauquier got

the Germans to pile all their small arms in the jeep and drove off back through the city.

And then on May 8 it was all over and the 150 pilots, navigators, bomb aimers, wireless operators, engineers and gunners realised they were going to have the same chance as ordinary people of walking down the years to a more natural death.

But no. Not quite. 617 and one other squadron were detailed for " Tiger Force," to be the R.A.F.'s contribution to the strategic bombing of Japan. They were to fly from Okinawa and drop their " tallboys " and " grand slams " on the bridges connecting Kyushu to the main Japanese island of Honshu to cut off reinforcements when the Americans invaded Kyushu, as they planned, in January, 1946. They were all set to go when the two bombs so much deadlier than " Grand Slam " fell on Hiroshima and Nagasaki and Japan surrendered.

" Hell ! " said the thwarted volunteers. " They must have heard we were coming."

EPILOGUE

617 is still flying, but all that is left of the old days now is the squadron number and the tradition. The men who won over 150 decorations and made the tradition are scattered, and many of them are dead.

Gibson is dead. When he came back from America he toyed with the idea of going into politics but soon perceived there is a little more to politics than wisdom and sincerity, so he politely declined the prospect of directorships and elected to stay in the R.A.F.

On July 11, 1944, he was disconsolately flying a desk when Micky Martin flew over in a Mosquito, and Gibson eyed the little plane wistfully. Martin took him up for a couple of circuits and then Gibson flew it himself ; he said when he landed, " I'm fed up with sitting on my tail. I'm going back on ops." He worried his seniors till they reluctantly agreed, and a few weeks later Gibson took off in a Mosquito for one last raid to act as master bomber of 5 Group on a factory at Rheydt, near the Ruhr. He guided the bombing, and when it was over they heard his voice on the R/T saying, " O.K., chaps. That's fine. Now beat it home."

No one knows exactly what happened after that. They think Gibson may have been hit by flak. He crashed into a low hill in Holland sixty miles from Rheydt on the way home, and the Dutch buried him there.

The Moehne Dam has been repaired, the lake refilled, but the valley below is littered with twisted, rusted girders and lumps of concrete and the earth still looks as though a giant's rake had scoured it. Where Himmelpforten stood the foundations still lie round the ruins of the church. Set among them is a rough wooden cross with neither name nor inscription. As far as sixty miles away the surviving villagers found the church's chalice, christening font, crucifix and some of the stones, and less than a mile away stands the new church of Porta Coeli built by the villagers. Around the altar is a Latin inscription, restrained and unmalicious : " The wreckage of the church of Himmelpforten, destroyed by flood in 1943, served six years later to build this new altar and this new Porta Coeli."

Martin distinguished himself as a night-fighter pilot, winning another bar to his D.F.C. After the war he shepherded the squadron of Vampires in the first jet flights across the Atlantic, nursing them skilfully through foul weather that nearly brought them to disaster. Then he broke the London-Capetown and return record in a Mosquito and added an A.F.C. to his two D.S.Os. and three D.F.Cs. That year he was awarded the Britannia Trophy, Britain's premier aviation award.

As I write this he is flying an R.A.F. desk in Whitehall. A conscientious administrator now, he wears an Anthony Eden hat when not in uniform, but not far under the hat lies the same old blithe and mettlesome spirit. He married the girl Wendy, who was so reluctant to lunch with him after the dams raid, and under her tuition has become a very accomplished painter in oils.

Cochrane is now an Air Chief Marshal, three times knighted and second in command of the R.A.F. Now that the pressure of war is off his austerity has thawed, except when he finds inefficiency, and then he is his old incisive self, still probably the best brain in the Air Force.

Not far from Whitehall, Willie Tait has also been patiently decorating an R.A.F. desk. Usually he wears mufti and a bowler, and looks deceptively shy and neat until someone blunders ; then the lips still tighten into that prim, pursed look that Cochrane once called his " mule face."

Fauquier retired with his old rank of air commodore and is now head of a big company in Toronto. His business, oddly enough, is building concrete structures. A change from knocking them down.

Cheshire ! Cheshire had a variety of ideas for after the war, most of them as original as himself. One was the " Modern *Mayflower*," to take picked comrades on a chartered ship and settle on an island. Another was to fly orchids from the Caribbean to New York, and another to grow mushrooms in disused tunnels. He had another scheme for forming a company with Martin, Shannon and Munro for experimental aviation. Cheshire said they might finish up flying to the moon, and they looked sideways at him, though it seems now that he was not looking impossibly far ahead after all.

Then the Prime Minister sent him to the Pacific, and he flew in an American plane as Attlee's personal representative to watch the atom bomb fall on Nagasaki. He came back, resigned from the Air Force and collected a band of unsettled ex-servicemen to form a communal group which he called " Vade in Pacem " (May you walk in peace) in an old house in Hampshire left him by an aunt. Cheshire's health broke down ; he went to Canada to recover, and for eight months in a forest hamlet in the Rockies the intellectual V.C. delivered groceries, cut wood and collected corpses for the local undertaker.

He sold his clothes to pay his fare back to England, arriving in Hampshire at Christmas, 1947, to find his settlement breaking up and £18,000 of debts on his head. He sold his furniture to pay his more pressing debts, and was sitting alone in the empty house when he heard of an old man dying of cancer nearby ; he had put his age back fifteen years to join the R.A.F. in the war and now had no one to help him. Cheshire borrowed a bed and took him in, nursed him, cooked for him, scrubbed the floors, carried the bedpans, washed the old man's pyjamas and lived off the garden. He heard of a bedridden woman of ninety-five with no one to help her, borrowed another bed and took her in.

The man was dying, and Cheshire was sitting with him in the middle of the night when he stopped breathing. There was a religious book on the bed, and Cheshire picked it up and started to read. When he had finished it he went to see the local Roman Catholic priest and four months later joined the Catholic Church.

Meantime, of its own volition, the house had grown into a hospital. Incurables kept knocking on the door and he took them in. The place had a strange spirit about it ; bed-ridden patients helped by sewing and darning ; a few who could walk put rags under their feet and shuffled over the floors to scrub them. Nurses and students came down to help in their spare time, and several men and women gave up their jobs for the privilege of living and working in the place. They had nearly forty patients and no money but somehow kept going.

Cheshire sold some cottages on the property, and some time about the middle of 1949 found he was free of debt. I've asked him several times how he paid it all off, and he always says, " I can't really explain it. Things just seemed to work out." He did, in fact, develop a fatalistic attitude that if he did not worry things would be all right. Peculiarly enough, they were.

A man called Cowie did his books, and one Wednesday he went to Cheshire and said, " Look, we're ten pounds short for our bills on Friday. We can't meet them."

" This isn't Friday," Cheshire said. " See me about it then. Something will turn up."

On Friday a letter arrived with £12 in notes from a woman in London. No one had been in touch with her.

Weeks later they were about £10 short again on the Wednesday. On the Friday a letter arrived from the same woman with another £12. Again no one had told her. The same thing happened once more a few weeks later.

Cowie, who has no faith (he is an agnostic) says that sort of thing kept happening. After a while, in spite of himself, he developed some of Cheshire's fatalism, and once, just before Christmas, when they had debts of £40 to pay and no money in the bank, Cowie went nervously to Cheshire and said : " I've sent off those cheques for the full amount. I only hope something turns up.

Next morning's post brought a cheque for £41.

The renown of the place spread until regular benefactors shouldered the burden of paying some of the bills. That left Cheshire with time on his hands, and it was Sir Ralph Cochrane who found him a job. A singularly appropriate job ! He is working for Barnes Wallis.

At Weybridge, Wallis is the white-haired patriarch, pink-faced, gentle and abstracted as ever, an old-fashioned doyen with new-fangled vision browsing over the same old drawing board, still getting outlandish ideas which unaccountably work. His friends urged him to claim a reward for his wartime inventions, but he said that if he did he would never touch such money for himself. I asked him why, and he said, " My dear chap, go and read your Bible. Turn up Samuel II, chapter twenty-three. You probably haven't got a Bible, so I'll tell you this story about David :

" He was hiding in the cave of Adullam after the Philistines had seized Bethlehem, and in his anguish he said, ' Oh that one would give me drink of the water of the well of Bethlehem, which is by the gate ! ' Now the three mighty men who were his lieutenants were with him, and I'm dashed if they didn't fight their way through the Philistine lines and draw a goatskin of water out of the well by the gate. They fought their way back and took the water to David in the cave, but when they told him how they had got it he would not drink it. They asked him why, and he said :

" ' Is not this the blood of the men that went in jeopardy of their lives ? ' "

THE END

(Just after this was written the Royal Commission on Awards to Inventors granted Barnes Wallis £10,000 for his wartime work. He immediately put it into a fund to help educate the sons and daughters of men who died serving with the Royal Air Force.)

INDEX

(Most of the ranks, titles and decorations listed in this index are those held at the end of the war, but in a few important cases they are those held at the present time.)

THE BOOK OF FAMOUS FLYERS

B.F.F.

Frontispiece

A BIRD'S-EYE VIEW.

What the earth and sea look like from the air! A colourful glimpse caught from
a low-flying 'plane, with a flying-boat in the foreground.

THE BOOK OF
FAMOUS FLYERS

EDITED BY
J. A. MOLLISON

*An interesting account of the history of aviation from the early
pioneers to present-day aces of the air*

LONDON AND GLASGOW
COLLINS' CLEAR-TYPE PRESS

PRINTED IN GREAT BRITAIN
BY WM. COLLINS SONS & CO. LTD.
LONDON AND GLASGOW

INTRODUCTION

IT has been a great pleasure to edit a volume of this nature, because throughout its pages there is that inspiration for others which led me, at an early age, to look to the air and aircraft for a career.

In just a few years, one sees the whole history of flight unfolded—the early adventures and difficulties of those who believed in the air as a medium of transport.

Their nationality is unimportant ; the air is essentially international, and knows no boundaries. Throughout this book you see the panorama of achievement revealed. You will realise that aircraft have revolutionised our conception of distance, and we will join in admiration for those early visionaries, as in their day they were thought, who paved the way and made air transport the accomplished fact it is to-day.

In conclusion, I should like to emphasise that, as editor, my main interest is the spacing and accuracy of the subject matter. The opinions expressed are not always my own. This applies particularly to the chapter concerning my wife and myself, which is unnecessarily flattering, and has only been retained at the insistence of the publishers.

J. A. MOLLISON.

VICKERS "VIMY."

[" *Flight* " *photo.*

*Fitted with two Rolls-Royce " Eagle "
engines of 375 h.p. each, this type has
to its credit the first crossing of the
Atlantic—Alcock and Brown—and the
first flight to Australia piloted by Sir
Ross and Keith Smith.*

CONTENTS

"HAWK MAXIMUS."   *"Flight" photo.*

Sq.-Ldr. Malcolm McGregor and Henry Walker reached Melbourne in their standard Miles "Hawk Maximus" 7 days 15 hours after leaving Mildenhall.

COLOUR ILLUSTRATIONS

THE WRIGHT BROTHERS.

Orville and Wilbur Wright, who were the first to fly in an aeroplane under its own power leaving the earth and landing on the ground as high as that from which it took off.

THE PIONEER AIRMEN

THE Wright Brothers, Louis Blériot, Henry Farman, Hubert Latham, Santos-Dumont, S. F. Cody, Hiram Maxim, S. P. Langley, Delagrange and Mademoiselle Peltier.

THE first faint glimmerings of the idea which led to the designing of mighty aircraft might never have entered man's brain but for a father's present to his sons.

The Reverend Milton Wright, an American subject, had two sons, both of whom were born at Dayton, Ohio. Like most other boys they were interested in things mechanical and, in 1878, when Wilbur was eleven and Orville seven, their father gave them a toy which in some ways resembled a helicopter. It thrilled them, and they set to work to construct one on a larger scale, one in which they might rise from the ground.

Imagine them at their task, the germ of a colossal idea in their minds. Imagine the unwieldy contraption at which all their friends laughed. Imagine their chagrin when the machine failed to move a yard. The puny efforts of these two immature youths were doomed to failure and, as printing and publishing and bicycle repairing claimed their attention, they forgot for years their early aerial experiments. Twenty long years elapsed before they again seriously turned their thoughts, as others were doing, to a craft which would fly.

The deeds of the experimenters in gliding had not passed them unheeded, but it was the death of Otto Lilienthal, a German, who crashed while testing a glider driven by an engine operated by carbon-dioxide, that at last reawakened in them the latent desire to rise from the earth.

Lilienthal had shown them that in order to fly successfully it was futile to allow the machine to be controlled entirely by air currents. It was this which led to his undoing, for he became confused over the operation of controls fixed to his head. His machine nose-dived and he broke his spine.

The Wright Brothers started experimenting where Lilienthal left off. They gave up their bicycle business and went completely over to aircraft. Other flyers of that day were of the opinion that the flyer should stand upright, but the Wrights believed that if the airman lay prone—on his stomach—there would not be so much wind resistance, and in this fearsome attitude they carried out many tests. They were also convinced, like Lilienthal, that the secret of flight lay in the use of an engine, but they turned to a petrol motor.

They approached most of the engine designers of America, but because America was then far behind Europe in mechanics, they were met with blunt refusal. Said a well-known designer: " I am one of the greatest builders of engines in the world, and I say that this engine you are asking me to construct for you is an impossibility."

With characteristic energy the Wrights set to work to make their own engine. Followed days, weeks, months of heart-breaking disappointment, but at long last it was ready and in 1903 fitted into a machine of their own design and build. In that year they actually flew—although their longest flight occupied only 59 seconds—and they covered a distance of less than 300 yards. Nevertheless, the Wright Brothers *had* flown, and theirs is the first recorded instance of an aeroplane under its own power leaving the earth and landing on ground as high as that from which it took off.

PAULHAN'S 'PLANE.

The famous Farman biplane with which, in 1910, Louis Paulhan won the *Daily Mail* prize of £10,000 for the first London to Manchester flight.

The quarter-size model aeroplane (known as the "Langley Aerodrome") with which, in the nineties of last century, S. P. Langley demonstrated the possibilities of heavier-than-air flying.

TAKING OFF.
Blériot is seen in full flight over the aerodrome.

14

Courtesy] [F. J. Camm.

Fokker, the famous aircraft designer, on his "glider."

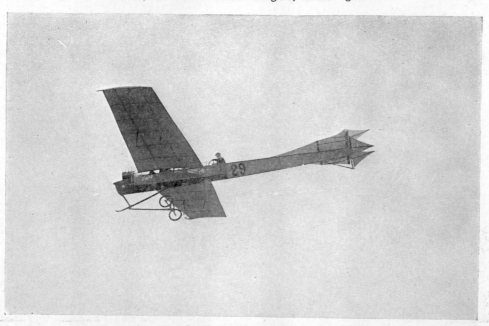

LATHAM'S 'PLANE.
Hubert Latham's Antoinette Monoplane, with which early records were made.

["Flight" Photo

["Flight" Photo

TWO EARLY TYPES OF 'PLANES.

Contrasted with the huge machines of to-day, which are capable of lifting many tons, it hardly seems possible that these 'planes with their frail structures and unreliable engines attained any success in the air.

The months passed and distances and times improved. The newspapers started to report the flights of the Wright Brothers, whereupon Wilbur and Orville immediately stopped experimenting, for they hated publicity. The result was that the stories of their attempts at flight were soon discredited, even though Orville had flown some miles.

In the midst of what the critics called their " gross exaggerations," the Wrights tried to find a buyer for the machine they had perfected. They were laughed to scorn. Even then they did not give trials in public, but hid themselves away and continued secret experimenting. What chance did they have, people asked, when engineers said that what they claimed was utterly impossible ? It is easy to imagine the sadness of the two Americans, knowing they could fly, and seeing all the credit going to French experimenters who were supposed to be making gigantic strides in aviation.

Eventually, in 1908, driven to desperation by the taunts of the European as well as their own press, they decided to give the world a lesson. Wilbur set sail for France while Orville remained in America. On both sides of the Atlantic they meant to prove that they were the greatest airmen of all time.

Without friends Wilbur put up a little shed at Le Mans, now the scene of the great French motor race, and prepared his ugly-looking machine for flight. He was dogged by ill-luck. His engine ran erratically no matter what he did to it and the French critics derided all his claims. Wilbur decided at this juncture to risk a death-crash in a now-or-never series of flights. Disregarding the faults of his engine, he flew, but as the distances covered were so poor compared with those of his French rivals, the " Wright bubble," as it was called, was said to have burst.

But Wilbur Wright's day was to come ; success was only round the corner. On September 21 he had France and the rest of the world at his feet. His engine, running as he hoped that it would, gave a splendid lead, and he made a record flight of nearly sixty miles, easily outdistancing the flights of all other aeronauts. Not content with this he soon began to take up passengers, and to make further records. A little later he was in the air for two and a half hours, covering 77 miles. Money prizes for record flights began to come in thick and fast. In a short while he secured £20,000 in this way.

Success now assured both in Europe and America—in the States Orville had created a sensation—the Wrights were asked by governments all over

HENRY FARMAN
Who flew 5000 feet in 1½ minutes (1908).

the world to give demonstrations. King Edward VII. watched Wilbur's trials at Pau, France, as also did members of the British Cabinet, and King Alfonso. The Italian Government asked for trials, ready to place orders if successful. In America, to which he returned in 1909, he was successful in his tests and received an order for a machine and £6,000.

To-day to this pioneer of flight whom the world scorned there is a beautiful monument at Le Mans. Wilbur died in 1912, but Orville Wright is still living, to note with satisfaction and pride the strides that have been made since those far-off days of 1903 when he and his brother taught the world to fly.

Following closely behind the Wrights came Louis Blériot, a man who was to be even more successful in his aerial accomplishments. He was born at Cambrai, in France, only a year after Orville Wright, and grew up in a world waiting and watching the French aviators at their task of conquering the air. Unlike the Wrights, however, Blériot did not commence experiments of any sort until he was nearly thirty years of age, by which time he could afford to spend unlimited sums, having made a fortune as a motor-car headlamp manufacturer.

Blériot soon came to the conclusion that propeller-driven machines were best, and it was he

LOUIS BLÉRIOT.
Louis Blériot (right), with his manager in England, M. Chereau.

who first placed an engine in the *nose* of a flying machine. Blériot is known as the man who crashed fifty times. Fortunately, not once did he seriously hurt himself, and each successive crash merely spurred him to further efforts.

Some of his machines were weird and wonderful. There was one, built in 1905, in which the back and front wings were great ovals. The machine had two twenty-five horse-power motors, but it was a complete failure.

Not until Blériot had spent £30,000 on experiments did he succeed in remaining in the air, and then his monoplane flew for just eight and a half minutes.

It was this successful flight after so many failures which served to bring another aeronaut to prominence. Henry Farman, born of English parents in France in 1875, had watched Blériot's work carefully, and it was a matter of luck that Blériot made history with his monoplane just a short while before Farman's name was added to air records. Farman had been in turn a painter, cycle maker and racer and a motor-car racer. Now, as an aerial experimenter, he was fast overhauling his contemporaries. Blériot no sooner created a record than Farman went up to beat it. These two intrepid conquerors of space fought a neck-and-neck duel—a duel which at any moment might send one or the other to eternity.

When Farman went ahead by flying from one town to another, Blériot immediately met the challenge by flying from one town to another and back again, covering a greater distance. For months these two engaged in this battle, but eventually Farman dropped out, to concentrate on designing. His biplane became world-famous in the Great War.

Aviators were now springing up everywhere, and there arose another pilot to fight for honours, again a Frenchman, by name Hubert Latham. Latham created a record by being the first man to take up a passenger in a monoplane, and later he raised the altitude figure by flying at the then great height of 450 feet. The reason why altitude records were so few was because many of the early airmen believed that the longest flights could be attained only by flying near the ground.

At last a test was set worthy of the great pioneers. The London *Daily Mail* offered a prize of £1,000 to the first man who could cross the English Channel by air. To you this may seem a simple test, but it must be remembered that while flights of sixty and more miles had been made, machines were still so untrustworthy that the idea of crossing a twenty-mile stretch of water was looked upon as next to impossible ; certainly a terrific hazard.

Latham determined to win the £1,000, as also did Blériot. In July, 1909, Latham took his queer-shaped monoplane to Sangatte near Calais, preparatory to flying the Channel. He wasted no time, for any day Blériot might make his attempt. In the same month at about 6.20 one morning he took off for Dover—just those few miles separating him from £1,000 and an achievement which would go down in history as the greatest flight to date.

["Flight" Photo

COLONEL CODY.
Colonel S. F. Cody, a pioneer of British flying.

A MAN-LIFTING KITE.
Colonel Cody's man-lifting kite, in mid-air, with an officer of the Royal Engineers in basket. (Right) Lieut. Bassel *en cerf volant.*

STARTING UP.
M. Tissandier's "Wright" machine (showing starting method).

22

AN AERIAL GYMNAST.
Reims Aviation Week. M. Lefevbre's "Wright" machine in flight.

CODY'S MACHINE IN FLIGHT.
Colonel Cody flying, during Doncaster Flying Week.

SANTOS-DUMONT.
A pioneer French flyer.

[I.E.A.

For one, two, three, four, even six miles, at a steady forty-five miles an hour, his engine behaved magnificently; but when seven miles had been covered it began to miss badly, and Latham was forced into the water. Could the 'plane float and so save him? Luckily it did and he was ultimately picked up by a French torpedo boat deputed to follow his course.

Blériot decided to make his attempt at once, for he knew that Latham would try again. On July 25 at four in the morning Blériot stepped into his machine. He was a sick man, with a fearful abscess on his foot, the result of a petrol explosion. It had kept him on crutches for days. He circled the coast once, circled again, then set his machine for Dover. The 'plane did not carry a single instrument. If he ran into a mist he would not know his altitude. His speed was an unknown quantity. Sight alone was his guide.

The weather remained fair. He expected to fail and yet, travelling uneventfully, he covered the twenty miles in a little less than forty minutes, landing behind Dover Castle.

The scene in Dover can scarcely be described. The streets were packed to suffocation. Flags were waved everywhere, guns fired. Never did Dover know such a demonstration, and never has there been one like it since. The Channel, hitherto an impassable barrier to all aircraft, had been flown. France was closer to Britain. Europe was no more than a few minutes' aerial journey from England. Visions of flights to India, to South Africa and Australia were no longer wild imaginings.

Hubert Latham was not downhearted because his rival had won the £1,000. He still wanted to fly the Channel, and be the second to conquer that expanse of water. Two days after Blériot's brilliant feat he took off again. His machine behaved splendidly. The cliffs of Dover loomed up.

He was scarcely a mile away—when again his engine failed and he dived straight into the sea. He was rescued, and he never tried again.

Another of the early masters of the air was Leon Delagrange, a sculptor. It was Delagrange who first gave a woman a flight. This was at Turin in 1908 when he took up a Mademoiselle Peltier.

The honour of taking two passengers into the air belongs to Louis Blériot, one of his passengers being Santos-Dumont, another pioneer.

Dumont's story is most interesting. He was born in 1873 on a Brazilian coffee plantation and, when only seven, could drive a steam tractor round

[" *Flight* " *Photo*

SIR HIRAM MAXIM.
An early British flyer. Like Colonel Cody, he was an American who became a British subject.

25

the fields. At twelve he was driving a locomotive with loads of green coffee on the sixty acres of his father's plantation.

Dumont predicted flight. With his boy friends, seated round a table, he used to play a game known as " Pigeon Flies." The leader in the game would call out " Pigeon flies ! " or " Hen flies ! " or " Crow flies ! " and so on, and the other players had to raise their hands unless " Dog flies ! " or " Fox flies ! " or any other thing which could not fly, was called. When anyone raised a hand wrongly a forfeit had to be paid, and it was Dumont who always made himself unpopular by his refusal to pay forfeit when his hand was put up on the cry " Man flies ! " He would assert that man would fly.

Santos-Dumont, however, was to work on balloons as well as aeroplanes. He made his first balloon in 1888 at the age of fifteen. In 1891 he went to Paris with his parents and on his first free afternoon there slipped away to watch some balloons, then the only known means of rising from the ground. The youthful Santos watched astonished, not at the flights, but because he discovered it was impossible to steer these cumbrous gasbags ; and immediately his thoughts turned in this direction. Santos-Dumont eventually flew a dirigible across Paris. On one occasion he set out to win a big sum of money for a flight of seven miles in thirty minutes, circling the Eiffel Tower. He succeeded after several attempts. During one of the failures his machine grounded on the Trocadero building quite close to the famous Tower, and Paris had the thrill and horror combined of seeing the envelope explode.

There were naturally other great pioneers of flight, amongst them Sir Hiram Maxim, an American who became a British subject, and renowned for his invention of the Maxim machine-gun. And there were the Americans S. F. Cody and S. P. Langley. To the latter we owe the idea of launching from ships.

[L.E.A.

M. DELAGRANGE.
The first airman to take up a woman passenger.

REAL MASTERS
of the AIR

PAULHAN AND HIS AEROPLANE.   [L.E.A.
Winner of the £10,000 prize in a flight from London to Manchester under 24 hours in April 27, 1910.

GLEN H. CURTISS. Claude Graham-White. Paulhan. The First Air Pageants. Curtiss prepares for an Atlantic Flight.

HAVE you ever seen an air display, and watched the daredevil evolutions of our most famous airmen ? How simple flying has become ! Very different indeed from the first air pageant ever held, when the greatest airmen of the day took their lives in their hands, even though they flew scarcely above the roof-tops.

Doubtless that first air display was much more thrilling to the spectators than are the pageants of modern times ; for flying then was something startlingly new, while to-day it has become commonplace.

This first of all air meets took place at Reims, in France, in 1909, and nearly forty aeroplanes were entered by a galaxy of great aviators. Amongst them were Henry Farman, Hubert Latham, Louis Blériot, Paulhan, a French aviator who was drawing to the forefront, and Glenn H. Curtiss, an American engine designer and clever experimenter in aeronautics.

27

From Britain, from all parts of Europe, from America also, people came in their thousands to watch the new marvel of flight. A quarter of a million spectators witnessed the exhibition and competitions during the five days of the display, and they were given thrills in abundance. Louis Blériot was fortunate to escape with his life, for his machine caught fire, and it was only with the greatest difficulty that he managed to land safely. Notwithstanding his presence of mind and courage he was severely burned.

The onlookers held their breath when Delagrange broke his propeller in mid-air. To any craft of that time the breakdown of a propeller was more than sufficient to put up the tail and send the machine swooping to earth. But the manner in which Delagrange coaxed his machine down earned for him a great ovation when he eventually reached *terra firma*.

Henry Farman provided a sensation by winning the Grand Prix de Champagne for distance—118 miles without stopping—for 50,000 francs in prize-money. Rarely was he more than ten feet above the ground, skimming the heads of the spectators, the roads and the fields during the whole of this epoch-making flight. The thrill, however, was not in his proximity to the earth; it was in the untried engine and propeller he was using. Farman was flying with a motor that had come straight from the test bench and which had been fixed into his 'plane only an hour or two before the actual flight. Added to this, his propeller had not been tested in any way; there had not been time.

The famous aviators whose names I have already mentioned were very successful, and it is worth taking particular note of the triumphant flights at Reims and contrasting them with the attainments of modern airmen and machines. The comparison is startling.

Glenn H. Curtiss won the fastest two-lap flight around the course. He travelled $12\frac{1}{2}$ miles in 16 minutes—approximately 47 miles per hour. That was the *fastest* time, it should be remembered!

Hubert Latham, who already held the altitude record, now broke the figure by flying at a height of over 500 feet.

Louis Blériot won the fastest single trip around the course at a speed of $47\frac{3}{4}$ miles per hour.

Henry Farman also won what was termed the " Three-men speed contest," by flying with two passengers a distance of 6.2 miles in 10 minutes 40 seconds.

From these successes it will be seen that France had established a definite lead in aeronautics. Britain's part was nil, unless we take into

THE " INFURIATED GRASSHOPPER."
Audemars on the " Infuriated Grasshopper," Bournemouth, July, 1910.

'CROSS CHANNEL.
Latham essays the Channel crossing, starting from Sangatte.

An R.A.F. 'plane of a type which did yeoman service in the Great War. Note the machine-gun mounted on the cockpit.

account that Henry Farman came of English parents. America had succeeded, but Germany had not even entered. This is because the death of Lilienthal made Germany set her face against aircraft. Yet the Reims meet had a far-reaching effect, the result of which is startlingly brought to light in the next chapter. It set Germany's eyes on aviation. She decided that, even though more of her sons die in their attempts to perfect aircraft, she must compete with those about her. And Germany built her first machine !

The world realised now that commerce via the air would give the foremost air nation a great advantage over rivals, and every nation began to encourage airmen in the new science.

Glenn H. Curtiss soon became the premier American flyer, and his name still lives in the engines of the Curtiss Company, which, for many years, have been fitted into types of American machines. Curtiss was born in 1878 and died in 1930. Like other aeronauts, he started as a motor-cycle builder and racer, and it was while racing that he attracted the attention and interest of Alexander Graham Bell, the Scotsman who settled in America and to whom we owe the ultimate invention of the telephone. Graham Bell gave Curtiss every assistance and he went from success to success.

An Englishman at long last entered the arena of aeronautics. Why Britain, with her huge Empire, had lagged behind is perhaps due to her natural disinclination to try anything new until she is really forced into moving. An Englishman, however, was ready to show the world that we were progressive—Claude Graham-White, born a year after Curtiss, and a motor engineer.

It was not until he was thirty years of age that he took up the

[L.E.A.

GLENN H. CURTISS.
A notable American flyer.

science, and then with characteristic resource and cleverness he quickly assumed the leading role. Graham-White was the first Englishman to receive a pilot's certificate, and certainly the first to challenge the supremacy of America as the English-speaking nation making the greatest strides.

Curtiss had by this time set the world agog. He flew at fifty-five miles an hour with a passenger at the first American air display ; he flew from Albany to New York, a distance of 150 miles, in less than three hours' flying time, for which he secured a prize of £2,000 offered by the *New York Herald*. A pupil of Curtiss won a prize for a return flight between New York and Philadelphia.

Graham-White had been making a name for himself at home, and he soon found himself opposed to the Frenchman Paulhan. Competition between the two reached its height when they both decided to try to win the £10,000 offered by the *Daily Mail* for a flight from London to Manchester —183 miles.

For his attempt Graham-White chose a Farman machine—Farman was now establishing himself as a builder of reliable aircraft. On April 23, 1910, he took off. The weather was miserable, and when he reached Lichfield he was forced to come down.

Now real bad luck set in for Graham-White. The wind became so boisterous as to play havoc with his machine, and next day there was no alternative but to have it returned to London.

Paulhan also selected a Farman and, four days after Graham-White started his attempt, he took off, reaching Lichfield without incident.

Graham-White noted his rival's progress apprehensively, but it so happened that on the day chosen by Paulhan, Graham-White's machine was ready once more. Graham-White did not waste a moment. Immediately he took off. Again luck was against him, for, because he had started in late afternoon, darkness forced him down at a spot some sixty miles behind his rival. Forced down by darkness, remember ! The aeronauts of that day had yet to master night flying.

At 2.30 next morning, long before dawn, Graham-White decided on a bold move. He would fly through the darkness in an effort to overtake the Frenchman. The machine was started up, Graham-White climbed into position and set off—the first authentic case of an airman flying by night. He sped on to Lichfield, but there was no sign of Paulhan. Dropping to the ground, he was told that Paulhan had left only five minutes before. Graham-White did not wait longer. He set his machine skywards,

AERIAL TRANSPORT.

A feature of military life in desert regions is the transportation of troops by air. Here is a detachment about to embark in a giant 'plane.

CLAUDE GRAHAM-WHITE.   [" *Flight* " *Photo*
On April 28th, 1910, Graham-White made the first night ascent in the London to Manchester race.

and did all he possibly could to overtake the Frenchman. But those five minutes were sufficient to keep Paulhan ahead all the way, and, when Manchester flocked to the flying ground in the hope that their hero, Graham-White, might be the first to land, it was Paulhan whose machine dropped first and won the £10,000. The time allowance set by the *Daily Mail* had been 24 hours. Paulhan took about half that time.

Graham-White was not downhearted, and he decided to take part that year in the second American air pageant. This time he scored a great personal triumph. He won easily a bomb-dropping contest, and at once followed this success by winning £2,000 for a distance flight. In both cases he relied upon a Blériot monoplane.

A month later another display was staged in America at which forty airmen and 'planes were on view. The Gordon Bennett speed contest for aeroplanes was also won by Graham-White at a speed of 61 miles per hour, although a French pilot would have beaten him but for ill-luck. Flying at 67 miles per hour, his petrol ran out on the last lap and he struck a telegraph pole and crashed.

Meets now followed one another in America and on the Continent, and because big prizes were offered records were made and broken almost daily. The result was that engines and aircraft improved out of all knowledge, giving the airmen an easier task in controlling them.

Germany also held air meets, and in 1912 the world's records were *long distance*, 627 miles; *speed*, 105 miles per hour; *altitude*, 18,000 feet —an increase in two years which almost takes one's breath away.

Just previous to this an attempt at an air mail service was made in England, a mail delivery being run between Windsor and Hendon. America followed with a rather more successful attempt.

Then Curtiss came into the limelight once more. Lord Northcliffe, then owner of *The Times*, offered a prize of £10,000 for a transatlantic flight. Curtiss started work to build an engine which would take a flyer across the great stretch of ocean, and he was within thirty days of having it ready for the attempt when murder was done! This seemingly unimportant murder took place in Europe, when an Austro-Hungarian royalty was killed. Within a few days Europe was at war. The Great War had started, and civil flying was at a standstill. But out of the holocaust of battle was to emerge an army of airmen whose daring will live for all time.

TWO GERMAN AVIATORS.

M. Ollivier and Baron Richthofen about to take off. Baron Richthofen was the leading German " ace "
in the Great War.

[L.E.A.

AIRMAN ACES OF THE GREAT WAR

ANTHONY H. G. FOKKER, the designer. Baron von Richthofen. Captain Fonck. Captain William A. Bishop. Captain Albert Ball. Captain George Guynemer. Captain W. Leefe Robinson. Count Zeppelin's mighty craft.

THE Great War—1914-1918—produced a number of super-airmen, and yet it can be stated with accuracy that many of these aces were scarcely more than boys at the outbreak of hostilities, new to the ways of warfare from above. For, as has been seen in previous chapters, aeronautics had just emerged from its infancy.

During the first two years of the war it was a constant game of attack and counter, until stalemate was reached when both sides had machines of equal quality and speed.

From the moment, a few years earlier, that Germany had realised the power in an air arm, she had steadily increased her budgeting for machines until, at the commencement of battle, she was far superior in men and machines to the Allied forces.

One non-combatant in particular caused the Allies to fear the German aircraft and airmen—not a flyer at all but a designer—a man whose services were actually offered to the Allies, but whom they rejected on the score that he was too expensive. This greatest aircraft designer of the time was Anthony H. G. Fokker, a Dutchman born in Java.

Nobody would have thought him, as a small boy, capable of one day evolving the world's fastest aircraft, to deal death in most cases whenever opposed to enemy machines. He was much like the native boys in his childhood, adept at climbing trees like a monkey, at picking up nails with his toes, and in doing all the wild and adventurous things beloved of native lads.

When quite young he built a model railway track to take up the whole of the downstairs floor space, but because his friends were not always available to work the points, he invented a system of automatic switching.

But this did not meet with his approval after a time. He found that, despite his system's efficiency, he was continually winding up the clockwork of his trains, and this was a nuisance. So he electrified the whole of the line.

But again he was not satisfied, for the renewal of batteries was too costly, so he arranged to make use of the domestic supply.

He made gas engines as a youth, steam engines, a " puncture-proof tyre," and even built an extremely seaworthy canoe at the age of twelve.

There came a time when he began to take an interest in the Wright Brothers and other

ANTHONY H. G. FOKKER.
The greatest aircraft designer of his time.

[L.E.A.

ARMY TESTS.
Army Aeroplane Tests on Salisbury Plain, 2nd August, 1912.

THE PILOT.
Cody pilots a 'plane in the Army Aeroplane Tests.

LANGLEY 'PLANE.
A Langley aeroplane piloted by Glenn H. Curtiss at Hammondsport, N.Y., 1914.

A 1912 MODEL.
An Army 'plane taking part in the Army Aeroplane Tests, 1912.

HANDLEY-PAGE, 1918.
A Handley-Page ready to start out on a bombing raid, Dunkirk, 1st June, 1918.

LAUNCHING A SEAPLANE.
Hoisting out a seaplane from the *Ark Royal*, January, 1916.

39

experimenters. He could not build an aeroplane—he was too young—but he certainly could attach wires and string to a chair in the attic of the house in which he lived, and work them as if he were actually flying. This " machine " greatly intrigued him. Even when, in 1910, he built an odd-looking monoplane, he had never so much as seen a machine in the air, and his knowledge was practically all self-taught.

At the outbreak of war he was busy building 'planes for Germany, and the Fokker soon became a grave menace to the Allies. The Germans had shot down a French machine in which was a crude contraption for shooting machine gun bullets through the propeller. The propeller was fitted with plates which, if struck, deflected the bullets without damaging the propeller. It was the best invention of its kind, but, as is natural, many bullets were wasted. The Germans asked Fokker to study the idea and see if he could produce something more serviceable. Fokker started his task on a Tuesday. By Friday he had perfected a machine gun which would shoot bullets through the propeller without the need for deflectors. Thus did the Fokker menace to the Allies grow, for the British and French observers were mostly using ordinary rifles when in battle in the clouds, or a type of machine gun which was particularly cumbersome for manœuvring. Fokker, therefore, paved the way for the German air aces, and helped to make it possible for Baron von Richthofen to bring down no fewer than eighty enemy machines before in turn being killed in an air duel.

Richthofen was undoubtedly the greatest of all war aces, and fearless to a degree. He led a " circus "—a squadron of fighters, each man an " artiste " in aerial duelling. His machines were painted a fiery red ; so the Richthofen circus could always be detected by friend and foe. In his memoirs, which were published only a few months before his death, he said of the British airman : " He is a dashing fellow. He used to come now and then and pelt our flying ground with bombs. He simply challenged one to battle, and always accepted it. I hardly ever encountered an Englishman who refused to fight."

It was in April, 1918, that his red-painted war birds went into an engagement with three British battle-planes, and in the general melee he and another member of his squadron were shot down and killed.

His French counterpart, who officially brought down seventy-five enemy machines, was Captain Fonck. He took up flying only two years before the war started, but by the time airmen were wanted was a daredevil of the first order. On one occasion, for example, he engaged a number

BARON RICHTHOFEN.
The great German " ace " responsible for bringing down eighty enemy 'planes before he himself was killed in an air duel.

[*L.E.A.*

of German biplanes and, fighting like a fiend, succeeded in bringing down six of them. As an adjunct to the British air force in Flanders he was immensely helpful, and he was awarded our Distinguished Conduct Medal and the Military Cross.

The greatest of the British " aces " was Captain William A. Bishop, Distinguished Service Order, Military Cross, V.C., a member of the Canadian Expeditionary Forces, credited with seventy-two victories over enemy aircraft. The official despatch of the exploit for which he was awarded the Victoria Cross makes thrilling reading, even though it is written in the matter-of-fact style of such statements.

" Captain Bishop, who had been sent out to work independently, flew first of all to an enemy aerodrome. Finding no machines about, he flew on to another aerodrome about three miles south-east, which was at least twelve miles the other side of the line. Seven machines, some with their

COLONEL BISHOP, V.C.
Credited with 72 victories over enemy aircraft.

[L.E.A.

engines running, were on the ground. He attacked these from about 50 feet, and a mechanic, who was starting one of the engines, was seen to fall. One of the machines got off the ground, but at a height of 60 feet Captain Bishop fired fifteen rounds into it at very close range, and it crashed to the ground. A second machine got off the ground, into which he fired thirty rounds at 150 yards range, and it fell into a tree. Two more machines then rose from the aerodrome. One of these he engaged at the height of 1000 feet, emptying the rest of his drum of ammunition. This machine crashed 300 yards from the aerodrome, after which Captain Bishop emptied a whole drum into the fourth hostile machine, and then flew back to his station. Four hostile scouts were 1000 feet above him for about a mile of his return journey, but they would not attack. His machine was very badly shot about by machine-gun fire from the ground."

Another British air " ace " was a boy killed at the age of twenty-one, Captain Albert Ball, V.C. Born at Nottingham in 1896, he was the son of a wealthy business man. He was in the Scout Movement as a lad, and had just entered an engineering business when the war broke out. He joined up, obtained a commission, went to France and was quickly transferred to the air service. On one occasion he attacked as many as twelve German 'planes single-handed. In all, he took part in over a hundred fights. He flew to attack hostile 'planes in May, 1917, from which he never returned alive. He came in contact with the Richthofen "circus" on several occasions, and the Germans claim that Richthofen's brother, also in the German air service, was responsible for shooting Ball down. Richthofen himself said of Ball that he was one of the most feared of all the Allied flyers—this boy of tender years !

[L.E.A.

CAPTAIN W. LEEFE ROBINSON, V.C.
The first airman to bring down a Zeppelin over British soil.

Just as young and just as skilful was the Frenchman, Captain George Guynemer, who was shot down and killed at the age of twenty-three. Over fifty victories were to his credit before a bullet through the head during a fight ended his life. His most thrilling battle was when he shot down two German machines in exactly one minute, and later in the day went up and accounted for a further two !

But perhaps the name which lingers longest in the memory of those who remember the war deeds of the airmen is that of Captain W. Leefe Robinson, V.C., the first man to bring down a Zeppelin over British soil —and he did this hitherto "impossible" task at the age of twenty-one.

Leefe Robinson was born in Southern India, travelled extensively in Russia as a lad, and entered Sandhurst during the month of the outbreak of war. He became an observer, but was wounded over Lille. On recovery, however, he learned to fly and was attached to various stations in England for night-flying.

On the night of September 2, 1916, an air raid was made on London

43

[*L.E.A.*

CAPTAIN FONCK.
During the Great War Captain Fonck brought down six German biplanes in a single engagement.

by Zeppelins, and Captain Leefe Robinson went up to help beat off the raiders. He had already engaged one airship, which escaped him, when he saw immediately ahead a second monster of the skies. Braving the accurate gunfire from the anti-aircraft defences on the ground, he carried on a running fight with the heavily-armed Zeppelin. The airship threw out black clouds of smoke in an endeavour to shake him off, and its machine-gunners kept up an intensive attack; but always Leefe Robinson stuck to his self-imposed task. When at last he felt the moment was right, he dived at a height of 10,000 feet straight at the intruder, pumping streams of lead into it. In an instant it burst into flames, to fall to earth a blazing, broken mass, at Cuffley, a few miles from London's northern suburbs. Strangely enough, Leefe Robinson did not die while fighting the enemy in the skies, like so many of his contemporaries. He died on a sick bed, as a result of influenza and his generally lowered condition as a prisoner of war in Germany. He was captured in 1917, after being shot down out of control: and for making several attempts to escape was placed in close confinement in a small cell. He returned to England about a month after the war, in a poor state of health. A few days later he caught influenza and, after only a week's illness, succumbed.

Mention of the Zeppelins would not be complete without reference to the man who built these huge craft. He made them actually to give Germany commercial power, but their use in the Great War was a step towards, it was hoped, breaking the morale of the people in England.

Count Zeppelin was born at Constance in 1838, and after a quite ordinary boyhood found himself an officer in the army at the age of twenty. At twenty-five he volunteered for the American Civil War, and it was when he went up in a balloon in the States that he became interested in this type of aircraft.

He took part in the war between Prussia and Austria in 1866, and he served against the French in the Franco-Prussian War. One of his devoted companions in this campaign was an Englishman!

After this war he gave his attention exclusively to the designing and building of airships, and it was not for many years, when he had almost broken himself, that the Kaiser expressed appreciation of his work and funds became more plentiful for his experiments.

The first Zeppelin to fly for any length of time created a great sensation, and Zeppelin's success was soon followed by still more impressive ones. Yet when he died in 1917 he was an old and disappointed man, for he saw his gigantic ships of the air gradually failing before the increasing efficiency of the Allied aircraft and air defences. At least twenty Zeppelins were destroyed by the time of his death, and the fear that more would suffer the same fate ended a great building scheme which was in the German programme. For a time, however, England went in fear of them, and they carried out their work of death and destruction unchecked for many months. The result of Count Zeppelin's experiments was the bringing about of the world's first planned campaign of air raids on a civilian population.

[L.E.A.

COUNT FERDINAND VON ZEPPELIN.
Designer of the giant airships by which German air raids were carried out in the Great War.

The First Transatlantic Flyers

HARRY HAWKER and Commander Mackenzie - Grieve. The American Attempt. Alcock and Brown. Major G. H. Scott and the R34.

HARRY GEORGE HAWKER. [L.E.A.
Known as " The man who won't be killed."

THE contest to be first to cross the Atlantic by air recommenced immediately the Great War ended, and it became evident that America, least hurt in the world struggle, would probably succeed in gaining the honour.

Contrary to expectation, the American authorities decided that a proposed official flight contemplated should be made of real value. The idea of flying non-stop did not appeal to them ; they desired to glean useful data from the costly experiment in view.

For their purpose the American Navy commissioned three Curtiss biplanes—NC1, NC3, and NC4—great craft which had originally been designed as bomb carriers.

While these machines were being prepared, civil airmen were making ready to attempt the flight, for the prize of £10,000 offered before the war was still to be won. The only stipulation was that the distance must be flown non-stop in not more than seventy-two hours, and in consequence each man who essayed the crossing chose to start from America, to benefit from the more favourable winds.

Amongst those who decided to try to win the prize was Harry George Hawker, known in Britain as " the man who won't be killed ! " A most popular contestant, he crossed to America with his friend, Commander

THE ATLANTIC FLIGHT.
Front view of the Vickers-Vimy machine standing on its nose in the bog at Clifden, Co. Galway.

ATLANTIC SEAPLANES.
Two American seaplanes, the NC4 and NC1, lying ready to start on an Atlantic flight. The NC4 completed the flight.

Mackenzie-Grieve, and a Sopwith machine, incorporating a single-engined Rolls-Royce Eagle motor of 320 horse-power. And at Newfoundland the two men waited for good weather. Hawker was confidently expected to succeed, for he seemed to bear a charmed life.

He was born in 1889, in Australia, the son of a blacksmith. At school he was actually backward; but school annoyed him. He wanted to become an engineer, and there was nothing in his lessons which would help him attain his ambition. His natural restlessness was manifest when he took it into his head to see the headmaster of another school and ask to be taken in there, his reason being that they had a cadet corps! He was allowed to enrol, but cadets soon palled, and at twelve he left this school, without even taking his father into his confidence, and obtained employment with a motor dealer.

Three years later he was one of the best drivers in Victoria, and before he was out of his 'teens was a leading motor expert with another employer. At twenty years of age, he decided to come to England, where he hoped to gain knowledge of the science of aeronautics, and get into the air.

His first few weeks in London nearly broke even *his* spirit. Friendless, lost in a great city, new to conditions, utterly strange, and with no hope of work, he began to think seriously of returning to Australia. By chance he came in contact with Mr. Sopwith, airman and designer of the famous aeroplanes after his name, and Sopwith said he would give this young Australian a chance.

Sopwith was well repaid, for he found in Hawker a brilliant student. It did not take him long to fly, or to start record breaking. Soon he had won a £500 prize for Mr. Sopwith, created a British record for a duration flight, and put up some amazing new altitude figures. In 1913 he made a thrilling attempt to win the Flight Round Britain contest. He knew little of seaplanes, in which the race was conducted, but took off. After flying over a thousand miles his machine was wrecked. He escaped little the worse.

Two months after his narrow escape he crashed at Brooklands, and this time had to be taken to hospital. He crashed again five months later, but escaped unhurt, and in the same year nose-dived while looping the loop. He hit some trees, and though his machine was wrecked, he once more escaped unhurt. A few months later the cowling blew off his engine in mid-air and, while his machine was damaged, he himself was not injured.

As a motor-racer he had miraculous escapes from death, on one occasion

IN FORMATION.

British Bulldogs—guardians of our coasts—are here seen flying in formation. Speed and perfect precision are in every well-timed movement.

smashing through some iron railings, damaging his car but still coming to no harm himself. This, then, was the man who was attempting to fly the Atlantic in one hop, with his fearless English navigator.

Hawker and Mackenzie-Grieve soon endeared themselves to the Americans, and on all sides it was hoped that they would get across the Atlantic and secure the £10,000 prize. They had rivals for the attempt—particularly from the British Rolls-Martynside machine to be flown by Mr. F. P. Raynham and his navigator Captain C. W. F. Morgan, R.A.F.—and it was doubtful which machine would start first.

But, while Hawker and Raynham waited for better weather, the American Navy 'planes started. Bad fortune attended NC1 and NC3.

[L.E.A.
LIEUT.-COMDR. MACKENZIE-GRIEVE.

The former lost its bearings in fog and came down in the sea. It was sighted by a vessel and taken in tow, but the towline broke and the aeroplane sank. The crew were all rescued. The NC3 had little better fortune. Caught in fog, it was forced down into the water, but taxied on the surface for over two hundred miles before reaching land—a magnificent feat on the part of its commander, J. H. Towers. The NC4 made up for the ill-luck attendant on its companions by reaching the Azores without incident.

It was at this juncture that Hawker decided he *must* make his attempt. He wanted particularly to reach England before the NC4 arrived at Lisbon, its next port of call, at which stage it could be said that America had first crossed the Atlantic. He planned that, as soon as he was in the air, he would loose the wheels of his 'plane to relieve his machine of weight, relying only on skids to land safely. He carried no sending wireless, trusting to ships to give him direction. Sufficient food was in the 'plane for three days. The moment came for handshakes, and all who saw the intrepid airmen off realised that it might be the last that the world ever saw of them. Once aloft, they turned straight for Ireland, crossing the aerodrome where Raynham waited. The latter, seeing them go, decided that he, too, must be away, for once Hawker got too far ahead it might not be possible to overtake him. The machine was started, he and his navigator took their places ; but a gust of wind caught the heavy machine as it was taxi-ing for a start, tipped it on to its nose and, the engine hitting the ground, was wrecked. Apart from bruises, the two airmen were unhurt, but it was the end of their attempt just then. As a matter of fact, ill-luck dogged Raynham, and he did not make an attempt on the Atlantic at all.

As for Hawker and Mackenzie-Grieve, the machine was sighted by the marine look-out on the hills above St. John's, Newfoundland, who reported her flying well at about eighty miles an hour. He watched her out of sight . . . and that was the last that was heard for several days. In the mean-time the NC4 arrived at Lisbon, having safely accomplished the first Atlantic crossing by stages. She then attempted to fly to Plymouth, but engine failure brought her down in Spain. Repairs were at once effected and she again set off, to be greeted with great jubilation on British soil

But what of Hawker and Mackenzie-Grieve ? As the days passed the world began to give them up for lost, and only one person refused to lose hope—Mrs. Hawker, wife of the airman. Never would she believe that her husband had been drowned ! Destroyers went out and searched for the wreckage of the machine, but returned without news. Hope faded. The airmen were lost for ever ! Questions were asked in Parliament ; it was suggested that these airmen had been allowed to attempt the crossing without support from the nation. The country was sad that two such gallant men should have died. And then the world was electrified. On May 26, eight days after they set out, a message was received in London :

Lloyds signal station at Butt of Lewis telegraphs as follows—" Danish steamer Mary from America, passing eastwards, signalled following : 'Saved hands with Sopwith aeroplane.'"

Station signalled : " Is it Hawker ?"

Steamer replied : " Yes."

Steps were immediately taken by the Admiralty. The *Mary* was inter-cepted by a British destroyer and the two airmen embarked. They were then landed at Thurso. Actually they had been in the sea only about two hours before the *Mary* rescued them, but the good news did not arrive because the vessel carried no wireless.

Their account of the flight is nevertheless a story of a struggle against terrific odds and hardship, even though Hawker makes light of it. He says : "We started because the weather was better. The moon was going off fast. If we did not start then we might miss the chance of being first across." He tells of the food they ate—one sandwich and a small portion of chocolate, with cups of coffee to keep them warm. . . . "And the next thing I ate was seventy-two hours after, for I was violently seasick."

Mackenzie-Grieve's words lend colour to Hawker's matter-of-fact statements. "It was like being in a small motor-boat in a heavy sea when we flew down to look for a ship (after flying 1050 miles). We were between the rough sea and low clouds, and were bumped about badly." When the 'plane alighted he adds, "We had water up to our knees. Waves were sloshing under the upper 'plane, the machine being nose up to the wind. Now and again a big wave rolled over."

["*Flight*" *Photo*

HEROES OF THE ATLANTIC FLIGHT.
Arrival of Alcock and Brown at Euston, after completing the first non-stop Atlantic flight.

Giving the reason for their failure, Hawker said : " My machine stopped owing to the water filter in the feed-pipe from the radiator to the water cock being blocked up with refuse, such as solder and the like, and shaking loose in the radiator. It was no fault of the motor. . . . *I had no trouble in landing in the sea."*

It is those last nine words which sum up Hawker's dare-devil spirit. *We* know what danger those two must have faced in dropping on the water, and yet in a few words Hawker dismisses it as an everyday occurrence.

The journey from Scotland to London was a series of receptions by local dignitaries and stationmasters. Everywhere thousands thronged the platforms to see the two airmen who had literally come back from the grave. At Edinburgh, at Newcastle-on-Tyne, at Darlington, at York they received congratulations. A telegram from the King was handed to Hawker at York inviting him that day to Buckingham Palace. America was equally enthusiastic. The world rejoiced that they had been saved.

Two years later Harry Hawker crashed for the last time. He had ascended in a machine while practising for an Aerial Derby a few days hence. His machine was at a great height when it began to turn over and over, as if in difficulties. Then it burst into flames and nose-dived for the ground. It was impossible for Hawker to save himself, and, though he jumped before the burning machine smashed itself to pieces, he was quite dead when found. Thus passed the first Briton to attempt the Atlantic crossing, a fearless flyer of the first order.

The Atlantic was to be crossed almost a month to the day after Hawker and Mackenzie-Grieve set out on their thrilling trip. Again two Britons made the attempt. Captain John Alcock, Distinguished Service Cross, was born in Manchester in 1892. His boyhood was devoid of anything which suggested that one day he would become a national hero. His technical engineering experience was obtained at a motor works in the city. In 1912 he obtained the Royal Aero Club's Flying Certificate at Brooklands, and distinguished himself in 1913 by running into second place in the London-to-Manchester-and-Back Flight.

At the outbreak of war he joined the Royal Naval Air Service, and was made an instructor at Eastchurch, very soon becoming Chief Instructor of the Aerobatic Squadron. He was drafted to the Eastern Front and found himself opposed to the Turks. He was mentioned for his long-distance flights when bombing, and quickly created a record for this special work. It was in this sector that he was awarded the D.S.C., but later, when

A WESTLAND-WESSEX MONOPLANE.

[" *Flight* " Photo]

In the picture above we are allowed to see through the walls of a modern air liner as it flies along with its passengers. You will notice how cosy is the interior, and how the cabin space is distributed before and behind the wings. Over forty people are travelling in the liner, as well as baggage, and every one has a comfortable seat.

53

This machine, which looks like a giant grasshopper, is an early type of Monoplane. Ever since the first 'plane took to the air, inventors have been striving to make improvements, till to-day there is much more security in air-travel.

Travelling by air need not mean discomfort, as we can see from this view of a luxurious cabin in the Dornier seaplane.

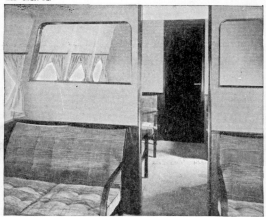

This is another view of the Dornier from inside. Air-passengers can sit here in comfort while they race the clouds.

In the picture above we see the famous German Dornier flying-boat taking to the water. This giant 'plane, which is fitted up to give the maximum of comfort to passengers, shows the rapid advance in aircraft in recent years.

his engine failed him, had the bad luck to be captured by the enemy, who held him prisoner until the Armistice. Which brings his career up to the momentous year 1919.

His companion of the Atlantic flight, Lieutenant Arthur Whitten Brown, was born in Glasgow in 1886, of American parents. In his case, also, his scholastic career was not especially meritorious, but immediately he turned to engineering he created a favourable impression. It was with the British Westinghouse Company that he received his practical engineering knowledge, but he soon became interested in flying and studied aerial navigation. At the beginning of the war he enlisted in the University and Public Schools Corps, but later received a commission in the Manchester Regiment and served with the 2nd Battalion during 1915.

He was transferred to the Royal Flying Corps (now, of course, the Royal Air Force), and became an observer. By a strange coincidence he also was taken prisoner of war. Thus the stage was set for these two Britishers to attempt the Atlantic crossing and win the £10,000.

Their machine was a Vickers-Vimy Rolls-Royce, built at Weybridge, Surrey, by the Vickers Company. It had two engines of Rolls-Royce design, with maximum speed of a little over a hundred miles an hour when fully loaded. It carried four tons of petrol, sufficient for nearly 2,500 miles, making a total load of over five tons.

When preliminary flights at Weybridge were passed as satisfactory, the machine was dismantled and shipped across the Atlantic. On arrival at St. John's, Alcock and Brown found that they were but two of several aspirants for the Atlantic crossing prize. They saw Hawker and Mackenzie-Grieve set off, and it is interesting to dwell for an instant on what their thoughts must have been when the days passed and no news was received of the flyers. They helped to rebuild the crashed machine of Mr. Raynham, but when their own machine arrived they had no time for anything but its assembling, for a big Handley-Page machine was almost ready to set off. The Handley-Page, however, was completely wrecked when eventually it did get away.

It was on June 14 at 5.28 p.m., British Summer Time, that the flight commenced. Weather reports were good, although there was a stiff gale blowing straight towards them. At first one of the engines refused to start, but after a little coaxing it fired and purred so healthily that Alcock decided there was nothing wrong with it.

Actually the time of the flight was to have been kept secret, but in a very short while the news got round that the two British airmen with the Vickers-Vimy were going to start. Thousands of people collected, yet there was more than a little doubt when the heavily-laden machine seemed unwilling to take off. Soon it was in the air, and when it rose steadily and set a course for Ireland cheer upon cheer rent the air.

The weather over the Atlantic was not generally good, and for many hours the two airmen had a rough passage. As night drew on they found themselves in thick cloud and mist ; they could see neither sea, sky nor stars. It was not till about 3 a.m. that Brown was able to obtain position when, for a few minutes, they struck an open patch of sky.

The machine went steadily on into the thick weather. The air speed indicator jammed through sleet freezing on to it. Alcock believes that, during the time when the indicator was not functioning, they looped the loop unknowingly, and went off into a steep spiral. Certainly from about 4000 feet they shot straight for the water ; it was not until they were quite close that they realised what was happening. This gave them their level once more, and the air speed indicator had recommenced work, doubt-less the result of their swift dive. They climbed again to about 6000 feet, only to encounter more fog.

Climbing still farther, they met heavy banks of cloud, while at 11,000 feet it was hailing and snowing. The machine was covered with ice, and Brown was continually chipping it off.

Their food was much the same as that taken by Hawker and Mackenzie-Grieve, but because of the noise of the engine they had to make signs one to the other when they required any.

Even as morning drew on the weather conditions did not improve, and it was not until the last hour of the journey that they could fly fairly low. At 300 feet they could look down upon the sea and, although the weather was still very cloudy, for the first time they saw the sun trying to break through.

Never once did they sight a vessel through that long, exhausting night, nor did they receive a single wireless message. Even when they felt they were at their destination they could not be certain, and it was with great relief that quite suddenly they sighted land ahead.

This was about 9.15 a.m., and very quickly they picked out those parts of the coastline of Ireland they knew well. Flying fairly low, they made out a beautiful meadow. Alcock decided to land on it, but it was nothing but a bog, and the machine toppled over on its nose with its wheels em-

MAJOR G. H. SCOTT

This well-known flyer was killed in an air disaster in 1930.

bedded in slime. They raised themselves out of their cramped positions, unhurt, and were free of the machine before soldiers and other helpers arrived.

The soldiers looked at them. Said one: " You're about at a funny time and in a funny place, I must say!" He did not realise that this 'plane had just flown the Atlantic.

Alcock replied simply: " We're the Vickers machine just arrived from Newfoundland."

For a moment the soldiers and other participants in this historic meeting looked askance. Then with one accord they cheered wildly.

The prize of £10,000 was presented to Alcock and Brown by Mr. Winston Churchill at the Savoy Hotel on June 20th, 1919, and only a few days later they were both knighted " in recognition of distinguished services to aviation in connection with the successful flight from St. John's, Newfoundland, to Clifden, Co. Galway, on the 14th-15th June, 1919."

Sir Arthur Whitten Brown is still alive, but Sir John Alcock was killed in December, 1919, when his aeroplane crashed in fog near Rouen, while he was flying from London to Paris. Their Atlantic Vickers-Vimy machine may still be seen, for it reposes in the Science Museum, South Kensington, London, for all the world to see and marvel at—the first aeroplane to cross the Atlantic Ocean non-stop.

Scarcely had the thrill of the Alcock-Brown flight died down when it was decided by the Admiralty that a British airship should fly from the British Isles to America and back—a pioneer flight for an airship, and the first attempt by any aircraft on a double crossing.

It had been suggested previously that an airship should fly to Newfoundland, turn and come back—flying non-stop. This idea was vetoed, and the new arrangement was that the ship should fly to Long Island, New York, remain sufficiently long to refuel, and return.

The airship R34 stationed at East Fortune, Scotland, was selected to make the attempt, under the command of Major G. H. Scott, and with thirty men aboard, amongst them General E. M. Maitland, senior officer in charge of Britain's Airship Fleet, a pioneer flyer of the old balloon days.

At 2.42 a.m., British Summer Time, on July 2, 1919, the giant airship rose from her base beside the group of scattered cottages, and pointed her nose for the west.

The Admiralty were in hourly communication with the ship throughout her trip, and Parliament watched her progress with interest. In America hurried preparations were made to receive her.

It was as the airship sighted the coast of Newfoundland that she ran into terrific electric storms, and but for skilful piloting might have been driven into the sea. On the night before her arrival, New York learned that the R34 was in distress over the sea in fearsome storms and using up her remaining supplies of petrol.

Naval vessels were rushed to her aid, also a supply of gas and large quantities of fuel ; but in the morning R34 was seen to be sailing serenely on her way. She landed at 2 p.m. on July 6th, after a flight of 3130 miles in 108 hours. When her nose finally rested at her mooring at Long Island, New York, she had but forty minutes' supply of petrol left in her tanks.

New York feted the airmen as only Americans can, while the remark of one of our flyers : " What's all the excitement about, anyway ? " became a classic example of the Briton's imperturbability and modesty.

The return trip of the R34 was started on July 10th, just before midnight. When over New York City searchlights were played on her ; hooters, sirens and motor-horns kept up an incessant salute, while the main thoroughfares were packed with watchers. Tram drivers stopped their cars so that passengers could alight and glimpse the British ship and her gallant crew. Never before did New York create such a traffic hold-up !

After an almost uneventful voyage, except for the fact that one of the five engines broke down completely, R34 landed at Pulham, Norfolk— exactly three days, three hours, three minutes after leaving Long Island. It had been an epic double voyage of perseverance and British technical skill.

As the years go on, however, these flights of the pioneers are thrust steadily into the background, and yet it is worth dwelling, if only for a moment, on them, and remembering that they were fraught with danger. For in no instance had engines reached the efficiency we expect of them to-day ; and communication was hard to establish.

In giving a thought to these heroes, it must never be forgotten that two Britons, Alcock and Brown, made the first non-stop flight of the Atlantic, and a British airship and British crew accomplished the first double crossing.

LONG-DISTANCE FLYERS

ROSS SMITH and Crew. Lieutenant van Ryneveld and Brand crash. Kelly and Macready Fly Across America. Gayford and Nicholetts. General Balbo's Air Armada of Italy.

SIR ROSS SMITH.
Who, with his crew, flew from London to Australia in 1919.

NOW that the Atlantic had been crossed, pioneer flyers with designs on existing long-distance records were beginning to search in other directions to show their prowess. For it must be remembered that the Atlantic itself—with its thousands of miles of water-waste—presented a grave risk. A flyer has but to fall into the sea to be in danger of losing his life. Also, the crossing meant flying through the night, with every possibility of fog and mist, making it impossible to see the water at all. Instruments could be used only when they functioned, so that the risks were considerable.

The air-minded in Britain and the Empire were planning to use aircraft in drawing closer to one another, and in this connection the Australian Government made a splendid offer. It would pay £10,000 to the first Australian or Australian crew who, in a British aeroplane, flew from Britain to Australia in not more than thirty days. The flight was subject to certain conditions as to engine replacements *en route*.

The winning of this £10,000 presented a formidable task, for such a flight had never before been made. There were stretches of sea and ocean to traverse, great forest and jungle areas, areas inhabited by unfriendly

60

natives and cannibals, and notoriously bad weather regions. Yet four flights were contemplated, as well as one by a Frenchman who, while not competing for the prize money, realised the value of such a record flight to French prestige.

One of the flights for the prize was to be made by Captain Ross Smith, M.C., who at this stage was only twenty-six years of age. Ross Smith was born at Adelaide ; a typical Aussie, energetic, hard as nails. And a distinguished career in the Air Force during the War, in which he won honour after honour, had fitted him for the hazardous undertaking he was attempting.

The machine he selected was very similar to that in which Alcock and Brown had crossed the Atlantic. In fact, it is not generally known that some of the actual parts from that amazing British 'plane went into the Ross Smith machine. His partners in what he hoped would be an epoch-making flight were his younger brother Keith, Sergeant W. H. Shiers and Sergeant J. W. Bennett.

Keith had been rejected for war service for a long time, and it was not until 1917, after undergoing an operation, that he managed to enlist. In England he became a cadet in the Air Force, eventually proving himself a most able instructor.

Sergeant Shiers, another Adelaide born flyer, also served in the flying corps during part of the war, and his knowledge of engines was second to none. Sergeant Bennett was born in Melbourne, and served in the air force, so that the crew could be said to be perfectly balanced.

The route selected by Ross Smith and his partners was chosen with the utmost care, and if you turn to an atlas the cleverness of it may be seen. The route was from Hounslow Aerodrome, London, via Lyons, Pisa, Rome, Taranto, Suda Bay, Cairo, Damascus, Ramadie, Basra, Bandar-Abbas, Karachi, Delhi, Allahabad, Calcutta, Akyab, Rangoon, Bangkok, Singora, Singapore, Kalidjatti, Bima, to Port Darwin. This made a total flying distance of 11,294 miles.

On November 12th, 1919, they set out, to meet decidedly uncomfortable conditions very early in the flight. Crossing to Lyons, they flew in 25 degrees of frost, so that their sandwiches froze solid and their breath iced on their face masks.

In Italy it rained so heavily that they could not fly to their schedule. Visibility was almost nil. When they did eventually start the engines and move off they were badly bogged. They got clear with Bennett sitting on the tail-plane and racing to the back cockpit like a hare immediately the machine moved !

They fought their way through terrific rainstorms near the Gulf of Corinth and were soaked to the skin. The storm was so severe that from time to time they had to take hasty glances, with shaded heads, over the side to obtain their position. Right through their flight they encountered in many places the first rains of the season, and, unfortunately for them, these were exceptionally heavy.

In certain parts, too, it was only their knowledge of the country, gained as war birds, which enabled them to continue flying instead of being forced down to await more favourable weather. Not until the ninth day did they have their first good flying weather.

It was at Akyab, below Calcutta, that they came upon their French rival, M. Poulet, who had started many days before. He was daringly flying a tiny machine with one mechanic. Ross Smith and his crew flew with Poulet as far as Bangkok, but hereabouts an equatorial gale blew Poulet back on his course, so Ross Smith now took the lead. So far as the other competitors for the £10,000 were concerned, one crew only had started, to be killed outright soon after leaving.

At Singora terrific rains put the aerodrome half under water, and during the night the gale was so severe that the airmen had to turn out and hang on to the machine to prevent it being blown away. In order to take off again two hundred convicts from the neighbouring prison were put to work to construct a runway, but many hours passed before the 'plane would rise.

Farther on their route they once more became bogged at an aerodrome, and the state of the ground may be gauged from the fact that the machine sank almost to the lower planes. Long planks and bamboo mats—many native houses had to be pulled down to get the latter—were made into a 350 yards runway before the aeroplane would take off. At the first attempt some of the mats flew up, swerved the machine off the track and badly bogged her again. Many hours' labour was required to get the 'plane into the air.

From then until Australia was reached the greatest of their difficulties had been overcome, and on December 10th they came down at Port Darwin. Needless to say, the machine and its crew fulfilled all the conditions, and the £10,000 was paid over. Later Ross Smith and his brother were knighted, while their companions were suitably decorated.

In April, 1922, Ross Smith was planning a great round-the-world flight —but scarcely a week later he was dead, having crashed in England with

CAPE-TO-CAIRO.
Sir Peter Van Ryneveld with his crew and the " Silver Queen."

AUSTRALIAN FLIGHT FINISH.
Ross-Smith with his crew and machine after completing his England to Australia flight, 1919.

TARRANT TRIPLANE.
Trial flight of the Tarrant Triplane at Farnborough. The machine before the crash.

THE TARRANT SMASH.
Front view of the crashed machine. Searching for the injured after the smash.

LIEUTS. O. G. KELLY AND J. A. MACREADY.   [L.E.A.

Who in April, 1923, broke the endurance record by staying aloft for over 36 hours, which was then considered a remarkable feat.

Bennett while testing the very machine they were to have used for the attempt. Smith had already been up in the aeroplane as a passenger, and it was when it landed and he took over as pilot that he dived to his death. Had he not succumbed in this singular manner he would doubtless have added to his achievements. As it is, the Empire will never forget his work in helping to blaze the trail for the Australian-Britain air service.

It was shortly after the completion of Ross Smith's epic flight to Australia that two South African Dutchmen—Colonel van Ryneveld and Captain Brand—both with distinguished careers during the war, determined to be the first to fly from Britain direct to Cape Town. Others had attempted it ; some were making the attempt, but van Ryneveld and Brand were not deterred. They knew the difficulties to be overcome—that there were parts of the great African continent where no 'plane could land, that

B.F.   65   E weather conditions would be most trying, that machines would need to be of the stoutest to reach the southernmost part of Africa.

They set out on February 4, 1920, from Brooklands aerodrome, Surrey, and landed at Turin on the first day. Then on via Rome to Sollum in Western Egypt. They crossed the Mediterranean in a fearful storm, but had no further real trouble until they left Cairo on a non-stop flight to Khartoum. At Wadi Halfa their 'plane crashed and was wrecked, which brought their attempt to an abrupt end. Not daunted, they returned to Cairo for another machine, fitting into it the engine of the crashed 'plane, as it had not been damaged. On February 22 they again set off, but came down at Wadi Halfa, scene of their crash, through head winds. Next day, however, they overcame what seemed such a stumbling block by reaching Khartoum. Here they were detained with engine trouble.

On leaving Khartoum they met whirlwinds, sandstorms, in fact every sort of weather dangerous to flying, and it was not until March 2 that they made Livingstone, just above the Victoria Falls. The natives were greatly impressed by the machine, and with much ceremony van Ryneveld was given a present from a chief. The gift was an ornamental fly-switch !

Bulawayo was reached four days later ; but while attempting to fly to Pretoria the second disaster befell the airmen, the machine crashing a mile beyond their starting-point.

A third machine was this time sent to them from the Cape, and at long last, on March 20, the gallant airmen reached Cape Town. It was a triumph of pluck and grim determination.

Airmen in other parts of the world were now noting the strides in long-distance flight being made by British airmen, and they began to plan similar and longer journeys. So far untouched in comparatively fast long-distance flying was the American continent, and it was not long before flights from west to east and east to west were in progress. The American continent had actually been crossed in 1911 by an American named Calbraith P. Rogers. He began his flight from New York and fifty-nine days later arrived at Pasadena. Of course, as a worth-while long-distance flight it counted as nothing, and could be beaten with ease by anyone who attempted it in a reliable 'plane.

On October 4, 1922, two United States army aviators, Lieutenants O. G. Kelly and J. A. Macready, started on a record-breaking flight from San Diego to New York. A few miles from their start, however, they found it impossible, with the heavy load of petrol being carried, to gain sufficient

[*Brazier*

Hawker " Fury " in flight.   This type is a modern fighting 'plane, the " British Bulldog " of the air.

[*Brazier*

Westland " Wapiti " flying over hills near Mosul, near Iraq.

67

[*Photopress*

A Short Bristol " Crusader " Seaplane.

Courtesy]

[" *Air* "

The Blackburn " Iris " Flying Boat. Used by the Royal Air Force for coastal patrol
and reconnaissance.

altitude to rise above the mountains, so they gave up their trans-continental flight and embarked at once on an endurance flight. They came down more than thirty-five hours later ; but, as the flight had neither been observed nor timed, the record could not be given official recognition.

Exactly a month later they began a second attempt to reach the east side of the continent. This time they managed to cross the mountains, but ran into shocking weather conditions and continually had trouble with their machine. Four hundred miles from their starting-point, after flying through a night of thunderstorms, they were forced down. They now began to plan carefully another endurance flight as well as a third attempt to cross America, and this time they took many weeks over the preparations. In April, 1923, they broke the endurance record by staying aloft for 36 hours, $4\frac{1}{2}$ minutes, and in the following month they set out from Roosevelt Field, New York, for San Diego. This they reached in just under twenty-seven hours, flying 2516 miles.

Quite a number of flyers now determined to beat this record in crossing America, and in the same year Lieutenant L. Maughan planned to fly from one side to the other *in daylight*. Twice he was unsuccessful, but at his third attempt flew from New York to San Francisco in a dawn-to-dusk flight, a distance of 2540 miles.

For four years this record remained unbeaten, then three times in quick succession it was lowered, the second and third flights being made by Captain Frank Hawkes, America's fastest flyer. Hawkes, having broken his own record with the third flight, then astounded the world with a swift there-and-back one-stop flight in under thirty-seven hours' flying time. Many of the deeds of this amazing speed-flyer are recounted in detail in a later chapter.

Yet the long-distance figures put up by flyers in non-stop flights were as nothing compared with the British Air Force record of 5341 miles, from Cranwell Aerodrome, Lincolnshire, to Walvis Bay, 781 miles north of Cape Town. The story of the Royal Air Force attack on long-distance flying goes back to 1929, when Flight-Lieutenant N. A. Jenkins and Squadron-Leader A. G. Jones-Williams were killed when they crashed in Tunis in an attempted London-Cape Town flight.

Four years later, on February 7, 1933, a great Fairey Napier Lion monoplane rose into the air before dawn, from Cranwell, and was watched with bated breath by officials and mechanics who were seeing off its gallant crew of two. The machine weighed $7\frac{1}{2}$ tons, of which quite half was petrol-load, and everything depended on whether it would reach flying speed before the enormous weight caused the machine to stall and crash. Fortunately she rose with hardly a falter.

The reason for such a flight was to determine the best type of aircraft for use in reinforcing air units in distant parts of the Empire, so it may be safely said that no record-breaking merely for the sake of putting up new figures was ever planned by our air officials. The chosen flyers were originally Squadron-Leader Oswald R. Gayford and Flight-Lieutenant D. L. G. Bett, both men of Suffolk. Bett died, and Flight-Lieutenant Nicholetts, a Devon-born flyer, was selected to take his place. The two men trained together, got to know each other almost as brothers, for such a flight might easily try them to the utmost. Gayford himself was a man of few words, but one of the most popular men in the air arm. Everyone at Hadleigh in Suffolk, where he lived, knew " Master Oswald," and the quietness which characterised him as a boy was in his make-up as a man.

When he was working for his father in their seedmills, as a lad, a boy fell into a pond nearby. When Gayford heard he rushed from the office, flung himself into the water and saved the boy's life. He went straight home as soon as he knew the boy was safe, changed his clothes and returned to his office stool. Scarcely anyone in the little town knew about the rescue for days !

Gayford, the man, was now in charge of the great Fairey monoplane, and at breakfast-time on February 7 the people of Britain learned that he and Nicholetts were attempting to fly without stop to Cape Town.

The machine carried wireless, and was in constant communication with the Air Ministry. Faultlessly, without once giving the airmen cause for alarm, the great 'plane sped onwards, crossing one country after another, turning one thousand miles into two, and two to three, and then four thousand. Had it not been for petrol shortage the 'plane would have reached the Cape ; but it came down at Walvis $2\frac{1}{2}$ days after setting out.

A large crowd was waiting to greet the flyers and, when they stepped from the machine, it was seen with astonishment that they had shaved and were as spick and span as if they had just done a fifty-mile run in an express train. They had no " shock tactics " to turn them into greater heroes than they already were. They showed themselves to be the efficient quietly working service airmen we have always known, and their calmness astounded the rest of the world, where such dignity and bearing are almost unknown.

R.A.F. LONG-DISTANCE FLYERS.   [" *Flight*" *Photo*
Flight-Lieut. Nicholetts (left) and Squadron-Leader Gayford (second right) with Lord Londonderry and
Sir John Salmond.

The machine was flown back by Gayford and Nicholetts in easy stages after a triumphant tour of the Union, which increased the return trip to England to nearly 10,000 miles.

Yet, splendid though this record was, it stood to the credit of Britain for only six months. Early in August, 1933, two French flyers, Codos and Rossi, flew 5915 miles in 55 hours, ending their flight at Rayak in Syria, where lack of petrol forced them to land. The amazing strides in long-distance flying can now be seen, in that Codos and Rossi started from New York, crossing the Atlantic Ocean as a prelude to their achievement. They did not even wait for favourable weather. It was bad when they started, there were storms in Nova Scotia, and for five hours they battled with Atlantic gales. The airmen reported at the end of their flight that all the way across the Atlantic to Cherbourg not once did they see the water, while for several hours of the grim struggle they could not even see their wing tips.

71

Undoubtedly the most spectacular and certainly the most brilliantly-conceived long-distance flight of 1933 was the Italian air armada's flight from Italy to America and back, in easy stages. Twenty-four machines, each carrying four men, set out under the personal command of General Italo Balbo, Air Minister of Italy, to demonstrate the possibilities of mass flights over long distances. The machines were hydroplanes with well-tried Italian engines, and it was Balbo's stated intention to take no risks with machines or men throughout the whole double flight.

For this reason the accidents which did occur were absolutely a minimum when it is considered that the lives of just on a hundred men were concerned. Two machines were wrecked—not over the Atlantic through failure, but while at landing-places; and only two of the flyers lost their lives. Most certainly the Italian air armada made world history in the summer of 1933.

In October, 1934, Scott and Black (Britain) won the great England to Australia air race, knocking 4½ days off the record by finishing the course in 70 hrs. 54 mins. 18 secs., surely a fine example of the speed and endurance of British aircraft!

Lieut. Cathcart Jones and Ken Waller, fourth in the Melbourne air race, set off almost immediately for the return flight. Though held up at Athens owing to storms in Europe they actually reached home only thirteen and a half days after leaving Mildenhall for Australia.

LEADERS OF THE AIR ARMADA. [L.E.A.
General Balbo (centre) with Lord Londonderry and Air-Marshal Clarke-Hall, General Pellegrini and Lieut.-Colonel Cogna, at Mountstewart, the residence of Lord Londonderry.

72

THE BLACKBURN PERTH FLYING BOAT.
[" *Flight* " *Photo*

Fitted with three 825 h.p. Rolls Royce Buzzard engines, it is built for long-distance flights.

SIR ALAN COBHAM AND HIS FLIGHTS

A BOYHOOD Aeroplane. Looking for a Job of Work. Amazing Flights as Air Taxi-man. Record Air Journeys and Knighthood.

THE story of Sir Alan Cobham is one of endeavour—of pluck and push despite all obstacles! Up against it for many years, he ultimately found his niche and received a well-earned knighthood. And all because he kept an idea in the forefront of his mind—that there were possibilities for himself in civil aviation.

He was born in London in 1894 and received his education in the metropolis. When he was fourteen years of age a prize was offered in Paris for the best aerial machine which would fly without the aid of a motor. Young

73

Alan and a friend, keen on the new idea of flying, went into partnership in the erection of a sailplane to win the prize.

The contraption they designed was a bicycle with wings on either side. There was a propeller, of course, worked by the cycle chain, and it revolved only a few inches ahead of the front wheel. Certainly the scheme of things was quite normal.

Alan was not the mathematical mind, so when his friend told him that if he pedalled hard enough he could work up to $3\frac{1}{2}$ horse-power, sufficient to give lift, he believed it. Needless to say, lift was always lacking !

At twenty Alan Cobham was in the army as a gunner, for the Great War had started, and it was the sight of so many aeroplanes on their various errands which reawakened in him his old desire to fly. He began to worry for a transfer to the air arm, and eventually found himself in the Flying Corps. As is only natural, he learned with a swiftness which took him to success. Quickly he became a first-class flyer, and then an instructor. At the end of the war he was a competent airman—but without a job.

His energy and confidence in himself were tested to the utmost now as he travelled hundreds of miles, interviewing first this company and then that, always with the set idea that there was a place for himself in the new business of commercial flying. Concerns were so few in number, however, that Cobham gave up hope of " getting in " from this angle ; and a new idea struck him. He joined forces with two brothers and commenced to travel the country, giving joy flights in an aeroplane they purchased between them with almost the total of their resources.

There was no organisation ; they had to create it out of their experience. Fortune smiled one week and turned her back the next. They made money and lost it. Then, when they could look to the future and had built up a joy flight organisation all over the country, promised financial aid was withdrawn. Soon their savings were swallowed up. Cobham and his partners agreed to go their own way, and this they did, each shouldering a burden of debt.

Within a short while Cobham was again making towards his goal, earning a living by taking aerial photographs for commercial concerns, newspapers, and so on.

Then the idea for air taxi-work came, and here commenced the first of Alan Cobham's big adventures in life, as a De Haviland pilot. From delivering in record time newspapers containing reports of big events, to

SIR ALAN COBHAM BROADCASTS.   ["*Flight*" *Photo*]
Sir Alan speaks into the microphone before making a flight at one of his popular air pageants.

rushing Americans from London to Cherbourg to catch Atlantic liners off to New York—everything he took as part of his job.

Gradually Cobham became known. He flew to every part of Europe on taxi-work, and there was no man who could fly so surely. He was called the pilot who flew Europe without a map! This was literally true, for he knew every landing-ground from Calais to Constantinople by heart.

Perhaps one of Cobham's most exciting aerial " stunts " of air-taxi days was to " cover " a big Royal marriage at Belgrade for an English newspaper. Despite rival newspapers' organisations, Cobham managed to get his own photographers back to England first—even though he had to make forced landings both in Europe and near the south coast.

His greatest hustle was when, one Derby Day, he was in a team of airmen to rush the Derby race film all over the country, so that it could be shown in a film corporation's forty odd cinemas the same day. This meant arranging for machines to take prints of the film to Bristol, Plymouth, Aberdeen, Newcastle-on-Tyne, and many other places. Thus it will be realised that without plans being worked out to the second the whole costly experiment would fail.

How was the scheme carried through ? The delivery was divided into twenty-five dropping-places, the films being thrown overboard in parachutes. Fields were selected over which the pictures were to be released, and white sheets were pegged there as a sign to the airmen where to drop their precious films.

Cobham's own story of that thrilling, breathless day is well worth the telling ; and this is how he recounts it in his fascinating book, *Skyways*. He says :

" It must be understood that the delivery of the printed films was one affair, but the transporting of the undeveloped negative by air from Epsom to the film works at New Barnet and the various prints from the works at Barnet to the waiting delivery aeroplanes at Stag Lane was another, requiring a certain amount of organisation, also. I cannot exactly remember what happened to every individual pilot, but if I tell you what happened to myself I think a fair idea of the whole stunt will be gained.

" We had previously obtained permission to use a small field near the racecourse to land our aeroplane, and twenty minutes after setting off from Stag Lane (the north-west London aerodrome of De Haviland's) had landed at Epsom and were waiting for the film negative. As the race was due to start at 3 p.m., the operators expected to be able to give me the

SEAPLANE AT REST.

A giant seaplane comes to rest by the banks of a Canadian river, followed by the interest and admiration of the onlookers.

BY THE RIVER-BANK.

A nearer view of the Seaplane seen on p. 77. Graceful and strong, it lies like a beautiful bird on the surface of the water.

negative at about 3.15 p.m. I had promised to land it in a special field at New Barnet about 3.30 p.m., and it was going to be an enormous scramble to develop the film and print it in less than two hours, which would be all the time available if Aberdeen were to be reached that evening.

"At 3.15 p.m. there was no sign of the film, and I continued to wait anxiously with the engine ticking over. At 3.30 p.m. I thought something must have gone wrong; at 3.45 p.m. I had switched my engine off. At 3.50 p.m. I saw two men tearing their way through the hedge with a black case; without waiting a second I jumped into the cockpit, and by sheer good fortune the engine started up at the first turn of the magneto.

"The moment the photographers got to the machine I ordered them to clamber in. One dear old boy had never been in an aeroplane before, and took rather a long time to settle himself, and as I could not wait for him, I just put my hand on the top of his head and pushed him down tight. The next second I had opened out, and in less time than it takes to tell it, we were in the air tearing north for Barnet. We covered the distance in fourteen minutes, and before the machine had come to a standstill, a horseman came galloping up to the aeroplane. The films were handed over to him immediately, whereupon he raced over three fields to the main road, where a dispatch rider on a powerful motor-cycle was waiting.

"The scene at the factory must have been very startling, for the film, once developed, had to be dried in an atmosphere that was almost liquid ether. I am told that the men who were doing the work could not stand it more than a few minutes at a time, and as they became faint and dizzy they were carried away and relays standing in readiness took their place. Owing to the time already lost through delay in the start of the race, it was a question of minutes as to whether the whole stunt would be a failure.

"Meantime I returned to Stag Lane, where all the machines were lined up in readiness. Soon after I had landed, a little school machine took off for Barnet to wait for the delivery, by means of motor-cyclist and horseman, of the first prints. These were to be flown straight back to Stag Lane, a matter of three minutes in the air, and would be put on the Aberdeen aeroplane, which would straightway set off on its long journey. After this the little machine would return to Barnet and await the arrival of the next lot of prints; and so on until all the deliveries had been completed.

"I was to do the Aberdeen trip; Captain C. D. Barnard was going to Glasgow, Captain Broad to Bristol, Exeter and Plymouth, and Captain

Wilson to Birmingham, Manchester and Liverpool. (Each was a famous flyer.) We had borrowed pilots for the other flights.

" The minutes ticked on, and the prospect of reaching Aberdeen, nearly five hundred miles away, diminished. At 5.55 p.m. we sighted our delivery machine in the air, and two minutes later it had landed. The prints were quickly transferred, each packet was attached to its respective parachute (this procedure had been rehearsed) and by six o'clock we were in the air heading north for York.

" It was a perfect summer evening, and we—for there was a passenger to throw the parachute out—were favoured by a slight following wind. An hour and a half after leaving Stag Lane, York racecourse was in sight. Hundreds of people had assembled to witness the films being dropped, and as we neared the white sheet pinned out on the ground I put my arm up, which was the warning to my passenger to prepare to fling the packet overboard.

" Everything went well at York, but as we had not a moment to spare, we could not wait to see the packet picked up. A few minutes later Darlington was in sight, and the same procedure gone through, and then we continued on to Newcastle, where also there was an enormous crowd waiting to see the film arrive. I heard that when the picture palace had advertised that a film of the Derby would be delivered and shown that night in Newcastle there had been heavy betting on the prospect ; this was possibly the cause of the vast crowd.

" It was getting dusk as we flew over the Lowlands of Scotland, and when Arthur's Seat at last came into view I began to get worried about the possibilities of reaching Aberdeen, a hundred miles farther on. It was half-past nine and very nearly dark when we dropped films in a field near Leith ; but not wishing to disappoint Aberdeen we flew on. We crossed the Firth of Forth when it was almost dark, but the curious fact was that the farther north we went after this the lighter it became, and so we were able to continue at comparative ease. The whole sky away to the north became quite light and bright, and when at last Aberdeen was reached at 10.25 it was far lighter than it had been at Edinburgh, especially at a high altitude. I felt that the higher I climbed and the farther north I went, despite the increasing lateness of the hour, the lighter it would have become, for I suppose if I had flown long enough I should have reached the Land of the Midnight Sun.

" There being only one film in our Aberdeen packet, the bundle was

THE AIR BOMBER.
A remarkable picture of a Torpedo Bomber dropping its deadly missile into the sea.

extremely light, and when we threw it from the machine the slip-stream of the propeller blew the parachute towards the tail, so that one of the strings became entangled on the show of my tail-skid.

"When I looked overboard to find out how the last packet was sailing down to earth, I could see no white parachute in the air at all, but discovered the whole bundle twisting round at a frightful rate at the end of my tail. For the moment I did not know what to do, and by this time I was over, not our field, but the town, and as the string might break at any moment, I feared that the film might drop on somebody's fanlight or roof. I turned and headed back in the direction of the dropping-field; but at the moment of turning the string broke, and we saw the packet no more.

"Imagine our feelings when, after we had created a record, the stunt should be spoiled at the last second. In a few moments I had found the improvised landing-ground. A party was waiting to receive us. In the middle of my explanations and apologies someone came dashing over from the telephone to say that the film had been shown on the screen in the town at 10.28 p.m., which was barely three minutes after it had broken loose.

"I was told afterwards that the packet had landed in somebody's back yard but a stone's throw from the picture house; and, as every man, woman and child in Aberdeen knew about this stunt, it had been rushed

[Brazier

Another graceful war-bird—a Fairey Long Range Monoplane being overhauled at the Baghdad aerodrome.

to the picture palace where the film was instantly put on the screen. All the other machines were completely successful."

Another exciting air-taxi adventure was when Cobham set out on a press photographic venture in Ireland, and finished up by making use of a rival newspaper's transport service—unknown to that journal—to get his pictures through to London for his own paper !

Alan Cobham was soon taking long flights, pioneer flights, each with a purpose in view of value to Britain. One flight of 10,000 miles, in 1923, set all eyes on this Britisher who had long since become chief pilot to the De Haviland Aircraft Company.

It was in 1925 that Alan Cobham and Sir Sefton Brancker (then Air Vice-Marshal, and eventually to die in the ill-fated British airship R101) set off on a journey to Burma and back in order to study the question of Imperial Air Routes. It was the first time that an important air official had undertaken such a mission, yet there was hardly any preparation. The flight was a huge success.

Two months later Cobham startled Europe by flying from Croydon to Zurich and back in fourteen hours, a distance of 1000 miles. A few months later he was carrying out the first survey flight round Africa with two companions. It was this flight and what it proved which did a great deal towards starting a South African Air Mail service.

Cobham's next flight was to Australia and back—the first such flight ever accomplished—but on the journey out a tragedy befell the machine and its occupants. Cobham was flying low towards Basra from Baghdad when an Arab took a shot at the aeroplane, and his bullet struck Elliott, Cobham's mechanic. In the terrific heat of the day Cobham flew at top speed for Basra, so that Elliott might go to hospital. Unfortunately, though everything possible was done for Cobham's companion (mechanic, too, on many previous flights), he died.

Cobham obtained another mechanic and reached Australia safely, where an amazing welcome awaited him at every town he visited. It seemed that the whole continent had suddenly become air-minded at this sudden arrival of an Englishman. Without fuss or bother Cobham set out on the return flight. He reached England without mishap and landed safely on the Thames at Westminster in front of the Houses of Parliament, to be received by Members themselves. He had flown 28,000 miles in the same machine—a seaplane—which had carried him on his survey of Africa ; a magnificent feat, and proof of the sterling quality of British aero-engines.

INTERIOR OF HANDLEY-PAGE.   [" *Flight* " *Photo*
An " inside view " of the controls and instruments of the Handley-Page 42 (Hannibal type).

Speeding over the Border. A Scottish express and an aeroplane have a friendly race across the Tweed.

[*Courtesy Handley-Page Aviation Co., Ltd.*

Handley-Page "Hannibal" type 40-seater on London-Paris Air Service.

84

It was a direct result of what Cobham had so far done for Britain and her aircraft that he was knighted, and no man could have more thoroughly deserved the honour.

In November, 1927, Sir Alan and Lady Cobham took off in a flying boat from Rochester, Kent, for a 20,000-mile African trip, and, despite the ill-luck which dogged their seaplane, carried through their objective, this being to obtain the necessary information at first-hand as to the possibilities of seaplane stations.

A few months after this Sir Alan was again making tours of this country, interesting municipalities in the need for aerodromes in their areas. When we realise to-day that there is scarcely a place of note in Britain without its landing-field, this work of Sir Alan Cobham was indeed that of a far-seeing air enthusiast.

He gave flights to thousands of school children in a big air liner, knowing that the growing generation needed just such an experience to begin educating their parents in the new means of transport. In all some 10,000 free flights to boys and girls were given.

In the summer months of 1929 he flew 60,000 miles and made a tour of over a hundred towns, taking up many thousands of adults.

Sir Alan then followed up his great scheme to make Britain air-minded by starting National Aviation Day, an air display given throughout the country in which many famous airmen took part with him. All over Britain Sir Alan and his air circus travelled, and flights in large and small machines for anyone interested were a regular feature. The number of people who have taken advantage of National Aviation Day to fly must run into millions.

Sir Alan is still a young man, but he can look back on a very full early life spent in the service of aviation. He has always had but one ambition —to prove that there was a future in civil flight. And he deserves the thanks of every Briton for giving us a truly brilliant lead.

ATLANTIC AIRMEN WHO FAILED

THE Disappearance of Captain Nungesser and M. Coli, Lieut.-Col. Minchin, Mr. Hamilton and Princess Lowenstein-Wertheim, Lloyd Bertaud, etc. The narrow escape of Miss Ruth Elder. Hinchcliffe and Elsie MacKay.

LIEUT.-COL. F. MINCHIN.

[L.E.A.

THE year 1927 witnessed a great mass entry of airmen intent upon flying the Atlantic—either from Canada or the United States to England or France, or from east to west. One after another they hastily completed their plans, for none would give way to the next. Each wanted to claim the distinction of flying across in record time. It is interesting to note that at this stage the Alcock and Brown success of 1919 had receded completely into the background, and there were many in the United States, at any rate, who believed that the first to cross in this 1927 campaign would be acknowledged as the first person to fly the Atlantic.

Tragedy followed fast in the wake of these plucky if somewhat rash contestants. By September of that year twenty-one lives had been lost, aeroplanes and passengers disappearing amidst the wastes of the ocean.

Why did these disasters occur so swiftly one after the other, when aircraft seemed to have reached a very advanced stage of reliability ? The reason is that, first, most of the machines in which the attempts were made were land machines, and therefore useless if forced to come down in water. Another reason is that in all probability few of the machines were tested sufficiently by long-distance flying and carrying the huge loads of fuel necessary for the Atlantic crossing.

86

Even in 1926 one or two attempts had been started, only to end as soon as they began, as in the case of Renee Fonck, the French wartime ace. He crashed on taking off from Roosevelt Field, New York, and escaped with one member of his crew. The remaining two were burned to death.

In May, 1927, another French airman who won distinction during the war essayed the Atlantic crossing. This was Captain Nungesser, who, with a companion, M. Coli, set off from Le Bourget, Paris, for New York. They were taking the more difficult east to west route; for in flying from Europe to America there is seldom a following wind. Usually a gale is blowing in the direction of Europe.

They started at dawn, expected to have nearly seventeen daylight flying hours, and finally a 1500-mile night flight before eventually reaching their destination. It was known next day that fog and storm awaited anyone flying the ocean, and an intensive look-out was kept from Canada down-coast to the United States.

Paris waited expectantly as the probable time of Nungesser's arrival drew near. A special edition of the newspapers was rushed on to the streets as a message was received that the two men had landed. Almost at once fresh editions were out contradicting the report.

Hours turned into days. Ships and aeroplanes searched the seas. The wireless stations were kept ready for conveying news as soon as received. But as the days passed and no sign of machine or men was discovered, the world realised with a new-found horror that the Atlantic had claimed two very gallant airmen. Here it is worth remembering that few anticipated failure of this flight. Aeroplanes were as near perfect as possible, while the vogue for Atlantic flights had become as commonplace as Channel swimming.

The disappearance of the two French airmen did not cause more than momentary consternation, for with the successful solo flight from west to east of Captain Lindbergh a fortnight later, all arrangements in hand to fly the Atlantic were hastened forward. (Lindbergh's amazing story is told in the following chapter.)

On the last day of August, 1927, a crew of three set off from Upavon Aerodrome, Salisbury, to fly to Ottawa. They were Lieutenant-Colonel F. Minchin, Mr. Leslie Hamilton and Princess Lowenstein-Wertheim. Both Minchin and Hamilton had an exceptionally good knowledge of aircraft, and they were confident of flying the 3600 miles quite easily.

The last seen of the machine was when it was half-way across, an oil carrier noting its position and features. Another vessel later reported seeing an aeroplane flying the white light—the recognised aerial distress signal—some 420 miles E.S.E. of New York. The report, however, could not be identified with the Atlantic 'plane, for as the first vessel's statement was doubtless accurate, the machine could not possibly have reached the second position at the time stated.

On September 6, before the fate of Princess Lowenstein-Wertheim and her crew had been definitely settled, a monoplane, *Old Glory*, left Roosevelt Field for Rome, piloted by Mr. Lloyd Bertaud and Mr. James D. Hill, and accompanied by an American newspaperman. The machine carried wireless, and reports were received from time to time that all was well. Then abruptly the tone of the wireless messages changed. An S.O.S. passed over the air, and four Atlantic liners picked it up. At once they altered their course and raced in the direction indicated by the stricken 'plane. The vessels searched over a wide area, but found nothing. It was felt, however, that *Old Glory* had some chance, for if the petrol tanks were emptied she would float indefinitely. Also, she carried a rubber raft, signal flares and rockets.

MISS RUTH ELDER.   [L.E.A.

Eventually the liners gave up the search. Days passed, and, as there was no news of the 'plane, hope vanished—and three more airmen were never heard of again. Wreckage was picked up some days later alleged to be part of the missing aeroplane, but how the three men came by their deaths could not be established. The secret is lodged with the Atlantic for all time.

On September 7 two Canadians, Captain F. B. Tully and Mr. J. V. Metcalf, started from Harbour Grace, Newfoundland, for Croydon, England. There was now grave misgiving throughout the world, and if the two had heeded the omen on the eve of their departure they might be alive

A GREAT FRENCH AVIATOR. ["*Flight*" *Photo*

Captain Nungesser, the French airman, who met with a tragic fate while attempting the Atlantic crossing from Paris to New York.

[L.E.A.

BEFORE THE RACE.

Princess Lowenstein-Wertheim (Lady Anne Savile) talking with her pilot just before the race for the King's Cup.

to-day. When their petrol tanks were being filled a kerosene lantern held too close caused an explosion. The machine, however, was not damaged.

As with the preceding flights, nothing more was ever heard of the machine once it took off, and there was a terrific outcry in Canada that this "gambling with death" should be stopped. It was suggested that legislation should be introduced through Parliament to forbid such flying.

Notwithstanding public opinion, on October 11 a Miss Ruth Elder, an American girl who had only just qualified for a pilot's certificate, set off from Roosevelt Field with Captain George Haldeman, an experienced flyer, their plan being to fly non-stop to Paris.

The aeroplane was sighted 500 miles out over the ocean, but the next message received was that the machine had been forced down in the sea beside a Dutch oil tanker. At this point the aeroplane was only 600 miles from Europe ! Unfortunately for the success of Ruth Elder's plan, they ran into bad weather, as had been predicted for them when they set out. For eight hours they fought their way onward, and succeeded in battling through. But when they were congratulating each other on their good fortune it was seen with dismay that the oil pressure had gone. Quickly the discovery was made that the feedpipe was fractured, but they decided to fly on and risk their engine seizing. Five hours later they sighted a ship and decided to give up, the engine now being perilously overheated. They dropped on the sea and were at once taken aboard the Dutchman.

The captain attempted to save the aeroplane, but during salvage operations petrol must have spilled on to the hot engine. In an instant there was an explosion, and the machine became a mass of flame. The ship was forced to push the burning 'plane away, and nothing whatever was left of the machine. Thus ended, somewhat more happily than the rest, another attempt to cross the Atlantic Ocean by air.

In the same month Mrs. Frances Grayson and three companions started from New York in an endeavour to fly to Copenhagen. The first attempt lasted only a few minutes. The second lasted but half an hour ; the machine would not rise with its huge load of fuel, and it was only after pulling a wire and releasing 260 gallons of petrol that the machine gained altitude. She was then nose-heavy, and the pilot decided to return to the aerodrome.

At the third attempt another large quantity of petrol had to be discarded, but missing on the cylinders caused Mrs. Grayson to abandon for the present all attempts to fly the ocean.

In December, with three companions, she set off from New York for Harbour Grace, preparatory to flying the Atlantic on Christmas Day. From the moment the aeroplane rose and was seen out of sight it disappeared for ever. It never reached Harbour Grace, and even though an American airship searched the route for the machine and crew no trace was ever discovered of this woman who kept trying until she met her death.

The next competitor in this life-and-death struggle with the Altantic was Captain W. R. Hinchliffe, the famous pilot of Imperial Airways. He had been chosen by Levine, the little American who flew the Atlantic from America some months before, to pilot his machine on a return flight ; but eventually Levine decided to fly to India instead. A forced landing in Austria ended the project, and Hinchliffe returned to England to arrange on his own account to fly to America. Levine's Atlantic adventure is detailed in a later chapter.

On March 13, 1928, at 8.30 a.m., his monoplane started off from Cranwell, his passenger being the Honorable Elsie MacKay, daughter of Lord Inchcape. The machine was seen over Ireland during a snowstorm, flying fast due west, and that was the last that was heard of Hinchliffe or his companion. The fact that both had kept their plans secret impeded all attempts to trace them, and the world came at last to add their names also to the legion of the lost.

In September, 1928, Lord Inchcape settled a gift on Mrs. Hinchliffe and her two daughters of £10,000, to be held in trust and administered for their benefit.

This was the sequel to the saddest chapter in the history of flyers. Thereafter designers wrestled with the problems set them by the Atlantic failures, and that they overcame them is evident from modern flight. The Atlantic crossing to-day presents very little more danger than flying the same distance non-stop over difficult country. As in all advances of science, however, the pioneers must risk their lives and die that those who come after may reap the benefit of their perilous adventuring.

THE HON. ELSIE MACKAY.   [L.E.A.
A passenger with Captain W. R. Hinchliffe on his ill-fated attempt on the Atlantic crossing.

LINDBERGH— LONE FLYER

COLONEL LINDBERGH.
Who made the first non-stop solo flight between New York and Paris.

EARLY Life. Father objects to Flying as Career. Becomes Stunt Flyer. Joins Flying Circus. An Air Mail Pilot. Rapid Rise. The Great Flight to Paris and Afterwards.

CHARLES A. LINDBERGH, the father of Colonel Charles A. Lindbergh, America's premier airman, did not want his son to fly! Had the young Lindbergh taken his parent's advice, it is problematical whether the first man to fly solo across the Atlantic from New York to Paris would have been an American. Instead of doing as his father wished, young Lindbergh eventually persuaded him to take a flight. It was quite a short trip, but Mr. Lindbergh enjoyed it so much that never again did he raise objections to his son continuing to fly aircraft in building up his career.

The older Lindbergh was born at Stockholm, but the family went to America and settled in Minnesota. Mrs. Lindbergh is of English, Irish and French extraction, but was born at Detroit, Michigan.

The " Lindy " we have come to admire was also born at Detroit, on February 4, 1902, and when only a couple of months old was taken to the family homestead at Little Falls, Minnesota, where his father was then a practising lawyer. It was at Little Falls that Mr. Lindbergh became interested in politics, and eventually went to Congress as representative of the area in which the family lived. From then on, the family resided one part of the year at Washington, as was necessary, and the remaining time in Detroit and Little Falls.

As a lad, " Lindy's " chief interest was in mechanical toys and contrivances, and a course of mathematical engineering fitted him to enter the College of Engineering of the University of Wisconsin. At the University he passed automatically to aviation. He had never touched a machine, never been nearer to one than some hundreds of feet, but the idea of flying fascinated him, and he decided at the first opportunity to investigate a cockpit and learn all he could about aeroplanes.

When the chance came to purchase an old army 'plane he was not slow in handing over the money to buy it, and soon he was learning to stunt. But this was not before he had been up as a passenger in an " old crock " belonging to a friend, and made parachute jumps for the entertainment of air-minded folk who flocked to see the machine and its two flyers.

He learned the whole art of barnstorming—the American equivalent of looking for likely fields near towns, and making use of the field to give flights for any sum up to £1 per head. With his friend he gave exhibitions, and even did a little wing-walking when required !

At last Charles A. Lindbergh became a flying student, but when his instructor learned that already " Lindy " had had some three hundred and thirty flying hours to his credit, the controlling of the learner-plane was handed over to him ! From that moment Lindbergh never looked back, and when he passed out of the training college, it was with the knowledge that he was a first-class flyer.

After leaving the college, Lindbergh started off on another barnstorming and air circus venture, but, hearing that the postal authorities were placing an air mail contract, he applied to one company for a position as flyer, to be told that if they were successful in getting the contract he would not be forgotten. The position of chief pilot would be for him. In 1926, the company having secured the contract, Lindbergh made his first flight as air mail pilot, and in the same year became captain of the St. Louis-Chicago air route—at the youthful age of twenty-four !

Night flying, day flying—it did not matter a scrap to him so long as he was in the air. He became known as the safest of airmen, and it is worth noting that in all the 9000 flights of his career he has had only four accidents, none of them causing serious harm to himself. With passengers —and he has taken aloft some 10,000—he has never lost a life.

It was while flying on the air mail route between St. Louis and Chicago one night that he began to wonder whether it was possible to cross the Atlantic by air. Of course, he knew that it had been done before by Alcock and Brown, although some of the world's historians do not seem so

["Sport and General"]

BRITISH AIRCRAFT TRADE SHOW AT HENDON AERODROME, MIDDLESEX.
A flight of three Blackburn B2 light training biplanes flying overhead.

ROYAL AIR FORCE ANNUAL AIR DISPLAY.
Aircraft flying over the new Type Park.

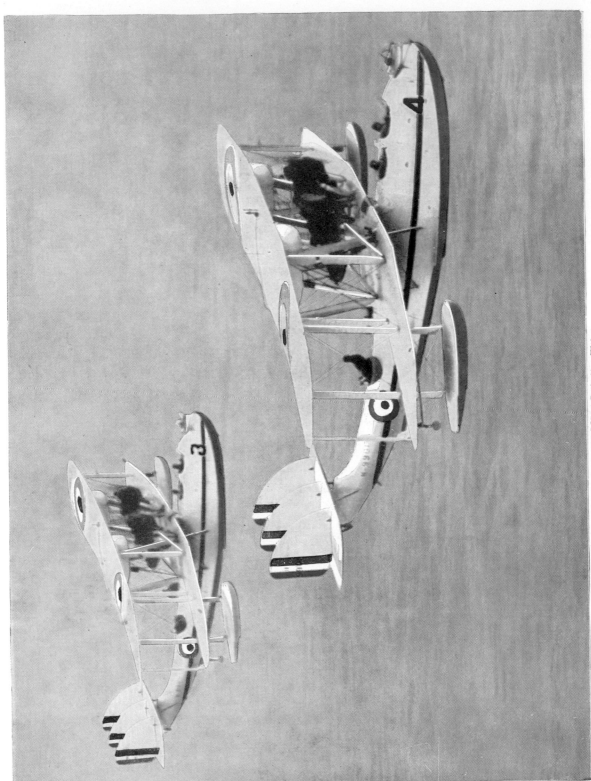

FLYING-BOATS.

I never tire of watching these big seaplanes rise slowly but steadily out of the water and soar into the air.

certain about it in their writings ; but a New York non-stop to Paris flight was in his mind. The backing necessary for such a venture would be considerable—he estimated it at £3000—and he had but £400 saved.

He pictured himself, as he sat in the cockpit of his air mail 'plane, out above the ocean, night flying over the vastnesses of water which would be ever ready to engulf him. And yet if only he could succeed he saw what it would mean to American aviation, to the world in creating a new friendliness between the old world and new, and to himself in his career as an airman.

He went to St. Louis and sought out certain far-seeing men whom he felt would help him. Maybe he expected deep down within him that St. Louis would laugh at his project, that he would have to search much farther afield for the necessary money. But the eight St. Louis citizens to whom he put his scheme literally patted him on the back. They told him that he could go ahead with his plans for the machine he wanted, that the money would be waiting to pay the expenses. As a sign of good faith, Lindbergh threw into the pool every penny of his savings—this was, as a matter of fact, the biggest contribution to the flight fund.

He went to New York to discuss the question of type of machine, for maps, and to obtain all the paraphernalia for such a perilous undertaking. After careful investigation he decided upon a single-motored monoplane, and that it should be constructed for one person only, passenger space being taken for extra fuel. He went to San Diego to have his 200-horsepower aeroplane constructed; and work at once started on the plan which was to sound a new triumph of engineering and a greater triumph for this fearless American youth.

As in all attempts of such magnitude—whether it be the construction of a racing motor-car, a racing motor-boat or an aeroplane—enthusiasm must be brought to bear on every tiny part, or the result will be lacking in some direction. It is a fact that some of the workmen in the aeroplane factory at San Diego worked twenty-four hours at a stretch more than once ; it is a fact that the chief engineer worked thirty-six hours at a stretch at his drawing-board. Every worker on the machine worked seven full days a week. If keenness could succeed for Lindbergh he was as good as at Le Bourget.

Meanwhile Lindbergh worked out his route, paying attention to winds, weather conditions, the mileage he would have to fly across open sea. He familiarised himself with the contours of the coastline from Ireland to Spain, so that he would know his position once the ocean was crossed.

By May 10, 1927, the aeroplane had undergone trials and been found satisfactory. On that day the great adventure commenced, for Lindbergh took his place in the cockpit and set the nose of the machine, christened *Spirit of St. Louis*, for the city of that name. He reached St. Louis without the slightest hitch, and on May 12 took off for New York. Again there was no hitch, and when he landed at Curtiss Field he had the satisfaction of knowing that he had crossed the Continent of America, from Pacific to Atlantic, as a preliminary to the most stirring adventure a youth had ever attempted.

The aeroplane at this stage was tested and found in perfect fettle, but weather conditions held up the flight for a few days. The story of Lindbergh's preparations and the flight itself are told by him in his book, *We— Pilot and 'Plane*, and a few passages from it give a vivid impression of the grim test which he was undertaking. It was decided that the attempt be made on May 20, and on the night previous Lindbergh allowed himself two and a half hours' sleep. But, as he says, "at the hotel there were several more details which had to be completed, and I was unable to get any sleep that night.

"I returned to Curtiss Field about daybreak. A light rain was falling which continued until dawn; consequently we did not move the ship to Roosevelt Field (which adjoins Curtiss Field and where final servicing was to be completed) until much later than we had planned, and the take-off was delayed from daybreak until nearly eight o'clock.

"At 7.52 I took off on the flight to Paris," he writes, and then calmly tells of his experiences. Reading, one cannot help but feel that Lindbergh writes down less than actually occurred, that he belittles the dangers and tucks them out of sight. He makes a most interesting point, however, about mirages over the Atlantic. . . . After experiencing bad banks of fog, which meant flying by instruments only, he continues: "The fog broke up in patches. These patches took on forms of every description. Numerous shore-lines appeared, with trees perfectly outlined against the horizon. In fact, the mirages were so natural that, had I not been in mid-Atlantic and known that no land existed along my route, I would have taken them to be actual islands."

Lindbergh flew the Atlantic and arrived almost on schedule. He was astounded at the warmth of his welcome, but he did not see what the world saw—that he had flown the Atlantic *by himself*, without wireless, risking his life; and this only a few days after the disappearance of Nungesser and Coli. Indeed, the French must be given great credit for the splendid way in which they received this American, while at the same time they

[" *Flight* " *Photo*

THE " LONE FLYER " ARRIVES IN LONDON.
Lindbergh lands at Croydon after his " lone flight " from New York to Paris. Here, as in France and America, he had a magnificent reception.

grieved for the loss of their own countrymen drowned somewhere out in the Atlantic. The landing and welcome make a thrilling pen-picture in Lindbergh's words :

" The lights of Le Bourget were plainly visible, but appeared to be very close to Paris. I had understood that the field was farther from the city, so continued out to the north-east into the country for four or five miles to make sure that there was not another field farther out which might be Le Bourget. Then I returned and spiralled down closer to the lights. Presently I could make out long lines of hangars, and the roads appeared to be jammed with cars.

" I flew low over the field once, then circled around into the wind and landed. After the 'plane stopped rolling I turned it around and started to taxi back to the lights. The entire field ahead, however, was covered with thousands of people all running towards my ship. When the first arrived, I attempted to get them to hold back the rest of the crowd away from the 'plane, but apparently no one could understand, or would have been able to conform to my wish and request if he had.

"I cut the switch to keep the propeller from killing someone, and attempted to organise an impromptu guard for the 'plane. The impossibility of any immediate organisation became apparent, and when parts of the ship began to crack from the pressure of the multitude I decided to climb out of the cockpit in order to draw the crowd away.

"Speaking was impossible ; no words could be heard in the uproar, and nobody apparently cared to hear any. I started to climb out of the cockpit, but as soon as one foot appeared through the door I was dragged the rest of the way without assistance on my part.

"For nearly half an hour I was unable to touch the ground, during which time I was ardently carried around in what seemed to be a very small area, and in every position it is possible to be in. Everyone had the best of intentions, but no one seemed to know just what they were.

"The French military flyers very resourcefully took the situation in hand. A number of them mingled with the crowd ; then, at a given signal, they placed my helmet on an American correspondent and cried : ' Here is Lindbergh.' That helmet on an American was sufficient evidence. The correspondent immediately became the centre of attraction, and while he was being taken protestingly to the Reception Committee via a rather devious route, I managed to get inside one of the hangars. . . ."

This lad of twenty-five had captured the imagination of the whole of Paris, and he had an equally great ovation in Belgium and England. Back in America—the United States sent a warship specially to convey him— his reception was even more exciting, and never did an American son reap such rewards. Soon it was arranged for him to make a tour of the American cities. St. Louis and Little Falls received particular attention. And then followed a big tour of the Latin-American states.

Next he was helping to lay the foundations for the present trans-continental air route, and carrying out surveys of a similar nature. To-day he is ever to the forefront in everything of use and value to American aviation, showing that he is indeed the greatest of all America's airmen.

But—and here it is worth pondering—what would Lindbergh be to-day had he given in to his father's wishes and not taken up flying as a career ? Would his inborn spirit of the conqueror have overcome so swiftly all the difficulties of any other profession ? It is worth pondering on. . . . Yet surely no son ever disregarded a father's wishes to more purpose !

THE WOMAN LINDBERGH

[L.E.A.
MISS AMELIA EARHART (MRS. G. P. PUTNAM).
The first woman to fly the Atlantic.

FIRST Atlantic Flight of Amelia Earhart. Her plan to fly solo. Stirring adventures during second attempt.

WHEN Charles A. Lindbergh flew the Atlantic Ocean solo from New York to Paris, the question which arose in the minds of many thousands of people—airmen as well as those who knew nothing of the intricacies of flying machines —was : could a woman emulate the feat ?

To fly solo across the Atlantic was considered at best a hair-raising adventure for a man—for a woman a wellnigh impossible task. And yet, in 1932, five years after Lindbergh's epoch-making flight, a woman was to span the Atlantic between New-foundland and Ireland. The woman was Amelia Earhart, in private life Mrs. G. P. Putnam, wife of the famous American publisher.

Amelia Earhart was born at Atchison, Kansas, in 1898, but her flying career did not start until after the war, and then she became interested in aviation as a sport. Even when she had grown into an accomplished flyer few of her friends knew of her prowess. This was doubtless because her life had so far been completely occupied with mercy work amongst poor slum children.

In 1928 she startled her friends and acquaintances by telling them that she was planning to fly the Atlantic. They could not believe her ; it was impossible that she would sacrifice herself in such a way. She smiled and went on with her preparations. She chose a seaplane for the venture and called it *Friendship*. Then, together with Mr. Wilmer Stultz and a mechanic, she set off on June 17 for Ireland.

The take-off was made at Trepassey Bay, Newfoundland, and their

101

destination was Southampton. The start, however, was delayed. As so often happens in Atlantic flights, it was found a most difficult matter to get into the air from the water with such a heavy load of fuel, and quantities of petrol had to be unloaded. Thus the idea of reaching the south of England was discarded. It was then decided to make for Valentia, Ireland ; but the machine eventually taxied along the water at Burry Estuary, near Llanelly, Wales, when there were but ten gallons of petrol left in the tanks.

The weather during part of the flight was exceedingly bad, and the flyers did not see Ireland at all. When they descended they firmly believed they were somewhere near Land's End.

Miss Earhart, as the first woman to fly the Atlantic, was given a splendid reception in this country. Before she returned to America she purchased the British light aeroplane used by Lady Heath in a Cape Town to England flight. Miss Earhart firmly believes that this type of machine is the finest of its kind in the world.

When she left our shores Miss Earhart made a statement which was not taken too literally. She said that the next time she flew the Atlantic she would do it solo. Who could believe that this woman flyer, who had already braved the dangers of Atlantic flight, would risk her life again ? And yet, on May 19, 1932, she left New Jersey for Harbour Grace, Newfoundland, the logical stepping-off place for Atlantic flights, ready again to fly the

[Brazier

WARCRAFT.
A new view of an experimental high bomber Fairey.

A FLOATING AERODROME.   [Brazier
Sopwith Camels are here seen on the deck of an aircraft carrier.

ocean separating America from these shores.   But this time she meant
to fly by herself.

It would have been, to a woman made of less stern stuff, a terrific
wrench when her mechanic said *au revoir* to her at Harbour Grace—he had
flown from New Jersey with her.   Amelia Earhart, however, did not allow
this to worry her—she would have quite enough to occupy her mind during
the perilous hours to come.

At twenty minutes past seven on the evening of May 20, local time, she
waved her last farewells and took off—in an aeroplane this time—her plan
being to make Paris.   For only four hours was the flight uneventful, then
a chapter of accidents set in which threatened to turn the attempt into a
catastrophe.   First, a section of the exhaust manifold—through which the
hot burned-up gases blow into the air—began to leak.   The hot gases came
through at the break.

At almost the same time the weather took a turn for the worse, so that
Amelia Earhart was forced to fly by her instruments only.   Even the
instruments let her down at this juncture, for almost as soon as she was

All kinds of aircraft on view at Kenley Aerodrome, 25th May, 1934.

An interested crowd of school children viewing one of the exhibits.

dependent upon them the altimeter failed—which meant that she could not tell whether she was rising or falling, a dreaded experience for any flyer. Not being able to glimpse the sea, the machine might be losing height, so that at any moment it might dive into the water.

There was only one thing for her to do—climb and climb until the meter which recorded the engine revolutions froze! Then she could *believe* with certainty that she was not near the water. She drove the machine up, ever upward, high into thick cloud, until ice caked on the wings of the 'plane. Adding to her discomfiture, she found she had to fly through lightning, storm areas being in the heavens just above.

And now the leaky manifold was growing infinitely more dangerous. It grew so hot that suddenly a portion broke clear away and dropped, to fall into the sea somewhere below the world of whiteness in which she was flying. At once terrific vibration set up in the machine; and still another danger threatened. The petrol gauge was leaking, allowing petrol to drop into the cockpit. At any moment petrol fumes, coming in contact with the red-hot exhaust, might cause an explosion, and then . . . it would be the end. Perhaps it was this danger which had threatened some of those flyers before her, men and women who had gone to their deaths without leaving the slightest trace of what had happened to them. . . .

Flames shot through the broken manifold. To look over the side at the red tongues was sufficient to unnerve the stoutest heart, and yet Amelia Earhart determined to fly on, until the machine burst asunder or the 'plane was forced down into the sea.

In the early hours of May 21 she passed a ship, and even then, though the temptation must have been great, refused to go down to the vessel. At long last Ireland hove in sight and the range of hills beyond—just when she was beginning to think she must be many miles off her route. Now, without the altimeter, she realised that the hills were to present a big difficulty. She could rise and fly into cloud, but she could not tell whether she was high enough to clear the hills. She did not intend now to make Paris; it was too far off the route Providence had chosen for her. Instead of trying to cross the hills, she ran parallel, looking for a town. Then one drew near—she did not know which it was—and now commenced a search for a landing-ground. She soon chose her field, and came down, just outside Londonderry, after only 13½ hours' flying—the record crossing! She taxied her machine almost to the door of a farm cottage, so that two dairymaids and a farm hand, coming into the open to find out what all the noise was about, received the shock of their lives.

Congratulations poured in from all parts of the world when the news of Amelia's arrival was flashed far and wide. There were messages from the American President, from the King and Queen, from the Continent. She was feted everywhere, and her homecoming was a veritable triumph.

But Amelia Earhart did not rest on her laurels. Only a month or two later she was making a record flight, for women, across the American continent, from Los Angeles to Newark, New Jersey. Perhaps most daring of all, however, was her solo flight from Honolulu to California in 18 hours, 15 minutes over that ocean which is anything but Pacific for the aeronaut. This pioneering record she established on January 11, 1935.

In the flights of others she has also taken a big part, helping with advice from her store of knowledge; and in American aviation to-day her suggestions are treated with the utmost respect. Amelia Earhart has been described as the Woman Lindbergh, and she certainly deserves the title for her contributions as a lone flyer to the history of flying and flyers.

[Brazier

HANDLEY-PAGE LIGHT BOMBER.
A modern "engine of war"—a "close-up" of a Handley-Page Bomber.

MORE ATLANTIC FLYERS

THE Amazing Story of Levine's Flight. Commander Byrd and his crew. Von Hunefeld's adventurous trip. Coste and Bellonte.

DURING the time that the youthful Lindbergh was making his preparations to fly from America to Europe, another American citizen, whose intention was almost the same, was the subject of derision in the United States. This was Mr. Charles Levine, millionaire at thirty years of age, and almost a novice at aeronautics. He had arranged for Mr. Clarence Chamberlin to pilot a machine, manufactured by the company of which he was managing director; but because he always seemed to be in trouble, legally and otherwise, over the proposed flight, he was derided through the length and breadth of the land.

Lindbergh completed his arrangements, flew from one side of America to the other, crossed the Atlantic, and was almost on his way back, and still the Levine aeroplane was on the flying ground waiting! Its owner was in the midst of fresh wrangling.

He could not now be first across to Europe, and America felt that his machine, named *Columbia*, would be used for some other flight. Yet in the faint, cold light of dawn on June 4, 1927, Mr. Chamberlin climbed into the aeroplane at Roosevelt Field, New York. Who would his companion be? So far, all arrangements Levine had made for someone to go with Chamberlin had come to nought. The onlookers saw Levine himself walk across the flying ground, bareheaded and wearing ordinary clothes with the exception of a leather waistcoat. He climbed into the cockpit. Mrs. Levine watched aghast. Surely her husband was not going to fly the Atlantic! She turned to the chief mechanic, to be reassured by the suggestion that the 'plane was off on a trial flight. Levine did not give a single glance at his wife—he kept his face averted. The machine took off, rose, and flew dead straight for the east. Levine *was* flying the Atlantic. He meant to show his critics that he *did* mean to send a 'plane across, and that he himself would go with it. According to his own account, it had been his intention throughout to fly with Chamberlin.

The machine was scarcely in the air before difficulties loomed up. The compasses were not agreeing, with the result that they did not know if they were on their right course. Should they turn back? The machine carried no wireless to find out their route. Levine decided that he would sooner drown in the Atlantic than let America laugh again. So, with no knowledge of their whereabouts, except through the agency of an old compass which they did not trust, they went straight into head winds.

They should have made Cape Race, but they were many miles from it when, two and a half hours behind schedule, they passed over Nova Scotia. Undaunted, they set the machine towards the open Atlantic, hoping sooner or later to meet land on the other side. At any rate, America should see that the Levine flight had all the pluck necessary for such an undertaking as the Atlantic crossing.

They met fog in abundance, but flew on. They would go on until the engine failed or petrol gave out. Eventually as the hours passed they found the temperature rising to such an extent that they knew they were flying too far south. Then came a thrill—sight of the *Mauretania* going back to America. They dropped down to try to obtain their position, but were unable to do this. It was a newspaper in the cabin, containing the movements of shipping, which helped them. They noted the day on which the *Mauretania* set sail, and worked out a course from its position below them in mid-Atlantic.

Ireland was sighted at long last. Previously, although Levine had had only a few hours' flying lessons, he had taken over from Chamberlin to give the pilot a little respite. They crossed land 399 miles south-west of Valentia, Ireland; then, determining to go as far as possible, flew over Plymouth, England, then Boulogne, and over Europe to Germany; they would land at Berlin.

How close they got to their destination! Lack of direction and shortage of fuel caused them to come down just a hundred miles away. Thus at 5.35 (local time) on June 6 they landed at Eisleben. Their flight had taken forty-three hours, and they had created a new long-distance record. They refuelled and again set off for Berlin, but had to come down at Kottbus, some sixty miles away. In landing their machine was damaged. Thus ended the Levine flight, although it should be added that the machine was repaired so that the flyers could finish the remainder of their " hop."

Less than a month later a 'plane called *America*, which had been waiting at Roosevelt Field at the time that Chamberlin and Levine set off, also taxied along the starting line. It contained Commander Richard Byrd, United States Navy and hero of a thrilling aerial survey of the Pole, Mr. Bert Acosta, Lieutenant Noville, late United States Navy, and Lieutenant

Balchen, late Royal Swedish Navy. The machine was exceedingly heavy as it moved away at 5 a.m. on June 29, and, despite the fact that an hour earlier not a soul but the mechanics were on the ground, at the moment of rising into the air a crowd of about a thousand had rushed up from the surrounding districts to see the gallant four into the skies.

Two months earlier Commander Byrd nearly lost his life in taking off, the machine crashing at the start. Also, on the very spot where the machine was starting another huge 'plane had crashed.

The onlookers were silent, heaving a sigh of relief only when the *America* rose with her five and a half tons weight and headed out for Newfoundland. Byrd was carrying a wireless installation, and it was almost entirely due to this that he and his companions came through alive. They were able to check their direction over most of the Atlantic, although at times wireless messages did not reach them.

As in the case of Chamberlin and Levine's flight, they lost their bearings for hours, and over France something went wrong with the compass. They flew over Le Bourget, the French air port, where all France was waiting to greet them, without knowing, for dense fog made it impossible to see a thing. When at last they thought they must be over Paris they were making back the way they had come !

For nineteen consecutive hours they flew without sight of land, sea or ship ; but the end of the flight makes even more thrilling reading— especially in the words of Byrd himself :

" With so much of our voyage completed, we got into trouble. I do not make any effort to say where we flew exactly. We were there in the dark, steering by a compass which had gone crazy. We must have been near Paris at least twice in those five hours of wandering in pitchy blackness, with rain pouring. We thought we were going right, but we were not. At one point I think we were only a few miles from Le Bourget, but we could see nothing. There was no way for us to know where we were going. Because of the lowness of the clouds and the darkness, we were hopelessly lost. We must have been near Paris, but we saw no lights. We did not know whether we were over town or country, over fields or mountains.

" It did not take us long to see that we had missed Paris and were just wandering around. We sent out one message about 1 o'clock to say that we were lost, but could get no reply. . . . Then came the surprise of our lives. We saw the sea beneath us. We did not know then where

COMMANDER R. E. BYRD AND FLOYD BENNETT (left).   [" *Flight* " *Photo*
In 1926 Commander Byrd flew from Spitzbergen to the North Pole and back, a distance of 1300 miles.

CHAMBERLIN AND LEVINE.   [L.E.A.
Mrs. Chamberlin photographed with her son and Levine after the arrival of the Atlantic heroes at Croydon.

we were. We knew then that we had done a half-circle and come back, doubling on our tracks—back to the coast, not far from where we had crossed it five hours before.

"Then we knew that in one hour, or perhaps half an hour, we could go no farther, because our petrol supply would be exhausted. We might at any moment have to make a forced landing, and we did not know where we were. . . . I then took the decision to land on the sea and to get ashore as best we could."

In a few seconds the 'plane jarred itself in the sea, but by good fortune the flyers reached shore. They had come down only a few yards from the

LIEUT. BELLONTE AND CAPTAIN COSTES,   [*L.E.A.*
who made the first non-stop flight from Europe to New York (September, 1930).

beach at Ver-sur-Mer, Calvados, France. The flight had taken some forty hours.

On April 12, 1928, at 5.38 a.m., two Germans and an Irishman set off from Baldonnel Aerodrome, Ireland, in a German Junkers machine named *Bremen* to fly east to west across the Atlantic. The pilots were Captain Hermann Kohl of the German Imperial Air Force and Commandant James Fitzmaurice, acting officer in command of the Free State Air Service. Also in the " *ship* " was Baron von Hunefeld, a former German officer of Marines, who was financing the attempt.

For eighteen days they had waited for favourable weather, and then, being told that they could expect no better, determined to set off. At daylight the five-ton machine ran slowly down the runway. Ambulances waited with engines ticking over in case the machine should crash on rising. She taxied slowly and, when it was feared a crash was imminent, the *Bremen* rose into the air. She carried no wireless, so that until she reached Newfoundland nothing more would be heard of her.

Very many hours passed before there was news. Various reports were received that the machine had passed over the coast, and yet the machine failed to materialise. What was the truth?

For half the journey the *Bremen* fought a fearful storm. Then, hundreds of miles from shore, in the pitch darkness of night, the machine's lighting gave out. Frantic efforts were made to repair it without avail, and an attempt was made to keep the instruments and compass illuminated with the light of an electric torch. The machine had to be flown blind in every sense, the pilot not knowing whether he was flying on an even keel, whether he was circling back the way they had come, or whether he was diving for the sea!

They must have travelled 400 miles in this fashion, and they had given up all hope of making the crossing when the first streaks of daylight came. Later they found that, fortunately, they had headed generally westward. At this stage dense fog drifted down, and again they were in difficulties. Eventually, when they knew that their petrol would last only an hour longer, they saw in the distance what they took to be a ship's funnel sticking up in ice. It was the lighthouse on Greenly Island! Behind it they saw a lake of ice. A perfect landing was made, but the ice broke, damaging the machine. And there, sandwiched between Newfoundland and the mainland, they waited for aid. Through the Labrador wilds the message of their safety trickled through, and in a world which had all but given them up, arrangements were at once made to rescue them. It was not until April 30 that New York could honour them, the first airmen to make an Atlantic crossing from east to west.

Following an Atlantic flight by stages of the German, von Gronau in July and August, 1929, Captain Costes and Lieut. Bellonte left Le Bourget on September 1, 1930, in their machine *Question Mark* on an attempt to fly non-stop to New York. For three years these two had been planning to fly the Atlantic. In July, 1928, they had started via the southern route, but were forced to turn back at the Azores through strong head winds. In the months between they had perfected their machine and also carried out a flight of over 4000 miles.

The *Question Mark* passed over Ireland early in the afternoon. An hour later, flying fast and very high, she was sighted over County Clare. On September 2, *Question Mark* landed at Curtiss Field, New York, and the flyers received a tumultuous reception. The weather conditions were as near ideal as they are ever likely to be on the east to west route. Nevertheless, the airmen had come through the ordeal after thirty-seven hours' flying.

At this stage it was seen that the Atlantic was providing real " sport," now being crossed from west to east with ease by more flyers. In this connection, therefore, little significance can be attached to such flights or the flyers. The pioneers had, as is obvious, shown the way, and therefore further Atlantic crossings by air were merely a matter of simple arrangement. Where world flights were contemplated, however, they are worthy of mention, and such flights that have added to the story of flyers are detailed in the next chapter, given to this subject.

Vickers Experimental Light Bomber (1932). [Brazier

Round the World Flyers

SQUADRON-LEADER A. Stuart MacLaren and Crew. The American Quartet who succeeded. Mr. Wiley Post and Mr. Harold Gatty. Post's Solo World Flight. Mr. James Mattern.

IN this chapter I shall deal with those who have accomplished the circum navigation of the globe, and also with certain gallant attempts which failed. And I would advise that you have at your elbow as you read this chapter a world atlas, for the studying of the routes taken by the world flyers is really fascinating.

As far back as 1922 Squadron-Leader A. Stuart MacLaren conceived the idea of opening up new aerial ways by flying round the world, and over British soil wherever possible. Owing to various difficulties the flight was postponed, but until its commencement in 1924 MacLaren was busily engaged in establishing petrol bases and supply depots.

MacLaren had had a distinguished career in the air force during the Great War, and afterwards did brilliant service in the Red Sea districts and in Somaliland keeping restive tribes under control. On one occasion, while dispelling a large band of marauding natives during the Aden campaign, he noticed the chief on a white horse. Flying after him, he swooped and suddenly let fly with a bomb. Horse and rider were blown up, and with that one bomb and single casualty the rising came to an end.

His pilot, Flying Officer W. N. Plenderleith, was a young man of twenty-five when the flight began, although he, too, had seen service against unruly natives and in the War. The third member of the crew was Sergeant R. Andrews, also with war-time experience. The machine selected was a Vickers Vulture, an amphibian of the latest type. Two were built, one for testing and the other to embody all the improvements required as a result of the tests. The first machine was sent forward, however, in case it might be of use later in the flight.

The flyers started from Calshot Seaplane Station on March 25, 1924, following the receipt of a special message from the King ; and particular interest was lent the flight by the fact that America had also been planning a world attempt, and her airmen were almost ready. Another point of interest was that, while the Britons would face ever eastwards, the Americans would follow the setting sun.

The British flight was soon marred, bad weather dogging the airmen for thousands of miles. At Corfu, Greece, there was mechanical trouble which necessitated the fitting of a new engine. This was sent across Europe to the flyers, yet after a further three thousand miles the same defect developed again. In the Desert of Sind they were forced down, and so hot was the weather that men had to be employed all day long throwing water over the fabric of the 'plane to prevent it cracking.

The machine was patched up sufficiently to get it to Calcutta, and here a new engine was fitted. Torrential rains now affected their plans, and, at Akyab, Burma, the machine ascended only to fall out of control and become a complete wreck. The accident was due to the exposure of the 'plane to extremes of heat and cold.

It was at this juncture—when the expedition seemed over—that the rivalry between the American and British round-the-world flyers was

[L.E.A.
SQUADRON-LEADER A. STUART MACLAREN.

shown to be of the friendliest. No sooner did the Americans hear that their rivals, not far away, were down and beaten unless they could obtain their second machine at Tokyo, than they arranged for it to be sent to them by an American cruiser. And it was while the Britons were resting, on the next stage of their flight, that the Americans actually passed overhead on the next stage of *their* expedition round the world !

The flight from Tokyo onward was a struggle against rainstorms which made flying absolutely impossible. Terrific rain and fog had delayed them almost from the start, and the result was that eventually, owing to thick fog, they were forced down after missing a cliff by only two feet, and the machine was badly damaged. The British round-the-world flight came to an end in the Bering Sea.

What, during this time, had happened to the Americans, whose expedition comprised four 'planes ? To hark back, they left Seattle on April 6. On April 19 three of the 'planes were still in the struggle. The other had been delayed by minor mishaps, and, in following up, had crashed. In fog and storm the Pacific was crossed and Japan reached. With new engines the three machines made Shanghai, then Rangoon, Akyab and Calcutta. At Karachi engines were again changed. Then on across Europe flew these world flyers, to be feted in England after 18,000 miles of arduous flying had been completed.

The Atlantic, perhaps the most difficult stage, remained to be conquered, but they flew by way of the Orkneys and Iceland. Only one 'plane reached Iceland, the remaining two being forced back by fog. Another attempt was made by the failures and again one got through. The third was forced down by engine trouble and the pilot, after drifting helplessly for four hours, was picked up by a British trawler. Thus the flight was reduced to two. The next port of call was Reykjavik, then on to Frederiksdal in Greenland, and so via Labrador and Newfoundland to Nova Scotia. The airman forced down had now been furnished with a new machine, and in Canada he rejoined his companions

On September 5 the three machines set off for Boston, but were forced down by fog. On September 6 they made another attempt, which they accomplished without further incident. On September 8 they were in New York, and Washington a day later. On September 14 they started on the final " hop," via Dayton, Ohio, Chicago, Omaha, and across Arizona and the Rocky Mountains to San Diego. Thence they made towards Seattle,

[*Central Press Photos., Ltd.*

SCHOOLBOY QUALIFIES AS "A" PILOT, April 10th, 1934.
Master John Stirling Creswell, aged 17, being congratulated after passing his test.

which they reached on September 28, 1924—the first round-the-world flight to be made successfully.

Major Kingsford Smith, Australia's own particular air hero, also made a round-the-world flight, as did the crew of the *Graf Zeppelin*, the great German commercial dirigible ; but the adventures in connection with these flights and flyers are detailed in special chapters given to them. The next great round-the-world flight of note, therefore, brings us to the most astonishing personality of all—Mr. Wiley Post, the American who decided that the world could be flown in a few days only !

Wiley Post understood aeroplanes from A to Z, and when he chose the machine in which he was to make his world attempt he first learned all there was to know about it. This iron-nerved individual from Oklahoma chose as his companion Harold Gatty, an Australian, an ex-naval man who also knew much about aeroplanes, and together these two determined to win a sum of £2000 offered for a flight round the world in not more than ten days.

Their route was carefully planned by way of England, Berlin, Russia, Siberia, Bering Strait, Alaska and Canada. On June 23, 1931, they left New York, and at 130 miles an hour headed for Newfoundland, the Atlantic and Britain. The first stage of their flight, from Harbour Grace, was almost uneventful, and they touched land at Sealand Aerodrome, Chester, ahead of schedule. They rested for one hour only before setting off for Berlin. It was here that their fatigue was manifest, and Wiley Post was actually found asleep in his bath !

Next morning they were on their way again, Moscow being the next port of call. Before evening they were in Moscow and taking a well-earned rest ready for the next day's work. Across Russia into desolate Siberia by way of Novo Sibirsk they flew, then on to Irkutsk and Blagoveschensk, where in coming down their machine was bogged. They obtained the services of a horse, but the 'plane would not move. It took the united efforts of horses, a tractor and Soviet soldiers to get the machine out of the bog and ready for taking off. Once in the air they flew via Khabarovsk to Alaska, and then on to Edmonton, in Alberta, Canada. They had previously had difficulty with their propeller in Alaska, and Gatty, struck by the blade, had received a badly bruised arm. But now that they were so near their goal they determined that nothing should stop them. And so, only *nine* days after setting out, they came down at Roosevelt Field, New York, having accomplished the circumnavigation of the globe in record time.

[L.E.A.

Wiley Post, the intrepid American airman who flew solo round the world in 7 days, 18 hours, 49½ minutes.

On paper the flight would appear a simple matter, for Post and Gatty had a fair share of good weather; but the crossing of the Atlantic, of Siberia and the Bering Sea formed part of a journey which only the hardiest and pluckiest would care to attempt.

Just two years later, on July 15, 1933, Wiley Post set off alone to try to beat the amazing record which he and Gatty had created in their joint flight. He was using the same machine, rebuilt, and was aided by a control which would fly the machine without human steering once it was in the air. Post, however, was so used to his own piloting that he relied on this rather than the mechanical flyer through most of the journey. Straight to Berlin he flew—the first man to make the non-stop "hop"—and then, two hours later, he set off again for Novo Sibirsk. He landed first at Konigsberg and called again at Moscow for minor adjustments to his machine. He arrived at his scheduled destination, and then went straight on to Irkutsk. At this stage he had taken less than eighty hours to cover the distance from New York, and he was some sixteen hours in front of the time established by himself and Gatty.

Unfortunately, he was forced down before he reached Khabarovsk, so

[L.E.A.

Harold Gatty, the Australian airman who accompanied Wiley Post on his first record flight round the world.

that when he made this town he was about level on time with that of his old flight. Yet he meant to regain the lost time, and took off again after a stay of less than three hours, thus establishing a big lead once more—for he and Gatty had remained at Khabarovsk for 26½ hours.

He had trouble in Alaska, but finally, with time still in hand, made the fastest hop of his entire flight straight to Edmonton and New York. The total time was many hours less than on the first occasion, being only 7 days, 18 hours, 49½ minutes.

All the world mourned when disaster overtook this fearless flyer and his friend Will Rogers, the film comedian, on a pioneer flight to Moscow, via the Arctic. Their 'plane crashed in Alaska on August 15, 1935, and both were killed.

While Mr. Wiley Post had been preparing to establish a new record for round-the-world flights, a native of Texas, Mr. James Mattern, got away first. A year earlier Mattern had started with a companion, but the flight had ended with a crash in Siberia. Now he was flying solo. On June 3, 1933, he took off from Floyd Bennett Field, New York, and set a course direct for Europe, via Newfoundland. He carried no wireless, and his only map was an ordinary one of the world, such as is to be found in the average atlas. He flew through severe weather which took him off his course, and when he at last came down he thought he was in Scotland. His surprise was great when he found he had crossed the British Isles and was in Norway.

Mattern soon reached Moscow, his next scheduled stop, having made slightly better time than Post and Gatty. His next point was Omsk, which he again reached with ease and his machine in splendid condition. His next stopping place was to be Chita, near the Manchurian border, and when he passed over Novo Sibirsk he was but two hours behind Post and Gatty's time.

It was now that trouble set in for him. Only an hour after he had been seen flying fast over Novo Sibirsk a petrol pipe leak caused him to come down. Suffering acutely from the effects of the fumes, he made a repair, but found himself too dazed—and doubtless too exhausted from want of sleep—to get into the air right away. But when he did rise again he found himself battling with head winds, and with bad weather generally. He was forced to make stops all along his route, and it was not till June 12 that he left Khabarovsk for Nome, Alaska.

It was now impossible for him to beat Post and Gatty's time, yet luck did not befriend him. For, the moment he left Khabarovsk all trace of him vanished. The Bering Sea and the coast of Alaska were shrouded in impenetrable fog; he might have been forced down on any part of the flight to Nome. Days passed. The cables were busy with inquiries. Not until July 7 did a message of hope come through, saying Mattern was safe near the far coast of Siberia. On July 9 fuller reports were to hand, and it was then learned that Mattern was unhurt. Later it was discovered that his machine was completely wrecked and unrepairable when it came down through lack of oil on June 15, fifty miles from Anadyr in north-east Siberia.

For a fortnight Mattern had lived in the wilds awaiting rescue, and kept himself alive by shooting birds and cooking them over log fires. A rifle given him by Russian airmen at Khabarovsk had undoubtedly saved his life. He nearly perished, too, from the intense cold. He was found on July 5 by Eskimos, and thus ended the Mattern flight round the world, and one of the pluckiest flyers of all time returned disconsolate to New York.

[L.E.A.

Captain Bennett Griffen and Lieut. James Mattern, two American flyers who crashed in Siberia while attempting a flight round the world.

["Flight" Photo

Kingsford Smith (right) with C. T. P. Ulm, his companion on the record-making flight, from California to Australia (1928), and from Australia to England (1929).

Nieuport Nighthawk over Baghdad R.A.F. Aerodrome. ⌊*Brazier*

KINGSFORD SMITH

AUSTRALIA'S AIR HERO

FLYING with an Umbrella. The great Pacific Flight. Flying to England, and completing Flight Round the World. His Disappearance and Death.

AIR COMMODORE SIR CHARLES KINGSFORD SMITH, the hero of many long-distance flights, was the Australian Lindbergh! Once he was plain Kingsford Smith, and certainly not regarded as likely to become the greatest of all Australian flyers.

He was born in 1897, the youngest of seven children. His father owned a sugar plantation, but Kingsford Smith remembers little about it, for at the age of six he was sent to Canada, where he remained until he reached the age of twelve. Then he returned to Sydney, Australia, where the family had settled. He knew nothing of flying in those days, and the urge had not struck him. He had a semblance of that necessary keenness about his sixth birthday, after he had seen a balloon giving exhibitions. Fired with the ambition to rise into the air, he got on to the chicken shed with an umbrella, his idea being to jump off in his " airship." Had it not been for the promptness of his older brother in catching him as he "took off" he might have severely injured himself.

At school he studied electrical engineering, and was apprenticed just as the Great War broke out. At eighteen he enlisted and went to France as an infantryman. He came to know the horrors and monotony of trench warfare, and it was in a state of complete boredom that he asked for a transfer to the air force. He could scarcely believe his good fortune when he knew that his wish had been granted. Very soon he was in the air fighting German 'planes. For his work in this connection he was awarded the Military Cross, but being forced down himself and injured in the leg, was transferred to England to act as instructor.

When the war came to an end he had no job of work to go to, and wandered to California, making a living there by taking up passengers.

On one occasion he landed at a farm where the wife of the owner had never before seen an aeroplane. She studied it critically, and was completely astounded by the propeller. Turning to Kingsford Smith she said eventually, " Surely it's breezy enough up above without the need for such a big fan ! "

Kingsford Smith returned to Australia and began flying, while at the back of his mind was a big idea. In California he had often stood on the seashore surveying the Pacific Ocean and asking himself how long it would take him to fly home ! He was certain it could be done, if only he had the right machine and the money to carry through such a proposition.

As his name became more known as a flyer, so he was listened to, especially when with Mr. C. P. Ulm, an ex-wartime pilot, he encircled Australia by air. At last he was granted Government backing for a flight from America to Australia. He went to California with his plans made, but in the meantime a new Government had taken the reins of office in Australia, and his financial backing was withdrawn. He could not give up the attempt at such an advanced stage, and began to look around for someone to lend him the necessary funds. When he set out from Oregon, California, on the momentous flight he was nearly £4000 in debt.

On May 31, 1928, at 9 a.m., he, Ulm and two Americans left Oakland to fly across the Pacific " home." Their first hop was to Honolulu, which they reached by the following morning. Then on to Hawaii. At dawn on June 3rd they set out for Suva, Fiji, and covered the distance in $34\frac{1}{2}$ hours—the longest flight so far over water.

The distance from Suva to Brisbane is 1530 miles. On this hop they encountered the worst weather of the flight, but, undeterred, though electrical trouble added to their worries, they flew on, to reach Brisbane at 10.10 a.m. on June 9, a total flying distance from Oakland of over 7000 miles. Thus were Kingsford Smith and his crew in the aeroplane *Southern Cross* the first flyers to brave the Pacific Ocean and reach Australia.

In April, 1929, Kingsford Smith and three companions set out from Sydney for England by air. This time they nearly lost their lives, for after flying 2000 miles through atrocious weather they were forced down, from lack of petrol, in the dreaded Australian bush. Here they remained for twelve days before they were found, despite the fact that aeroplanes scoured the skies for them in all directions. On several occasions they saw aeroplanes a few miles from them, but could not make their presence known. When they were discovered they were four starved men who could scarcely stagger to the rescue 'plane which brought them food. Their condition may be judged from the fact that when they attempted to lift their rescuer shoulder high the effort was too great for the four of them!

Safe, and later on no worse, they flew their machine back to Sydney and then recommenced the flight to Britain on June 25. Their route was Derby in north-west Australia, then via Singapore, Rangoon, Allahabad, Karachi, Baghdad, and Rome to London. This time the weather and luck were more or less on their side, and they landed at Croydon on July 10.

On June 24, 1930, Kingsford Smith and three companions were ready for a new flight—to reach America on the east to west route from the British Isles. The *Southern Cross* was ready for the momentous flight, as it had been in the case of all the others. She took off from Portmarnock Strand, Ireland, on a two-and-a-half-mile runway—very necessary in view of the fact that the large aeroplane weighed something like nine tons.

The machine carried wireless, as on the previous flights, and during the whole of the Atlantic crossing messages were being received. Amateurs with wireless receivers were thrilled time and again to pick up messages from these men who, according to their reports, were in a world of impenetrable fog out somewhere in mid-Atlantic. After $31\frac{1}{2}$ hours' flying the 'plane landed successfully at Harbour Grace. But for the fog they would have gone on to New York. They arrived there on June 26, and on July 2 took off for Oakland, California. It will be realised now that if the *Southern Cross* reached the west coast of America it would have completed a round-

["*Flight*" *Photo*

Kingsford Smith's aeroplane, the "Southern Cross."

the-world flight. It was on July 4 that the circuit was completed, and Kingsford Smith received a mighty reception at Oakland airport.

Kingsford Smith did not rest on his laurels, but at once commenced preparations for a new flight from England to Australia. This time he chose a small British aeroplane with a single engine—120 horse-power against the 675 h.p. of the three-engined *Southern Cross*. On October 9, 1930, he set out from England, and only eleven days later had landed at Port Darwin, Australia. In making this amazing flight Kingsford Smith just beat another competitor on a speedy England-Australia journey— Flight Lieutenant Hill, who was forced down on the last lap and passed by Kingsford Smith. Hill was also flying British—in the cheapest type of light aeroplane in the world. The two flights were a triumph for British aircraft. For his splendid efforts Kingsford Smith was created Air Commodore, the highest rank in the Australian Air Force.

In October, 1931, he set out in an effort to fly from Australia to Britain in only seven days. The record was made by Mr. J. A. Mollison, who took just over eight and a half days. Kingsford Smith failed to beat the record, for on the ninth day he was forced by indisposition to come down at Milas, ninety miles from Smyrna. Sickness prevented his taking off for England for some days, so he decided to try for a record on his return journey to Australia. But even this was not to be, for in England his medical men forbade him to fly for four months, his nerves being in a bad state.

He returned to Australia by liner, but in December of the same year he was flying again, despite the doctors' warnings. This time the journey was most adventurous. Christmas mails for England had been stranded in Malaya and he was asked to pick the bags up and fly them to England.

Needless to say, the mails from the Australian cities and the backblocks were delivered by the adventurous airman in England in time for the Christmas festivities.

Then, in January, 1933, he attempted to fly to New Zealand for the third time, and for the third time his efforts were crowned with success.

On October 4, 1933, Kingsford Smith set out from England for a flight to Australia. He said before his departure that he did not intend to break the record standing to the credit of C. W. A. Scott, the Englishman, of 8 days 20 hours 47 minutes.

His route was well worn for the flight to Down Under—via Brindisi, Baghdad, Karachi, Akyab, Alor Star, Sourabaya, and across the sea to Wyndham, Australia. So well, however, did his light British aeroplane behave that he found himself steadily beating Scott's time, and the result was that he reached his destination in 7 days 3 hours 15 minutes, close on two days ahead of the next best time.

In October, 1934, Kingsford Smith set off with Capt. P. G. Taylor and was successful in crossing the Pacific from Australia to the United States.

After a false start on October 23rd, 1935, he left Croydon with Mr. J. Pethybridge on an attempt to beat the record flight to Australia.

They flew well until they reached the Burma region where all communication with them stopped, and on November 8th they were reported missing. Search parties were organised and watch was kept for any sign of the missing fliers. No trace of them was found, however, and they were reported dead on December 7th, 1935.

Thus died Air Commodore Sir Charles Kingsford Smith, Australia's hero, and one of the world's finest airmen. Burma holds its secret well and so far not the slightest trace of their bodies or machine has been found.

NOCTURNE.
Night-flying over a tranquil sea—the low-flying 'plane makes a beautiful silhouette against the moonlit sky.

CROYDON—THE AIRPORT OF LONDON.

THE AMAZING MOLLISONS

AN Attraction for Aeroplanes. Two People with Great Ambitions. A Girl Flies Alone to Australia. Amy and Jim meet. Record Flights. Dual control in the conquest of the Atlantic.

THE story of the amazing Mollisons must inevitably commence with Amy Mollison herself—or, rather, Amy Johnson, as she then was.

She was born in Hull, and, being a scholar above average, was intended for the teaching profession. Viking ancestry gave Amy a power of leadership at a very early age, and if there were pranks which required a girl to show the way, Amy's personality asserted itself. Even when it came to riding for the first time on a motor-bicycle, it was Amy who took the risk—and incidentally received the fright of her life when she could not stop the machine.

Instead of studying to be a teacher, Amy took a job in an office at the princely salary of £1 weekly. So far as flying was concerned, it did not then interest her at all, for, to use her own words, she had once " wasted " five shillings on a joy flight at an air pageant not far from her home.

From a pound to thirty shillings a week, then to London in a solicitor's office was a moderately quick step. But it was a Sunday walk which began to change her whole life. She was enjoying a stroll near Stag Lane Aerodrome when she saw machines landing and taking-off. She was so thrilled at the sight of the 'planes and the airmen in their picturesque attire that she walked straight into the 'drome, despite notices warning strangers off. But she could not bring herself to ask how one became a flyer. It was a subsequent visit which evinced the information that by joining the London Aeroplane Club she could learn to fly.

The secretary put her name on the long waiting list. One month, two months, three, and six months she waited patiently. Then when six months became twelve without word she lost patience and bearded the secretary in his den—an astounding thing for her to do, considering she was normally so shy. Then and there she was enrolled.

Her first lesson was disappointing, for she was told she would never make a flyer. Actually, owing to the noise of the engine, she could not hear one word of the instructor, so that she appeared not to have learned a single thing. Her second lesson was more satisfactory, and within a few weeks she was making her first solo flight.

Her father did not look favourably on his daughter's new pastime, but so insistent was she as she became more and more proficient that he gave her £150 with which to learn to become a commercial pilot. Now she started to look ahead—to Australia! She wanted to fly for miles and miles, and on the map Australia seemed to fit her idea of a long flight.

But flying to Australia required funds, and nobody would listen to her. Who could believe that this stripling of a girl intended to brave the dangers of a journey across deserts, mountain ranges and jungle lands? To advance her money was to send her to her death. Not unnaturally, too, the male mechanics of the club did not take kindly to the intrusion of this girl, who would insist on learning everything she could of aero-mechanics. Yet she did not mind the dirtiest of jobs, nor how much her hands and face were oil-begrimed. Because of this the mere males came to look upon this first girl to work side by side with them with a new friendliness and a certain admiration.

Everyone turned her down, nevertheless, until she forced herself upon Sir Sefton Brancker. He was interested, and after an interview, in which he realised shrewdly that here was no ordinary girl, gave her an introduction to Lord Wakefield, that splendid sponsor of flights and flyers, and he advanced £300. Her father now came to the rescue with the other £300 needed to purchase an old but valuable aeroplane offered her. It belonged to Captain W. L. Hope, the well-known air-taximan, and although it had already done 35,000 miles, was good for many more. What was as important to a girl with little money, its fitments were essentially those necessary for long-distance flying. At long last Amy was ready to go ahead with her plans, and she began to select a route and to learn all she could of weather conditions. But despite help on the one hand there were many who did their utmost to dissuade her from what they believed was a mad-brained scheme.

She persevered ; she was going to fly to Australia. But it was not for notoriety. The love of flying was deep within her, and she wanted to show that a woman as well as men could fly fast to Australia, and solo. The lack of interest in her flight is manifest in *The Times* announcement of May 5, 1930, at the commencement of the ordeal. It occupied two inches of space

AMY AND JIM. ["*Flight*" *Photo*
The well-known flyers who have created many records in recent years.

only, and told the world that a Miss Amy Johnson, a member of the London Flying Club and the first woman to qualify as a ground engineer, intended to set out for Australia. " Although she has an expert knowledge of aeroplanes," said this national newspaper, " she has had little experience of long-distance flying." Which was perfectly true, for all her " long-distance " work so far had been the hundred odd miles between London and her home at Hull. Thus Amy Johnson was plucky beyond comprehension. She set off on May 5 at about 8 a.m., only her father and a handful of people seeing her into the skies.

The first stage of her journey to Vienna was made in almost perfect weather. The second, to Constantinople, passed without incident, but there was no sign that the world was interested. Now came mountainous country, and great cloud banks. The little light aeroplane was up against very formidable country, but the flight was so far passing off splendidly. She met a fearful sandstorm on the run to Baghdad, which caused her to alight in the desert, and it was as much as she could do, hanging on to her machine after chocking it with whatever luggage she carried, to prevent its being dashed away and overturned. It was not for hours that she could take off for Baghdad.

Then via Bandar Abbas, Karachi, and on to Calcutta and Rangoon went the tiny 'plane and the indomitable girl aviator. Actually she did not land at Rangoon as she intended, for severe storms took her down at Insein, a tiny town which she mistook for Rangoon, on the edge of the jungle to the north. She landed on a football field between the goalposts, which again shows her prowess in the control of a machine. In coming down, however, she damaged her propeller, wings and under-carriage. Eventually the machine had to be hauled by road to Rangoon, for the football field was too small as a taking-off ground.

It is worth remembering here that, had Amy reached Rangoon in the first place unhindered and got away without damage, she would very probably have broken the record for a flight from England to Australia— beating the time of Bert Hinkler in 1928 of $15\frac{1}{2}$ days. She had nevertheless set up a new record for a solo flight between England and India. Again and again on further stages of her flight she met weather which terrified her, and yet the little 'plane carried her onward, despite forced landings caused by the unbending elements. At one time the world, now thrilled by her feat, gave her up for lost, but she turned up in a tiny village which did not boast a single telephone. In the final stage across the Timor Sea

IN FLYING KIT.   [" *Flight* " *Photo*
A charming portrait of Miss Amy Johnson (Mrs. Mollison), who startled the world by her amazing solo
flight from England to Australia.

a vessel kept watch for her, and was ready to wireless Port Darwin as soon as she was sighted. She came out of the sky and passed overhead and Port Darwin made ready to greet this young woman, the first to fly solo from England. Never mind that she had not beaten Hinkler, although she did not set out with this intention. She had lost by only two days, but Australia was astounded that a girl who had never before so much as crossed the English Channel should be so near them in so short a time.

From Port Darwin she flew in stages down to Brisbane, being received in jubilation everywhere she went. But disaster befell her at Brisbane, for the machine in landing struck a fence and was badly damaged. She journeyed to Sydney in an Australian air liner, piloted by a young man who strangely interested her. She could not hear what he had to say on the flight because of the roar of the engines, but when he passed across a note asking her to dance with him at a reception being given for her that night she readily agreed. The pilot was Jim Mollison; but she did not see him at the reception because of the crush, nor for many months afterwards. For her time was soon occupied with a voluminous correspondence, offers of lecture tours, and all sorts of business opportunities. She returned to England by liner and air, to receive £10,000 from the *Daily Mail* to help her continue her flying. And England greeted her wondrously.

On New Year's Day, 1931, Amy Johnson left London in a new aeroplane for a solo flight via Russia to Pekin. She had been told by various experts not to attempt such a flight on account of the bad weather she was likely to meet, but she persisted. For one thing she wanted solitude, to escape from the fame which had come to her, and which caused her everywhere to be received in tumult. She intended to make Berlin on the first stage of the journey, but was forced by fog to land at Liége. She also had to come down at Cologne. After Berlin fog persisted right across Germany, and she came down again at a village called Amelin, some fifty-five miles north of Warsaw, damaging the machine badly. On January 7 she decided to postpone her flight, for she now saw that in the depths of winter Russia and Siberia could not be flown over without great difficulty. When her machine had been repaired she set out for England, but until she reached home she was dogged by vile weather.

On July 28, soon after midnight, she again set her machine east and intended to make for Tokyo. Her route was by way of Berlin, Warsaw and Moscow, along the trans-Siberian Railway through Omsk, Irkutsk, Chita and Tsitsihar. Late that night she was in Moscow! On August 6, after just under eighty hours' actual flying time, they were in Tokyo, again demonstrating the reliability of British light aeroplanes. On September 9 she and her companion were back in England, having flown over the route again, mostly in bad weather.

On her arrival it was to receive a pleasurable surprise. Jim Mollison was in England, having just broken the record for a flight from Australia to England. His time was less than nine days. Amy and Jim did not meet, for Amy was due to go on a lecture tour, and Jim was never able to get to the same town as she was appearing. But they were destined to meet again, in much more romantic circumstances.

It happened this way. Mollison had started out in November, 1931, to lower the time for an England to Cape Town flight, but when nicely on his way crashed and his machine was wrecked. In March of the following year he had accomplished this feat, creating a new record by reaching his destination in 4 days 17½ hours. For four days he had had no sleep whatever, and at Walvis Bay was feeling the effects badly. Which is probably why he came down on the outskirts of Cape Town, landing in the dark on a beach. And at Cape Town 'drome, where he was whisked by a taximan who was on the coast road when he landed, he met Amy. She was waiting to greet him, having landed by liner that very day, on a voyage on which she was recuperating after an operation for appendicitis. In May, 1932, the engagement of Amy Johnson to Jim Mollison was announced, and a little later they were married in London.

They determined now that they would carry out all the solo flights they had planned, and in August, 1932, Mollison took off by himself on a flight across the North Atlantic. He left Portmarnock Strand, Ireland, just before noon on the 18th, crossed the ocean and landed in New Brunswick, first to have flown the North Atlantic from east to west solo.

In the meantime Amy Mollison had been pushing forward with her plans for a record flight to the Cape, and on November 14, 1932, she took off from Lympne. Only four days later she dropped to earth at Cape Town, to beat her husband's record by several hours.

Not content with this new aerial conquest, Amy determined to beat the existing record for the return flight, and this she did easily, by nearly three days, the previous best having been by Captain Barnard and the Duchess of Bedford in 1930. Her record was not beaten till Flying-Officer David Llewellyn and Mrs. Joe Wyndham landed at Hamworth aerodrome on November 11, 1935, 6 days, 12 hours, 17 minutes after leaving Cape Town.

Mollison then planned a flight across the South Atlantic, to beat the record from Europe to Brazil of 4½ days. He accomplished the flight in just under 3½ days, and thus was the first airman to make the solo crossing of both the North and South Atlantic. This was also the first flight from England to South America.

In June, 1933, the Mollisons embarked on a dual flight across the Atlantic. They took off from Croydon, but almost before they left the ground had smashed their machine. It hit a bump which collapsed the under-carriage and unseated the engines. Less than two months later, caring nothing for such ill-luck or the dangers, they again attempted the flight, their plan being to make New York non-stop, turn about after resting and fly to Baghdad non-stop, thus creating a new long-distance non-stop record. All Britain watched their progress on the outward journey, and when it was known that they had crossed the coast of Newfoundland joy knew no bounds. Yet within fifty miles of New York they were forced to come down through want of fuel, and here they crashed, wrecking the machine completely. They were taken to hospital, badly bruised and shaken, and Mollison in need of several stitches in his forehead ; but when they were well once more New York staged one of its astonishing welcomes for them.

The Mollisons have proved British light aeroplanes up to the hilt, for every flight they have made, singly or in dual control, has been in De Haviland light machines. These two flyers have been the means of selling these well-tried, highly-efficient British products, with their baby engines, in every part of the world. They have shown that they are the equal, though much less costly, of the massive-engined aeroplanes of our competitors for world trade in aeronautics.

In October, 1934, they took part together in the race from England to Melbourne for a gold cup and a prize of £10,000 presented by Sir Macpherson Robertson. The distance to be covered was 11,000 miles. After being first to Baghdad, which they reached non-stop at an average speed of over 200 m.p.h., they experienced bad luck in the form of serious engine trouble. They struggled on to Allahabad but had to withdraw from the race.

DR. ECKENER AND HIS AIRSHIP

[" *Flight* " Photo

DR. HUGO ECKENER (right).

COUNT ZEPPELIN'S Critic. A Visit to the Zeppelin Sheds. Eckener Flies to America.

DR. HUGO ECKENER, one of the greatest airship designers and navigators in the world, first became associated with airships through his severe criticisms of their utility! This German airman, whose exploits in the *Graf Zeppelin* have astounded the world, was probably the most caustic of all Count Zeppelin's many critics, deriding his earlier attempts, which, like so many new ventures even to-day, more often than not resulted in miserable failure.

Born in 1868, Eckener received a good education, and fitted himself for a political career. Indeed, his degree of Doctor was obtained in political economy. As a youth he heard of, and probably saw, some of the many wild attempts which were being made by the pioneers to conquer the air, but except in a contemptuous way he never took an interest in them.

By the time he was in his early thirties, however, the new craze had made startling strides, and Count Zeppelin was building airship after airship, most of which came to an untimely end. Although at this stage Dr. Eckener looked upon airships with such contempt, he had his own ideas on the reason for the failure of the Zeppelins, and in consequence his criticisms led to his being invited to visit the Zeppelin works at Friedrichschafen. The immediate result was that his idea changed somewhat ; he came to realise that after all airships *could* be made and utilised with safety. It is well known that a convert often becomes the staunchest upholder of his new creed, and Eckener was no exception to the rule. He saw things in a new light, and realised the enormous future of aerial travel

GRAF ZEPPELIN.   ["Flight" Photo
The giant German airship, Graf Zeppelin. This type was designed by Count Zeppelin and perfected
during the war years by Dr. Hugo Eckener.

—especially the airship. All his previous prejudices were cast overboard, and he became enthusiastic in his new belief. In 1906 he joined the staff of the Zeppelin company, and such was his enthusiasm, that barely four years later he was appointed to the position of manager. Although he had previously interested himself but little in flying, he soon discovered that his mind was perfectly adapted to the new science, and his skill as an airship commander developed steadily with experience.

With the coming of the Great War, Eckener took his place as an instructor to airship commanders, at the same time superintending the training of crews. By exercising his enormous energy, he also managed to find time to continue in the capacity of manager to the great Zeppelin works. Then he was appointed to the position of adviser to the Naval

Airship Branch, which with its huge fleet of airships carried out the numerous raids on London and other cities in those dark days of the War.

This phase passed, and Eckener devoted his attention to building two small airships for commercial purposes—the *Bodensee* and the *Nordstern*. The first of these carried out for some considerable time a highly successful service between various German towns until both ships were confiscated by the Allies under the Peace Treaty.

By this time Eckener's fame as an airship designer was spreading, but in 1921 he had to build for America an airship as part of the peace arrangements. Work was commenced and eventually out of the great sheds at Friedrichschafen there emerged the giant airship, to be named *Los Angeles* by America, a vessel of 2,500,000 cubic feet gas capacity. After various trials she was flown across the Atlantic to Lakehurst in October, 1924, Dr. Eckener being in command. So successful was this ship that she was used for years without the slightest mishap.

A MODERN BALLOON.   [*Brazier*

Above we see a Naval Observation Balloon leaving an aircraft carrier.

[Flight Photo]

THE WORLD'S LARGEST AIRSHIP, THE *HINDENBURG.*

A sectional view of the airship showing the passenger accommodation. This monster dirigible is propelled by four 900 h.p. Mercedes-Benz Diesel engines, and in one minute actually rose 1000 ft. during its trials over Lake Constance.

Fame came with this airship, and it was arranged with an American company that Eckener should assist in the building of three more great ships. The result was seen in the *Macon*, and the ill-fated *Shenandoah* and *Akron*, both of which eventually met with disaster.

As soon as the ban on airship construction in Germany was lifted, Eckener began work on what was to become the most famous of all airships—the *Graf Zeppelin*. From the outset he was handicapped by the limited space of the erecting shed at Friedrichschafen, so that he could not build his ship to the proportions which he estimated. Nevertheless, as everyone now knows, the ship has had a wonderful career, demonstrating for many years the possibilities from a commercial point of view of this type of craft.

October, 1928, saw Eckener flying the *Graf Zeppelin* to Lakehurst and back. Then followed a series of European cruises, after which yet another flight was made to Lakehurst in August, 1929. From there Eckener headed his craft eastwards and flew right round the world, the first airship flight of its kind ever made.

Encouraged by his success, Eckener planned a flight to the Arctic, but difficulties arose and the project was abandoned. There is no doubt that but for this hitch Dr. Eckener would have added his name to that select band of successful Polar flyers.

May, 1930, found Eckener and his crew heading for Brazil, and after visiting Rio de Janeiro by way of Seville and Pernambuco, the airship was turned towards New York, and thence across the Atlantic to Germany. So successful was this flight, that a regular programme of flights to South America has been carried out each summer since, interspersed with flights through Europe. Bad weather does not bother Dr. Eckener overmuch, for he not only seems to have an uncanny sense of navigation, but his ship is as near perfection as the best of all other types of aircraft. Truly, Eckener is a worthy successor to his master, Count Zeppelin, whose persistent optimism in the future of airships finally overcame Eckener's doubts and scorn, and laid the foundations of a career which was to produce airship history.

On March 4, 1936, at Friedrichshafen the new Zeppelin, the *Hindenburg*, made its first trial flight piloted by Dr. Eckener. With the *Graf Zeppelin* the *Hindenburg* will fly regularly every fortnight to Pernambuco and Rio. This journey will take $3\frac{1}{2}$ days. The airship has cabin accommodation for 50 passengers and is faster than the *Graf Zeppelin* by nearly 10 miles an hour.

Some Famous Women Flyers

["Flight" Photo]

Lady Heath, the Irish airwoman.

*L*ADY HEATH. Lady Bailey. Miss Winifred Brown and Winifred Spooner. The Duchess of Bedford.

*A*MONG the women flyers there are some half-dozen, apart from Amy Mollison, who are acclaimed pioneers; and the first we shall deal with is the Irish-woman, Lady Heath. She was born at Limerick, and for some years as a girl studied agriculture in Dublin, as a preparation for a farming career in South Africa. It was when she obtained her pilot's certificate, and there followed many offers by British aircraft manufacturers for her to demonstrate the quality of their products, that she relinquished her earlier intentions.

She was a Mrs. Elliott-Lynn when she carried out several attempts on the height record. She made some splendid long-distance flights, amongst the most successful being one from Cape Town to London.

Perhaps the most spectacular and astonishing flight of her career was when she set off at 9 a.m. one morning from Manchester to discover how many aerodromes it was possible to visit in a day. A second notion was to see where there were fields near towns which could be turned into landing grounds. Six times she refuelled, and she called at fifty aerodromes and landed on some seventeen likely fields !

She was eventually created a pilot on the Royal Dutch Air Line between Amsterdam and London, but a year later while visiting America was un-fortunate to crash over Cleveland. Her injuries were so severe that for a time her life was despaired of.

Lady Bailey, another pioneer woman flyer, was born in London in 1890 and also learned the rudiments of flying at the London Aeroplane Club. In

B.F.F.

BEAUTY AND SPEED.

Like a wild sea-bird free in two elements is this giant seaplane, winner of the
Schneider Trophy in 1931.

K

a light machine in 1928-9 she flew solo from Croydon to Cape Town, and then after a lapse of a few months back again to England. The remarkable thing about the return flight was that she flew for part of the time over a route that had never been selected before on account of the complete lack of landing grounds.

She was the first woman to obtain her certificate for blind flying; and a word might be added here regarding this test she underwent to gain the distinction. Blind flying is necessary when passing through fog—the instruments being the only guide; and flying by the dials is known as "flying blind." In the test the flyer is placed in a hooded cockpit and must fly entirely by the instruments in front of him, disregarding his own personal beliefs as to whether the machine is upside down, side-slipping or dropping. To the uninitiated, the need to fly blind always creates the

WELCOMING AN AIR HEROINE.   [" *Flight* " *Photo*
The Duchess of Bedford and Captain Barnard after their flight to India and back in 7½ days.

[" *Flight*" *Photo*

CONGRATULATIONS.

Miss Winifred Spooner, who finished second in the race for the King's Cup in 1928, congratulating the winner, Captain W. L. Hope.

[" *Flight*" *Photo*

Frau Elly Beinhorn (in centre), the well-known German lady pilot, who has many good flights to her credit.

horrible feeling that the instruments have suddenly gone wrong. Many pilots have, in fact, crashed through disregarding the dials and flying according to natural direction which has been badly at fault!

In 1933 Lady Bailey again set off solo for Cape Town, but she was forced down in the desert in the French Niger Colony and returned to England instead of continuing her journey. Lady Bailey has competed in several King's Cup Air Races.

Mention of this race immediately calls to mind Miss Winifred S. Brown, who actually beat every male competitor in the race of 1930. Miss Brown hails from Cheshire and was born in 1899. During the Great War she served in the Red Cross, but only obtained her pilot's certificate in 1927.

In the 750-mile race round England in July, 1930, she flew at an average speed of 102.7 miles an hour, and by consistent rather than extraordinary flying won comfortably.

Another girl flyer who came into prominence with a London to Cape Town flight is Miss Peggy Salaman. Born in London, she was only nineteen when she set out for Cape Town, accompanied by an instructor of the London Aeroplane Club. The pair reached the South African extremity in $5\frac{1}{2}$ days, beating all the then existing records.

Never was there a cleverer woman pilot than Miss Winifred Spooner, who died in 1933 following an illness which lasted only one day. At the time of her death Miss Spooner was definitely the only woman in Britain earning a regular living as the personal pilot of a private owner of machines.

She was born at Woolwich, London, in 1900, and when she began her study of aircraft, learned to know the aero-engine through and through. For just two years she was what might now be termed air chauffeur to a Leicestershire Member of Parliament, and never once, though she flew him and his friends thousands of miles, did she cause them a moment's anxiety. She had taken her employer across Europe to Turkey, Egypt and Palestine through foul weather without the suggestion of risk.

Only once, in 1930, did she encounter real trouble in the air, and that was when, with Flying-Officer E. C. T. Edwards, she set off on a quick flight to South Africa. A mysterious defect set up in the machine and, without warning, while flying at night by the Italian coast, the machine dived into the water. Miss Spooner and her companion had to swim a mile to shore, so that had they not been expert swimmers they would assuredly have been lost.

Miss Spooner entered many big air races, and in one round Italy

148

A SOLO FLYER.   ["*Flight*" *Photo*

Lady Mary Bailey, the first woman to receive her certificate for blind flying. In 1928-29 she flew solo
from Croydon to Capetown, returning after a few months.

received the congratulations of the Italian air chiefs on finishing fourth. She finished second in the King's Cup Race of 1928.

A chapter on women flyers, brief as this is, would not be complete without a reference to the Duchess of Bedford, who astounded the world by flying solo in her sixty-first year. The Duchess with Captain Barnard the famous flyer, made many long flights, and in one to Cape Town and back, in which 19,000 miles were covered, completed the return journey in only twenty-one days.

In May, 1934, Miss Jean Batten, the young New Zealand flyer, flew from Britain to Australia in 14 days, 23 hrs., 25 mins., thereby winning the women's record for that flight held by Mrs. Mollison.

Miss Batten was also the first woman to accomplish the double journey, arriving at Croydon on April 29, 1935. But she met with considerable difficulty on the homeward flight, which covered 17 days, 16 hours, 15 minutes in all. She was the first woman to fly solo across the South Atlantic when, on November 13, 1935, she accomplished the journey in 13 hrs., 15 mins. She thereby beat Senor Campo's time of $16\frac{1}{2}$ hrs. for the 1700-mile ocean trip, and Jim Mollison's 82 hrs., 8 mins. for the flight from Lympne to Port Natal in February, 1933, by covering the same distance in 61 hrs., 15 mins.

THE HAWKER TOMTIT.
A graceful picture of an aeroplane in flight.

[*Brazier*

THE BRITISH SCHNEIDER TEAM.   *[" Flight " Photo*
The Schneider team for 1931 (left to right), Stainforth, Boothman, Orlebar, Long and Snaith.

THE SCHNEIDER MEN

SCHNEIDER'S Trophy. The first race and the great 1931 record.

IN 1912 Jacques Schneider, a Frenchman, offered a magnificent trophy for the greatest speed reached by seaplanes over a triangular course of 150 miles. The trophy was to be won outright, subject to certain conditions, by the country succeeding three consecutive times. It is doubtful whether the trophy would ever have been offered had M. Schneider foreseen the advance in danger which the competition promoted. How could he possibly have guessed that the winning speed of 45.75 miles an hour in 1913 would be increased in the comparatively short space of eighteen years to the incredible speed of nearly 350 miles an hour ?

This fantastic speed has not been attained merely by the increased power of engines, or the advanced design of machines alone ; it has been reached also with the aid of a small band of supermen trained to handle flying projectiles driven by motors. Some idea of their task can be gained

THE 1929 TEAM. ["Flight" Photo
The British Schneider Trophy Team of 1929, with H.R.H. The Prince of Wales.

from the fact that in any Schneider machine attaining 300 miles an hour the velocity created would be sufficient to knock a man's head off were he to put it above the cockpit. The physical strain of flying at such a speed is enormous, and these supermen have had to undergo special training to fit themselves for the ordeal. Contrary to general belief, this does *not* consist of being placed in powerful wind-tunnels, being hung upside-down or being whirled round at a terrific rate! The training methods, while rigid and different in one or two ways, are merely intended to produce physical fitness of both mind and body.

A special section of the Air Force, known as the High Speed Squadron, was created and into this were drafted all those youngsters who showed keenness in achieving fast flight. Actually, the training methods were little different from those used for ordinary service pilots, but of course they were somewhat more strict. At Calshott, opposite the Isle of Wight, and also at Felixstowe, the small group of daring men were put through their paces in the fastest of machines, so that they gradually

152

A SCHNEIDER ENTRANT.   [" *Flight* " Photo
Gloster Napier 6.   A Schneider Trophy contestant.

became accustomed to handling those to be used for the actual
race.

The Schneider Trophy aeroplanes take off at approximately three times
the speed of an ordinary service 'plane, and taking off is one of the first
things the Schneider man has to learn. Once in the air, the machine is as
easy to fly as an ordinary 'plane. Where, then, you may ask, is the danger ?
First, there is the danger of a crash, which would obviously be more than
serious. This is because these " human bullets " do not fly high, which is
a safety factor in normal aircraft. The race itself is flown at a height of
150-200 feet only, and at six miles a minute it would take but the slightest
error to crash the machine into the sea. Such tragedies have occurred.
Another danger ever-present to the Schneider Trophy pilot is that known
as " blacking out." This occurs when the machine banks to round one of
the pylons marking the course, and is caused in simple language by the
blood in the pilot's head trying to continue in the direction it was taking
a moment before. It has been estimated that the strain on both man and

machine when cornering is something like seven times the force of gravity, and it is this " pull " which causes the blood to drain away. For a little while everything goes black. The airman's head throbs as though it will burst ; he cannot see—momentarily he is blind—and there comes a second when he loses consciousness. It is now that the danger is greatest, for should the pilot lose control the penalty is death. In another moment the " black out " has gone, and he is safe until the next banking turn arrives, when the drama is re-enacted.

There is grave danger, too, in landing the high-speed 'plane, for the slightest deviation and the machine would put its nose under water and plough to the bottom. A bad landing, according to Squadron-Leader Orlebar, who had charge of the Schneider Team in the final races, whilst not endangering the life of the pilot, will often cause the 'plane to skip across the water in half-mile jumps !

Such, then, were the dangers which beset the airmen who were to defend the trophy in 1931 after Great Britain had already won it twice in succession. Could we hold it yet again, thus making the coveted trophy

GRACE AND SPEED.   [" *Flight* " *Photo*
A high-speed air-boat, the Vickers Supermarine S.6.B.

154

ours for all time ? Rumours were current of startling developments in Italy, where machines were said to be capable of flying at a speed of over 400 miles an hour. The French were whispered to have equally fast machines, and it was generally felt that the great speed of 328.6 miles an hour put up by Flight-Lieutenant Waghorn for Great Britain in 1929 would be as nothing compared with the speeds of 1931. Indeed, events seemed to point this way, for the contest in 1929 had seen an increase in speed of 82 miles an hour over the speed of the winner of the previous race.

Despite the rumours of their opponents' prowess and super-machines, the British team—consisting of Orlebar, commanding the men (who had previously put up a world speed record of 358 miles an hour), Hope, Boothman, Long, Leech, Stainforth, and Snaith—went steadily forward with their training, taking-off, taxi-ing along the water, and landing countless times to accustom themselves to the conditions. Then came the shock—neither France nor Italy were to compete ! Both had withdrawn at the last moment—a wonderful tribute to our men and machines.

It was necessary, however, for Great Britain to fly the course if the Trophy were to be secured for all time, and for the purpose Boothman was selected. The day of the flight was dull and miserable, and soon heavy rain was falling. It was decided, therefore, to postpone the attempt until the following day. This proved to be a wise move, for the next day was ideal for high-speed work. To the cheers of a large crowd, Flight-Lieutenant L. Boothman took his 'plane up and swept round the course at a record speed for the Trophy of 340 m.p.h.—an increase of over 11 m.p.h. over the speed reached in the previous race. There was a slight feeling of disappointment, but it can safely be said that Boothman was holding the 'plane in, for two hours later Stainforth took the machine out and, flying over the straight three-kilometres speed course, made four flights with an average speed of 388 m.p.h. At one time he travelled at well over 400 m.p.h., thus proving that our machines had a really big reserve of speed. Thus ended the last of the Schneider Trophy contests, for having won the Trophy outright, it became ours for ever. A few days after the race Stainforth reached 407.5 m.p.h.

In October, 1934, Lieut. Agello established an unofficial air speed record of 441.1 miles per hour at Denenzon. He thus broke his previous record of 423 m.p.h. which had beaten Stainforth's record of 407.5 m.p.h.

Bulldogs of No. 19 Squadron performing smoke evolutions at the R.A.F. Display, Hendon, 1934.

FLYERS WE MUSTN'T FORGET

CAPTAIN C. D. BARNARD. Frank Hawkes, the " human bullet." Glen Kidston. C. W. A. Scott. Bert Hinkler, the Flyer the world forgot.

[" Flight " Photo
BERT HINKLER.

BESIDES those airmen who have separate chapters in this book, there are other famous flyers who must not be forgotten. Thousands of words could be written of each, but our space will not permit it, and therefore we have to tell in brief what each has done to go down in air history.

First, there is Captain C. D. Barnard, whose knowledge of aircraft is second to none. To-day he is prepared to go to any part of the world—for anyone and at any time ! His early work as a surveyor of new flying routes has been of great value to Britain, while his long-distance flying ranks him as one of the finest of British flyers.

He was born in London in 1896 and educated at West Buckland, Devon. When war broke out he enlisted in the H.A.C., and in France soon found himself with a commission in the air force. When war ended, Barnard joined the famous aircraft firm of Sopwith, but in 1928 he really became famous, astonishing the flying world with a 5000 mile " hop " from India to Britain in four and a half days.

A year later, with the Duchess of Bedford, of whose machine he is pilot, and Mr. R. F. Little, a double journey between India and Britain was completed—in less than eight days. The important point about the flight was that all flying took place in daylight. Had they flown by night as well their time would undoubtedly have been better. The machine they used had already taken part in an unsuccessful attempt on the Atlantic, also two unsuccessful attempts to fly to India ; but when the Duchess of

Bedford purchased it she had it thoroughly overhauled and installed new engines.

The next big flight of Captain Barnard was to Cape Town and back, again accompanied by the Duchess of Bedford and Mr. Little. They accomplished the double journey of 18,500 miles in two hundred hours' flying time.

In 1930 Captain Barnard set out to prove that a British light aeroplane could fly 1000 miles per day non-stop, and that therefore light mail 'planes might make similar flights without the need for landing on foreign air grounds. He set his machine straight for Tangier, 1240 miles from Croydon, which he reached in twelve hours. The return flight was even more successful, for the aeroplane reached Croydon in just under eleven hours.

Five years' progress has borne out Captain Barnard's principle in full,

THE " HUMAN BULLET." ["*Flight*" Photo
Captain Frank Hawkes, nicknamed the " Human Bullet," who has made more speed records than any other private airman living.

for on June 17, 1935, Captain E. W. Percival flew from Gravesend to Oran, Africa, and back to Croydon, 2300 miles, within 17 hours. For this he was awarded the Johnson Memorial Trophy for the best air navigation feat during a period of 12 months by the Guild of Air Pilots.

An altogether different type of flyer is the famous American, Captain Frank Hawkes, who believes that the future of aircraft lies in speed.

He was born in Iowa in 1897, and had his first aeroplane ride when a "barnstormer" was giving flights in the district at £5 each. Hawkes had nothing like this sum to spend, but he told the airman that he was a newspaper reporter and that, if given a flight, he would "write him up" in the press. The flyer agreed and Hawkes experienced the delights of flying, which made him vow that soon he would have a machine of his own. Then, sorry for the deception he had practised, he told the flyer the truth. Instead of being kicked off the landing ground, he was shown the intricacies of the machine, and the two became firm friends. The airman even gave Hawkes his first lessons in the handling of a 'plane.

Hawkes was seventeen when war started, and though he joined up he did not go to France. He was given air training in America and then told off to instruct others. At the end of the War he took up farming, for there were too many flyers "barnstorming." As a farmer he was a dismal failure, so he went to Mexico as an air soldier. Taking pay across mountainous regions, transporting government officials, and running air circuses took up the next six years of his life. Then he decided to be the first to fly across the Atlantic to Paris non-stop, but when Lindbergh did it before he was ready he gave up that notion. He had now come to the conclusion that speed in aircraft was everything, and to demonstrate his ideas he flew across the American continent from Los Angeles to New York in exceptional time, and capped the performance with a hectic flight back. America now began to look into the career of this speed flyer.

He came to England in 1931 and flew from Brussels to London—195 miles—in an hour! Then he set off on another fast flight, from London to Rome—900 miles—which he accomplished in 5 hours, 24 minutes. On April 30 he flew from Croydon to Baldonnel Aerodrome, Dublin, 320 miles, in exactly an hour and a half. After lunching he visited Cork, Limerick, Galway and Athlone in less than two hours for the lot!

In May he tried to beat the existing speed record for the London-Paris flight, of 1 hour 12 minutes, put up by Glen Kidston, but was beaten by two minutes. He succeeded, however, when he tried to beat existing

159

SCOTT, THE ENGLISH-BORN AUSTRALIAN FLYER.   ["Flight" Photo
C. W. A. Scott, the English-born airman who flew from England to Australia in less than nine days.

records for the flight between London and Berlin. He covered the distance in 2 hours 57 minutes. In the same month, too, he carried out another remarkable flight. He left Le Bourget soon after eight o'clock one morning, breakfasted in London, flew to Berlin for lunch, and had dinner in Paris at night! In June, 1931, he flew from Rome to Croydon in 5½ hours, and later in the month flew from England to Rome and back in just over 9½ hours. Captain Hawkes has been well nicknamed the "human bullet."

In recent years time has become of real commercial value. So De Haviland Comets set about lowering the record for the London to Paris flight. On April 11, 1935, the distance was covered in 53 minutes, the average speed being 220 m.p.h. But Capt. Hubert Broad capped this performance by piloting a Comet at the approximate speed of 250 m.p.h. on July 30, 1935, reaching Paris 48 minutes after leaving London.

AN AERIAL ROLLS-ROYCE.

Another view of the Vickers Supermarine Rolls-Royce, which in 1931 won the
Schneider Trophy outright with a speed of 407 m.p.h.

A famous airman who bore a charmed life for years was Lieutenant-Commander George Pearson Glen Kidston, who was killed in an air accident in Natal in May, 1931. Kidston had been interested in aircraft only since 1927. During the War he saw service in the Navy, and early in the campaign his ship was torpedoed. Then he was interned in Holland for a time. Later he went in for submarine duty and saw service in China.

From 1920 onward he became interested in motor-car and motor-cycle racing. He had many lucky escapes as a motor-cycle racer representing this country, on one occasion crashing into a hedge at nearly a hundred miles an hour. He scored some notable triumphs in motor-cars, and then turning to motor-boats had another thrilling escape when his boat broke in halves in the Solent.

He now took to aeroplanes, buying several for his own use. In East Africa on one occasion his engines failed, and he was forced down in a swamp. But again he escaped unhurt, though his machine was wrecked.

["Flight" Photo
COMMANDER GLEN KIDSTON.
The hero of many hairbreadth escapes before his final crash.

In 1929 he was concerned in a terrible air liner disaster near Caterham, Kent. A big German machine caught fire and Kidston was the only occupant to escape alive. Even when he got out of the machine his clothing was a mass of flames, but in his fuddled state he still had presence of mind to roll himself in the wet grass, which undoubtedly saved his life.

By the law of averages, however, this escaping death and injury could not go on indefinitely, and 1931 saw the end of this promising young airman.

A flyer, born in London but acting as an air pilot in Australia, came into prominence in April, 1931, with a flight from England to Australia in 9 days 40 minutes. This was Mr. C. W. A. Scott, who created this new record at the expense of Kingsford Smith. The flight was filled with dangers and difficulties, but Scott smoothed them all out in his speed dash from one side of the world to the other. In June of the same year Scott again lowered a Kingsford Smith record by flying the return journey in two days' less time than that taken by the Australian.

In November, 1931, his time for the outward flight was beaten by Mr. G. A. Butler, so Scott left Lympne in April of the following year to recover the record. He used the same Gipsy Moth light aeroplane which brought him back from Australia, and he succeeded, after faultless navigation, in beating Butler's time by over five hours.

These experiences must have proved invaluable to Scott when, with C. Black, he entered the Melbourne Air Race in October, 1934. These intrepid flyers and their gallant little D.H. machine astounded the world by covering the distance between England and Melbourne in 70 hrs. 54 mins. 18 secs.

Bert Hinkler, another famous flyer, has been termed "the man the world forgot," for while no finer airman lived, the business men turned their backs on him, so that he was unable for years to obtain the employment that his talent warranted. Perhaps this was because he shrank from publicity, also because he rejected all offers which did not appeal to him. He was born at Bundaberg, Queensland, Australia, on December 8, 1892, and as a boy developed a love for gliders. He made several and carried out some successful flights. During the War he became interested in serious flying, and afterwards was a demonstrator in Australia for the famous British aircraft firm of A. V. Roe, makers of the "Avro" machine.

For seven years he was on the Avro books, and during that time he won several competitions, besides going to America with the Schneider Trophy Team in 1925 as a pilot.

In 1928 he planned to fly to Australia, but wherever he turned he was unable to raise the money. Newspapers refused to take an interest in the proposition, and it was only by accepting schemes he would much rather have rejected that he was able to set off. The record then stood at twenty-eight days, and he at once brought the time to about fifteen. His greatest flight of all was from New York to London via Brazil and West Africa. From New York to Jamaica he flew practically the whole of the way over sea. From South America to the West Coast of Africa was the hardest flight of his career. There were 2000 miles of open sea, and at times he was reduced to flying only five feet above the sea. Then for safety he rose some thousands of feet, only to find himself engulfed by great cloud banks. He also went through a terrific thunderstorm, during which he expected the machine to be struck at any moment. In all he flew twenty-two hours "blind," yet when he reached Bathurst, in Africa, he was only a hundred miles off his course—an amazing piece of navigation.

His last flight, on January 7, 1933, was to Australia, and he intended to reach his homeland in five to six days. He was using the same machine as that which took him safely across the seas from South America to Africa, and few expected him to crash. His send-off was practically nil; yet when no news was heard of him across Europe the world was suddenly struck with remorse. The question was asked—why was this man, with such a record, allowed to go off in such a way; why was he always so forsaken? As the days passed, and no news came, it was realised that Bert Hinkler had indeed been the loneliest of all the great flyers. Not until late in April were his remains found, in the mountain wilderness not far from Arezzo in Italy. A very sad end to a very gallant airman!

PUSS MOTH. ["Flight" Photo
The De Haviland "Puss Moth" Light Aeroplane.

Nobile and other Polar Flyers

THE Andrée Catastrophe. Commander Byrd's Polar Attempt. Amundsen's Airship Attempt. Adventures of Nobile.

ON a warm Sunday afternoon in July, 1897, three intrepid explorers set out from Spitzbergen for the North Pole. Their venture was doubly hazardous, first because any Polar expedition is fraught with danger, but mainly because this one was to be made in an entirely new way—by air ! For

[L.E.A.

Umberto Nobile, the famous Italian airman.

some time past Salomon August Andrée, the leader, had watched the progress of this new method of travel, and he was convinced that a balloon could be profitably employed in the conquest of the Polar regions. Scientists scoffed at the idea, yet Andrée persisted in his belief, and he eventually succeeded in winning to his side Nils Strindberg and Knut Fraenkel, who made up the little party which set out on that fateful day. With the cheers of a large crowd ringing in their ears the three men entered the basket of their balloon, cast off the holding ropes, and soared into the air. Two messages were later found in buoys dropped from the balloon on the day of the ascent, and a carrier pigeon, released on July 13, conveyed a message to a sealing ship, giving the position of the balloon, together with the assurance that all was well. After that—complete silence !

Nothing more was heard of the gallant adventurers until August, 1930, *thirty-three years later*, when the mystery of their fate was solved by the finding of their frozen, shrunken bodies on White Island, together with Andrée's diaries and a number of undeveloped photographs which the party had taken. So intense was the cold, that the negatives were wonderfully preserved, and yielded invaluable pictures when finally developed.

164

The diaries told clearly of the tragedy which had overtaken the party two days after setting out—how the balloon had come down on the ice; how the three men had started to march south in the hope of reaching one of the outlying settlements; how the intense cold overcame them one by one until only Andrée was left, who, with the calm fortitude which one has learned to expect from such men, leaned wearily against a wall of rock, waiting for death. . . .

Thus perished the first of the Polar flyers—pioneers indeed, for it was not until twenty-nine years had passed that a successful attempt was made to fly to the North Pole. This was accomplished without mishap by Commander Byrd of the U.S. Navy. The intervening years had naturally seen a great advance, not only in the science of flying, but also in the knowledge of what was required for a successful Polar expedition, so that Byrd arrived at his base with aeroplanes (not airships or balloons) and the best-equipped party that had ever set out for the Arctic. He had, as co-operators at the base at Spitzbergen, no fewer than forty-six men; nothing at all was left to chance. Six flights were planned, and on May 8, 1926, Commander Byrd left on the first. Success was achieved immediately, and the other flights were abandoned. It must not be supposed, however, that this flight was really as easy as it seems; it had taken many days to prepare a track on which the machine could rise, and it was not, as Byrd himself said a few days after the fine performance, until their hearts had almost broken in the persistent labour of replacing broken skids to the undercarriage that the machine got into the air.

An hour's journey from the Pole an oil leak developed in the third engine, and some anxiety was felt, not only for the success of the flight, but also for the safety of those engaged upon it. Byrd passed a note to his pilot asking what could be done, and with typical coolness came the reply, " Let's get to the Pole first, and discuss that after." Happily, the defect was remedied, and the return journey was made without accident.

At the time that Byrd and his crew set out, another explorer of fame, who intended to fly over the Pole by airship, was making ready at Spitzbergen. This was Roald Amundsen, the Norwegian, who had already conquered the North Magnetic Pole, and who had been the first to reach the South Pole—both, of course, by marching across the ice. Three previous attempts which Amundsen had made to fly by aeroplane to the North Pole had failed, and he now chose the airship as the more satisfactory means of carrying out his plan.

There were with him Lincoln Ellsworth, an American, and Umberto Nobile, an Italian who designed and built the craft ; and two days after Commander Byrd's return *Norge I* started from the same base. Seventy-two hours later the ship landed at Teller, a small village on the Alaskan coast, having passed over, and twice round, the Pole. Although the flight was without incident, it had not been lacking in danger or discomfort. The solar compass had frozen to a solid block and ceased working. Ice had been sucked into the propeller stream of the airship, to be flung into the outer part of the balloon envelope, so that it had become badly battered and in need of constant repair. Sandwiches which were on board were as hard as slices of wood, and the meat cakes supplied to the party had to be thawed out in the explorers' pockets before they could be eaten. And, to make matters worse, damp fog in the form of ice settled on the external metal parts of the ship and made navigation extremely difficult. Again, whilst they were over open sea, strong winds rose which tossed the airship about like a ball. Yet *Norge I* came through !

Two years later yet another successful and uneventful Polar flight was undertaken, this time by Captain (now Sir) Hubert Wilkins, who had been taught to fly in 1910 by Graham-White. Wilkins' object was to try to discover whether any land existed in those regions which had hitherto only been found to contain fields of ice, and the great flight was made in the smallest craft ever used in Polar explorations. Not long after this Arctic venture, Wilkins also set out on a flight over the South Pole, which was equally successful.

Umberto Nobile, the Italian who had accompanied Amundsen on his North Pole flight, formed the next expedition for yet another airship flight over the same area, but, unlike the previous one, his was marred by a series of tragedies. The voyage in the *Italia*, Nobile's ship, commenced from Milan on April 15, 1928. The airship flew to King's Bay, Spitzbergen, and left there on May 23, passing over the North Pole on the following day. Although the ship hovered over the North Pole for some hours, it was not possible to lower anyone, as no landing-ground could be found. Accordingly, the ship was steered on a homeward course, but trouble commenced almost immediately. Within a short time the *Italia* was battling against furious head winds, which lessened her speed and threw her off her course. Then, for some unexplained reason, on May 25, she suddenly began to fall quickly, and in spite of all that was done she continued to drop until she landed heavily on the ice. Nobile, his arm and leg

["*Sport and General*" *Photo*

Thousands of children watching the full rehearsal of 1934 R.A.F. Display at Hendon. A refuelling 'plane taking off over the children

ROALD AMUNDSEN,   [L.E.A.
Pioneer of flight in Arctic exploration.

fractured by the impact, was thrown out, together with eight others, one of whom also suffered a fractured leg. Another was killed outright. Then, with the remainder of the crew still aboard, the *Italia* rose swiftly into the air, sailed off, and was never heard of again!

At first Nobile thought that he and those left stranded on the ice had but a few hours to live, but luckily the position was not so bad as at first supposed. Packets of provisions, tins of petrol, and other articles had fallen out with the men, and best of all, a waterproof bag containing among other things a little tent and a wireless outfit. These were to be the means of eventually saving all but one!

At intervals they sent out radio messages, but for some days these were not heard. Food began to run short, so that it became necessary to kill a polar bear on which to live. Since the wireless messages were not answered, it was decided that the strongest members of the party should attempt to reach the coast on foot, and after some discussion three set off. They suffered incredible hardships and, at his own request, one was abandoned on June 14. The remaining pair were rescued by a Russian ice-breaker on July 11.

But what of the others? They had remained in their little tent, and at long last on June 8 they succeeded in establishing wireless contact with the outside world, in particular with the ship *Citta di Milano*, which was supporting the expedition. Aeroplanes began to arrive and drop food, and for the time being the outlook was brighter. Eventually Lundborg, a Swede, landed in an aeroplane, and insisted on taking Nobile away. It was intended that the Swede should return at once and bring off the rest, but on his next trip his 'plane capsized, and he was himself held a prisoner until rescued by another Swede in a Moth aeroplane.

In the meantime Amundsen volunteered to assist, and started out by aeroplane to the rescue. Disaster overtook him and his companions, and they were never heard of again!

The ice-breaker, which had rescued the two on foot, was fast in the ice and unable to give further help for the time being. To make matters worse, a magnetic storm on July 7 interfered with all wireless communication and hopes began to sink. But later, when things were at their blackest, the ice-breaker in a magnificent effort broke through the ice and rescued all the survivors on the same day, after nearly two months of hardship.

Courtesy] ["*Flight.*"

No. 43 Fighter Squadron of Armstrong-Whitworth Siskins "in flights astern."

AMONG THE ETERNAL SNOWS.

Here one has an idea of the perils which mountain flyers have to face. A forced landing on these glacial heights would mean almost certain death.

THE EVEREST EXPEDITION. ["*The Times*" *Photo*
The Mount Everest Air Expedition, formed in 1933 for the purpose of flying over Everest

THE EVEREST FLYERS

AMAZING Photographs. The Terrors of Mount Everest. A Flight Against Orders.

BY the end of 1932, few places in the world had been left unexplored by air. There remained practically only one spot which had consistently defied the many expeditions sent out—a mountain so formidable that all hopes of ever reaching or surveying the top by ordinary means were fast disappearing. This was Mount Everest, 29,000 feet high, the highest mountain in the world.

Early in 1933 an expedition was formed with an idea of conquering the mountain by air, and a number of experienced airmen enlisted from the Air Force were selected for the purpose. The failure of ordinary climbing expeditions on Mount Everest was generally attributed to the intense cold, and to the difficulty of breathing in the rarefied **air** at great heights. Accordingly, special aeroplanes were built, and special precautions had to be taken to ensure not only warmth, but also a supply of oxygen to enable the airmen to live at the height it was expected to reach.

A long period of training took place at Yeovil, during which time the two machines to participate in the flight were rigorously tested. Various flights were made by the members of the expedition to test the conditions of the upper regions of the air, and heights of 35,000 feet were reached with ease. The cold at such a height was intense—over 60 degrees below zero—but it was found that the special electrically-heated clothing which had been made was ample protection. The main object of the flyers was the securing of a series of photographs of the summit, and in order to ensure success special cameras were built, fitted with heated jackets to prevent the freezing of the working parts.

After many weeks of testing machines, cameras, scientific instruments and heated clothing, the party set off on February 16, flying by easy stages to India. The flight was led by Air-Commander Fellowes, who was accompanied in his Puss Moth cabin aeroplane by his wife. Following them came Flight-Lieutenant D. F. MacIntyre, in a Gipsy Three Moth, and then Squadron-Leader Lord Clydesdale, Mr. C. H. Hughes, a mechanic, and the correspondent of *The Times* in a Fox Moth. The start was made with no more fuss than a cross-country flight from a London airport might have done. Lieutenant-Colonel L. V. S. Blacker, who was to be the chief observer of the expedition, left for Karachi by Imperial Airways. And the two Westland aeroplanes in which the attempt was to be made were dispatched to India in advance.

By the end of March the whole of the expedition, which comprised, besides those already named, a number of mechanics and two cinematographers, was ready for the great test, and many flights were made with the reassembled machines. All that the party waited for now was good weather, and when in April 3 the Indian Meteorological Office at Purnea reported that the conditions were favourable, the two machines took off.

Lord Clydesdale and Colonel Blacker occupied the Houston-Westland 'plane, and the Westland-Wallace was piloted by Flight-Lieutenant MacIntyre, with whom was Mr. S. R. Bonnett, the aerial photographer for the Gaumont-British Film Corporation. After thirty minutes' flying they passed their emergency landing-ground at Forbesganj, and from a height of 19,000 feet they glimpsed Everest. Chamlang was passed at an altitude of 31,000 feet, and then both 'planes flew over Everest, clearing it by a bare hundred feet ! For the first time in history the great peak had been conquered and the summit observed at close quarters by human eye.

The story of the flight itself makes graphic reading, and shows the courage and skill necessary in order to achieve this signal success. Nothing untoward happened till Chamlang was reached, and here the flyers tasted the difficulties they were to expect. Over the huge edge of the mountain a terrific downdraught was experienced, caused by the wind striking the steep side of Everest, shooting first upwards over the summit and then being forced down for twelve miles beyond. Both machines were caught in this swirling, raging wind, and 2000 feet of height were lost in a few seconds. Nothing daunted, the 'planes were driven onward.

Over the summit itself the wind was not so strong, but it forced the machines close to the mountainside, and the pilots had to be prepared to turn back at any moment for fear of being dashed against the solid wall of rock. It was at this point that MacIntyre missed his passenger, Mr. Bonnett, who had previously been standing head and shoulders above the cockpit using his camera. A mishap with his oxygen mask had caused him momentarily to lose consciousness, and he had been forced to sink on to his little seat in the 'plane, where he noticed a small leak in his oxygen air-tube. Happily, by tying a handkerchief over it he was able to avert disaster, and carried on his work of photographing the mountains ahead.

All the time that the 'planes were close to the summit, Colonel Blacker was firing off plate after plate as fast as his camera would take them. This in itself was no mean achievement, for the camera, owing to its heating jacket, was extremely heavy, while the rarefied air made every movement an exertion, and the cumbersome clothing hampered still further.

The airmen's goggles were being constantly misted over through the intense cold of the air striking the warm heat from the elements in them. Ice rattled into the cockpits of the machines out of the frozen snow plume of the mountain, and the whole position was decidedly uncomfortable. Added to which there was always present the danger that if the engines failed nothing short of a miracle could save the occupants. For fifteen minutes the flight round Everest continued, during which Colonel Blacker managed to obtain nearly forty photographs. Then they commenced their 160-mile flight back to the base.

Thus ended the first flight over Everest, and with it the expedition should have terminated. But it was found that the aerial survey camera installed on one of the machines had developed some slight defect which had caused it to cease working for some time, with the result that the series of pictures was not complete. Permission for another flight was sought, but owing to the risk of life it was not granted. It was therefore decided to make another attempt in secret !

The flight was begun with never a word to anyone, and it was believed by those who remained behind that the two aeroplanes had merely set off on a final short flight for cinematograph purposes, to be expected back after about two hours. At the end of that time, however, it began to dawn upon the watchers, waiting for the machines to come back, that something was wrong. What had happened, of course, was that Lord Clydesdale and Flight-Lieutenant MacIntyre had, in secret conference, decided to disobey orders and make a more prolonged flight of the summit of Everest. They were accompanied this time by Colonel Blacker and Mr. A. L. Fisher, the second cinematographer, who, as a result, secured the world's finest films of mountain scenery. This flight, contrary to all orders, was actually more fruitful than the first, since the airmen had profited by their experience and were now more sure of their movements. Thus for the second time in a few days Everest, hitherto unsurmountable, had yielded up her secrets to these intrepid navigators of the air.

[*Topical.*

DORNIER FLYING BOAT

The Dornier Do X Flying Boat taking off. Designed with 12 engines developing 6000 b.h.p., it can carry 170 passengers.

[" *Sport and General* "

R.A.F. ANNUAL AIR DISPLAY AT HENDON, 1934.
A flight of 'planes over the heads of the spectators.

AMONG THE CLOUDS.
Formation flying by army aeroplanes—an art brought to a pitch of perfection by constant training and manœuvres.

[*" Flight "* *Photo*

Capt. G. de Haviland receiving the King's Cup from Lord Gorell.

The Daring of Professor Piccard

[Associated Press

PROFESSOR PICCARD.

THE Experimental Balloon. The Balloon which Refused to Come Down. The Second Exploration of Space. The Russian Balloonists.

OF all the heroes of the air, surely the strangest is Professor Piccard, the man who, whilst being in no sense an aeronaut, had until comparatively recently ascended higher into the air than any other human being. His story reads something like a fantasy of H. G. Wells, and shows to what lengths men of science will go in their search for enlightenment.

Tall, thin, and nervous-looking, Professor Piccard of Brussels University was engaged in 1930 upon the study of certain rays. In his laboratory he worked for days on end, seeking to find the properties peculiar to these rays, until he was forced to the conclusion that successful experimenting would have to be done on the rays themselves before they reached the earth. To do this would necessitate travelling through space for miles until the outer atmosphere of the world was reached—an astonishing idea, even in these days of advanced aeronautics.

The greatest height ever attained by man at this time was 45,000 feet, but it was not sufficient for Professor Piccard's plans. He estimated that he would have to soar upwards for at least 52,500 feet—a height generally regarded as impossible to achieve in any form of aircraft. Professor Piccard, despite difficulties with which he was faced and the scepticism of fellow-scientists, set to work upon his scheme of reaching the upper atmosphere, or stratosphere. He proposed to use a specially-constructed balloon for his flight, and, though he knew little or nothing of aeronautics, by means of scientific calculations he soon evolved a plan for a balloon which he hoped would take him and his assistant to the desired height. This craft was to have a new type gas-bag, and in place of a basket a huge metal globe. The latter was to be airtight and to contain oxygen in tubes, necessary for breathing. Also, of course, numerous scientific instruments were to be carried.

In due course the curious craft was built, and on September 14, 1930, was ready for its first flight into the unknown. In order to allow for expansion of the gas in proportion to the decrease of atmospheric pressure as greater heights were reached, the balloon was only partially filled, and the result was that on the first attempt it would not rise perpendicularly, so that the globe in which Professor Piccard and his assistant sat did not leave the ground.

Far from being discouraged, Piccard overcame all difficulties, but it was not until May of the following year that he again set out on his attempt to explore the air at a height of ten miles. At 3.30 a.m. on May 27 he and M. Kipfer climbed into the aluminium sphere and pulled the lid down after them, screwing it tight and thus hermetically sealing themselves in. As they did so the weather suddenly became boisterous. The balloon was given added impetus and shot upward at an alarming rate, tossing the gondola about in the process. This caused some of the instruments to become dislodged, and one struck the metal wall of the cell, creating a small leak. The fracture was not noticed until later, when it was mended with all haste with materials they were carrying.

Twenty-five minutes from the start the balloon had attained a height of nine miles! And this without any ballast having been thrown out. Everything pointed to success if only the walls of the gondola were strong enough to withstand the terrific pressure being exerted upon them.

TEN MILES UP.
Professor Piccard, at the risk of his life, soars into the sky to an altitude of almost ten miles above the earth.

Professor Piccard, in describing the flight afterwards, told of the fantastic sights they saw; how the sun was glimpsed rising above the horizon long before the earth beneath them had been touched by its rays; and of the wonderful panorama which stretched for miles beneath them. But the nature of the work to be done inside the gondola prevented the two intrepid explorers from feasting their eyes upon the wonders outside.

At the nine-mile mark Piccard steadied the balloon and checked its upward flight, whilst observations were taken. Then up they went again, slowly now, for the rarified air necessitated careful management of the craft. Very soon the unpleasant discovery was made that the valve mechanism was out of order, which meant that they would go higher but could not descend! From the very beginning of the flight Piccard had calculated that the balloon would descend of its own accord during the afternoon owing to the cooling temperature after sunset, and his supply of oxygen had been estimated accordingly. But when five o'clock in the afternoon came, after hours of work and study, and the balloon was still soaring gently upwards, matters began to look serious. Six o'clock, and still no sign of the balloon starting to descend! By seven o'clock things were critical, as the supply of oxygen in the tubes was beginning to run low. To have opened the screwed-down lid of the gondola would instantly have been fatal.

Eagerly the two scientists waited, unable themselves to bring the balloon down! Had their calculations been wrong? Had something happened which they had not allowed for? Was there some sinister quality in the upper regions of space and thin air about which they knew nothing? With bated breath they waited anxiously, watching their altitude meters. Critical as the situation was, however, the gallant men remembered the errand upon which they were engaged and continued their scientific observations in the very teeth of death. . . .

Resigned to their fate, they watched the setting of the sun just after eight o'clock. Then, almost as their hopes were at an end, the cooling air began to help, and the needles of the height-measuring instruments started to travel back. They were coming down! At 8.45 they had descended sufficiently to be able to expel some of their used air with safety. What a relief that was! Eagerly they waited for the exact moment when the air pressure inside the gondola should correspond with that outside; and as soon as it did the scuttles of the cabin were opened and the sweet air rushed in, reviving these air-starved men.

They prepared for a landing, and this was accomplished about nine o'clock at an altitude of 2700 metres, on the side of a glacier in the Austrian Alps. Overcome with fatigue, the two men fell asleep. In the morning, seeing no signs of human habitation, they decided to climb down into the valley, first arranging signs near the balloon to show they were alive and well. After a difficult climb they entered the nearest village, chatting

[Planet News.

THE U.S.S.R. BALLOON.

Commander Prokofier in the spherical metal gondola of the Russian balloon which achieved an altitude record in 1933 by climbing 11¼ miles into the atmosphere.

OBSERVATION BALLOON.

Reconnoitring the enemy's lines from the basket of an army observation balloon. The balloon is "captive." Communication with the ground below is by telephone.

181

AFTFR THE FLIGHT.   [E.N.A.
The Professor, with the Italian Air Minister, standing beside his famous
balloon, which is attracting the attention of curious onlookers.

merrily to those they met, as though their wondrous ten-mile flight upward had been an everyday affair.

On August 18 of the following year Professor Piccard made another flight into the stratosphere, this time rising to a height of $10\frac{1}{2}$ miles. He was accompanied by M. Cosyns, and the ascent was made from Zurich. Starting at 5.15 a.m., the terrific height of 54,450 feet was reached at 12.12 p.m., and although the gondola was considerably warmer inside than the atmosphere without, the thermometer at Piccard's side registered 15 degrees below zero. So great was the change in temperature between the upper regions and ground level that the two all but fainted as they stepped out of the cell on landing.

Professor Piccard's record stood until the autumn of 1933, when it was broken by three Russians who, in a balloon similar in construction but larger, ascended to twelve miles! No doubt the Russians benefited from Piccard's pioneer flights, for, whilst outside the gondola the temperature was 67 degrees below zero, inside it was comfortably warm for the occupants. Also, the commander, M. Prokofieff, was an experienced balloonist, and his two assistants were airmen. It was intended that this balloon should stay aloft for 18 hours, but it came down after only seven.

It is interesting to note that at the end of 1931, Henry Farman, the famous pioneer airman and manufacturer of aircraft, commenced work upon a special plane which was intended for a flight into the stratosphere, having a hermetically sealed cabin. It was estimated that at a height of ten to twelve miles this machine would develop a speed of more than 500 miles an hour ! So far, nothing more has been heard of this project.

Now, however, balloonists are turning to the stratosphere. On January 30, 1934, a Soviet balloon, after reaching 68,892 feet above Leningrad, crashed and all the occupants were killed. This record was held till November 11, 1935, when an American stratosphere balloon taking off near Rapid City, South Dakota, attained a height of 74,000 feet.

PARACHUTE DESCENT.
The first successful parachute descent from a balloon was made by a Frenchman, Garnerin, in 1797.

THE "AUTO-GIRO." [*Topical*

The Cierva "Auto-Giro" or "Windmill" aeroplane, designed with overhead propeller for vertical ascent and descent.

CIERVA AND HIS AUTO-GIROS

A Boy and His Kites. The Problem of Slow Flight. The great Channel Crossing. What Cierva is Trying to Do.

AT the time when the first bird-men were making their desperate efforts to conquer the air, there was born at Murcia, Spain, a boy who was eventually to set the whole world talking. Almost from the moment that he could run he was interested in flying, the chief outlet for his feelings at that time, of course, being the ordinary schoolboy's box kite. As he grew older he began to fly kites of his own design, queer things which differed greatly from the accepted kite designs.

From kites it was an easy step to gliders, which Cierva designed and built in great number. Not satisfied with their flying power, however, he set to work to install a motor in one.

Engines for aeroplanes and gliders were by this time an accepted practice in aeronautics, but to Cierva fell the honour, whilst in his 'teens, of designing an astonishing tri-motored biplane. For a time this machine was successful, but eventually it crashed, through stalling—losing flying speed—and was destroyed. This set the young man thinking seriously on the problem of slow flying and how it could be achieved, for he was convinced that only by having the power to fly slowly could the aeroplane or glider be made a really safe vehicle.

In 1920, therefore, he conceived the idea of a rotating wing. Not until 1923 was the finished product able to take the air, and although this machine was sufficient of a success to prove Cierva's ideas practicable, it was yet too crude to be really serviceable. The first models were built round the fuselage of an ordinary light aeroplane, and the drawback to these models was that the four rotating blades which revolved above the pilot's head and gave the machine the necessary " lift " had to be rotated by hand before the machine could take off, and even then the 140 revs.

CIERVA WITH HIS FAMOUS INVENTION.   [" Flight " Photo
Don Juan de la Cierva (left), inventor of the Auto-Giro, which solved the problem of slow flying.

THE AUTO-GIRO IN MOTION.   [*" Flight"* Photo
Cierva's invention, doing away with the necessity for huge aerodromes, may be regarded as the aerial
equivalent of the privately-owned small car.

per minute required could not be obtained always. As a consequence
the machines needed a run somewhat longer than that of the ordinary
'plane before rising from the ground. Once in the air, however, Cierva
could tell that he was on the right lines, for his machines would hover
slowly or travel at nearly 100 miles an hour. His idea in building
his auto-giros was to create a machine for the man in the street, who,
he contended, did not necessarily want great speed, but did want safety and
comfort. He also desired, Cierva contended, to be able to enjoy the countryside over which he flew, a thing not possible with orthodox aircraft which
flew at a height of 1000 feet or more, and had to attain and keep to 80
miles an hour minimum to maintain flight.

The first of these necessities—safety, comfort and the ability to fly at
slow speeds—had more or less been overcome with his first models, but

AUTO-GIROS.

Auto-Giros in motion, demonstrating Sr. de la Cierva's famous invention for stabilising aeroplanes and making them safe for the private owner.

Cierva felt something more was needed. The man in the street had no huge aerodrome, and his machine would be required to come down and rise in very small space. Cierva felt he could guarantee this if only he could make his rotating blades move fast enough to take the machine straight up into the air. So he set to work to embody gear-driven blades. Again difficulties arose which he had not foreseen, but eventually success was achieved.

His machines can now take off in less than five yards, can hover, fly more slowly than a man running, or at 100 miles an hour, can change direction and move upwards, down or sideways—and all this merely by tilting the horizontal rotators. He does away with rudders, elevators, or ailerons.

The auto-giro, while still in its infancy, had, under the command of Senor de la Cierva, done wonderful things. A few years after the first demonstration was given in England, Cierva flew his machine across the English Channel, leaving at 10.5 in the morning and landing near Calais at 11.6. From there he flew to Le Bourget. A passenger was carried throughout, and experts declared this flight to be the most significant since Blériot's nineteen years before.

The new method of flying advocated by Cierva is rapidly gaining a hold, and a British company has purchased world rights, with the exception of those for Spain. Cierva believes in the future of auto-giros for private owners.

Apart altogether from its usefulness as a medium of transport, the air has made possible a new kind of sport. Gliding has become very popular, particularly in Germany. On July 30, 1935, four German glider pilots landed in Czechoslovakia 310 miles from their starting place, and Fraulein Liesel Zanglemeister beat the world's duration gliding record for women by remaining in the air in an engineless plane for 12 hours, 57 minutes.

["Flight" Photo

AN A.D.C. GLIDER, 1922.
Gliding in a motorless 'plane has become a popular sport in Britain and Germany. In 1931 an Austrian made a flight of 70 miles in a little over 3 hours.

SOME FLYERS AND THEIR EPOCH-MAKING FLIGHTS

1903, December 17.—ORVILLE WRIGHT makes the first authentic machine-driven passenger-carrying flight, lasting 12 seconds, and covering 120 feet. At Kitty Hawk, N. Carolina, U.S.

1905, September 26.—ORVILLE WRIGHT flies 11.12 miles in 18 min. 9 sec. At Dayton, Ohio, U.S.

1907, April 5.—LOUIS BLÉRIOT flies the first monoplane. At Bagatelle, France.

1908. January 13.—HENRY FARMAN flies nearly 5,000 feet in 1½ min. At Issy, France.

1908, July 4.—ZEPPELIN L.Z.4 makes a 12-hour flight of 235 miles, including crossing of the Alps.

1908, September 21.—WILBUR WRIGHT makes flight of 60 miles in 1½ hours. At Auvours, France.

1908, December 31.—WILBUR WRIGHT wins £1000 for world's endurance record of 2 hrs. 20 min. 23½ sec. In France.

1909, July 19.—HUBERT LATHAM endeavours to fly English Channel. Forced down after covering 7 miles.

1909, July 25.—LOUIS BLÉRIOT flies the English Channel from Sangatte to Dover in 37 minutes.

1910, April 27-8.—PAULHAN wins £10,000 for a flight from London to Manchester in under 24 hours.

1910, April 28.—CLAUDE GRAHAM-WHITE makes first night ascent, in the London-to-Manchester race.

1911, September 9.—Air Mail Service started in England between Hendon and Windsor.

1913, September 2.—PEGOUD makes first loop-the-loop flight.

1913, December.—BONNIER and VEDRINES make long-distance flight between Paris and Cairo.

1917, November 12-16.—ZEPPELIN L.59 creates world's distance record of 4225 miles in unsuccessful attempt to carry hospital supplies to German East Africa.

1919, May 16-27.—N.C.4 makes first trans-Atlantic flight from America via Azores.

1919, June 14-15.—ALCOCK and BROWN, British airmen, make first non-stop trans-Atlantic flight. From St. John's, Newfoundland, to Clifden, Ireland.

1919, July.—R.34, British airship, makes first lighter-than-air double Atlantic crossing.

1919, November 12–December 10.—ROSS SMITH and crew fly from London to Australia.

1920.—DE LA CIERVA conceives rotating vane for fitting above aeroplane cockpit.

1924, April–September.—American flyers circumnavigate the globe.

1926, May 8-9.—COMMANDER BYRD and FLOYD BENNETT fly over North Pole, in monoplane.

1926, May 11-15.—AMUNDSEN flies over North Pole in the airship *Norge*.

1927, May 20-21.—LINDBERGH makes first non-stop solo flight between New York and Paris. In 33½ hrs.

1928, February 6-22.—BERT HINKLER makes first solo flight between England and Australia. In about 15½ days.

1928, February 12–May 17.—LADY HEATH flies solo between Cape Town and London.

1928, April 12-13.—GERMAN aeroplane *Bremen* makes first east-to-west trans-Atlantic flight.

1928, May 31–June 10.—KINGSFORD SMITH and companions fly approximately 7400 miles from Oakland, California, U.S., to Sydney, Australia.

1928, June.—AMELIA EARHART, first woman to fly Atlantic, makes non-stop flight with companions from Newfoundland to Wales.

1928, September 18.—DE LA CIERVA flies auto-giro across English Channel.

1929, April.—SQUADRON-LEADER A. G. JONES-WILLIAMS and FLIGHT-LIEUTENANT N. A. JENKINS makes flight of 4130 miles non-stop, from England to India, in 50½ hours.

1929, June 17–July 1.—KINGSFORD SMITH, C. T. P. ULM, W. McWILLIAMS and H. A. LITCHFIELD fly from Australia to England in 12 days, 21½ hours.

1929, August 2-9.—DUCHESS OF BEDFORD, R. F. LITTLE and CAPTAIN BARNARD fly from England to India and back in 7½ days.

1929, August 8-29.—GRAF ZEPPELIN makes first lighter-than-air round-the-world flight.

1929, November 28-29.—COMMANDER BYRD and companions fly over South Pole.

1930, May.—AMY JOHNSON makes first woman's solo flight from England to Australia in a Puss Moth.

1930, September.—COSTES and BELLONTE makes first non-stop flight from Paris to New York, 3700 miles, in 37 hours.

1931, April 1–June 5.—C. W. A. SCOTT flies from England to Australia and back in 19 days, 19 hrs. 40 mins. flying time.

1931, June–July.—POST and GATTY fly round the world, 16,500 miles, in 8 days, 15 hrs. 51 mins.

1931, July.—BOARDMAN and POLANDO fly 4984 miles non-stop from New York to Contantinople in 49 hours.

1931, August.—J. A. MOLLISON flies from Australia to England in 8 days, 22 hrs. 25 mins.

1931, September 30.—FLIGHT-LIEUTENANT STAINFORTH creates world speed record of 408.288 miles an hour.

1931, November.—BERT HINKLER makes first solo flight across South Atlantic from West to East, in smallest aeroplane ever to cross the Atlantic.

1932, March 24-28.—J. A. MOLLISON flies from England to the Cape, 6350 miles, in 4 days, 17½ hours.

1932, April 19-27.—C. W. A. SCOTT flies from England to Australia in 8 days, 20 hrs. 47 mins.

1932, May 20-21.—AMELIA EARHART makes first solo flight for women across Atlantic in 13¼ hours.

1932, August 18-19.—J. A. MOLLISON makes first solo flight across North Atlantic from East to West.

1932, August 18.—PROFESSOR PICCARD ascends 10½ miles in balloon, after reaching approximately 10 miles in 1931.

1932, September 24.—C. F. UWINS breaks aeroplane altitude record by reaching 43,976 feet.

1932, November 18.—MRS. AMY MOLLISON beat her husband's Britain to the Cape record. Her time was 4 days, 6 hrs. 54 mins.

1932, December 18.—MRS. MOLLISON flew to London from Cape Town in 7 days, 7 hrs. 5 mins.

1933, February.—GAYFORD and NICHOLETTS create non-stop record of 5341 miles, England to Walvis Bay, S. Africa.

1933, April.—Mount Everest conquered by air. British expedition.

1933, April 10.—LIEUTENANT AGELLO, Italian airman, creates new high-speed record of 423 miles an hour.

1933, July 1-August 13.—Italian Armada of seaplanes crosses Atlantic, and returns.

1933, August 7.—CODOS and ROSSI, French, create new long-distance non-stop record of 5,915 miles from New York to Rayak, Syria.

1933, October 1.—Soviet Balloon *Stratostat U.S.S.R.* attains height of 12 miles.

1933, October 11.—KINGSFORD SMITH sets up new record for flight from England to Australia in 7 days, 3 hrs. 15 mins.

1933, October 14.—C. P. ULM flies from England to Australia in 6 days, 17 hrs. 56 mins.

1934, April 11.—COMMENDATORE RINATO DONATI (Italy) breaks existing aeroplane altitude record by reaching height of 47,349 ft.

1934, May.—JEAN BATTEN flies from Britain to Australia in 14 days, 23 hrs. 25 mins.

1934, September 9.—Slutz Aerological Institute, Leningrad, sent up crewless balloon with automatic recorders. It reaches altitude of over 13 miles.

1934, September 20.—C. J. MELROSE flies from Australia to England in 8 days, 9 hrs.

1934, October.—LIEUT. AGELLO (Italy) establishes unofficial air speed record of 441 m.p.h.

1934, October.—C. W. SCOTT and C. BLACK fly from England to Australia in 70 hrs. 54 mins. 18 secs.

1935, In January, MISS AMELIA EARHART took off from Honolulu and flew over 2000 miles across the sea to California.

1935, March 30.—H. L. Brook makes a record solo flight from England to Australia in 7 days, 19 hours 50 minutes.

1935, April 29.—Jean Batten arrives at Croydon after her return journey from Australia in 17 days, 16 hours 15 minutes. First woman to accomplish the double flight.

1935, May 20.—Herr Heine Dittmar, a German, gliding with a passenger, reached 8860 feet, 3280 feet more than his previous record.

1935, June 17.—Capt. E. W. Percival left Gravesend, Kent, at 1.30 a.m., reached Oran, Africa, at 8.48 a.m. and was back at Croydon at 6.30 p.m., having flown 2300 miles within 17 hours. Awarded the Johnson Memorial Trophy by the Guild of Air Pilots.

1935, September 7.—T. Rose, flying Viscountess Wakefield's Miles Falcon, wins the King's Cup at an average speed of 176.28 m.p.h.

1935, November 9.—H. F. Broadbent beat the existing record for the solo flight from England to Australia, taking 6 days, 21 hours 19 minutes from Croydon to Port Darwin.

1935, November 11.—Flying-Officer David Llewellyn and Mrs. Joe Wyndham broke Amy Mollison's Cape to Britain record by 18 hours 48 minutes. Their time was 6 days, 12 hours 17 minutes.

1935, November 11.—American stratosphere balloon, Explorer II., took off near Rapid City, S. Dakota, and reached a record height of 74,000 feet.

1935, November 13.—Jean Batten arrived at Port Natal, Brazil, first woman to make the solo flight over the S. Atlantic. She took 13 hours 15 minutes for the 1700-mile ocean trip and 61 hours 15 minutes for the flight from Lympne to Port Natal, both records.

1936, February 9.—Flight-Lieut. T. Rose beat Mrs Mollison's Britain to the Cape record by 13 hours 19 minutes. His time was 3 days, 17 hours 37 minutes.

1936, March 4.—The new Zeppelin airship *LZ*129, the *Hindenburg*, climbed 1000 feet in 1 minute on its trial flight at Friedrichshafen.

1936, March 9.—Flight-Lieut. T. Rose arrived at Croydon, having broken the Cape to London record set up on November 11 by Flying-Officer Llewellyn and Mrs. Wyndham. He took 6 days, 6 hours 57 minutes for the flight.

LONDON AND GLASGOW: COLLINS CLEAR-TYPE PRESS